THE
GREAT EXPERIMENT

THE
GREAT EXPERIMENT

*An Introduction to the History of the
American People*

BY

FRANK THISTLETHWAITE

FELLOW OF ST JOHN'S COLLEGE, CAMBRIDGE

'... to show the world by one great
successful experiment of what man
is capable.'   LYMAN BEECHER

CAMBRIDGE
AT THE UNIVERSITY PRESS
1955

PUBLISHED BY
THE SYNDICS OF THE CAMBRIDGE UNIVERSITY PRESS

London Office : Bentley House, N.W.1
American Branch : New York
Agents for Canada, India, and Pakistan : Macmillan

Made and printed in Great Britain by
William Clowes and Sons, Limited, London and Beccles

To the memory of
ERNEST ALFRED BENIANS

CONTENTS

MAPS

      The particulars given in this map are derived from a map
      in *Atlas of American History* by James Truslow Adams and
      R. V. Coleman, by permission of Charles Scribner's
      Sons, publishers

PREFACE

THE impulse behind this book has been the conviction, formed as a result of several years' teaching American history to Cambridge undergraduates, of the need for a new introduction to the history of the American people written by an Englishman. Although it has been only since the Second World War that American history has been given an integral place in the curricula of British universities, undergraduates have taken to the subject with zest. In venturing on these hitherto sketchily charted waters teachers and students have been fortunate in the help of distinguished visiting American scholars and of growing collections of books made available in part through the generosity of American foundations. But in the matter of general works we have been less well placed. Existing introductions to American history and especially the many ably written text-books, even when their cost is not prohibitive, do not give the intelligent British student or reader a satisfactory starting point for study, do not suggest answers to many of the urgent questions which an English layman asks these days when faced for the first time with the phenomenon of the United States. The reason is not far to seek: they are very largely written by Americans for American readers and the assumptions on which they are grounded are not those which an Englishman instinctively understands. This book has, therefore, been written to satisfy a special need. Its main purpose is to provide the British student with a point of departure.

This book is, however, an introduction, not a text-book; and it is cast in a form which may make it more widely acceptable. In particular, American readers may find some interest in an account which, in attempting to answer questions raised by outsiders, emphasizes the special characteristics that distinguish Americans from Europeans. I hope, therefore, that although I shall hereafter address myself to the British undergraduate, what I have to say may have some value to a wider public on both sides of the Atlantic.

ix

Preface

As every good host knows, an introduction must be more than a pronouncing of names and titles. This book, therefore, attempts to present not merely a condensed factual narrative, but what your host, so to speak, believes to be the chief distinguishing qualities of the American people as they have developed in time, and especially those qualities which, perhaps more by contrast than affinity, may make the American people stand out in three dimensions for you, the British undergraduate. Selection has not been easy. But in making the presentation I have been guided by some knowledge of the misconceptions which you most naturally harbour and which it is the object of an introduction to dispel. For there is nothing like a meeting face to face to banish an image known from hearsay. These misconceptions have governed the form of the book.

Let me say at once that I am not accusing you of cherishing the grosser prejudices which are conversational gambits in pubs and even in clubs (where they ought to know better), such as that American society is especially materialistic or that culturally America has become 'rotten before it was ripe'. I am thinking, in the first place, of the misconception which arises in approaching American history from the standpoint of constitutional theory. An exposition of American Federalism in a strictly political context has not often left you convinced that the American Constitution is a sound instrument for the present day, nor that within it American politics are conducted in a spirit which has much traditional wisdom; and you have all too often been left with *arrière-pensées* such as that the Americans in the end will have to come round to British parliamentary government. The danger of a purely political approach for us British has always been that of projecting our own assumptions about politics to a system which has its origins in a common tradition but which has diverged markedly from our own; and it is here that the proverbial barrier of a common language operates most formidably. Only when one digs deep below the surface does one begin truly to understand the genius of the American political tradition expressed classically in Federalism. Again, I am thinking of misconceptions which arise from approaching American history in the strictly economic mode. The most insistent questions which you whose chief concern is economics have asked in studying American economic growth are susceptible to answer, not in economic terms, but in terms which relate to the social framework. Thirdly, there are more general misconceptions which arise because you approach the new subject from the frame of reference of European history and because, in these pinched days, so very few of you have had the opportunity to travel, let alone live, on the North American continent. I am thinking here, for example, of the belief, hard at first to shed, that the United States is still a young country which in time will follow the pattern of older countries; that with frontiers vanished and immigrants regulated, American society will harden into classes in a European sense; that in time this settlement may produce a cultural tradition of a European order; that the New Deal was but a delayed version of the Liberal government of 1906, and so on. All these misconceptions point to the need somehow to define the unique quality of American society. For your unasked question behind the rest has always been, not 'How did the United States become the overwhelming Power she is?', but 'Why do Americans regard themselves as a special sort of people?' And so this book has gone beyond a conventional political and economic treatment in an attempt to describe the evolution of American society as a whole and in the round.

Such an approach presents difficulties. 'Social' history is difficult to write; and my attempt to suggest causal relationships among political, economic, social and cultural factors has inevitably been empirical and amateurish. But in order to bring out the deeper meanings of the story the attempt has had to be made. Fortunately, the main clues have been at hand. The writing of this book has strengthened the conviction that one set of influences has dominated American development: I mean those which relate to migration; and the underlying purpose of the book has been to show how as a result of the grand process of migration from Europe across the new continent a new variant of western society has come into being.

This approach has had two distinct sets of advantages.

In the first place, by emphasizing the inter-connectedness of American and European history it reaffirms the fact that the United States has developed, not in truth in isolation, but as an integral part of the Atlantic basin. The transcontinental trek began, not at the Cumberland gap, nor even in New York, but in Surrey and County Mayo, in Westphalia, Lithuania and Sicily; American wealth derives in part from the know-how of Rochdale and Swansea, the confidence of Lombard Street and the markets of western Europe; American culture grew to maturity within an Atlantic world with nerve-centres in Chelsea and Manchester, as well as in Boston and Philadelphia. In developing this theme the British elements have been given prominence for two reasons, neither of them chauvinistic; first, to provide you with a springboard of known experience for your imaginative leap into American history, and second, because the role of Britain in that history since the Revolution has not usually been sufficiently defined. For reasons of geopolitics rather than kinship Britain has remained a vital factor in American affairs. Like bats from a musty old world we have always been getting in the Americans' hair; and I hope that transatlantic readers will not take amiss this dwelling on some of the less obvious reasons why.

In the second place, the migration theme, while emphasizing the inter-connectedness of America and Europe, provides the greatest insight into the unique qualities of American society as it has developed in the continental hinterland. For in their uprooting, European emigrants and westward-moving Americans alike, in spite of the cultural baggage they took with them, learned to order their social affairs in ways which are subtly, but profoundly, different from ours. In important respects American values have come to be the very antithesis of those of the 'old countries'. The line of least resistance, for the Englishman who stayed at home, has been to conform; for the Englishman who became an American, it has been to 'go some place else'; and this deep-seated psychological contrast must be taken into account in any attempt to establish the true affinities between Americans and ourselves. The American variant of western society is a new thing, which I have attempted to define as 'the mobile society'.

One further quality of American history must be mentioned: the dynamic pace of change. The peculiar conditions which shaped American institutions ceased to be effective some time between

1890, when, with the disappearance of the frontier, F. J. Turner believed the first chapter of American history to have closed, and the restriction of immigration in the early 1920s. But since that crucial period the United States has continued to develop with astonishing velocity; and this makes the writing of American contemporary history exceptionally difficult. I have not, therefore, attempted to do more than emphasize continuities in the hope that these will provide the most useful clues to the interpretation of current events. But in the United States, as American friends never tire of pointing out, almost anything can happen; and as a historian I have had to make an end without prediction.

Finally, I should like to thank the people and institutions who have made this book possible. Something of what it owes to Cambridge undergraduates may, perhaps, be gathered from the foregoing. I must acknowledge a special debt of honour to the Commonwealth Fund which, in its wisdom, sent me to the Middle West, to the University of Minnesota, for my first introduction to American history and institutions. I should like to record my thanks to the Salzburg Seminar in American Studies; to the participants in the Fulbright Conferences on American Studies of 1952 and 1953, particularly to Mr Alfred Kazin who was good enough to read Chapter Ten; to successive Pitt Professors of American History and Institutions at Cambridge, especially to Professor Dexter Perkins who gave me the opportunity to teach at the University of Rochester, and to Professor Corwin Edwards who commented critically on the final chapter. I am particularly glad of the opportunity to express my warm gratitude to Professor D. W. Brogan—who read the manuscript at an early stage—for his unfailing generosity and learning, and to Mrs E. A. Benians, who most kindly, and with great insight and skill, undertook the immense work of criticizing in detail the style and content of the text. The book has benefited immeasurably from their criticism; only its failings and errors remain my sole responsibility. Lastly, I should like to thank the staff of the Cambridge University Press, and especially Mr F. R. Mansbridge and his colleagues of the New York branch, for their helpfulness in preparing the manuscript for the press. My wife's

Preface

contribution, in terms both of her American birthright and her trenchant criticism, cannot be adequately indicated.

F. T.

BILL HILL,
LYME, CONNECTICUT
4 *July* 1954

ACKNOWLEDGEMENTS

Acknowledgements are due to the publishers for permission to quote from the following works: to Henry Holt and Company, Inc., for passages from 'Chicago', in *Chicago Poems*, by Carl Sandburg, Copyright 1916 by Henry Holt and Company, Copyright 1944 by Carl Sandburg, and from F. J. Turner, *The Frontier in American History* (1920); to Doubleday and Company, Inc., for passages from *My Life and Work*, by Henry Ford with Samuel Crowther, Copyright 1922, and from *The New Freedom*, by Woodrow Wilson, Copyright 1913; to Harcourt, Brace and Company, Inc., for passages from *American Humour, a Study of the National Character* (1931), by Constance Rourke, and from *Main Currents in American Thought* (1930), by Vernon L. Parrington; to the Harvard University Press for passages from *The Letters of Theodore Roosevelt*, edited by E. E. Morison and others, and from *The Atlantic Migration* (1940), by M. L. Hansen; to the Macmillan Company for passages from *The Irrepressible Conflict* (1934), by A. C. Cole, from *The Completion of Independence 1790-1830* (1944), by John Krout and D. R. Fox, and from *The Literary History of the United States*, edited by Robert E. Spiller and others; to *The Atlantic Monthly*, for passages from *Towards an American Language*, extracts from the Charles Eliot Norton Lectures by Thornton Wilder; to Crown Publishers, Inc., for passages from *A Treasury of American Folklore* (1944), by B. A. Botkin; to E. P. Dutton and Co., Inc., for a passage from the book *Three Essays on America*, by Van Wyck Brooks (1934); to Houghton Mifflin Company, for a passage from *Henry Adams and his Friends* (1947), by Harold Dean Cater; to Alfred A. Knopf, Inc., for passages from *Democracy in America*, by Alexis de Tocqueville; to Rhinehart and Company, Inc., for a passage from *The Farmer's Last Frontier* (1945), by F. A. Shannon; and to Charles Scribner's Sons, for passages from *John D. Rockefeller: the Heroic Age of American Enterprise* (1940), by Allan Nevins. Thanks are also due to Charles Scribner's Sons for permission to use material from a map in the *Atlas of American History* by James Truslow Adams and R. V. Coleman, and Henry Holt and Company, Inc., for material from a map in the *Historical Atlas of the United States*, by C. L. and E. Lord.

CHAPTER I

PROVINCIAL SOCIETY IN AMERICA
IN THE TIME OF GEORGE III

'The settlement of our colonies was never pursued upon any
regular plan; but they were formed, grew and flourished, as
accidents, the nature of the climate or the dispositions of private men, happened to operate.'

EDMUND BURKE, *An Account of the
European Settlements in America.*

IN the time of George III a full-rigged ship took from six weeks
to three months to make the uncomfortable Atlantic voyage
from England to the British plantations in North America. Land-
fall might be anywhere along some fifteen hundred miles of difficult
coastline whose shoals and forested islands concealed the entrance
to great rivers like the Hudson and the Delaware and bays like
Chesapeake and Narragansett. Here along the shores of these rami-
fying waterways, often separated from one another by a tangle of
forest and scrub, were scattered settlements which were to be bridge-
heads for the conquest of a continent.

In 1763 at the close of the Seven Years' War, which the colonials
called the French and Indian War, some of these settlements had
become thriving ports with a low silhouette of brick dwellings,
counting-houses and warehouses, pierced by steeples and a forest of
masts. A few merited the dignity of provincial capitals: Boston with
its Assembly House on a hill; New York with its Dutch gables;
Charleston whose sea breezes made it a fashionable watering-place
for the elegant planters of Carolina. The most considerable was
Philadelphia with nearly 40,000 inhabitants, Penn's Holy City,
planned like a gridiron and the model for many a future city in the
wilderness. But such towns were exceptional. Most colonials lived
in villages, hamlets and isolated homesteads or plantations. Of the

two and a half million people scattered along the two-thousand-mile fringe of the continent probably over ninety-five per cent lived in places of less than 2,500.[1] Charleston was the only city in the entire south. Even a generation later the average density of population was less than ten per square mile of settled area.[2] Most Americans lived within a stone's-throw of uncleared land, extracting subsistence from the soil, the forests and their wild life, or the sea, depending on themselves, their families and the occasional help of neighbours for the provision of necessities and a few bare amenities. If land was plentiful, labour and capital were scarce; and for many who attempted to carve a holding out of the wilderness there were too few hands and too little credit to do more than eke out a homespun existence from a corn patch and the game of the forest.

Yet even the backwoods were not without the quickening influence of trade. Necessities like salt or hatchets had to be 'swapped' for pelts or skins; and the ports drew upon an ever-widening hinterland for provisions and articles which could be turned to good account in foreign trade. Fur traders, penetrating far beyond the mountains in search of the ever-retreating beaver and deer, sent back packs of pelts and skins to Albany, Philadelphia and Savannah. Charcoal burners in the wilderness smelted bog iron, some of which found its way to England. The lumbermen in Maine were attacking the stands of white pine and oak on the first stage of an epic march which would take their successors to the Pacific coast; and the sandy pine barrens of the Carolina shore produced pitch, tar and turpentine for the Royal Navy. Plentiful timber enabled the ways of a score of little New England ports to launch ships which earned profits for Yankee merchants and found ready sale in Bristol and London. The fishing ketches of Massachusetts brought cod and mackerel from the Grand Banks to the West Indies, and the whalers of New Bedford and Nantucket returned from the Arctic with whale oil. Even the stony soil of New England yielded a surplus, and from the rich limestone country of central Pennsylvania a wagon road brought to Philadelphia abundance of grains and live-

[1] U.S. Bureau of the Census, *Historical Statistics of the United States*, Series B, 145–59 (henceforward abbreviated to *Hist. Stats.*).
[2] U.S. Bureau of the Census, *A Century of Population Growth* (Washington, 1909), p. 58; in contrast with 150 per square mile for England and Wales in 1801.

stock destined to provision the West Indies. Farther south the long, warm growing season encouraged the planters of Maryland, Virginia, the Carolinas and the infant colony of Georgia to grow tobacco, rice and indigo for export.

Of these exports Britain took the greater part, largely in the form of the subtropical staples, which in 1769 amounted to some £1,200,000. In the same year about £700,000 worth of provisions, livestock and timber products were exported to the West Indies, and some £500,000 worth of fish, grain, rice and timber to southern Europe.[1] Some of this trading was a simple, two-way affair like that in southern staples handled by British merchants and ships; but most was an indirect carrying trade from which Yankee merchants with keen noses for a bargain and a full cargo brought a profitable living to northern ports. A ship from Salem or Boston exchanged New England fish or timber in the West Indies for sugar which it then carried to England, whence, if the ship itself were not sold, it returned with manufactures or immigrants to the colonies. Quaker merchants in Rhode Island sent their ships to the African coast for slaves to be delivered either to the southern colonies or the West Indies. From the West Indies they returned to Newport, laden with molasses to be distilled into the rum which the Puritans used for trade as well as to keep out the New England winter cold. A similar search for cargo brought salt and wines from southern Europe and the Wine Islands.

Exports from the southern plantations were twice as valuable as exports from the rest of the colonies put together. But, although the southern colonies sold slightly more to Britain than they imported, this by no means compensated for the sharply unfavourable balance in the British trade carried on by the middle and northern colonies. The temperate climate north of Maryland, more nearly like that of the British Isles, did not yield enough products of the sort in demand in Britain to pay for the needs of a rapidly growing population for manufactures. The direct trade of the colonies as a whole with the mother country showed a deficit which averaged well over £1 million a year. This deficit was made good largely from West

[1] C. W. Wright, *Economic History of the United States* (New York, 1949), Fig. 8, p. 130.

Indian and southern European trade from which the colonies earned a supply of coin, bills of exchange and goods which could be sent to Britain to settle the account. In the last resort it was the enterprise of colonial merchants in manipulating the margins of a far-ranging ocean trade which kept the colonists solvent.

The continental colonies were constituent parts of an Atlantic trading area which embraced, not only the British Isles, but the West Indies, the Wine Islands, the Iberian Peninsula and southern France. That oceanic area was dominated by the British colonial system, which regulated all its colonies in relation to their function in the Atlantic community. Traditionally, the much prized sugar islands of the West Indies were the more important; but the rapid growth of the continental colonies, which increased their value both as markets and as sources of raw materials, had made them the centre-pieces of empire.

The old colonial system had come to prosperity within the paternalistic framework of mercantilism. That framework had been developed on seventeenth-century assumptions about trade. National wealth depended on trade; and trade must be fostered and fought for. Empire was the only effective way of prosecuting trade; and empire meant monopoly. The object of colonies was to provide the mother country with goods which could not be produced at home and with markets for her products. Although complementary and benefiting from the mutual monopoly, colonies were subordinate to the mother country and existed to augment her wealth. Since national wealth was thought of in terms of treasure for peace and war, the mother country must strive for a favourable balance of trade which would bring in bullion, and for a flourishing mercantile marine as the basis for a navy to protect that trade.

But by the mid-eighteenth century the old Acts of Trade, which embodied these assumptions, had been supplemented by a more sophisticated corpus of regulations, duties and bounties which governed colonial trade, on the whole, to the mutual advantage of colonies and mother country alike. Englishmen in the colonies as well as Englishmen at home benefited from laws which largely confined the carrying trade, both within and without the empire, to English ships. The regulations which canalized trade to and from the great *entrepôt* of the British Isles were to the advantage of colonial as well as home merchants. If the colonists were forced to market an increasing number of 'enumerated' exports in Britain they enjoyed not only bounties and, in the case of tobacco, a monopoly of the British market, but the benefits of British credits and the world trading opportunities of the British mercantile community. If they must buy their major imports from Britain they enjoyed the superior quality and cheapness of British manufactures. British capital developed colonial enterprise and helped sustain in the new lands a rapidly growing population swollen by immigrants provided by British agency. Above all, during the half-century of conflict with the imperial power of France they rested secure behind the protection of the Royal Navy, the cost of which was borne by the home government. Although local interests might chafe at particular regulations there was little disposition among colonials to question the validity of the mercantile system as a whole.[1] Britain and her American colonies were members of an Atlantic partnership which brought prosperity to both. Britain, the dominant partner, provided the impulsive energy for colonial expansion.

The colonial was very conscious of his place in an Atlantic system whose centre was the British Isles and whose links were the ocean trade routes. From the rice planter of Carolina to the horse breeder of Narragansett, from the trapper on the Ohio to the fisherman off Newfoundland, from the wheat farmer of Pennsylvania to the lumberman of Maine, most colonials, however remote they might be from the bustle of the ports, felt the pull of the ocean, and looked eastward along the trails and down the rivers to the seaboard; and the Bostonian, New Yorker or Philadelphian from his provincial capital looked across the ocean to the great metropolis of London. It was more natural for him to look to the mother country than to the neighbouring colonies of his own continent with which he communicated by difficult coastal sailing or by a tenuous post road open only in summer. Ultra-marine in outlook, he had his back to the vast unknown continent on the edge of which he made his living. His face was towards the ocean whence came much that he

[1] See O. M. Dickerson, *The Navigation Acts and the American Revolution* (Philadelphia, 1951).

needed to sustain him in his outpost: supplies and the credit to pay for them; immigrants to provide labour and skills, for he was always shorthanded; furnishings; newspapers; books; musical instruments and a host of other amenities which were the badge of his European culture.

The character of colonial society was determined by the Atlantic. The profits of overseas trade had brought affluence to a small but powerful class of merchant and planting families whose outlook and manners were familiar to one bred in Bristol, Norwich or the English shires. In Boston the great-grandsons of the Pilgrim Fathers gave more thought to the fortunes of the latest trading voyage than to their spiritual duties as members of a 'gathered community'; in the Quaker bosoms of Philadelphia the inner light was too often smothered by a complacent prosperity derived from trade; in fox-hunting Virginia the easygoing planting squire preserved his century-old tradition with the support of Negro slaves and a London overdraft secured by tobacco crops yet unplanted. Sustained in their business dealings by British mercantile houses, this class enjoyed the patronage in politics of the home government, which looked to them to support the royal authority and to do the business of government. If they formed their manners on St James's and Bath, they modelled their political habits on the Westminster and Whitehall which the Duke of Newcastle knew. They ruled the colonies by influence, manipulated through family, business and political connections.

As families they were for the most part long established. The family of Thomas Hutchinson, Lieutenant-Governor of Massachusetts, had enjoyed three generations of affluence from foreign trade; William Byrd was the third of that name to occupy the family seat of Westover, Virginia, which, after the fashion of the Tory squires of England, was rebuilt in Georgian brick and stone. They enjoyed a monopoly of offices in the patronage of the Crown or the proprietors and, like their English peers, were not above feathering their own nests in the course of business. Many an estate was carved out of the wilderness by an obliging friend or relation in office. Land holdings were vast. English magnates, whose forbears had been courtiers, owned enormous tracts. Lord Granville

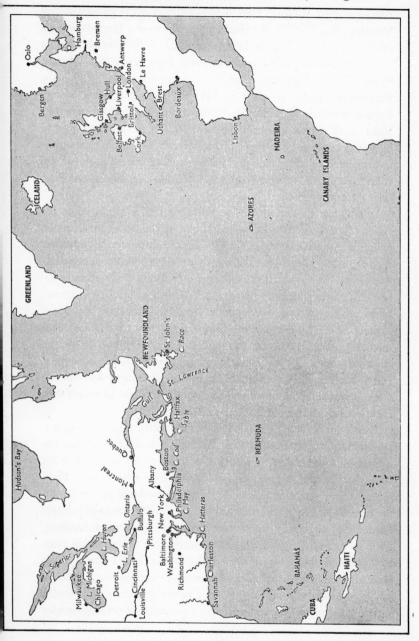

1. The North Atlantic

owned a third of North Carolina; Lord Fairfax the greater part of Virginia's Northern Neck; the Penn estates were a formidable part of the proprietary interest in Pennsylvania. A few Dutch families were patroons of great manors in upper New York. Sir William Pepperell, merchant and conqueror of Louisburg, could ride for thirty miles along the coast on his own land at Kittery, Maine. Boston merchants held the land title to many a blockhouse settlement on the upper Connecticut frontier. The tendency of land to be concentrated in a few hands was fostered by the English common-law practice of entail and by primogeniture. The hunger of the ruling oligarchy for new land was insatiable and land speculation their overriding passion.

In addition to the profits of property and administration the ruling oligarchy controlled colonial politics. The Governor administered his colony only by binding to him the all-powerful oligarchy. The oligarchy in turn, for the most part, controlled the representative assemblies to which the Governors looked for advice and support in carrying out the royal policies. They filled the upper house, which, in many cases, was appointive; they dominated the lower, elected, house by keeping the franchise severely restricted to substantial property owners, by their controlling influence in the constituencies which made some of them virtually 'rotten boroughs' and by refusing full representation to newly-settled areas not susceptible to control. In addition, as justices of the peace and lawyers they controlled the administration of justice.

Thus a comparatively small class of merchants, planters and great landowners, together with their lieutenants in the professions, the lawyers and the clergy, disposed of colonial affairs by a few quiet words at the county court or over the madeira after dinner. Their rule was competent; but their vision, determined as it was by family interest, was narrow, and the British Government was to pay dearly for relying so heavily upon their good offices in administration. True to their class and time, they regarded the unpropertied mass as a rabble unfit to have a voice in colonial affairs; and fearful of the growing numbers of such men as a result of immigration, they consciously pursued a policy of restriction to preserve their rights intact against all comers. Their monopoly of positions of privilege under the Crown identified them to a dangerous degree with the mother country. Grouped as they were round the royal governor's throne they came to be associated, in the minds of onlookers, with the Royal Standard.

But if the colonial oligarchs enjoyed the sun of British favour, they were by no means passive agents of Britain. It was recognized that the colonies were no longer merely plantations to be commercially exploited, but had become autonomous societies with rights and interests which must be respected in practice, however much they were denied in theory. A new awareness of their consequence for Britain had bred an independent temper which emboldened the colonists to scrutinize British policies. Certain points of friction, certain tensions between perimeter and centre of the Atlantic system, gave planters and merchants a new sense of common interests as Americans and a feeling that those interests were not fully understood at home.

The New Englanders fitted awkwardly into the colonial system. Unlike those favoured sons of mercantilist theory, the planters, they had no tropical staples to offer in return for much needed manufactures. Instead they kept solvent by competing with British shipowners and merchants in an extensive carrying trade. The most critical area of this trade was the West Indies, where they sold fish and timber for the molasses which, when distilled into rum, became in turn a cardinal article of New England commerce. The most lucrative part of this trade was with the French and Dutch islands. Since the passing of the Molasses Act in 1733 the import of foreign molasses was subject to a heavy duty; but, fortunately for New England's prosperity, customs procedures were lax and French molasses could either be smuggled in direct or imported by way of Jamaica as British produce. Whether or not as a result of the disrespect for law encouraged by the smuggling habit, trade with the French islands continued throughout the Seven Years' War; in colonial eyes the fact that this was trading with the enemy was a mere technicality. In 1761 the Royal Navy, in an intensive drive against French West Indian commerce, seized colonial cargoes as contraband along with those of the enemy; and the conclusion of hostilities left New England merchants aggrieved at the Admiralty courts and apprehensive about prospects for that accustomed, if clandestine, trade in French molasses which was so important for their prosperity. Then again, the Board of Trade and Plantations, in the interests of British manufacturers, prohibited the colonists from manufacturing, except for local sale, iron and steel products, woollens and hats; and although there is no evidence that these prohibitions hobbled successful enterprise, they were resented. Again, bullionist theory prohibited the export of sterling from Britain, the establishment of a colonial mint and the use of paper money as legal tender. While the governing oligarchy approved the proscription of paper because of its inflationary effects, the absence of a reliable circulating medium handicapped trade. The colonists were forced to rely on the louis, pieces-of-eight and guilders which they earned abroad; but since these were in constant demand to settle British accounts the colonies remained chronically short of currency and dependent for day-to-day transactions on barter and commodity money like tobacco and pelts.

The tobacco planters of Maryland and Virginia also, despite their favoured position as staple growers, were suffering from pressures which they believed to be caused by the operation of the mercantile system. The obligation to send their tobacco to Britain gave them a protected market there and the considerable advantage of British marketing *expertise* on the European continent. But it appeared to stack the cards against them and in favour of the British merchants. Like colonists in general the planters were dependent on British credit to carry on their affairs; and like farmers everywhere they believed that the middlemen obtained undue profits from the risks they ran. The planter was kept going until his crop was raised by the credit of the London or Glasgow merchant, who not only charged high interest rates but captured all the profits from shipping and marketing, and from selling the planter his imported necessities. Long credit terms tempted the planter to overdraw on his British account and to mortgage his crop for years in advance. In addition, while the price of tobacco remained level, costs of production increased sharply. Slaves cost more; and the fixed charges on the English selling price—notably the heavy excise duties—became so burdensome that in times of depression the planter took big losses.

As a result most plantations were encumbered with debts to British merchants which were often passed down from father to son. As Jefferson put it, 'the planters were a species of property annexed to certain mercantile houses in London'[1]; and there were no more unpopular men in the colonies than the Scottish factors, agents of Glasgow tobacco merchants. At the mercy of his creditors, the planter was unable to diversify his farming and had no option but to work his slaves and land year in year out at steadily decreasing returns. Land on tide-water became exhausted and the planters began to open up new lands in the back country which, although less accessible to navigable rivers, promised a better yield. Planters made a policy of acquiring title to larger holdings of uncleared land than they could hope to cultivate and, as their tobacco profits dwindled, looked more to profits from land speculation. In their efforts to acquire western land titles they sometimes came up against British investors with greater resources and influence with government.

The colonial conviction that their interests were not fully understood at home found political expression in friction between governors and assemblies. Although the oligarchy did not scruple to use the royal authority to further their own interests, they were increasingly sensitive about its exercise. The assemblies had grown in power and constitutional authority with the growth of the colonies. The basis of that power was financial, the assembly providing the expenses of administration, including the governor's salary. A half-century of squabbling between governors and assemblies, largely over matters affecting taxation, led the assemblies to assert a constitutional position *vis-à-vis* the governor analogous to that of the British Parliament against the Crown. The home government never admitted the validity of such arguments by colonial lawyers and politicians whose training at the Inns of Court had made them apt pupils of Whig theory. But in practice power of the purse proved in the long run irresistible and against it the governor became well-nigh helpless save for his skill in diplomacy.[2] Through their control of the assemblies the oligarchy were in a position to resist policies

---

[1] Quoted in C. P. Nettels, *The Roots of American Civilization* (New York, 1938), p. 620.
[2] See L. W. Labaree, *Royal Government in America* (New Haven, 1930).

to which they took exception. Dominant factions in colony after colony fought the interests of the Crown or proprietors where these clashed with their own. Unfortunately, these factions took a parochial view of their own interests, refusing taxes to meet legitimate demands, especially defence. Urgent pleas from the frontier for protection against Indians fell on deaf ears in comfortable Boston or Philadelphia; and successive attempts at a common mobilization against the French had broken before the determination of the Albany fur magnates to preserve their trade with Montreal or the refusal of the Carolina planters to see that they had an interest in the Nova Scotia frontier. By the end of the Seven Years' War the colonial assemblies had become sounding boards for an increasingly outspoken opposition to British policies where these fell foul of the local oligarchy; and the narrow vision of that opposition was the despair of a good governor with a broad view of his responsibilities.

If the dominant society was oriented towards the Atlantic, the colonies supported a growing population whose preoccupations lay elsewhere. The most important fact about the continental colonies at this time and for a century to come was their uniquely rapid growth in population and settled area.

Between 1715 and 1776 the population of the colonies grew from some 400,000 to some 2,500,000, an increase of over one-third in each decade.[1] Some of this enormous growth resulted from a remarkable natural increase in a society where labour was scarce and children an economic asset: but the most significant part was the result of immigration. Of the generation which lived through the events of the Revolution, something like a third were foreign born. Between 1718 and 1754 the colonies had absorbed the first of the great 'modern' waves of European emigrants which have peopled the American continent. Most of these emigrants were of non-English stock. The largest groups were Scotch-Irish and Germans. Scots whose families had colonized Ulster had been driven thence to America by the decline of their textile industries, by rack-renting English landlords and by the discrimination they suffered, as Presbyterians, under the Test Acts. Some of the Germans had left the

---

[1] E. B. Greene and V. D. Harrington, *American Population before the Federal Census of 1790* (New York, 1932), pp. 4 and 7.

Rhineland, devastated in the War of the Spanish Succession; others had come in bands of pietistic sects from Germany, Austria and Switzerland. In addition, there were Lowland Scots who had come to trade, and Highland Scots who had emigrated rather than face the consequences of supporting the Young Pretender. These non-English ethnic groups, when added to the French Huguenots, the Swedes and the Dutch already in the colonies, had already given to the colonial population that polyglot character which was to be the essence of the American people.

The newer arrivals were scattered throughout the middle and southern colonies: but they were to be found in especially large numbers in Pennsylvania whither they had been attracted by the accessibility of fertile lands and the liberal religious and immigrant policies of the Quaker proprietors. Filtering through the coastal settlements, immigrant German and Scotch-Irish families were pushing inland up into the mountain valleys of the Appalachians, and into the backwoods of Carolina. From the Pennsylvania mountains the tide of settlement was seeping south-westwards along high, fertile *intervalles* like the Shenandoah into the mountain wilderness of back country Virginia and the Carolinas. In places an advance guard had found its way through the mountain passes out on to the western slopes of the Alleghenies which fell away to the Ohio; and shrewd gentlemen like George Washington of Virginia were buying up the title to as much land as they could engross between the Ohio and the headwaters of Atlantic-flowing rivers.

In this surging movement into the wilderness native migrants also played their part. The townships of New England were no longer able to support their growing population on the produce of an infertile soil. New settlements were launched, not only within New England itself, in the less attractive back country, but outwards: north into New Hampshire, north-west into the forests of Maine, up the Connecticut River into the Green Mountains of what became Vermont, across into western New York and south-west into New Jersey and the Susquehanna Valley. Planters of Virginia, like the elder Jefferson, had moved up under the shadow of the beautiful Blue Ridge in search of virgin soil where tobacco could once again be made to pay.

As a result of this restless land hunger the frontier of settlement had been pushed back within a single generation from the fall line of the eastward flowing rivers to the crest of the great mountain ranges and beyond, a matter in some cases of hundreds of miles of penetration. Already the advance demonstrated that law of geometrical progression which seemed to govern American expansion; for while the frontier had taken a century to reach the fall line it leaped the entire Appalachian Range in half the time and was to reach the Mississippi River in as much time again. It was an inexorable pressure which neither the French nor the Indians could do more than bring to a temporary halt.

Behind the frontier from Georgia to the Maine coast a vast back country was being filled up by settlers whom circumstances had impelled outwards from the older communities. Here in this 'lubberland' life was very different from that of the well-established counties and townships. The existence of the isolated settler was conditioned by the inexorable demands for survival in a cruel wilderness. The unending struggle with forest and undergrowth, mountain pass and swamp, with death by freezing, by summer sickness, with the depredations of wild life and hostile Indians, absorbed the vital energies and induced a hard tempering. As the flow of settlement moved slowly south-west across colony boundaries from New York to South Carolina, these homespun communities began to sense that they had more in common with one another than with the seaboard of the colony which happened to have a shadowy claim to their allegiance. Most of the settlers moving down the Shenandoah Valley belonged to the more recently arrived stocks: Germans for whom the colonies were an alien world and who wished only to be let alone to cherish their peasant culture and their individual religions; or Scotch-Irish with the habit of migration in their blood, independent and sturdy, and with an ingrained hostility to English control in politics and religion. In the Carolina back country, debtors and runaway indentured servants started a new, anonymous existence hidden from authority. They had turned their backs on the ocean and their hopes and fears were concentrated on what the next western horizon would bring. They had become continental-minded, and their values were subtly different from those of the

14

mercantile, seaward-looking communities of the coast. As a result they began to find control from the provincial centres irksome.

For their part, the ruling oligarchy, fearful of the effect that this expansion into the hinterland would have on their own power, rode it with a tight rein. Men of property acquired title to some of the richest western lands from Virginia to New Hampshire, speculating thereby on a handsome increment from future sales or rents. The Ohio Company, for example, a syndicate with both British and colonial investors, in 1763 acquired control of a vast area between the forks of the Ohio and the mountains. These gentry, busily surveying their claims, were determined to prevent the frittering away of their investment by allowing settlers to squat on their land. The whole tide of settlement had been deflected south from New York, leaving the rich Mohawk Valley undeveloped and the frontier pinched in, far to the east of its general line, owing to the strict terms offered to settlers by the Livingstons and other New York magnates who owned the title deeds. The settlers, ignorant of the law and remote from its officers, believed that the hazards of clearing the land and cultivating it were enough price to pay without the addition of rent to an absentee landlord living in the comfort of a plantation or a Boston town house. But even where the gentry, such as those Virginia planters beginning to cultivate tobacco up towards the Blue Ridge, proposed themselves to settle, they had difficulty with the Scotch-Irish and Germans whose south-westward trek from Pennsylvania had brought them to squat on these rich lands of the Virginia mountains; and the struggles between Tuckahoes and Cohees became an important element in southern politics.

As with land so with credit. The back country districts were chronic debtors to the provincial centres, just as the colonies as a whole were debtors to the mother country. The back country dweller was sustained by the credit of the town merchant, from whom he obtained necessities in exchange for such produce as he could market. His expectations seldom equalled his obligations, and his tendency to get into debt increased his resentment at what he regarded as the unjust intervention of the comfortably established in his secluded and difficult life. The burden of debt and the severity of the merchant's credit terms became a political issue in colony after colony. The debtor parties found an instrument to hand in paper money, the issue of which had been a practical necessity ever since Queen Anne's War owing to the scarcity of metallic currency. The inflationary possibilities of paper, with the consequent lightening of the debt burden, led to extravagant issues of paper currency where-ever the popular party could obtain control of the assembly. Land banks were established to lend money to *bona fide* settlers on the security of their land, and this device also led to wild excesses of depreciation. In retaliation, the propertied element had called in the home government to prohibit land banks and the issue of paper money as legal tender in New England in 1751, and this prohibition was extended to the colonies as a whole by the British Parliament's Currency Act of 1763. These measures increased the resentment of the back country debtor against the governing oligarchy and Great Britain. One of the men financially ruined by the declaring illegal of the Massachusetts Land Bank in 1751 was the father of Samuel Adams, the revolutionary leader.

This friction was increased by the tight political control which the provincial centres exercised over the back country. Colonial assemblies were slow to grant representation to the more newly settled communities, which were often unable to make their interests effectively felt. As a result the special needs of the frontier areas went unheeded. Time and again assemblies failed to grant taxes for de-fence against the Indians, leaving the border wide open to the pillag-ing of war parties. The bitterness of frontiersmen against their rulers on this score was such that on one occasion the scalped bodies of a Pennsylvanian settler family were transported all the way to Phila-delphia as a demonstration against the Quaker oligarchy which hid its interest in the Indian trade and its parsimony in defence matters behind a complacent pacifism. Colonial governments were also slow to build bridges and improve roadways. They were reluctant to bring the machinery of justice to the back country, and the distance of the county court and the expenses of the law forced many a remote litigant to let judgment go by default. Even the elements of local government were denied to the back country settlements, such as those New England townships where the privilege of nominating the selectmen rested with the Boston landlords.

To these specific sources of friction must be added a more intangible sense of social difference alienating back country from tidewater. This is nowhere better illustrated than in religion. Although not entirely a back country affair, the great religious revival of the 1740s, known as the Great Awakening, had found fertile ground in the back country, where the harsh conditions of life brought a yearning for a more simple and emotional religion to sustain the spirit against the relentless wilderness. This swamp fire of religious conversion, which had swept the colonies after the teaching of Jonathan Edwards and the revivals of Whitefield, Wesley, Frelinghuysen and others, split sect after sect into 'old and new lights' and sharpened the contrast between the emotionalism of rural America and the deistic urbanity of the educated people. This led to conflict where there was an 'established' religion. German Moravians or Scots Presbyterians resented paying taxes to support the Church of England establishment in the Old Dominion or in the Carolinas. When the young Patrick Henry attacked the Government's attempt to pay the Anglican clergy of Virginia in over-valued tobacco currency in 1760, he voiced the protests of the up-country Virginia which he represented.

With the expansion of the continental colonies into the hinterland, there had developed tensions between the periphery and the centre in each colony which came increasingly to determine the character of colonial politics. These tensions were the result of conflict at all levels—economic, social, religious, political, ethnic. The diverse circumstances which prevailed from Maine to Georgia produced a complex pattern which varied with the individual colony. But in the last analysis those tensions were set up by the efforts of a well-established mercantile-planting oligarchy to maintain and extend their control over a rapidly expanding society. Because this expansion was geographic, the conflicts of colonial politics were predominantly sectional in character. With a spreading population, class contrasts never became fully explicit; and this was to be so as long as America had a moving frontier. The least favourably situated groups in the community—the less well off, the more recently arrived, the rebellious—were pushed outwards willy-nilly from the provincial centres towards the periphery. This did not necessarily mean the frontier itself; the characteristic back country could be found in eastern Connecticut, along the Maine coast and the coastal pine barrens of the Carolinas. In the comparatively dense communities of New England there were highly charged relations between provincial capitals like Newport or Boston and the farmers of the adjacent countryside. Indeed, opposition to oligarchic control existed within the very citadel of the provincial capital. For as Boston, New York and Philadelphia grew in size and importance, they harboured an increasing population of artisans, mechanics and shopkeepers who felt themselves shut away from the sun of mercantile prosperity. In most cities ordinary men were denied political rights. In Philadelphia in 1775 only a tenth of the taxable males had sufficient property to entitle them to vote.[1] Further, their very freedom to trade was curtailed by powerful combinations of merchants. In Philadelphia, again, the merchants for many years tried to obtain a monopoly of the retail trade by abolishing the system of free markets and auctions, an operation which, in 1771, led to a most remarkable outburst of popular feeling. In the eyes of the propertied few, the 'townees', like their back country cousins, were an ignorant rabble to be held in check by an armoury of political, legal and economic devices. The discontent of artisans and shopkeepers found expression in a turbulence which on occasions rose to mob violence like that of their brethren in London and Bristol. This condition was not dangerous so long as the masses of Philadelphia, New York or Boston remained unorganized and leaderless. But the merchants and their lawyer allies were to discover that it could be formidable when exploited by unscrupulous demagogues.

These tensions were not new to colonial politics. They had existed as early as 1675 in Bacon's Rebellion; but they had gradually become more taut with the great expansion of the eighteenth century. However, colonial politics remained manageable so long as the governing power was supported by the unchallenged supremacy of the British Government. Once this was called in question the unstable equilibrium of colonial life was at an end. Unfortunately for the old British Empire the character of imperial control came urgently under review, both at home and in the colonies, with the triumphant close of the Seven Years' War.

[1] M. Jensen, *The Articles of Confederation* (Wisconsin, 1948), p. 17.

CHAPTER II

THE REVOLT IN THE COLONIES

1763-83

'The continent must in the end be conqueror.'
TOM PAINE, *The Crisis*.

IN 1763 the Peace of Paris transformed the British colonial system into a continental empire. The decision to take Canada, and not Guadeloupe, from the French shifted the system's centre of gravity from the West Indies to the American continent. It not only added the vast hinterland of Canada and the eastern part of the Mississippi Valley to the seaboard colonies, but, by eliminating the French, it left the way open to a further expansion across the Appalachians into the heart of the continent.

British policy had to be adjusted accordingly. The basis of empire still remained the Atlantic trading system; but its strategy became increasingly concerned with the needs and resources, not of island and littoral, but of a continent. Instead of limiting her commitments, as of old, to trading positions which could be easily exploited, Great Britain found herself saddled with the problem of administering an empire which was territorial in character and continental in scale.

Had this island people, three thousand miles distant from the very fringe of the new continent, the technical and political resources to rise to this occasion for statesmanship? Economically, Britain was well placed to develop her traditional role. With a rapidly growing population she could continue to provide the main market for the produce of the continent. Her newly productive industries could supply that continent with more, cheaper and better manufactures than her rivals. She could draw on her financial strength for capital to extract the riches from the wilderness. But the cost of supporting this role had become prohibitive. The burden of preserving the empire as a closed system against trading pressures from without and of defending that empire against a possible revival of French military power was too great for the mother country to shoulder unaided. The question was whether the political ties which bound the colonies to the mother country were strong and flexible enough to allow the latter to shift some of the burden to the former so that both could enter into a new and mutually profitable relationship.

It was here that the weakness of the British tradition of colonial control became apparent. The colonies were developing too rapidly to be held within a political system which, however apt for an homogeneous, island, trading people, was less effective for the sprawling, disparate, frontier-conditioned communities of a new continent. The special conditions of that continent were nurturing a society which was coming to differ, in important respects, from the society of Englishmen. England could no longer supply all the emigrants which colonial expansion demanded; American society had become ethnically mixed, and the instinctive allegiances and discipline which bound colonials to their parent society were in a measure relaxed. Even among the dominant English stock, local conditions had fostered a way of doing things which both Englishmen and colonials were surprised to find differed from the habitual at home. In these circumstances, the reshaping of empire, for which the Peace of Paris was the signal, called for imagination, insight and daring. Unfortunately for the old empire those qualities did not prevail in Whitehall and Westminster.

Characteristic of the narrow, if well-meaning temper of British administration was its handling of defence. Part of the general problem was that of defending the western frontier against the Indians, a problem which came urgently to the front as a result of Pontiac's conspiracy in 1763. In the days of the French and Indian wars the colonists had proved incapable of performing this duty. Rather than face the expense of stationing British regulars in the wilderness, the Board of Trade and Plantations sought a solution by guaranteeing hunting grounds to the tribes west of the Alleghenies and preventing settlers from encroaching on them. The Proclamation of 1763, therefore, drew a line along the crest of the Alleghenies west of which settlement was prohibited. This measure, which has every mark of having been drawn up over a map in the quiet of a White-hall office, shows clearly how out of touch was the Administration with American conditions. The tide of settlement was already beyond the line at several points, and with the end of the war a new westward movement was already under way which would be difficult to police. The settlers, who cared little about trespassing, resented the Government's tenderness towards their natural enemies, the Indians, and suspected it to be not unconnected with British interests in the fur trade. The Proclamation was a major grievance of those men of property, especially in Virginia, who were already investing heavily in western lands. Moreover, the Americans were justified in their suspicion that one of the motives behind the Proclamation was a desire to restrain westward movement, not only to promote a more intensive settlement on the seaboard, but for fear that settlement beyond the mountains would be altogether beyond the range of imperial control. This fear was specially marked among the London merchants, who saw no way of pursuing their debtors across the mountains. The attempt at control represented by the Proclamation was shrewd in its ultimate purpose; but the means were unrealistic; and indeed, as the Americans themselves were subsequently to discover, there were no effective means, apart from Indians and natural hazards, of restraining the flow of westward migration.

The Indians were not the British Government's only defence worry. The possibility that the French might renew hostilities and the vastness of the newly acquired territory persuaded the Government that it would be impolitic to rely entirely on command of the sea. In addition a regular force of 10,000 was to be stationed in the colonies. This novel step caused ill-feeling among colonials, who had an inherited prejudice against standing armies and who suspected, with the French threat removed, that the army was intended for domestic coercion. This suspicion was strengthened by George Grenville's Mutiny Act of 1765 which, quite innocently, provided for the quartering of troops in private premises. But colonial irritation was multiplied a thousandfold when it was discovered that the cost of this army was to be met by the colonists themselves.

Hitherto the cost of defending the colonies and of administering the mercantile system had been the recognized duty of the mother country. But the Seven Years' War had left British finances so straitened that it was felt to be just for some of the burden of defence and colonial administration to be shifted to the colonies, which had, on the whole, done well out of the war and were far less heavily taxed than the squires of England. And so a fiscal system designed to make the colonies pay their way was the central feature of the British Government's plan to reorganize and streamline the colonial system.

This scheme was technically well conceived and, from the British point of view, fair. But it raised a host of questions concerning the status of the colonies within the British system. These questions were not new; but they had remained implicit so long as the easygoing temper of Walpole prevailed in Whitehall and the French remained a menace to colonial security. The new situation created by the peace demanded a more positive policy; and this inevitably made the underlying questions explicit. The new temper of Whitehall was conscientious. But it was the conscientiousness of men of limited vision whose viewpoint was narrowly insular. It has been said that Britain lost her American empire because George Grenville read the American dispatches. If he read them to sufficient purpose to formulate a policy, he repeatedly failed to understand the underlying issues which were pointed out to him by the more able of the colonial governors. The result was a policy which raised more questions than it solved. By inadvertently running foul of important interests and deeply held beliefs, it precipitated a political crisis which resolved itself into constitutional terms.

Grenville first attempted to raise revenue by tightening the mercantile system. In place of the old and ineffective Molasses Act a new Sugar Act in 1764 reduced the duty to 3d. a gallon but made clear that this was to be strictly enforced. Customs procedures were made more elaborate; the customs service was increased in size; the powers of the Admiralty courts were strengthened; and the Navy was retained in its anti-smuggling efforts. These measures touched the colonists on a sensitive spot. For, as noted above, it was only by trading outside the Empire that they managed to balance their trading account with the mother country; and the most important commodity in that trade was the French molasses needed for the New England rum distilleries. This trade was central to the operations of New England shippers. The result was a commercial crisis in the northern ports which, coming at a time of post-war depression, made it hard for many houses to keep their heads above water. Such was the outcry that the Government was forced in 1766 to reduce the duty to 1d. and to make it uniform on all molasses, British or foreign. But this did not altogether placate the mercantile fraternity who claimed that the object of the Sugar Act was not to regulate commerce but to tax the colonies to support a new army of British placemen.

The Sugar Act directly affected the northern merchants only. But Grenville's next revenue-raising device touched sensitive nerves all over the continent. The Stamp Act of 1765 imposed on legal transactions, licences and newspapers, stamp duties which pinched the shoes of property owners generally and certain important moulders of popular opinion in particular—tavern keepers and printers. So powerfully did the Stamp Act attract the opposition of all who were irritated with British policies that the agitation against it surprised not only the Government, but colonials of influence who had obtained the new, lucrative office of stamp master. The agitation culminated in the Stamp Act Congress, an inter-colonial meeting of protest which so impressed the home government that, with a change of administration, the Act was repealed.

The next essay in colonial taxation came in the following year when Townshend sought to avoid colonial opposition to a direct tax by imposing import duties on a variety of articles. Although the duties were so small as to be no financial hardship, they were protested against even more vigorously than the Stamp Act had been. In colony after colony groups of indignant men bound themselves to non-importation agreements until the duties should be repealed. In the ports popular feeling ran high, and in Boston the arrival of British troops led in 1770 to a brawl in which several citizens were killed or wounded. As with the Stamp Act, the British Government was forced ultimately to bow to the storm, and in the same year all the duties save that on tea were repealed.

After seven years of trying, the British Government had failed to find an acceptable solution to the main problem of colonial policy.

Taxation on the scale considered appropriate in London could not be imposed except by force. And there was neither the will nor the means of resorting to force; for the army which had been the immediate reason for the new policy still existed largely on paper. The chief result of the British efforts had been to attract to the tax measures the hostility of all those in the colonies with a sense of grievance against British policies in general.

For the colonial animus against the Sugar Act, the Stamp Act and the Townshend duties drew its strength not only from the merchants and property owners most directly affected, like John Hancock, but from lawyers like James Otis and John Adams, who opposed writs of assistance and Admiralty courts; from publicans and printers; from frontiersmen and land speculators like Washington, who disliked the Proclamation line; from paper money advocates like Sam Adams, who resented the Colonial Currency Act of 1763; from debt-ridden planters; from those who feared a British standing army; from Presbyterians and Baptists, who were restive under the Church establishment; and in general from all those who regarded the authority of the Crown as limiting unwarrantably their freedom of action.

By forcing upon the colonies an ill-conceived fiscal programme, successive British administrations had inadvertently chosen for a political duel weapons most suitable for their opponents. The mercantilist reforms had affected only the trading classes of the northern ports, and although held misguided they were consistent with traditional economic policy and no exception was taken to them on principle. But the Stamp Act not only affected all colonies equally but was a direct tax imposed by the imperial Parliament on the colonial population for the support of the colonial administration. It was the traditional policy that local expenses should be borne by the colonies themselves and voted by the assemblies. The whole strength of representative government in the colonies rested on this. The colonists therefore, ignoring the fact that the British Parliament's action resulted from long experience of the inadequacy of colonial requisitions, feared it to be the thin end of a wedge whose thick end would be full parliamentary control. This was a threat to that autonomy which the colonial assemblies had won after hard-fought struggles with royal governors over the power of the purse. With so much at stake, it was natural for colonial lawyers and politicians to take the view that Parliament had no right to tax the colonies, which were responsible, through their own assemblies, direct to the Crown.

This was the question of principle which had always been side-stepped before. Whether or not Acts of Parliament might be extended to the colonies was a question constitutionally obscure, although the colonial oligarchs themselves had not scrupled to call upon Parliament to act in this way when it was in their interests, as with the prohibition of paper money in 1741. But in the new circumstances the colonial cry 'No taxation without representation!' revealed a wide divergence between the implicit assumptions prevailing in England and in the colonies about the Constitution. In England the theory of virtual representation, which justified the denial of parliamentary representation to Birmingham and Manchester, equally justified the extension of parliamentary sovereignty to the colonies. In America, on the other hand, representation, although narrowly based on property interests, was more nearly related to the spread of population. Moreover, its theoretical formulation derived not from eighteenth-century England but from the seventeenth-century thought of the Cromwellian radicals which had taken root in the direct democracy of the New England town meeting. Behind that theory lurked an attitude to politics markedly different from that of the mother country. Thus the colonial cry ' No taxation without representation!' rallied a public opinion against the British financial measures which united diverse interests and cut across inter-colonial jealousies. It was the expression of an instinctive attitude.

It was in the nature of colonial society to resist external control. Many of the colonies owed their very origin to conflicts which had led to a conscious rejection of customary authority at home, and to the creation in the American wilderness of a new society by a dissident group. The 'gathered communities' of the Puritan Separatists were only the first of a series of migrations of this kind. Even in the colonies themselves the instinct to reject unpopular authority led to repeated separations like those which founded Connecticut

and Rhode Island. A limitless and unclaimed wilderness, however unpromising, beckoned to individuals (either in the colonies
themselves or in Europe) who felt their circumstances—political,
religious, social or economic—to be intolerable. The great wave of
eighteenth-century migration, with its German pietists and its
Scotch-Irish rebels, with its indentured servants straining to be free
of their bonds, had only deepened the tradition that authority, where
intolerable, might be rejected. Society might be disowned. The
existence of the back country meant that this rejection took the
form of migration rather than revolution; but in any case sub-
mission and conformity were never regarded as socially virtuous, as
in Europe. As a result, colonial society was a much more loosely
woven fabric than the tightly drawn society of the mother country.
Allegiances were less compelling and committing. The diversity of
ethnic stocks and religious sects did not permit that high degree of
instinctive social cohesion characteristic of the English at home. The
fact that colonial society was in a state of constant and restless movement lessened those loyalties to place and family which made for
stability in the old world. Authority was never unquestioned; and
the more distant the more suspect. In the colonies themselves, as we
saw in Chapter I, the writ of the provincial capital ran but shakily
in the back country. And this resistance by the periphery to control
by the centre was magnified a thousand times when the centre was
the British Isles and the periphery the American continent. Given
these social conditions, the demand for self-government was no
mere slogan used by interested groups. It represented a deeply felt
emotional conviction born of the individual colonist's heredity and
environment.

This heightened awareness by the individual of his separateness
found articulate expression in an apt political philosophy which,
when translated into popular terms, became a powerful ideology.

The starting point of this philosophy was the Calvinistic belief
in a society of the elect. For, although the Saints of Massachusetts
Bay had preached a merciless determinism, and had legislated as
absolutist theocrats, the sense of an immediate relation of the individual to God, which had led to their separation from the corporate
Church in England, carried within it the seed of a new individualism

which flowered in the village life of New England. As the harsh conditions of the seventeenth century gave place to the comparative ease and leisure of the eighteenth, the old rigidities of Puritanism relaxed. The total depravity of man seemed belied by the fact of his capacity for betterment; and with physical betterment came a new emphasis on the possibility of moral betterment. Determinism gave place to a new affirmation of free will; and the centre of religious conviction shifted from the doctrine of the elect to that of conversion. The emotional fervour of the Great Awakening quickened the individualistic temper and, as a result of the teaching of Jonathan Edwards, gave Calvinism a new lease of life. More sophisticated minds, unaffected by revivalism, as they moved towards Deism or Unitarianism, gained a new sense of individual freedom.

This in turn became translated in secular terms into the philosophy of natural rights. The strain of English seventeenth-century thought which flowered with Sidney, Harington, Milton and John Locke found in America its most fertile ground. Here, in these communities bordering on the wilderness, the illusion of man's preexistence in a state of nature carried complete conviction. The existence of natural rights which antedated the State, the idea of the State created as the result of a compact among free men for certain specific purposes, came naturally to men who regarded the bonds of society as limited commitments. Above all, in the writings of Locke, Americans found a brilliantly explicit formulation of what they regarded as common sense; and his doctrine of the right of revolution against arbitrary rule provided a completely satisfying basis for opposition to the new colonial policy. The *Two Treatises of Government* gave Americans an ideology for revolution to be revealed plainly in the Declaration of Independence and in Paine's *Common Sense*.

In their resistance to parliamentary taxation, Americans in colony after colony were moved by convictions which were deeply felt at all levels of society. That so many of them not merely felt the same way but came to act in concert, resulted from the fact that the British Parliament presented them with a simple issue which all could recognize in the terms of an almost universally held political philosophy. The conflict between that philosophy and the assumptions of British imperialism was profound. It could only be resolved by thinking out afresh the whole basis of political obligation between mother country and colonies; and this demanded an exacting degree of statesmanship which was beyond the powers of British politicians.

Few colonials were thinking in terms of a complete break with Britain. The failure of the mother country to impose her policy by 1770 resulted in a slackening of tension and in hopes that the crisis could be weathered. With the repeal of the Stamp Act, even the passing, at the same time, of a Declaratory Act asserting the sovereignty of Parliament over the colonies failed to dampen the general relief and rejoicing that the immediate issue of direct taxation had been disposed of. When the Townshend duties were withdrawn, with the exception of that on tea, the merchants believed they had won their point and, with trade reviving in 1770, were content to turn from politics to business. Non-importation agreements languished; and those Virginia gentlewomen who had appeared at the governor's ball in homespun once again flaunted the silks and brocades of the London houses.

The peace was, however, deceptive. The oligarchy might, as a whole, be content with the positions they had gained and held; but the crisis had shaken the whole basis of confidence upon which colonial administration rested. The agitation against British policy had stirred new forces in colonial politics which were to prove no longer easily amenable to oligarchic control. In their campaign of protest merchants and planters were prepared to work up against Britain a popular opinion much more far-reaching than conventional politics; and in so doing opened a Pandora's box of troubles for the established order. The people who rallied most vociferously to the cry of natural rights in danger included those who felt themselves to be most discriminated against within the colonies. A decorous debate among gentlemen about the conditions of trade, the propriety of certain kinds of taxes and the niceties of constitutional theory was transformed into a rough and tumble by the admission to the debating chamber of a rude and sweaty multitude of back country farmers, artisans, shopkeepers, sea lawyers and psalm singers only too anxious to take a knock at the Crown. By attacking the Crown they saw an opportunity of striking at their betters, so many of whom were grouped round the royal governor's throne. The natural rights argument justified resistance not only to parliamentary tyranny but to arbitrary authority at home. So long as colonial politics rested on the unquestioned authority of British power, those interests which were outside the ring of favour could not force their way in; but once British authority came under attack the whole basis of the colonial oligarchy was undermined, and what that oligarchy persisted in regarding as an unorganized rabble was given a chance to stake out for itself a place in the sun. And so when men of property turned back to their counting-houses, their ships and their estates, they were too complacent in assuming that things could be again what they had been before the French and Indian War. By 1770 those peripheral interests which had been squeezed out of the centres of power had become grouped together and their influence was felt from Carolina to Maine.

In colony after colony the voice of the back country was heard ever more stridently in the assemblies. In Virginia, the resolves which were carried against the Stamp Act were the work of Patrick Henry, who, along with Richard Henry Lee and others, represented the back country and set the pace for the tide-water gentry. In the sea-port towns the influence of the mob, swollen by more respectable artisans and egged on by the merchants themselves, intimidated not only stamp masters and customs officials but the very centres of provincial government. Stamp Act mobs revealed their subconscious motives by riotous and indiscriminate attacks on property. In Boston, Governor Hutchinson's mansion was sacked, and the manuscript of his *History of Massachusetts Bay* had to be retrieved from the mud. In New York, Governor Colden's state carriage was burnt after being driven round town with a drunken Indian in the seat of honour.

The disorders of the mob and the strident oratory of radicals in the assemblies were not in themselves dangerous to the established order. They could be controlled within the existing political framework. But under the pressure of colonial agitation, back country and urban elements became organized outside that framework. A mushroom growth of Sons of Liberty, turbulent political clubs, not above tarring and feathering the objects of their wrath, agitated town and countryside and, operating with a rough cohesion, provided the nucleus of a rudimentary political party.

All this, however, was the politics of agitation; and when the political temperature dropped again in 1770 there was every chance that this incipient organization would disintegrate, leaving the interests it represented as defenceless as before against the force of reaction. Fortunately for the radical cause, there had emerged in certain key colonies leaders who were determined to keep the agitation against Britain alive until that cause could be supported by an effective political party, even if this meant forcing the issue to the point of armed rebellion against the Crown.

The most effective leadership came from Massachusetts, where Samuel Adams was a remarkably talented agitator and organizer. On his initiative the Boston Sons of Liberty effectively directed the activities of the town mob. By a mixture of propaganda and intimidation the popular party secured control of the Boston town meeting and thereby of the town's government. But Adams and men like him in other colonies were shrewd enough to perceive that this narrow basis of power must be widened to include those sympathizers in the back country who, by their nature, were disorganized and leaderless. Committees of correspondence were established throughout the colonies. These enabled leaders in the provincial capitals to conduct a co-ordinated campaign which was politically effective at the seats of power and which by 1774 had become continental in scale. During the years of reaction between 1770–4 the radical leaders perfected their organization and took advantage of every incident which could be worked up against the British, such as the burning of the revenue boat *Gaspée* by a Rhode Island mob in Narragansett Bay. At last, in December 1773, the British Government presented the radical party with a splendid opportunity for direct action.

In order to help the East India Company out of difficulties, the Government, by granting the Company a drawback, gave it a virtual monopoly of the tea trade with the colonies, to the detriment of colonial merchants. This led to an immediate boycott of the Company's tea in colonial ports and, in Boston, to the dumping of a cargo of tea into the harbour. With this deliberately staged 'tea party', the quarrel with Britain flared up again with full force. For the British Government, coercion seemed now the only possible course; but the passing of a series of measures designed to reduce the people of Massachusetts to obedience only played into the hands of the radicals, who once more had the backing of an inflamed public opinion throughout the colonies. Formal protests by conventions and assemblies were followed in September 1774 by the calling of a Continental Congress at Philadelphia.

Only the most statesmanlike of compromises could now have prevented an open rebellion. But neither Lord North's attempt at conciliation nor Joseph Galloway's proposals for what was in effect a kind of 'dominion status' had a real chance of acceptance. The radical party was in the saddle and its leaders were determined on independence. When, in April 1775, British troops, detailed to destroy stores at Concord, retired to Boston in a running fight with improvised companies of Massachusetts farmers, the first shots had been fired in a rebellion which was to end in revolution. In May there met a second Continental Congress which, on 4 July 1776, passed Jefferson's Declaration of Independence. The radicals had become rebels: they were about to become revolutionaries.

If the crisis had created a united public opinion throughout the colonies against Britain, only a small minority were prepared to push resistance to the point of independence. John Adams later estimated that at most a third of the colonial population were active radicals or Whigs, a third were active loyalists or Tories and the indecisive remainder drifted with the tide. But the radical third were led by an effective cadre of revolutionaries who, by manipulating a political organization outside the conventional framework of politics, managed at the critical moment in colony after colony to seize control of the real centres of power. This revolutionary cadre contained leaders from most groups in colonial society: merchants like Hancock, planters like Washington and Jefferson, lawyers like John Adams, a financier like Robert Morris and a *savant* like Franklin. But its most active leaders in the early stages were demagogues like Samuel Adams with a talent for the rowdier kinds of agitation and intimidation in the local communities. Moreover, these men agitated, not so much the considered opposition of men of property and education to the principles of British colonial policy, as the instinctive grievances of small men everywhere against the restrictions of authority in the colonial centres. The emotional force which generated a revolutionary party and ultimately an army had its origin in hostility to the colonial, rather than the British, regime. For the radical the two were identified; but in attacking Parliament and George III he was primarily concerned to strike at the colonial oligarchy who pressed so tightly upon his daily life.[1]

As for the oligarchy itself, when it came to the sticking point, merchants, planters and professional men divided according to their dominant convictions and interests. The merchants, as a class, were not men to convert an argument about trade and taxes into a shooting affray. For most of them the radical cause became associated with tarring and feathering and riotous attacks on property by the 'baser sort'. Fearing for the established order, most urban families of property and position turned conservative after 1770 and worked for conciliation. Some, as in New York, played along with the radicals in the vain hope of moderating the activities of the committees of correspondence and the first Continental Congress. A few played on both sides in the hope of preserving their position. But the great majority of merchants, lawyers, office holders and clergy remained loyal, helped, no doubt, in Philadelphia, New York and Boston by British military occupation during the early revolutionary years. Over a thousand families followed the lead of Governor Hutchinson, Chief Justice Oliver and other luminaries in joining General Howe's evacuation of Boston in 1776; and here and elsewhere the well-to-do did their best to support the British military administration. They provided officers for the loyalist regiments and, after British defeat had made their position untenable, they left the continent for exile in England or Canada whence they carried on a weary and vain correspondence for the recovery of their property. In the plantation colonies, also, most of the more prominent families and those closest to the administration remained loyal to Britain; and here as elsewhere families were divided by the bitterness of civil war. But the proportion of Whigs among the gentry was higher than in the towns. The ingrained independence of mind fostered by the sequestered plantation life; a quick-trig-

[1] M. Jensen, *op. cit.* ch. i.

gered sense of personal honour; the absence of British occupation; the absence of towns with their turbulent and frightening lower orders; the deeply felt grievances about western land investment; and the nagging burden of plantation debt held in England were some of the influences which kept many of the Virginia gentry within the Whig fold and provided the patriot party with its most respectable leadership. But even in Virginia it was the newer, poorer and more rebellious of the gentry who took this initiative: Henry, who represented the back country; Jefferson, who was brought up under the Blue Ridge and had to make his way in the world; Washington, the self-made businessman-planter; Richard Henry Lee, who, although of good family, had been ostracized for exposing the peculations of Speaker Robinson of the Virginia House of Assembly, which involved a number of the 'best families'. In general, the oligarchy were divided in their allegiance, and sorted themselves out variously according to local conditions; but the majority, especially in the towns and of those closest to administration, were Tory in sympathy and many suffered for it as displaced persons. In the last resort, what told was their loyalty, not merely to a regime or a king, but to an entire social order whose underpinning was the social structure of Great Britain herself.

As for the Whigs, despite the fortunate leadership provided by a minority of men of gentle birth or education, the strength of their rank and file came from back country and town streets, and they were drilled by self-made warrant officers of similar background. The impulse which led such men to leave their spring fields and, with their long hunting rifles, to pick off straggling redcoats, sprang from deeply felt resentment, not against British rule in the abstract, but against the restrictions of provincial authority which denied to the ordinary colonial subject what he regarded as a natural and fitting measure of local self-government. And in taking up arms the New England farmer or the Scotch-Irishman from up-country Pennsylvania failed to distinguish between his enemies in England and those in his own colony who had done the British bidding and had thereby profited in the exercise of power.

The fundamental character of the Whig Party as a fusion of back country and town was complicated by the inevitable variations between colony and colony. This fusion was most complete in New England, where town and back country were closest together, and in Pennsylvania. In Virginia the back country found important allies among the controlling oligarchy. In North Carolina, on the other hand, the conflict between back country and tide-water was so marked that since the tide-water planters were predominantly Whig, the back country remained Tory. But these variations merely serve to show the importance of these internal conflicts in setting the pattern of revolutionary politics.[1]

In the last resort, the Whig cause drew its strength from those groups at the periphery of colonial life who saw an opportunity to break the power of the centre. Without these tensions between periphery and centre in the colonies, the tensions between the colonies as a whole and their own centre of government three thousand miles away might never have come to breaking point. Those internal stresses were the result of conflict between the pull of the Atlantic and the pull of the continent in colonial society. The Whigs were continental-minded. Although the British Government had failed to get the individual colonies to act as a continental unit against the French, who were a continental threat, they succeeded in spite of themselves in forcing a continental union against British Atlantic power. These are the overtones to the names Continental Congress and Continental Army. And when Jefferson drafted the Declaration of Independence, just as when he wrote his *Notes on Virginia,* his frame of reference was the vast hinterland of the continent whose great mountains, forests and rivers would provide a natural setting for a free society.

The same conditions which created a Revolutionary party made for the military success of the Revolution. British strategy, like British civil policy before it, was thought out in Atlantic, not in continental, terms. The colonies must be reduced to obedience by an effective show of British military and naval power at the provincial capitals on the seaboard and along the St. Lawrence. With British pressure on these nerve-centres resistance at the extremities must surely collapse. But however ingratiating Sir William Howe might be in Boston, New York and Philadelphia, however forceful

[1] M. Jensen, *op. cit.* ch. ii.

and competent Sir Henry Clinton and Lord Cornwallis might be in deploying their splendidly professional armies from coastal bases into New Jersey and the Carolinas, the British always failed to extinguish entirely the quickening spirit of the Revolution. That spirit drew its moral and physical strength not from the organized centres of colonial life, but from back country and plantation and the semi-underworld of the towns.

That spirit proved an illusive will-o'-the-wisp during the first critical years. From the first enthusiasm of '76 to the news of the French alliance of '78, the Continental cause was always at the point of disintegration. For all its continental character the Congress was not an effective government. It was often on the run and had no powers to enforce upon the States the provision of adequate supplies not only of munitions and food and clothing but of men. Recruiting for the Continental Army was always far behind what was needed for a minimum campaigning programme. However critical the moment, men left the colours for their families and farms when their short seasons of service were at an end. The army had perforce to rely upon the State militia, ill-disciplined and poor-spirited drafts who often refused to operate beyond their State boundaries. The commander-in-chief, General Washington, was constantly worried by a state of affairs which led him to write: ' If every nerve is not strained to recruit the new army with all possible expedition I think the game is pretty near up.'[1] The army's supplies were improvised throughout the war. Army contractors made great profits out of the dire needs of the soldiery. There was a chronic and crippling shortage of powder and of woollen clothing, neither of which was made in sufficient quantities in the colonies. The shortage of food was equally severe; for farmers preferred hoarding or selling to the British for silver to selling to the Continentals for paper money. And paper money was ever-proliferating testimony to the political weakness of the Revolutionary cause. The Continental Congress, a mere diplomatic conference without the taxing power of government, succeeded in coaxing from the States only a fraction of their promised financial contributions.

[1] Washington to John Augustine Washington, 18 December 1776; quoted in D. S. Freeman, *George Washington* (London, 1951), vol. IV, p. 295.

It was forced repeatedly to pay contractors for supplies by manufacturing paper money which, through lack of backing, depreciated so rapidly that by 1781, in spite of attempts at reform by Robert Morris, it was worthless, and the phrase 'not worth a continental' became a byword. The States also, although newly sovereign, failed to raise money by taxation. The newly styled patriots, who were fighting a tyranny symbolized by taxation, were not prepared to see the odious office usurped even by State assemblies of their own choosing. The States, by resorting in turn to the manufacture of paper, contributed to a galloping inflation which by 1781 had exhausted the entire body politic. From almost every point of view the revolutionary war effort was a picture at best of parochial endeavour and at worst of self-defeating jealousies, treacherous neglect and criminal self-seeking. It displayed nakedly all the vices of its character as an insurrection of men who distrusted authority, were impatient of discipline, ignorant of the need for controls, and bent only on achieving a liberty bordering on anarchy.

The virtues of such a revolution were less obvious, but in the end proved more telling, than the disciplined force of the British professionals. Only a few may have been passionately or doggedly convinced enough to commit themselves without reserve; but those few were sufficient to keep a political mechanism and an army functioning and by their example to draw new recruits to the colours when that army seemed on the point of disintegration. The very dispersed nature of Whig support was its strength. For as the hunting shirt was better camouflage than scarlet, so the Continental soldier easily faded into the back country citizen when he had had enough of fighting, to return refreshed at the opening of the next campaign. And although he fought in a European-style army, his seasoning in the wilderness made him a light infantryman of exceptional resource and endurance. Enough of such men stayed with the colours to keep the army in being in spite of the almost incessant retreats from Brooklyn Heights to Morristown.

But that army would not have survived without its commander-in-chief. Washington, the aloof Virginia gentleman who had never commanded more than a regiment, acquired a slow but unshakable conviction in the justice of the Whig cause which enabled him to master all self-doubts and to emerge as an iron-willed commander, the epitome of a revolution purged of all cant, self-seeking and doubt. Although no brilliant tactician, he remained true to his strategic purpose, which was to keep an army in being and to avoid a show-down on British terms. After the gruelling test of the Valley Forge winter, the army's survival was no issue. But the problem remained of how to take the initiative in wearing down British forces which were too strong to be decisively beaten in the field. Fortunately, Washington could rely on the mistakes of his opponents; and it was the characteristic failure of the War Office and General Burgoyne to understand the full hazards of the latter's thrust southwards from Quebec to the wilderness of Lake Champlain which led to the first positive American victory, the surrender of Burgoyne's army at Saratoga.

But although the Whig cause survived because of the secret resources of the continental back country, that cause could not triumph so long as the British were in a position to reinforce their strong coastal bases by sea. Happily the French, whose expulsion from North America had given the Americans their first opportunity, saw in the colonial rebellion a chance to re-establish some of their lost positions in the Atlantic area. The French alliance not only provided the Americans with supplies, volunteers and encouragement, but powerful naval forces to threaten British sea communications. It was Admiral de Grasse's temporary wresting of the ocean command from the British Navy off Chesapeake Bay which led to Cornwallis' surrender at Yorktown in 1781 and the virtual end of the Revolutionary War. Thus, while the absence of sea power had lost the French their American empire, the seizure by the French of the initiative at sea twenty years later lost the British their American empire and set the seal on American independence. Without sea power the Continentals, although strong enough now to survive out of reach of British authority, were still unable to achieve any real measure of independence. The continent had achieved much; but the Atlantic still had the final say. It was still necessary for the Old World to intervene to redress the balance of the New.

CHAPTER III

THE REVOLUTIONARY
ACHIEVEMENT
1776-1801

'The genuine Liberty on which America is founded is totally
and entirely a New System of Things and Men.'
THOMAS POWNALL, His Majesty's late Governor of
the Provinces of Massachusetts Bay and South Carolina, *A
Memorial Addressed to the Sovereigns of America* (London, 1783).

'The Revolution was in the minds and hearts of the people.'
JOHN ADAMS to Hezekiah Niles, 13 February 1818.

THE independence of the thirteen colonies, formalized in 1783 by
the Treaty of Versailles, was the high point of triumph for the
radical revolutionaries. In the *élan* of their success the insurgents
consolidated their control and in each of the new States proceeded to
transform institutional life to fit their own beliefs and interests.

The colonial structure of politics was revamped according to the
assumptions of natural right. The convention of the State as a compact among free men, to whom self-respect reserved the right of
withdrawal if those natural rights were threatened, had been given
incandescent form in the Declaration of Independence. It was also
reflected in the preambles to new State constitutions like that of
Massachusetts which declared that 'the body politic is formed by a
voluntary association of individuals : it is a social compact, by which
the whole people covenants with each citizen, and each citizen
with the whole people, that all shall be governed by certain laws
for the common good'.[1] The radical aim was local self-government.
In a sprawling community resistance to authority took the form of
resistance to any form of distant control, whether from England or

[1] Massachusetts Bill of Rights, Constitution of 1780; H. S. Commager, ed., *Docu-
ments of American History* (New York, 1946), p. 107.

from the provincial capital. Pains were taken to ensure that State governments should have no opportunity to exercise a tyrannous authority over the local communities. The old colonial assemblies were transformed into virtually sovereign State legislatures more directly representing the interests of the mass of small farmers. Constituencies were reorganized to give a greater measure of equality to the back country. Maximum power rested with truly representative assemblies whose members were delegates rather than true representatives. The Pennsylvania constitution, for example, dispensed altogether with an upper house. Governors were vouchsafed a minimum of authority and were for the most part creatures of the dominant party in the legislatures. Suspicion of the executive went so far that assemblies assumed both legislative and executive functions, to the confusion of both. The Continental Congress had fought the Revolutionary War without an executive and, in spite of the grotesque ineptitude of the system, of which Washington and the Revolutionary financier, Robert Morris, were only too painfully aware, the radicals remained content with the primitive practice of government by committee.

With this new instrument shaped to fit their purpose the radicals proceeded to attack those customary institutions transplanted from the Old World which had embodied a corporate social order and had protected the privileges of a ruling class.

They confiscated the Crown lands and most of the Tory estates, large and small, redistributing some of the land to small farmers and old soldiers. They abolished quit-rents, entails, primogeniture and titles of nobility. By these means they not only removed the restrictions which had preserved vast tracts of land from piecemeal settlement, but swept away the legal devices, some of them feudal in origin, which had moulded colonial society on the traditional pattern of English life. Henceforward the aggregation of great estates, which remained a typical feature of American growth, had no longer as its sanction customary privilege with attendant duties, but property right. The change loosened the social bond between landlord and tenant; it increased the mobility of real estate and shifted the basis of proprietorship from social position to mere wealth. It was a change which reflected the inner convictions of small men everywhere on a continent where the exploitation of abundant land in the expectation of profit from rising values was the primary preoccupation of most citizens.

The radicals also disestablished the Church of England where established. The new Episcopalian body, bereft of its ancient authority as the corporate, and indeed catholic, Church of a total society, was reduced to the somewhat anomalous position of being merely another independent sect, cherished among the conservative and well-to-do, but insignificant in the religious life of America as a whole. Its dethronement marked the final success of those sects which had resented the payment of taxes to support an exclusive and alien establishment whose clergy were for the most part English, condescending and slovenly in the performance of their duties; and it is significant that hostility to the Church of England came from bodies like the Presbyterians, Baptists, Lutherans and German pietists who were strong in the back country. Disestablishment was an integral part of the radical programme. But there was more in this than hostility to a Church whose head was King George III of England. It was a logical consequence of both Puritan and natural rights traditions. The Puritan idea of a 'gathered community' of the elect and John Locke's view of the Church as a voluntary society were equally a denial of a catholic Church embracing a complete community. Such a conception belonged to the customary societies of the Old World, but had no natural place in the sprawling, experimental communities of the New, with their eclectic sects, their disparate ethnic groups and their suspicion of authority whether secular or religious. Henceforward the English tradition of religious liberty was to be pushed to its ultimate limit of absolute equality for all Christian belief within a neutral and secular State. This was another fundamental doctrine of American society which Thomas Jefferson crystallized into shining phrases, in his Virginia Statute of Religious Freedom. Connected with the disestablishment of the Church was the attack on colleges which had received their charters from the Crown and which were popularly identified with the education of a privileged group for royal service in Church and State. Even the College of William and Mary, *alma mater* of so many Virginia statesmen including Jefferson himself, was tainted with this suspicion; and Jefferson finally created the University of Virginia to provide an American education without religious bias for young Virginians of talent. He also wrote into what became the North-west Ordinance the principle of State-supported secular education for the new territories to be created west of the Alleghenies.

Other institutions were also transformed by the radical touch. The Revolution had dealt a severe blow to the legal profession. The colonial judges and most attorneys had joined the Tory exodus, and the profession, which had always relied partly upon the Inns of Court for training, was diluted in talent. These circumstances, together with radical hatred of royal administration of the law, led to a marked shift towards the election of judges and the decentralizing of the administration of justice. This tendency, while egalitarian and satisfying the grievances of the back country, diverted the stream of English legal tradition into new channels in America. The old suspicion of military authority, ever present in the radical mind, was directed against what remained even of the Continental Army. The hard core of officers received short shrift from the politicians in the matter, not only of pensions, but of arrears of pay; and their ex-service organization, the Society of the Cincinnati, appeared in radical eyes in the sinister light of what would today be called fascism. Even the reputation of Washington himself suffered under this cloud. As for the navy, the thin veneer of naval discipline was quickly rubbed off, leaving the basic stuff of merchant seamen and fishermen. When the time came for the permanent establishment of U.S. armed forces, its officers were to be recruited, not from any well-defined officer class, but eclectically on a basis of talent and political patronage.

These measures subtly transformed American society and were in themselves a social, as well as a political, revolution. The radicals disestablished not only the Church, but all the institutions which made up the highly integrated, customary communities of Europe. Henceforward king, squire and parson, those symbols of a society of status where authority devolved in an inbred and unquestioning allegiance, lost their magic. Instead there was the groundwork for a society based on the idea of contract, where authority was imparted from below and hedged with restrictions, and where allegiance to institutional forms was tentative and conditional. The centrifugal forces of a continental society with an expanding frontier had proved too strong for the governing balance of a colonial system fashioned by an island people. In this new context the conflict between authority and liberty, between order and variety, had to be newly resolved.

The assumptions from which the radicals started led them quickly into difficulties which they were reluctant to face. Positive State action was so minimized that the condition of public order approached anarchy. The drunken inflation through which the Americans had worked off the financial effects of the war left the economy in a state of almost total collapse. Both State and Continental currencies were discounted so heavily as to be worthless. Fixed incomes shrank into insignificance and debtors forced into the hands of reluctant creditors bundles of paper money. The sudden stoppage of war orders and the inflooding tide of British manufactures after the peace resulted in a severe post-war depression in commerce and in those mushroom manufactures which the war had stimulated. The merchants of New England, New York and Philadelphia, now excluded from trade in the British Empire, had to endure hard times until they could open up new markets. Meanwhile, the British dominated America's foreign trade, and in American ports a forest of idle masts flying the Stars and Stripes testified to the stagnation of American shipping. Until 1786, when confidence slowly revived, those Americans who lived by commerce, manufacture or investment had to withstand a state of siege.

The radical parties were complacent about this state of affairs. The small farmers, like peasants everywhere in wartime, were the one group able to improve their position. The real value of land was enhanced, and its produce could be bartered advantageously or consumed at home. The back country was comparatively insulated from the effects of commercial depression, and its representatives, taking a narrow view of their interests, could afford, where they were in power, to ignore the major issues of economic policy. That shrewd observer Franklin believed that the mass of small men were better off than those of any other country.[1]

---

[1] Franklin, in the 'American Museum', January 1787; quoted in D. M. Potter and T. G. Manning, *Nationalism and Sectionalism in America, 1775–1877*, p. 44.

The Revolutionary Achievement, 1776–1801

The radical attitude of mind determined the relations between the individual States. The Revolutionary War had been conducted by a Continental Congress representing all thirteen States; and in terms of strict constitutional chronology it is possible to maintain, as Abraham Lincoln did, that by making a formal declaration of independence on behalf of all the colonies, the Congress had assumed the sovereignty wrested from Britain. But in truth, real power remained with the individual States. Only a profound crisis had forced the colonies to combine; and once the military crisis was at an end the impromptu union was in danger of breaking up into its constituent parts. The Continental Congress was little more than a conference of ambassadors. The constructive side of the Revolution regarded as a social movement was carried through within the States, which embodied separate societies.

Continental loyalties were insubstantial compared with the more immediate and more traditional loyalties to one's State. When Jefferson referred to 'my country' he meant Virginia; a Massachusetts soldier of the Revolution thought of his country as New England; and John Adams described his membership of the Continental Congress as his country's 'embassy'.[1] This local loyalty reinforced the radical suspicion of external authority. The radicals, in demanding local self-government, resisted the idea that the States should give up any significant measure of power to a central, continental authority. And so, although the committee appointed by the Continental Congress to draft a declaration of independence took only some five weeks to do its job, a second committee, appointed on the same day to draw up permanent articles of confederation, took five years to bring its proposals into effect; and the Articles of Confederation of 1781, which were the result, merely gave the *de facto* revolutionary Congress a more permanent constitutional form. The States kept their sovereignty intact. The Federal Congress could not move a foot without the consent of the States, each of which had the right of veto. Congress had no power to tax, to regulate commerce or to negotiate effectively with foreign countries or Indian tribes. In the enthusiasm of their newly won sovereignty the States carried

[1] John Adams to his wife, 18 September 1774; quoted in Potter and Manning, *op. cit.* pp. 29–30.

43

on independent relations with foreign Powers, issued their own currencies and, with an inherited mercantilism, constructed tariff walls at the expense of their neighbours. New York State not only prosecuted its ancient war with Connecticut over the Long Island trade, but even taxed the vegetables brought over for sale to the citizens of New York City from the New Jersey shore; and New Jersey retaliated by imposing a tax on Sandy Hook lighthouse at the entrance to New York harbour, which happened to be on Jersey soil.

As the 1780s drew on, it became increasingly clear that many of the problems facing the individual States were common to all and could only be solved by a common effort. No single State had enough bargaining power to force from the British reasonable trading rights or the evacuation of the western frontier posts still occupied in violation of the Treaty of Versailles. No single State could develop its commerce on a continent divided into thirteen trading areas, with thirteen separate and fluctuating currencies, and in the absence of a legal system recognized by all.

But the Congress of the Confederation was powerless to provide a remedy. Radical-dominated States resisted all pressures to impart greater authority to the Federal Congress by revising the Articles of Confederation. They could afford to be complacent about the evils of the time which affected most the mercantile and property-owning classes; and their objection to the delegation of authority to a distant and central seat of authority was magnified a hundred-fold when the authority in question was continental in scope. For the radicals, the Articles of Confederation represented the judicious limit of Federal authority; any increase in the Federal power was likely to have just those tyrannous effects which Americans had resisted in the British rule. Only in one significant direction were the powers of the Federal Congress augmented during the period of radical ascendancy. As a sop to the small State of Maryland, which feared domination by its larger neighbours, those States with claims to western land handed over their rights to Congress, which, in a series of ordinances, laid down the political conditions to govern the settlement of the American hinterland.[1] Only in the matter of western land did the radicals show themselves sensitive to the need

[1] See ch. v below.

for effective continental direction. In this, too, the back country spoke out in its own interests.

It must not be supposed, however, that merchants, planters and men of property generally bowed before the triumph of insurgent radicalism. The *élan* of the Revolution, although sweeping away the ancient social sanctions of wealth and property and instituting a more egalitarian framework for politics, had by no means routed the old colonial oligarchy. The dominant Tory element had disappeared, although a few families, protected by more fortunate Whig connections, returned quietly from exile after 1783. But the void left by the Tory exodus was quickly filled by new men. The Revolutionary War provided ample opportunities for the enterprising to make money. There was the profitable business of army contracting and of financing Revolutionary loans which brought affluence to such men as Elbridge Gerry. New England merchants quickly discovered that patriotism could be combined with profit by fitting out their fast schooners as privateers to prey upon the richly laden and slow-moving merchantmen of England. The risks were great; captured ships must be written off; and captured men had to face a grim internment in the Royal Navy's prison hulks off New York. But Yankees who could lay their hands on small ships made fortunes, which, at the conclusion of hostilities, were invested in overseas trading ventures. Many a New England family of merchant princes owes its origin to Revolutionary privateering. Elias Haskett Derby of Salem, for example, who started in this way from nothing, died in 1799 worth over a million pounds. This new money was used to buy up State and Continental securities and land. Some royal and Tory estates had been distributed to small men and veterans; but much real property ultimately found its way into the hands of speculative investors who discovered, as a result of the Revolutionary changes in land tenure, a splendid opportunity to pick up land titles on the cheap. Choice tracts of western lands were available to men of political influence in the States and in Congress; a radical politician like Samuel Gorham became part-proprietor of a vast estate of some six million acres in western New York. Southern planters who had backed the right side were busy picking up what windfalls they could from the collapse of British interests in the Ohio Valley; and the ever-assiduous Washington had left the army, not like Cincinnatus for the plough, but for his ambitious land development scheme on the western slopes of the Alleghenies. In these and other ways the opportunities of the Revolution had created a class of *nouveaux riches* to fill the depleted ranks of the old colonial oligarchy. And, although that oligarchy was no longer entrenched in the privileges of British rule, it occupied positions of great potential power.

Throughout the Revolution, men of property and position had sought to moderate Whig policies in the interest of the conservative order. Joseph Galloway of Pennsylvania had attempted to persuade the second Continental Congress to adopt a Plan of Union which might have kept the colonies within the Empire; and, although at the sticking point he turned Tory, others of his outlook and position continued to resist the extremism of the radicals within the Whig camp. They opposed all levelling and decentralizing tendencies and advocated strong government in the interest of property and trade. With a broader and more urbane outlook on affairs they understood that the prosperity of the States depended not only on effective State governments to enforce the law, to service their debts, to protect commerce and manufacture and to develop unsettled territories, but on a continental union strong enough to guarantee these conditions for the continent as a whole. Their mercantile interests convinced them that the States could only preserve their independence and grow in prosperity and power by joining in a union which could present a united front to the world. The same outward looking vision which had made them reluctant to break with the British Empire impelled them towards an embryo nationalism which contrasted sharply with the radical hatred of all national forms.

In the States the conservatives worked to recapture power from the radicals in the interest of effective law enforcement, sound money and commercial expansion. They succeeded in tipping the balance of political power in their favour in several States during the reaction against radical success which came with the years of confusion and depression from 1783 onwards. But radical resistance continued to impede progress towards economic recovery and a stable order. In 1786 the up-state farmers of Massachusetts, exasperated by a conservative regime which refused to issue fiat money and sought to enforce the collection of land taxes and private debts, rose in armed revolt under the leadership of an ex-army captain, Daniel Shays. Such anarchic conditions strengthened conservatives everywhere in their conviction that there could be no guarantee of effective government until the Articles of Confederation had been reinforced to provide the elements of law and order for the entire continent.

A group of Virginia gentlemen led by George Washington, who were interested in developing land between the Alleghenies and the forks of the Ohio, were promoting a scheme to extend the navigation of the Potomac and to link it with the Kanawha across the mountain watershed.[1] For this the right of navigation up the Potomac must be safeguarded; and since that river marked the boundary between Virginia and Maryland it was desirable to reach agreement between the two States to open trade and navigation on the river on equal terms. Commissioners, therefore, met in the summer of 1785 at Mount Vernon, Washington's country house which looked down on the Potomac. So satisfactory was the understanding they reached that like-minded men in the States bordering on Chesapeake Bay were encouraged to take the experiment a stage further. The assemblies of five States were prevailed upon to appoint representatives to discuss the liberalizing of trade for mutual advantage. The movement had, however, acquired such momentum that when the meeting took place at Annapolis in 1786 it was decided to adjourn it in favour of a more general convention which all States be invited to attend. This meeting was fixed for the following year at Philadelphia. The conservative forces behind the proposal were strong enough to ensure official delegations from key States; and this induced all the others with the exception of Rhode Island to appoint delegates. The Federal Congress, which had hitherto resisted all such proposals, was therefore presented with a *fait accompli* which considerations of face-saving forced it to recognize to the extent of passing a resolution empowering the Convention to consider ways and means of amending the Articles in order to make possible a greater freedom of trade. Thus Congress had been manoeuvred into

[1] The route afterwards followed by the Chesapeake and Ohio Canal and the Baltimore and Ohio Railroad.

the position of having to set the seal of its authority on the revision of its constitution by what was in fact an unofficial and largely partisan Convention. In so doing it signed its own death warrant.

The delegates who met behind closed doors in that upper chamber of the State House at Philadelphia on 25 May 1787 bore a faintly conspiratorial air. Radicals were suspicious; and Patrick Henry, for one, although nominated as a Virginia delegate, refused to have any part in it. A few of the delegates had been Tories, and the very great majority were men of property and position determined to remedy what was primarily an economic situation unfavourable to their interests. They faced a difficult job. Representing nobody but themselves, they were in an ambiguous and somewhat presumptuous position. The chance of getting agreement to a satisfactory revision of the Articles seemed remote. Many of the delegates must have travelled to the City of Brotherly Love feeling, like James Madison, that although the experiment must be tried it was a forlorn hope.

But, fortunately for the future of the Union, these men were no mere lobbying group of merchants, planters and investors. They were the spokesmen for a class, aristocratic in temper and used to handling public affairs with ease and assurance. Men like Elbridge Gerry, whose fortune came from shipping dried codfish from Marblehead to Barbados and from army contracting, or John Langdon, the timber magnate of New Hampshire, remained essentially the business men they were. But Robert Morris, the Lancashire-born export merchant of Philadelphia, had an imaginative flair which led him from private banking and real estate investment to the position of financier of the Revolution, and his career was hardly sullied by its *dénouement* in bankruptcy and ruin, the result of that characteristic 'big thinking' which had made him so valuable a public figure. James Wilson, a Scots immigrant, had made a fortune in land speculation and multiple business interests; but he was also a jurist of distinction, trained at the University of Edinburgh in the high noon of its brilliance. General Charles Cotesworth Pinkney, of South Carolina, whose father was a provincial Chief Justice and whose mother was the pioneer of indigo planting, was a cultivated land magnate, educated at Westminster, Christ Church and the Middle Temple. Gouverneur Morris, son of the lord of the Manor of Morrisania, belonged to the landed aristocracy of New York and had turned Whig 'at no small cost to his family and social connections'[1]; his half-brother was a major-general in the British army and married to the widowed Duchess of Gordon. Among the delegates were some of the best brains and talent in America. Apart from Wilson and Robert Morris there was the late military secretary to General Washington, Alexander Hamilton, and a brilliant delegation from Virginia which included George Mason, who drafted the Virginia Bill of Rights, and perhaps the ablest draftsman of them all, James Madison. Also among the Virginians was George Wythe, of William and Mary College, the most distinguished jurist of his generation. Indeed, in an age when reading for the Bar was the conventional education of a gentleman, most of the delegates were lawyers, at least in name. W. S. Johnson, of Columbia College, who had been a Tory, was one of two college presidents among the delegates. The aged Benjamin Franklin, F.R.S., gave the lustre of his name to the Convention, as did Washington himself, whose authority and judicial detachment made him the obvious choice for President. These men, whose average age was only 42, had an inbred confidence which gave them the courage to act with independence. Drawing on similar backgrounds and united by a common and specific purpose, they formed an effective committee which could keep to the main issues and draft proposals of enduring quality. Working within a common legal discipline they had a natural aptitude for constitutional forms and for the philosophic bases of politics.

Such men took no narrowly selfish view of their own interests. In seeking to protect their position as creditors, as owners of real estate, as investors in government securities and as merchants, they acted to redress the political balance towards order and away from that liberty which the radicals had pushed to the point of anarchy. In so doing their personal view was projected into a broader vision of the public interest; and because they were the men they were, the result was a political solution of surpassing statesmanship.

[1] *Dictionary of American Biography* (henceforward abbreviated to *DAB*).

The Convention had no option but to pursue a bold course. The persistent and doctrinaire refusal of the radicals to take adequate measures for the economic welfare of the States had forced the conservatives to seek a constitutional solution at the continental level. They had been empowered to suggest amendments to the Articles of Confederation which would strengthen the federal powers. But they quickly concluded, what the more discerning had known all along, that by their very nature the Articles were incapable of amendment for this purpose. A stronger federal executive, with power to override the States on the central issues of government, meant an abrogation of State sovereignty. And this was precluded by the existing constitution. Therefore, the Convention had no alternative but to go behind the Articles and to draft a new constitution of sufficient strength and yet one which the peoples of the States might be lobbied into accepting. But in proposing a new constitution, instead of an amendment to the old, the Philadelphia delegates went far beyond their terms of reference: they were acting not only *ultra vires*, but illegally. The success of such a scheme involved a direct appeal to the peoples of the States over the heads of the State governments and the Congress. The radical suspicion of the gentlemen at Philadelphia was justified. Behind the closed doors of the State House they were conspiring to depose the existing order and to substitute a government of their own design. In their elegant, statesmanlike way these conservative gentry had in turn become revolutionaries. The *coup d'état* they plotted was a counter-revolution. It was an American Thermidor.

If the delegates were at one in their desire for a stronger central government, their early discussions revealed wide disagreement about the form it should take and the extent of its powers. A hot-head like Hamilton, who wanted a single and powerful government at the centre, narrowly based on propertied interest, attracted little support. The Virginians made the running with proposals whose starting point was British practice towards the colonies before the Revolution. In feeling their way towards a central authority which would bind the States it was only natural that conservative constitutional lawyers like Randolph and Madison should hark back to the British connection and think in terms of an imperial authority

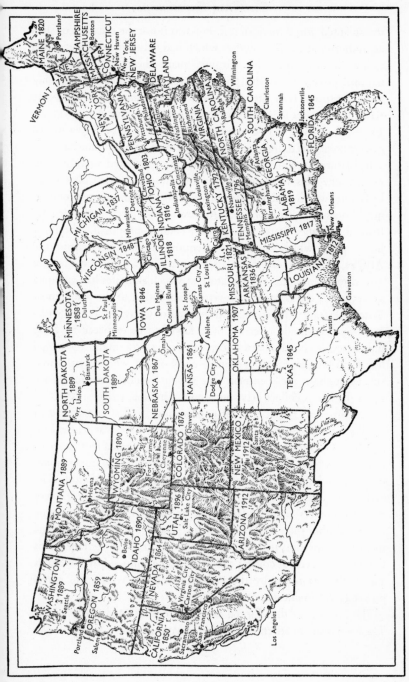

2. The United States

transplanted into American soil. For was it not the removal of such an authority at the Revolution which had led to the excesses of the radical insurgency? The Virginia plan, therefore, proposed a national government with power to veto State laws contravening the constitution (*vide* the veto of the Privy Council) and to coerce recalcitrant States by armed force (*vide* the Coercive Acts of 1774). Even this proved strong meat for many stomachs. The national government was to include, not only an executive and judiciary, but a legislature in which States would be represented according to population. This went counter to the interests of small States like Delaware, which feared the domination of richer and more populous neighbours like Pennsylvania. Accordingly, a group of delegates from the smaller States put forward counter-proposals. The New Jersey plan, which was a conscientious attempt to amend the Articles, retained most of the latter's weaknesses, including a federal government limited to a legislature in which all States had an equal voice; but it did contain the germ of a solution to the problem of State sovereignty. By stipulating that acts of Congress framed within its powers should override State laws and be enforced by State judiciaries, it abandoned the idea of coercing the States by armed force and favoured instead a single body of law whose writ would run throughout the continent and which would be enforced, not upon the States collectively, but upon individual citizens.

The time had now come for compromise; and after a period of deadlock in the sweltering heat of July, agreement was reached on a Federal Government with executive, judiciary and a legislature of two houses; the States were to be represented in the upper house equally, and in the lower house according to population. The Federal powers under the Articles were augmented by further essential powers including taxation and the regulation of commerce. Within the precise limits of its powers the Federal Government was supreme; its laws were to be enforced on the citizens of the States by Federal courts; they were to be enforced by the States and in the last resort by the Federal executive, which was given power to command the State militias.

The instrument thus forged was therefore, as Madison wrote in *The Federalist*, 'in strictness, neither a national nor a federal Constitution, but a composition of both'.[1] The central legislature had a dual character: its upper house, in which each State was equally represented, was federal; its lower house, in which each State was represented according to population, reflected more directly the opinions of the people of the United States as a whole. Similarly, the President was to be appointed by electors chosen by the State legislatures, but in proportion to population. The central government was supreme within its sphere, acting directly upon the people of the United States; but outside that sphere the States retained the residue of their powers, including the power to determine the basis of the suffrage for Federal as well as State elections. Central and local governments functioned as 'co-ordinate powers' under the canopy of a written constitution.

In their drafting and counter-drafting, the Founding Fathers had produced a document which was the embodiment of political expediency; but the compromise they had achieved was formulated in terms of constitutional principles which reflected some of the most discriminating political thinking of the day. Shunning, as they did, the idea of an absolute sovereign authority, either in the form of the old imperial Parliament or the new State legislature, the delegates took their stand on a rule of public law the sanction of which was, not that immemorial custom from which they had rebelled, but a written constitution based on natural rights. The Constitution they evolved had its starting point in the sovereign people whose will it embodied. Its overriding concern was to guard against tyranny by preventing the concentration of authority in any one place. It did this by a specific apportionment of powers to different organs. Those powers were to be held in equilibrium by an interlocking relationship of checks and balances which may be discerned at all levels of the constitutional structure. State and national elements were mutually contained by the opposition of Federal and State legislatures, of Federal president and State governor, of Federal and State judiciaries. In some respects the Federal Government was related directly to the States, as in the Senate; in others to the people as a whole, as in the House of Representatives. At the Federal level, the three organs of government

[1] James Madison, *The Federalist* Papers, No. xxxix.

were circumscribed, but interlocked so that each could function effectively only with the co-operation of the others. The President was removed from Congress, although charged with the duty of executing its Acts and subject to Congressional impeachment. Yet he held a partial veto over legislation and extensive powers to act independently, especially in a national emergency. Mutual checks within the Congress itself gave the lower house the sole right to initiate money bills and the Senate a powerful restraining role in foreign relations. The Federal courts had not only the duty of up-holding legitimate Acts of Congress but, by implication, the logic of which was subsequently established by the great Chief Justice, John Marshall, the duty of deciding whether those Acts were within the powers of Congress under the Constitution.

By devising this ingenious system the Founding Fathers sought to deal with the problem of power in the terms which came most naturally to them. In an age dominated by Newtonian thought it was as if they had worked by analogy from mechanics to construct a constitution on the principles of engineering; a constitution which, like a bridge, would be held in a state of perpetual equilibrium by the interlocking tensions of its parts.

Yet the result was not doctrinaire, but a practical solution apt for the needs of the expanding continent. The division of central and local power was an acute assessment of continental conditions where the overriding demand for order must be tempered by the greatest possible local freedom and where genuine regional entities must be protected from the indiscriminate demands of a mere majority. It was a continental solution to the problem of empire. Where the British Government had failed to contain the expanding forces of the continent, the Federal Constitution gave those forces freedom to find their own levels within a single political framework. The new Constitution expanded the power of the Federal Government to regulate western settlement, and made provisions for the establishment of new States with the same powers as those of the original thirteen. The Constitution was capable of the multiple expansion of its standardized parts. When the United States began to colonize westwards it did so on the novel principle of automatic self-government.

It was one thing for the men of Philadelphia to draft a constitution; it was another to get it accepted in the teeth of radical opposition. The critical moment in this counter-revolution came not at Philadelphia, but in the campaign to have the Constitution ratified by three-quarters of the States. The conservatives, however, newly confident, carried on a campaign of propaganda distinguished by the eminence of Washington and the brilliant arguments of Hamilton, Madison and Jay in *The Federalist*. Madison and others negotiated a gentleman's agreement with certain doubting independents in Virginia whereby the rights of individuals and States were to be further defined and strengthened by articles to be written into the Constitution as amendments. The momentum of this offensive ultimately overwhelmed the flagging forces of radicalism with the capitulation of New York, and the new Constitution finally came into effect in 1789.

The inaugurating administration of President Washington was the high point of conservative success. The Constitution was but a colourless abstraction; it could receive definition and quality only in action. And from the phaetons and chaises which rolled into New York for the first session of the new Congress there stepped gentlemen in powdered wigs, buckled shoes and ceremonial swords, determined to bestow upon the new form of government the accolade of their own stylish respectability. General Washington was in every inch of his tall frame a head of State, conducting himself like royalty, holding levees and travelling in a state coach with uniformed outriders. John Adams, elected Vice-President, although a self-made lawyer,[1] a stubborn republican and a revolutionary of the finest vintage, hankered after the establishment of orders of nobility and the ceremonial trappings which symbolized the puissance of government in Britain. Washington's cabinet were men of distinction in the new order: General Knox, Secretary of War, had been his able lieutenant as General of Artillery; Edmund Randolph, of the Virginia Randolphs, was Attorney-General; Thomas Jefferson, the brilliant dilettante and statesman-author of the Declaration of Independence, was Secretary of State. But it was the Secretary of the Treasury, Colonel Alexander Hamilton, joint-author of that

[1] With the help of Harvard College.

most distinguished series of political pamphlets, *The Federalist* Papers, who chiefly gave the stamp to the new administration and to the Constitution.

There is little recognizably American about Alexander Hamilton. Perhaps it was only the handicap of his obscure and illegitimate birth in the West Indies which attracted him to New York to make his way in the world instead of to Scotland. From his Scots father and his French Huguenot mother he inherited an intellect which would have brought him eminence at the University of Edinburgh or Glasgow in the days of Hume and Adam Smith instead of at the provincial King's College. As it was, his natural distinction as a lawyer, a man of affairs and staff officer to Washington, reinforced by marriage into the Livingston-Schuyler clan, had led him to easy ascendancy in the elegant society of New York. With a lucid mind, aristocratic temper and charm of manner he was effective and forceful in politics. With rare singleness of vision he looked at the problem of America's future from his vantage point at the pinnacle of New York's mercantile oligarchy. He believed that the United States, having achieved its independence, had the opportunity to become a great nation. But he characteristically assumed that the qualities making for greatness were those which had brought Britain power and eminence in the world.

He had nothing in common with agrarian radicals. He had a temperamental distrust of popular government: 'the people', he said, 'are a great beast'; and he yearned to restore in American society that balance in favour of wealth and position which made for stability in Britain and which he felt to be the right ordering of society. Moreover, he was convinced that the kind of propertied interest which had made Britain great was not mere land. Trade, banking, manufacture—these were the sinews which brought wealth and empire. The energies of the American people must be harnessed to the end of making the Republic a great mercantilist power. Hamilton became the spokesman for those men of property on the seaboard whose fortunes and way of life were determined by Atlantic influences. He was a New Yorker; and like New Yorkers from that day to this he was something more and yet something less than American. He who never went to Europe faced the ocean and had his back to the sprawling continent. He sought to foster the overseas trade and manufactures on which depended the prosperity and, indeed, in a world where trade and war seemed inseparable, the very independence of the United States. He therefore worked to strengthen the Federal authority and to attach to the new regime those propertied interests which had most to gain from strong government and most to give to a mercantilist state.

As Secretary of the Treasury, Hamilton was in a position to orient the new Government towards his objectives. Most of the immediate problems were fiscal, and by taking a broad construction of his powers he assumed the position of first minister. The debts of the Confederation and the States were assumed and re-funded at par; and the new national debt was promptly serviced by the imposition of excise and import duties. This step established the credit of the Republic at home and abroad, and ranged behind the Federal Government and the Federalist Party the moneyed men who had invested in Government securities. The creation of a National Bank, on the model of the Bank of England, gave facilities for handling Government finances and stimulated credit for new enterprises in a country which boasted only three rudimentary private banks. Hamilton was also anxious to buttress American economic independence against Britain by fostering those manufactures which were revolutionizing the English midlands. Despite his reading of Adam Smith he retained the mercantilist assumptions of his day. The new industries of the Revolution must be preserved from the hot wind of British competition by a protective tariff. Like other enterprising gentlemen with money to invest, he was also personally concerned to develop new enterprises in the speculative boom which his policies had stimulated. The motive which had prompted men like Washington to follow the Duke of Bridgewater with plans for canals led Hamilton and his associates to promote a company to harness the water power of the Passaic Falls for textile and other 'manufactories'. But if Hamilton and the Federalists worked for a greater measure of self-sufficiency they were aware of the overriding need for new trade relations with Britain. The Federal Government could now talk with sufficient authority to send the former Chief Justice, John Jay, to Britain to negotiate a trade treaty. Jay's treaty, in 1794, only provided the barest foothold for American merchants within the British Empire; but while this reflected the superior bargaining power of Lord Granville it also demonstrated how far the Federalist merchants were prepared to go to cultivate the good will of the alienated mother country. For the Federalists, peace and trade with Great Britain was the foundation of American foreign policy.

Brilliant though he was, Hamilton's career fell short of the highest point of statesmanship. His vision for the United States, although far-seeing, was too narrow to take account of much that was basic to American character. The model he had constructed fitted the facts of the United States as an Atlantic trading power; but he failed to adjust it to satisfy the most deeply felt needs of an agrarian and continental society. For Hamilton, greatness lay in trade and manufacture rather than farming; in capital rather than land; in the culture of port-cities with their windows opening on the greater world, rather than in the culture of sequestered country houses; in the virtue of merchant princes, not in that of modestly independent yeomen. Because the Federalist connection stood mainly for the mercantile oligarchy of the north-eastern seaboard, it alienated the men of the back country and in the end, the planters of the South. It was thus forced into the unwelcome position of a minority party which, after its first run of power, was never again broadly enough based to dominate a national administration.

Hamilton's policies inevitably created an opposition even though party was still regarded as factious and out of place in a republic based upon a delicate balance of multiple interests. The assumption of State debts benefited the more deeply indebted States, mostly in the north-east, at the expense of the more lightly burdened. The re-funding of securities brought rich profits to men of means with enough inside knowledge to buy up the worthless paper; but it brought bitterness to small men, including war veterans, who had been forced long since to sell their scrip for the little it would bring. The National Bank would be of direct benefit to merchant capitalists rather than planters; its monopoly power was feared and thought, by its opponents, to be unconstitutional. The excise irritated the old prejudice against direct taxes. That on whisky pressed especially hard on the frontiersmen of the Appalachians who distilled their corn into highly negotiable 'moonshine' which could be transported to market along the difficult mountain trails. These prickly gentry were goaded into an insurrection in 1794 which was put down in person by Washington, accompanied by Hamilton, in a rare excursion from his metropolitan haunts to the 'lubberland' of the west. The import duties benefited the infant manufactures of the North but raised the price of imports, whether from the North or from abroad, which were essential to plantation and homestead. The Federalists' eagerness for trade with Britain in Jay's treaty offended the susceptibilities of many. The interests alienated by these Federalist measures were gradually drawn together into a political connection which, by the turn of the nineteenth century, had emerged as the dominant political party in the United States.

With the assumption of power by the Democratic Republican Party in 1800 the Federalist Party shrank into little more than a 'high Tory' interest of merchants, lawyers and professional men in the towns of the north-eastern seaboard. The mutual antagonism of Hamilton and Adams who, as Washington's presidential successor, acted out the 'third term' of the Federalist administration, contributed to the Party's decline. Hamilton was killed on the Palisades above the Hudson River in the early light of a July morning in 1804 in a duel with Aaron Burr, which he had brought on himself by the violence of his partisanship. His death, further loosening the hold of the Federalists in New York, left the Party largely New England in character. No longer nationalist but sectional, it took an ever more narrow view of its interests. The New England merchants, with their concern for foreign trade and their close cultural affinities with Britain, set their faces against continental expansion and took their stand on peace and trade at all costs with the United Kingdom. And when continental nationalism once again clashed with British power in North America, the New England Federalists were drawn down a slippery slope which led, in the War of 1812, to passive resistance and a demand for the secession of New England from the United States. The pull of the Atlantic almost proved too strong for a political system designed to span a continent.

The creation of the Democratic Republican Party was largely the work of Hamilton's colleague in Washington's Cabinet, Thomas Jefferson. Like his colleague, Jefferson was a cultivated gentleman brought by his talents to the front of revolutionary statecraft. But there the likeness ends; for the two men were temperamental opposites. It seems inevitable that they should have become political antagonists; and that because of their contrasting personal magnetisms they should have polarized two distinct sets of values in American life. Hamilton's mind brought all before it into sharp focus; Jefferson's was diffuse and luminous; Hamilton was analytical, Jefferson intuitive. The one reduced problems to simple forms; the other was content to give his omnivorous curiosity free rein to pursue the varieties of experience. Hamilton's bent was political economy, Jefferson's, natural philosophy; and whereas one concentrated on statecraft, the other's influence permeated many levels of American experience. While the New Yorker gave force and consistency to one political interest, the Virginian's prismatic personality caught and refracted a variety of interests.

In that Age of Enlightenment, which set a premium on gentlemanly accomplishment, Jefferson was a dilettante. The interstices of his routine as a gentleman farmer allowed him leisure to practice the violin and piano, study astronomy and botany, invent household devices like the dumb-waiter, and to design and build his own country house, Monticello, and his University of Virginia according to the fashionable Palladian taste. Above all he read widely, cultivating that feeling for words which made his occasional writings, like the *Notes on Virginia* and his state papers, the literary masterpieces they are. His political convictions, like those of his Virginia acquaintance, were those of the English natural rights school which he distilled so brilliantly into the Declaration of Independence. But he admired not English, but French culture and his thinking was coloured by the *philosophes* and the physiocrats.

As a southerner and a planter, Jefferson's political outlook differed profoundly from Hamilton's. For Jefferson the good life was the life of the country gentleman. The labour of raising food from the earth had a moral value which ought to earn it a special regard in the Republic. The soil and the rhythm of the seasons gave to the cultivator a virtue which counting-house and work-bench could

not impart to the merchant and artisan. He had the farmer's prejudice against the merchant who earned profits from his toil and to
whom he was so chronically in debt. Capitalism was a corrupting
influence, creating a breed of arrogant monopolists whose concentrated power could wreck the State. He knew enough of Lancashire
to fear the rise of factory industry in America; and like most Virginians brought up on remote plantations he hated towns and
crowds which bred ignorance, disease and squalor. For Jefferson the
Revolution offered a providential opportunity for Americans to
escape from the evils to which the British Empire, with its concentrated power and wealth, was subject. In that vast continent, insulated from European pressures, it should be possible to create a
republic where the natural virtues of men could flourish. Rural
communities, dispersed on the land, required a minimum of external
government, and must be protected against the tyranny of centralized government backed by moneyed power.

Jefferson's ideal was a republic of yeoman farmers; and he believed that such a society would make possible a degree of self-
government such as the world had hitherto not dreamed of. For
although Jefferson, like Hamilton, was bound by their common
horizon to a belief in the need for an intimate connection between
property and political power, he differed in his broader vision of
the unique potentiality of the American continent to create a State
truly based upon the principles of the Declaration of Independence.
A republic of yeoman farmers, unmolested on the one hand by
great landed proprietors and on the other by merchant capitalists,
could achieve a degree of equality in land holding which would
carry with it a similar measure of equality in the distribution of
political power. He was aristocrat enough to assume that political
leadership would remain in the hands of those brought up to it; but
his University of Virginia, with its dignity and comfort, provided a
gentleman's education open to youths of talent.

The unique guarantee for such a society was the inexhaustible
land of the continent, enough, he thought, to provide a livelihood
for countless generations of Americans. For Jefferson, brought up
under the shadow of the Blue Ridge, within easy reach of the frontier, thought naturally in continental terms. He knew the back

country and understood its westward yearnings. It was he who had sketched the first framework of government for the old north-west; he who, as President, seized the opportunity to acquire for the United States in the Louisiana purchase the title to the great heartland of America; and he whose scientific curiosity sent Lewis and Clark on their explorations to the Pacific. Jefferson, the student of Montesquieu, saw the great forests, mountains, rivers and prairies of the American continent as a fit environment for a free people. This rich and spacious hinterland would provide means to counteract those pressures which, in the densely populated states of Europe, made for domestic tyranny, nationalism and war.

Jefferson, and those who thought like him, believed that these conditions would permit the growth of a society in the New World radically different from the nation states of the Old. The United States was founded on the belief that Americans had the unique opportunity to establish a political society on a higher moral plane than the 'corrupt monarchies' of Europe would allow. This society was to be based not upon the sanction of custom, but upon certain political principles. These famous principles of the Enlightenment rested upon assumptions about the perfectibility of the individual and his capacity to combine with his neighbours to order his political affairs exclusively according to the dictates of reason. Subscription to those principles, embodied in the Declaration of Independence, the Bill of Rights and the Constitution, was the sole absolute test of citizenship. Membership of the Republic was, therefore, a matter for affirmation, almost for political conversion. It involved personal choice and an act of will. It was not clear to this first generation of Americans that the new State would carry with it any corollary of 'nationality'; indeed its object was to get away from the irrational compulsions of the nation states of the Old World. Members of the revolutionary generation like Tom Paine and Joel Barlow regarded themselves as citizens of the world, blood brothers of all who believed in the sacred principles. 'National' loyalties, in the compelling social sense, remained local and sectional. The Americans were not an homogeneous people with a single ethnic inheritance to determine their folk pattern and national tradition; no one understood better than Jefferson, who had known the Scotch-Irish and the

Germans on the Virginia frontier, how many ethnic, linguistic and religious groups went to make up the American—'this new man' whom that French sojourner, Crèvecoeur, had so eloquently apostrophized in his *Letters from an American Farmer*. Only subscription to the political faith made a man an American. 'He is an American', wrote de Crèvecoeur, 'who, leaving behind him all his ancient prejudices and manners, receives new ones from the new mode of life he has embraced, the new government he obeys, and the new rank he holds.'[1] For the Jeffersonian, the immigrant from Europe was not to be resented as an outsider: he was to be welcomed, not only for the work he did, but for the affirmation of political faith he had made in becoming a citizen of the United States.

[1] Hector St John de Crèvecoeur, *Letters from an American Farmer* (London, 1782), Everyman edition, p. 43.

CHAPTER IV

THE ATLANTIC OUTLOOK

1790-1850

'See, through Atlantica's depths pulses American,
Europe reaching, pulses of Europe duly returned.'
WALT WHITMAN, *Starting from Paumanok.*

NEITHER independence nor more perfect union had by any
means established the position of the struggling ex-colonies
in the comity of nations. The snapping of the tie with
Britain left the infant Republic adrift and losing way in the heavy
swell of international politics. Independence, negative in itself, was
no positive solution to external problems. The United States had
to win for itself a standing abroad befitting its independent status.
How that should be done—what, in other words, should be the
foreign policy of the Republic—was a dominant issue in politics for
its first twenty years of existence. That issue was shaped by the conflict between Atlantic and continental impulses in American society.

In practice, foreign policy meant policy towards Britain. In spite
of the loss of the greater part of her American empire, Britain
remained the dominant power in the North Atlantic; and the course
of the Napoleonic Wars, determined in so large a measure by sea
power, ensured that, in furthering their interests abroad, the
Americans should meet the British at every turn. The Union Jack
still flew at St John's, Nova Scotia, at the head of Lake Champlain,
and over forts to the south of the Great Lakes by means of which
the Governor-General of Canada exerted control over the Indians
of the Ohio territory. His Majesty's frigates in American waters
still enforced the maritime policies of the naval and mercantilist
Power. Moreover Britain was, for the Americans, more than a
foreign Power. In spite of the political break, Britain and her ex-
colonies still impinged upon each other in a multitude of ways. The

revolution which had transferred political sovereignty from White-hall to Philadelphia had modified, but not fundamentally changed, the deep-seated relationship between the American communities and the Atlantic world. For almost a century to come, American growth was to retain its character as a process of settlement, an integral part of the expansion of Europe; and in that expansion Britain was to continue to play an important role. There had been no economic revolution in 1776. Americans were still dependent on overseas resources for immigrants, credit and markets to sustain their independence. The Napoleonic struggle only enhanced the position of Britain as the prime agent for the supply of these re-sources and underlined the importance of North America as an object of British enterprise. The purpose of Anglo-American dip-lomacy was to draw up the terms of a new partnership which would foster American expansion to mutual advantage and which would give complete recognition to American independence.

This purpose was at first only fitfully understood. Thomas Pown-all, His Majesty's late Governor of Massachusetts Bay Colony, might plead for a 'real family compact' between Britain and the United States and for the building of a 'great marine Atlantic Alliance'.[1] But the British as a whole, sceptical of American pretensions to independent nationality, and soon preoccupied by the vital struggle with France, ultimately forced the United States to assert its free-dom of action by resort to arms. Josiah Tucker, Dean of Gloucester and economist, spoke for many Englishmen when he wrote of 'the highest probability that the Americans never can be united into one compact Empire, under any species of Government whatever. Their Fate seems to be—A DISUNITED PEOPLE, till the End of Time.'[2] And a less unfriendly critic, the Rev. Andrew Burnaby, wrote: 'An idea, strange as it is visionary, has entered into the minds of the generality of mankind, that empire is travelling westward . . . But if ever an idea was illusory and fallacious, I am fully persuaded that this will be so. America is formed for happiness, but not empire.'[3]

[1] T. Pownall, *A Memorial Addressed to the Sovereigns of Europe and the Atlantic* (London, 1803), quoted in M. Kraus, *The Atlantic Civilization, 18th Century Origins* (Ithaca, 1949), p. 302; Pownall first developed this theme in *Three Memorials addressed to the Sovereigns of Europe, Great Britain and North America* (London, 1784).
[2] Josiah Tucker, *Cui Bono* (London, 1781), pp. 117–19.
[3] The Rev. Andrew Burnaby, *Travels through the Middle Settlements in North America,*

And so the Great Lakes posts were occupied until the new Federal Government could prove its sovereign authority by guaranteeing the payment of British debt. Royal Navy captains, in impressing merchant seamen in the western Atlantic, refused to recognize American citizenship by naturalization—a fundamental provision for an incipient nation recruited so largely from immigrants. In trading rights the British were equally intransigent. They believed that commercially the Americans needed the British more than the British needed the Americans; and in employing the machinery of the Navigation Acts against the United States, British policy followed the advice of Lord Sheffield that: 'the solid power of supplying the wants of America, of receiving her produce, and of waiting her convenience, belongs exclusively to our own merchants. If we can abstain from mischievous precipitation, we shall learn, to our great satisfaction, that the industry of Britain will encounter little opposition in the American market.'[1]

For their part the Americans were at one in wishing to be let alone to develop their republican institutions in the new continent. But they came to hold two broadly differing views, determined by those two agglomerations of interest, the Federalist and Republican Parties—the one Atlantic, the other continental in outlook.

The Federalists, under the guiding hand of Hamilton, were preoccupied with the need to establish the financial probity of the Republic abroad, to promote foreign trade and to foster a greater measure of self-sufficiency through the growth of domestic manufactures. The cardinal point of foreign policy for the Atlantic-looking merchants of Philadelphia, New York, Boston and lesser ports was an understanding with Britain which would permit a resumption of old trading relations and attract British capital for land improvements, canals, turnpikes, textile mills and iron foundries. Advantageous terms if possible; if not, whatever could be obtained. Jay's Treaty of 1794, however humiliating to Republican pride, was ratified as a result of pressure from Hamilton, because it re-established trading relations with Britain and American financial respecta-

in the Years 1759 and 1760, reprinted from the Third Edition of 1798 with Introduction and Notes by R. R. Wilson (New York 1904), p. 149.

1 John, Lord Sheffield, *Observations on the Commerce of the American States* (sixth ed., London, 1784), p. 5.

bility in the eyes of the world. Direct trade between the two countries was placed on a completely reciprocal basis. If American trade continued to suffer as a result of virtual exclusion from the British West Indies, New England shipowners were quick to discover new areas of indirect trade, notably the Far East (the *Empress of China* made the first voyage from New York to Canton in 1794) and the Mediterranean, which offset the loss to the United States' balance of payments. Precarious survival became a heady prosperity when, owing to hostilities in Europe, there went begging a profitable carrying trade which Americans, as neutral traders, were quick to take over. Between 1790 and 1807 American exports rose from 20 million dollars to 108 million dollars, and re-exports jumped from practically nothing to over 50 per cent of the total.[1] Such profits were ample compensation for the high risks run by the traders of a small neutral nation in wartime; and, although the Federalist merchants protested at the losses suffered by American cargoes under the British Orders in Council as well as under the Berlin and Milan Decrees, the Federalist Party was never prepared to press the issue to the point of rupture with the British. It was different with the French. The mercantile community of the north-east, anglophile for reasons of both culture and self-interest, saw in the French Revolution a threat to religion, morals and property. The hostility of the Federalist Party to French intrigues almost led to war with France in 1798, and underlay Washington's advice on foreign affairs in his farewell address (which was drafted by Hamilton) to beware 'the insidious wiles of foreign influence' and to steer clear of European entanglements save for commercial relations. Neutrality and commercial friendship with Britain at all costs was the basis of Federalist foreign policy. It was sound doctrine; and although its unpopularity accelerated the decline of the Federalist fortunes and in early days found little favour with the British, it was in the long run to triumph because it harmonized with the natural process of American expansion. As Hamilton saw, the interests of Britain and the United States were complementary, not competitive. 'I cannot', he said to an Englishman in 1790, 'foresee any solid grounds of difference between us.'[2]

[1] C. W. Wright, *op. cit.* p. 202.
[2] Quoted in S. E. Morison and H. S. Commager, *History of the American Republic*, vol. i, p. 346.

The Jeffersonians placed a different emphasis on American independence. A self-reliant republic of yeoman farmers on a remote continent need not truckle to the British whose baleful influence in war and empire was to be feared. With their revolutionary belief in a new order they hoped that the Atlantic would provide security from the contagion of the world's slow stain and for peaceful expansion into the heart of the continent. But if in this sense isolationist, they were ideologically drawn towards the conflicts of Europe. The revolutionaries in France were kindred spirits in a universal movement for the betterment of men; and in that movement Americans had a prominent part to play. The United States was not simply another nation state but a novel experiment in government—what Lord Sheffield sneered at as 'the whimsical definition of a people *sui generis*'[1]; and its citizens were, in a measure, citizens of the world. The conflict of the Republican Party with the Federalists on the French issue went much deeper than foreign policy; it was concerned with what sort of a people the Americans should become. While the Jeffersonians gave welcome and asylum to immigrant British radicals like Priestley and Cooper, as a sign that the revolutionary experiment was renewing itself, the Federalists, panic-stricken at 'the insidious wiles of foreign influence', passed, in 1798, the Alien and Sedition Acts which reflected a much more nativist and restricted view of American nationality. It was the Jeffersonians who waxed most indignant at the impressment of American seamen by the British: for the unique right to American citizenship by naturalization, by act of will, was fundamental to the revolutionary philosophy. The policy of the Jeffersonians, in power after 1800, was to protect American neutrality in the turmoil of Anglo-French conflict. In spite of aggressive naval action against the pirates of Tripoli to protect American commerce in the Mediterranean, Jefferson understood too little of sea power to build a navy strong enough to stand up to the high-handed British maritime policy; and when, after 1807, friction increased as a result of the intensified blockade and counter-blockade in Europe, he had recourse, as a landsman, an anti-militarist, a countryman and an isolationist, to economic sanctions. But the embargo of 1807 and the Force Act of 1809 did not

[1] Sheffield, *op. cit.* p. 2.

succeed, any more than the neutrality legislation of the 1930s, in insulating the United States from foreign conflict. Jefferson succeeded only in playing ducks and drakes with America's foreign trade. The growing tension with Britain led to a demand for war, not by the Federalist merchants who had suffered most from blockade and embargo, but by the Republicans of the continental hinterland, who saw in the British occupation of Canada an impediment to westward expansion. The war hawks of 1810–12, like Henry Clay, spoke for a new generation of westerners from the forest and river settlements of Kentucky and Tennessee whose brash nationalism would brook no obstacle to the westward-moving frontier either from the Indians of Tecumseh's Confederation or from the Canadians whom they wrongly suspected of prompting the Indians to revolt.

The War of 1812 was predominantly a naval affair and fought ostensibly over maritime commerce. But the aggressive spirit which pushed the issue to the point of arms came largely from the west.[1] It was a continental impulse and its war cry was 'Canada, Canada, Canada!' The mercantile classes of New England were against the war, and the Federalist rump who met in the Hartford Convention went so far in their seditious opposition as to preach passive resistance under the cover of States' rights. For Atlantic interests, both American and British, the war was unnecessary and disastrous. Only the time-lag of slow communications prevented the acceptance of a formula which would have avoided it; and the Treaty of Ghent, which ended it, settled none of the points in dispute.

Fortunately for Anglo-American relations, none of these outstanding points was vital to the interests of either country; indeed, as both countries emerged into the calmer weather of peace after 1815 it became clear that their true interests lay in the promotion of a tacit *entente*. With peace, neutral rights and impressment ceased to inflame American passions; and after the blood-letting, so satisfactory for Americans, at New Orleans, the turbulence of their feelings subsided. Henceforward, in spite of moments of friction,

[1] See J. W. Pratt, *Expansionists of 1812* (New York, 1925); see also, however, A. L. Burt, *The United States, Great Britain and North America from the Revolution to the establishment of the peace after the War of 1812* (New Haven, 1940).

there was no occasion when both sides were prepared to go to war over outstanding issues, which were largely confined to boundary and fisheries disputes. Within three years of the Treaty of Ghent it was possible for Richard Rush and Charles Bagot to negotiate an agreement whereby both countries ceased to maintain naval forces on the Great Lakes—a principle which, after 1846, was extended to land fortifications on the Canadian boundary, the first example of the limitation of armaments by voluntary agreement. In 1818 a convention established the Canadian boundary on the 49th Parallel from the Lake of the Woods to the Rockies, and the Webster-Ashburton Treaty of 1842 rectified the north-eastern boundary. The latter was the peaceful culmination of a series of incidents arising out of the Canadian rebellion of 1837 which, not for the last time, touched the old annexationist nerve. Similarly, the Oregon boundary was settled in 1846 only after the jingoist agitation which claimed the greater part of British Columbia for the United States. But in each case the two governments were determined on a peaceful settlement.[1] American expansionist energies were occupied elsewhere, notably in Mexico, and the Liberal Government of Aberdeen was not prepared to fight for territory in a corner of the globe where free trade was already paying such substantial dividends.

These piecemeal settlements were possible because the United States had at last come to terms with its principal rival in foreign relations and in doing so it had acquired a viable foreign policy. By the 1820s the mood of grudging recognition of an American sphere of interest had been replaced in the British Foreign Office by a more positive recognition that Anglo-American interests were complementary. When, in 1823, it seemed that the Powers of continental Europe were about to meet to consider intervention against the revolutionaries in Latin America, Canning proposed to the United States Government a joint declaration warning them off the American continent. Such a joint declaration would have demonstrated to the world that the United States and Britain were, in a measure, partners in an Atlantic sphere of influence with a common liberal outlook hostile to legitimacy. But it was to be a long time before Uncle Sam felt able to link arms with the suspect John Bull. The

[1] S. F. Bemis, *A Diplomatic History of the United States* (New York, 1936), p. 283.

Administration of James Monroe represented the last phase of the Jeffersonian era when, with the Federalist Party in eclipse, American politics were fought out largely within the framework of the Republican Party. Isolationism, though still its dominant mood, had been modified by the experience of twenty years in office. Its leading exponent of foreign affairs, Secretary of State John Quincy Adams, had broken with his hereditary Federalism, and after he had represented the United States abroad for some twenty years, part of which he had spent as Minister to the Court of St James, he had returned with a shrewd sense of the way in which his country's policy should be set. He preached isolationism; but not the negative withdrawal of the early Jeffersonians, rather a positive assertion of the United States' special destiny in North America and the need to protect that destiny by making an impassable gulf between the New and the Old World. A declaration against European intervention in Latin America there must be; but it must be an independent assertion by the United States alone. The United States should not, he said, 'come in as a cockboat in the wake of the British man-of-war'. The message to Congress which he drafted, and which has come down to history as 'the Monroe Doctrine', solemnly warned the European Powers that any intervention in the affairs of any of the American Republics would be an unfriendly act towards the United States.

That doctrine, with its implication of isolation and a special sphere of influence in the Western Hemisphere, made explicit what was to be the cardinal feature of American foreign policy down to the twentieth century. Yet the doctrine obscured rather than clarified the realities of power on which the United States took its stand. The American Government, with its tiny navy, was in no position to enforce so all-embracing a threat. The Monroe Doctrine was but windy rhetoric without the unseen hand of the Royal Navy. It made sense only in terms of an underlying Anglo-American partnership. Such a partnership did, in fact, exist. Why could it not be made explicit? Because the American people were still too much pre-occupied with their special destiny on the American continent, too ignorant of the realities of sea power, and too suspicious of Britain to look candidly on their position in the world. The pull of the continent was too strong.

The Peace of 1815 left the United States and Britain free to resume that mutually profitable exploitation of the American continent which had been interrupted by the revolutionary upheaval. In place of the old, unequal partnership of colonial times, a new, tacit agreement provided the British with a market for their manufactures and a profitable field of investment, and the Americans with capital to exploit their resources, markets for their surplus produce and immigrants to provide labour and technical skill.

As in colonial times, Americans still worked largely in field, forest and on the sea; and to rise above a primitive subsistence they must trade abroad. This was the mercantile age of the United States. If between 1816 and 1860 her foreign trade grew more slowly than her national income as a whole, the growth of foreign trade, which represented an increase of 230 per cent, was greater than that of Britain.[1] Americans still exported largely raw materials—cotton, tobacco, wheat and corn, rice, meat and fish, timber, potash and leather—in exchange for manufactures, predominantly textiles and iron and hardware, and tropical foodstuffs like coffee, sugar and tea. In addition, they earned an indispensable income, as they had done in colonial times, from a carrying trade now worldwide in its conditions. Merchantmen whose home ports were Salem, New York or Philadelphia dropped anchor not only at Lisbon, Havre and Liverpool, but as far away as Canton, Calcutta and Buenos Aires.

If Americans traded in the Far East, South America and the Mediterranean, they did most business with north-west Europe, and by far their most important customers were the British who, in turn, found the United States their best export market. Between 1821 and 1860 nearly half of American exports went to Britain whence came about 40 per cent of American imports.[2] This was the golden age of Anglo-American commerce. In the England of Huskisson and Peel, the lesson of the American Revolution, taught by Pitt, but rejected by the old Toryism, had at last been ruefully understood, and men came to believe with Cobden and Bright that true empire came through private trade, not political control. After 1816, trade barriers were gradually relaxed, and once again Ameri-

[1] G. R. Taylor, *The Transportation Revolution, 1815–60* (New York, 1951), p. 177.
[2] *Ibid.* Appendix A. Tables 10 and 13.

cans traded freely with Britons, but without the political sanctions of mercantilism. The British admitted American ships to their West Indies in 1830, freed the trade in corn in 1846, and finally abolished what remained of the Navigation Code in 1849. The Americans kept their coastwise trade as an exclusive preserve; but if they raised a tariff against British iron and textiles in 1828, the southern interest in the export of raw cotton was strong enough to lower it again to an innocuous level until the Civil War.

Anglo-American trade was a simple exchange of raw materials for manufactures, reflecting the complementary nature of the two economies. British exports were chiefly textiles and metal products of all kinds from rails to hardware; Americans, as noted above, exported mainly cotton, tobacco, wheat and potash. But one single commodity overwhelmingly dominated the exchange. Between 1820 and 1860 from forty to sixty per cent of American exports was raw cotton shipped across the Atlantic to be spun and woven into cloth in the mills of Lancashire. The cotton bale largely paid for America's imports, which included a high proportion of textiles woven in Lancashire from that same American cotton. Cotton was king, not only of the southern States but of the entire Atlantic world. That revolution in technique, which was transforming Lancashire into Britain's first industrial society, was vitally linked with a similar revolution which was rescuing the American plantation States from the decay of tobacco and indigo growing and creating a new South dedicated to raising a single staple for export largely to Britain. Spinning frame, carding machine and power loom would never have been geared to factory production without the cotton gin. Manufacturers and merchants, taking advantage of these inventions and of the growing demand for cheap clothing in Europe and America, set the pattern for the entire Atlantic economy.

That economy rested on the New York–Liverpool axis. With the industrial growth of Lancashire, Liverpool became the British *entrepôt* for the American trade. On the other side of the ocean New York rapidly drew away from Philadelphia and Boston as the pre-eminent trading port in the North Atlantic.[1] A magnificent harbour, a tributary hinterland which, after the opening of the Erie

---

[1] R. G. Albion, *The Rise of New York Port, 1815–60* (New York, 1939), *passim.*

Canal in 1825, tapped the remote region of the Great Lakes, and superior enterprise on the part of its merchants contributed to New York's growing metropolitan status. Its liberal auction laws led to its being chosen by British exporters, after the War of 1812, for the dumping operations by means of which the pent-up stocks of British warehouses were released on to the American market with the successful object of recapturing it for British manufactures. Even before the war, the agents of Lancashire and Yorkshire textile firms had ventured to take up office space in the Pearl Street warehouses to sell cloth. Men like Jeremiah Thompson, of Rawdon in the West Riding, and Benjamin Marshall, of Huddersfield and Manchester, stayed to become leaders of a mercantile fraternity, American and British, engaged in importing dry goods and exporting raw cotton. These families formed a British community in exile round the then fashionable Greenwich Village neighbourhood of Manhattan, with their St George's Society and *Albion* newspaper. Although American houses acquired a share, the export-import business with Britain continued to be dominated by British merchants, who could command greater capital resources than their American competitors. It was not only that great risks had to be faced from wreck, spoiled cargoes and wild market fluctuations, but American wholesalers, dealing up-country, needed credit terms of as long as twelve or eighteen months; and the great power of the City of London was drawn upon to sustain not only the North Atlantic trade but a line of credit reaching back to the storekeeper, farmer and planter of the remote interior.

For the New Yorkers it was an easy step from importing manufactures, some of which were sold south, to buying the South's cotton for shipment to Liverpool and Havre. The cotton planters, like their tobacco-growing predecessors of colonial days, were too short of credit to market their own crops and became increasingly dependent on their merchants for credit. With their Liverpool connections, control of shipping and the backing of British credit it was inevitable that the great New York houses should seize the opportunity to market a crop which, although highly speculative, brought good prices on the Liverpool exchange. New York agents bought the crop when still in the field, shipped it either direct from New Orleans or Savannah to Liverpool or by coastal schooner to New York for trans-shipment as outward cargo on the North Atlantic run. The other side of this triangular business was the import, as return cargo, of British merchandise from Liverpool from which the Southern planter would be supplied with clothing for his slaves, tools and machinery for the plantation and the latest novels and *haute couture* for his elegant family. By the 1840s, New York firms had acquired control of the bulk of the cotton crop and in some cases of the plantations themselves. Georgia planters travelled north with their families each summer to Saratoga Springs to escape the intolerable heat and to negotiate with their New York merchants for next year's credit and imported wants. Temperamentally unbusinesslike, the southern gentry were increasingly in debt to their Yankee merchants. The nineteenth-century cotton planter was as much at the mercy of his merchant as the eighteenth-century tobacco planter. The merchant had merely shifted his ground from London or Glasgow to New York. In the planter's eyes the enemy was no longer the rude Scots factor from overseas; he was the ungentlemanly Yankee representative of a New York firm. The produce of the southern plantations still went largely to Britain; but the profiteering, or so the southerner thought it, was enjoyed in the North. 'The "Lord North" of these days was a greater oppressor than the Lord North of the British Ministry', proclaimed a southern newspaper in 1851.[1] The inexorable pressures of an extensive colonial monoculture still played into the hands of the merchants with metropolitan resources. In the eighteenth century those resources had been British; now they were, in part, American. The balance of the Atlantic system had been shifted westwards.

The growth of North Atlantic trade depended on radical improvements in ocean communications which made more distant markets accessible to the factories of Britain and stabilized a world market for raw cotton. Ships became larger. The full-rigged merchantman of the 1850s of about 1,000 tons had three times the capacity of that of the 1820s. Her streamlined design enabled her to sail nearer the wind, with a smaller crew, and to make port with the wind in a more unfavourable quarter. She was also faster. Packets

[1] A. C. Cole, *The Irrepressible Conflict, 1850–65* (New York, 1934), p. 64.

on the North Atlantic shuttle cut their westbound time from 39 to 33 days between 1820 and 1850. The use of sail was pushed to its ultimate limits with the clipper ship designed to race passengers and light cargo from the Far East or the California gold mines. The clipper *Lightning*, designed by Donald McKay, the Yankee king of shipbuilders, covered 436 miles of the Liverpool run in twenty-four hours. Their day was short; but while it lasted, the clippers, which outsailed their British rivals, were the pride and joy of the American nation. These developments prompted that same Yorkshire importer, Jeremiah Thompson, to use sailing ships, not as tramps on individual voyages, but as a 'line' with regular fortnightly sailings between New York and Liverpool. When, on the fifth of January, 1818, his *James Monroe* moved down New York harbour in a snowstorm, dead on schedule, Thompson inaugurated an experiment, the Black Ball Line, which not only made him the biggest shipowner in the United States, but resulted in a network of packet lines across the Atlantic. On St George's Day 1838, to the excitement of New Yorkers already in the habit of celebrating the comings and goings of famous ships, there appeared in the Narrows the British paddle steamer *Syrius*, the first ship to steam all the way across the Atlantic. Within two years, Samuel Cunard, a Nova Scotian with a British Government subsidy, had started a regular steamship line between Liverpool and Boston, switching to New York in 1847. Thenceforward with the iron, screw-propelled ship, steamers took over more and more of the fast traffic on the Atlantic. These improvements made for regular delivery of freight and correspondence, and for better market intelligence; and comfortable and quick journeys for passengers transformed the Atlantic crossing from a tedious and hazardous enterprise into an habitual convenience for business and professional men.

In maritime enterprise the Americans had the edge on their competitors. For twenty years after 1816 over eighty per cent of American foreign trade was carried by the American merchant marine, which between 1820 and 1860 multiplied nearly four times.[1] Its ascendancy depended on the cheapness of wooden ships built by superior craftsmen on ways accessible to first-class timber. The

[1] Taylor, *op. cit.* p. 122 and Appendix A., Table 1.

success of these methods blinded Americans to the dangers of competition from iron steamers built on industrialized Clyde and Merseyside. When they had recovered from their Civil War they found that iron steamers flying the red ensign had captured most of their commerce.

As in colonial days, Americans imported more manufactures than they could pay for by exporting raw materials. Until as late as 1873, the United States had an unfavourable balance of trade which neither the earnings of her merchant marine nor, after 1850, Californian gold were sufficient to make good. The deficit was, in the last analysis, made good by loans from abroad.[1] In their drive across the continent the American people still depended on the Old World, and especially on Britain, not only for manufactures but for credit to sustain them until they had subdued the wilderness. The role of British merchant bankers was not limited to extending commercial credit. By marketing in London the securities of American banks and plantation States they made possible the rapid growth of the new cotton South and the consequent boom in cotton and land. Nor did the London merchant bankers limit themselves to the cotton trade and its adjuncts. In England, after Waterloo, there was a marked belief in the future material prosperity of the American people, reinforced, among radicals, by an ardent faith in the moral superiority of American institutions. Opportunities for investment in the young Republic were much sought after. The bonds of the Federal Government found a ready sale in London; but the greatest avenue of British investment was into the State-financed canals, railways and turnpikes, those 'internal improvements' in transport which were so essential for the commercial development of what came to be called the Midwest. Between 1821 and 1837, foreign capital to the value of about 125 million dollars, most of it British, was invested in the United States. If the ordinary English country gentleman who bought the bonds of Indiana or Illinois was ignorant of all but an imposing State crest and seal and a high rate of interest, his London banker was conscious of a high purpose in the transaction. The dramatic success of the Erie Canal, the stock of which

[1] See C. J. Bullock, J. H. Williams and R. S. Tucker, 'The Balance of Trade of the United States', *Review of Economic Statistics*, Preliminary, 1 (1919).

passed almost at once into the hands of Englishmen, opened a shining vista of rich prairies growing golden crops of wheat which could be economically transported by canal and lake, not merely to the seaboard, but to British markets.

Unfortunately, this Anglo-American partnership in the development of the American continent was too impatient for results.[1] The over-extension of British commercial credit was alone sufficient in 1838 to bring about a financial collapse which halted for a time the westward advance of settlers, who laid the blame for their bankruptcy not merely on eastern merchants but on sinister British bankers. Even so, despite State bankruptcies of 1839–42 which brought forth a classic case of Anglo-American friction characterized by the mordant reproaches of Sidney Smith, the westward flow of British capital was soon renewed by the glowing prospects of mining and, above all, railways. North America became Britain's greatest market for iron. American contractors paid British ironmasters for their iron rails partly in the form of railway bonds. From this there developed a new British investment boom. During the '50s nearly 200 million dollars-worth of new capital flowed into the United States, mostly into railways. Richard Cobden, whose imagination had been fired by the promise of American life, invested in the Illinois Central the sum raised for him by admirers after the repeal of the Corn Laws. Until the Civil War accelerated America's industrialization, the old Atlantic partnership held firm.

The North Atlantic trade route also stimulated the flow of emigrants. Freighters which had unloaded cotton bales in the Mersey or the Seine, or tobacco at Bremerhaven, returned to New York packed to the hatches with emigrant families who camped as best they could in the converted holds.[2] Timber ships returning to the Maritime Provinces brought Irish peasants to St John whence they drifted south to Boston and other New England cities. The emigrant trade became an important by-product of the North Atlantic, and Jeremiah Thompson was again a pioneer when, in 1828, he organized the Union Line of immigrant packets. And because it was the

[1] L. H. Jenks, *The Migration of British Capital to 1875* (London, 1938), ch. 3.
[2] M. L. Hansen, *The Atlantic Migration, 1607–1860* (Cambridge, Mass., 1945), ch. 8.

queen of the Atlantic, New York, with its Castle Garden immigrant control, became the chief port of entry for immigrants. Many an immigrant stayed in the United States instead of pushing on into Canada, indifferent about whether he was squatting on land subject to the British Crown or under the protecting wings of the American eagle.

The stream of immigrants, which had been but a trickle during the Napoleonic Wars, reached tens of thousands a year in the 1820s and hundreds of thousands in the 1840s. In 1854, the peak year before the Civil War, nearly half a million immigrants entered the United States. In 1860 there were over four million foreign-born in the United States, fifteen per cent of the population.[1] The great majority came from the British Isles. The severe dislocation due to the industrial revolution and the reactionary temper of politics after Waterloo, led thousands of English, Welsh and Scots annually to seek their fortunes in the United States. Pauperized farm labourers from Sussex were helped to emigrate by the parish overseers instead of being forced to drift to London or the industrialist north. Impoverished Welsh hill-farmers emigrated rather than face working in the iron works and coal mines of South Wales. Dispossessed Highland crofters sailed westwards instead of tramping south. East Anglian tenant-farmers hoped to better themselves by buying freehold tracts in Illinois and Ohio. Blacksmiths, cobblers, weavers, potters, carpenters hoped to make a better living from their trade in the new country. Some returned, like the Lancashire cotton operatives, in the American depression of 1840–2. Most stayed to go under or prosper in an American community. Irish peasants formed an important part of the total from the beginning. But after the potato famine of 1846, the same exodus which brought the Irish to Lancashire and Glasgow sent hundreds of thousands to the United States, so that in 1860, of slightly over four million foreign-born, over a million and a half were from Ireland. Similar conditions of agricultural depression, crop failures and the displacement of handicrafts induced a large migration from North and Central Germany, much of it by way of the North Sea, Hull and Liverpool. By 1860 there were over a million German-born in the United States.[2]

[1] *Hist. Stats.*, Series B, 184–92, 304–30.
[2] *Ibid.*

Most of these immigrants were farm labourers who had little more than their bare hands. Only the fortunate few with capital were in a position to farm the rich, but remote, lands of western New York, Ohio or Illinois. Most remained to provide manual labour on the more thickly settled seaboard. Irish navvies dug the canals and railway cuttings of America as well as of England; and their wives and daughters worked as domestic servants. But a significant few brought badly needed skills: English bricklayers and carpenters, printers and steamboat engineers, Cornish miners, Welsh foundrymen and textile operatives from the Pennines. In spite of the laws prohibiting the emigration of artisans and the export of machinery, Lancashire spinners and weavers had been in the habit of quietly embarking in American-bound freighters at Liverpool ever since 1790 when the young Samuel Slater, with the design of Arkwright's machinery in his head, left Belper for New York at the call of an advertisement by Hamilton's friends of the Philadelphia Society of Arts and Sciences. Just as Slater, who was put to work by Almy and Brown, a firm of Quaker merchants in Rhode Island, was the father of America's cotton manufacture, so the Scholfield family of Saddleworth in the West Riding performed the same service for woollens.[1] These pioneers were followed in the twenty years after Waterloo by hundreds of skilled technicians bringing from the industrial metropolis improved designs and superior operating skill. Although the New Englander, Francis Lowell, by building the first comprehensive factory, set the Massachusetts cotton industry on to new paths, the mills of Fall River or New Bedford were manned by a cadre of key operatives whose Pennine accents withstood the influence of the Yankee drawl. These artisans also brought with them the radical ideas of a more advanced industrial society. More class-conscious than their native-born mates, they became so prominent among the organizers of trades unions that the labour movement of the 1830s was looked upon as a foreign conspiracy.[2]

[1] George S. White, *Memoir of Samuel Slater, the Father of American Manufactures* (Philadelphia, 1836); Arthur Cole, *The American Wool Manufacture* (Cambridge, Mass., 1926); also *DAB*.
[2] Caroline Ware, *Early New England Cotton Manufacture*, pp. 203–7; R. Ernst, *Immigrant Life in New York City, 1825–63* (New York, 1949), pp. 99–100.

The North Atlantic packets also brought more sophisticated travellers from Britain intent on satisfying their curiosity about the American experiment. Some, like Harriet Martineau or Captain Marryat, returned to publish their findings for an eager reading public. But many British radicals, discouraged by the resistance to privilege at home, sought greater opportunities by emigration. These men and women ranged from the self-educated artisan such as Francis Place to the well-to-do reformer like Joseph Hume and differed from these prototypes only in their decision to pursue their programmes in the new land of freedom rather than in the reactionary England of Lord Eldon. There were the Utopians, like Robert Owen and Frances Wright, who wished by their example to demonstrate to unreformed society that an ideal community based upon the best rational principles, the blue-prints of which they brought in their valises, could be made to flourish in the uncorrupted American wilderness. There were the Benthamites who wished to reform existing institutions according to the precepts of the Master. There were the land reformers, disciples of the Englishman Thomas Spence, like George Henry Evans who started the movement which led directly to the Homestead Act. There were the Chartist exiles, like Thomas Devyr or John Cluer, who communicated the fervour of their crusade for co-operatives or shorter hours to mechanics in the cities.[1]

As with political radicals, so with religious reformers. The Evangelical Revival was a transatlantic movement which galvanized British Nonconformists and American sects into common action. By means of indefatigable correspondence and frequent Atlantic journeys, British Quakers, Methodists, Baptists and Unitarians cultivated intimate relations with their American brethren, establishing theological colleges, Bible, tract and missionary societies, and new church communities in the west. Fired by the American experiment for the moral progress of the human race, they built a transatlantic empire of humanitarian endeavour which transcended political boundaries.[2] The anti-slavery, temperance, peace and feminist

[1] H. S. Zahler, *Eastern Workingmen and National Land Policy, 1829–62* (New York, 1941), pp. 19, 22, 76–9.
[2] See especially A. H. Abel and F. J. Klingberg, *A Side-Light on Anglo-American Relations, 1839–58, furnished by the correspondence of Lewis Tappan and Others with the British and Foreign Anti-Slavery Society* (Lancaster, Pa., 1927).

movements had their origins in the evangelical impulse which also gave moral stiffening to the free trade movement of the 1840s and '50s. Philanthropists like William Jay in America and Joseph Sturge in England bore witness to a common belief in the special duty of Englishmen and Americans towards the betterment of men.

The evangelical faith in spiritual regeneration, the radical belief in moral betterment, the mercantile drive for free trade and technological progress, the investor's trust in the American future, the emigrant's vision of a higher standard of living and a freer way of life, all were manifestations of a common climate of opinion deriving its force from the Anglo-American partnership which, between Waterloo and the first Battle of Bull Run, dominated the Atlantic world.

Overseas trade gave wealth and a blue-water horizon to a score of port towns from Portland, Maine, to Baltimore, Maryland. On the rocky New England shore, ports like Salem, Newport or New London became little city-states trading proudly in their own right with Canton or Calcutta. The leathery seamen of New Bedford, Stonington and Nantucket sailed their stout little brigs to the waters of both Poles to harpoon whales for candles and oil lamps. The unassuming fishermen of Gloucester or Newburyport earned good profits from the Grand Banks. Each of these ports boasted its shipyards, ship chandlers, ropewalks and counting-houses, supporting proud families in growing comfort and style from the profits of distant voyages. Their simple, but pleasantly proportioned wooden-frame houses acquired the quiet elegance of classic-revival fanlights, pediments and pilasters. Their panelled parlours had the air of ship's cabins, and their roofs were surmounted by 'widows' walks' with a clear view of harbour-mouth and horizon. Oak, maple and pine furniture was supplemented by Turkey carpets and *chinoiserie*; painted shutters by Chinese brocade curtains. And on their bookshelves, beside the sermons of Cotton Mather appeared Bowditch on navigation and the novels of Walter Scott. Their lives were governed, as their ancestors' had been, by the vagaries of the ocean, the routine of the counting-house and the discipline of the Congregational Church.

By the 1840s, the day of the little ports of New England was over, and grass grew on the cobbled quays of Salem whose decay prompted Nathaniel Hawthorne to muse on New England's past. For the growing scale of shipping and commerce had drawn business increasingly to the great ports of Boston and New York, Philadelphia and Baltimore. Here, as early as 1794, Thomas Cooper had found society 'much the same as in the large towns of Great Britain such as Birmingham, Bristol, Liverpool and Manchester'.[1] Among the great ports New York drew ahead. Her 1860 population of over a million made her nearly twice the size of her nearest rival, Philadelphia, and had increased ninefold since 1820. New Yorkers with means were moving across the East River to Brooklyn and up Manhattan to brown-stone terraces in streets with paved sidewalks, gas lighting and the marvellous new Croton water piped all the way from Westchester. A jostling crowd of carriages, carts and horse buses carried merchants and tradesmen along Broadway down town to the busy commercial maze between Trinity Church and the river wharves. The temper of life, as Dickens found it, was quick and thrusting; but it was also more urbane. An opera house, theatres which ran the latest London successes of Fanny Kemble or Macready, clubs, restaurants and hotels, provided a varied background for men about town like Philip Hone, New York's mayor in 1825, who set a high tone for fashionable society.[2] Although Boston suffered from the lack of cheap inland transport, she remained the second most important city in the foreign trade. The proud capital of New England, she eclipsed Philadelphia as America's intellectual metropolis. In the parlours of Beacon Hill, Louisburg Square and across the Charles River in Cambridge, circulated the intellectual currency of Theodore Parker, Emerson, Thoreau, Bronson Alcott and Margaret Fuller. The culture of New England, which had as much in common with Britain as with the continental west, was based on the profits of foreign trade. As trade was concentrated in the great ports, it brought power and wealth to city families—the Grinnells and Griswolds of New York, the Jacksons, Lees and Cushings of Boston, the Biddles of Philadelphia. These merchant princes had their fingers on the pulse of American growth.

[1] Thomas Cooper, *Some Information Respecting America* (London, 1794), p. 48.
[2] See *The Diary of Philip Hone*, edited with an Introduction by Allan Nevins (New York, 1927).

By the 1820s, the widespread interests of the great mercantile houses extended beyond foreign trade. After the first substantial earnings from improved ocean transport foreign commerce became relatively less profitable than domestic. The merchants began to divert capital and enterprise to developing an inland market. The key to this, too, was communication; and the greater part of American energies went into solving the transport problem. The cost was prohibitive of transporting manufactures inland, and also of carrying bulky grains from western New York, or coal from the Pennsylvania mountains, to seaboard. From 1790 onwards, merchants had promoted turnpike, toll-bridge and canal companies to improve the links between seaboard towns. The success of the Erie Canal held out the first real hopes of a great western market, and started a mania of canal-building among competing cities. Money also went into the steamboat after Fulton's experiments on the Hudson in 1807 had demonstrated its feasibility for American waters.[1] Steamboat lines up the Hudson to Albany, along the Sound to Providence and Boston, up the Raritan and down the Delaware to Philadelphia, quickened and cheapened seaboard communications. These improved waterways were supplemented in the 1830s and '40s by tributary railways which shortened, and by stages replaced, the steamboat routes, linked inland towns like Springfield, the quarries of Vermont, and the mines of the Alleghenies with Boston and Philadelphia. By 1853, trunk railways, notably the Baltimore and Ohio, the Pennsylvania and the New York Central, provided continuous rail-links which had negotiated the Alleghenies on their way to Chicago and St. Louis. The drive behind railway construction came partly from civic and county initiative, partly from new men like the ferryboat captain Vanderbilt, but mostly from the great established merchants of the ports, like the ex-China merchants John Murray Forbes, who organized a Boston syndicate to build the Michigan Central and other mid-western roads, and William Osborn of New York, who controlled the affairs of the Illinois Central. This revolution in transport put the banking and trading facilities of eastern ports at the service of Buffalo, Cincinnati,

---

[1] The engines for Fulton's famous *Clermont* were by Boulton and Watt and her hull was built in New York by an Englishman; Albion, *op. cit.* p. 236.

Pittsburgh and Chicago, and encouraged Philadelphia enterprise to invest in the coalmines and ironworks of the Allegheny region.

The profits from overseas trade helped to launch the first machine-driven, factory-organized industry. It was Almy and Brown, Quaker merchants of Providence, who gave Samuel Slater his start. The Englishman Benjamin Marshall, for twenty years a cotton merchant in New York, organized the first large-scale manufacture of fine cottons up the Hudson River after the imposition of the textile tariff in 1824: and his career is symbolic of the way in which the cotton kingdom, expanding westwards, planted the first modern industry on the western shores of the Atlantic. But the most significant excursion into textiles was made by the merchants of Boston. Francis Lowell's ambitious ventures at Waltham and Lowell, where for the first time all the processes of manufacturing cotton cloth by machinery were carried on in one factory, were financed by large drafts of capital provided by the Lowell family and their connections, the Jacksons and Appletons, merchants in the overseas trade.

The technical complexity of textiles, gifted leadership, high profits and the legal device of incorporation, encouraged the growth of a manufacturing interest independent of mercantile control. But the circumstances of this advanced industry were not typical of American industry as a whole.[1] In general, the merchant, whose financial resources and enterprise were fully stretched in exploiting the growing market for a variety of commodities, was uninterested in revolutionizing the methods of production of one. Industry remained backward by British standards, and was still organized on a mill and cottage basis. Household manufacturing actually increased up to 1830, as settlement moved inland in advance of transport. In the back country, industry was largely a matter of small grist and sawmills, iron foundries and smithies, catering for a strictly local market. Even where industry tapped a wider region it often remained a cottage affair. The shoemakers of Lynn, Mass., worked in the 'ells' built on to their cottages, using materials provided by a merchant to whom they sold the finished product. Until the 1840s, even in the textile firms of Rhode Island the men

[1] L. M. Hacker, *The Triumph of American Capitalism* (New York, 1946).

continued to weave the cloth at home, leaving the spinning and finishing processes to be handled by their wives and children in the mills. Lack of cheap transport hobbled the iron trade, which remained an affair of small, back-country ironworks using charcoal for fuel.

Until the 1850s, the colonels and captains of American economic life were merchants, land speculators, transport promoters, ironmasters, millers, lumbermen. Manufacturers were still hardly distinguishable from the labouring class from which they emerged. They were usually master craftsmen or superior journeymen who had accepted responsibility to the merchant for the execution of orders in his shop. These 'bosses', as they were called in the Dutch slang of New York, were often ignorant about their future role in industry. They were hostile to the merchants who passed on to them the lower prices which were often the result of competition in wider markets, denied them funds to develop new production methods, and appeared in general to be responsible for the ills of longer hours, depressed wages and unemployment. In the workingmen's parties of the 1830s, the boss took his stand with the journeyman against the tyranny of a mercantile oligarchy which controlled markets and capital and, with its political connections, acquired monopoly privileges in the form of exclusive corporations to promote banks, toll-bridges and railways. In the 1840s, manufacturers began to demand elbow-room. They agitated for general incorporation laws which would permit them to draw upon the public for capital, and attacked the mercantilist policies of State governments which still regulated economic life with an eighteenth-century paternalism, granting monopolistic powers to privileged groups and conducting vast public works, like Pennsylvania's Main Line canal, as State enterprises. The manufacturers successfully undermined this traditional structure in the interest of a *laissez-faire* policy which would ensure the maximum freedom of action for commercial enterprise and put an end to special privilege in the economy. Only in the 1850s, however, did *laissez-faire* become part of the American creed[1] : and its adoption was the work of this insurgent manufacturing class.

[1] See Louis Hartz, *Economic Policy and Democratic Thought, Pennsylvania, 1776–1860* (Cambridge, Mass., 1948).

The journeyman awakened slowly to his new position in an industrial community. He had been brought up as an independent craftsman, working in his own time, often combining his trade with other pursuits and regarding it not as a lifetime's calling but as a stepping-stone to a prosperous business or freehold in the expanding west. Even the New England farmer's daughter, who took her temporary job in Lowell's mills in the hope of earning a trousseau, felt, when she took up residence in one of the model boardinghouses, that she was not only preserving her respectability but doing a patriotic duty in providing much-needed labour. The shoemakers of Lynn were often fishermen or small-holders in the summer. But with an expanding market, many craftsmen were forced to abandon making bespoke goods in favour of supplying cheap articles for distant markets. They received lower piece-rates from the merchant, who was himself harassed by increasing competition. Greater demand led to the employment of a scratch labour force with rudimentary training, to the detriment of craft standards and the discipline of apprenticeship. In order to scrape a subsistence, the journeymen had to work daily at their benches from sun-up to sun-down. In trade after trade, they found themselves compelled to live in sweat-shop conditions in the slum cellars and tenements of Boston's waterfront or New York's lower East Side. As 'wage slaves', not only did they earn less, but they had lost that sense of self-respect which went with their traditional status.[1]

The labour movement of the Jackson period represented the blind struggles of the journeymen to recover their old status. From the 1790s onwards, sporadic strikes, largely against the lowering of piece-rates, had been condemned by the courts under the common law of conspiracy. The boom periods of the 1820s and '30s, which strengthened the journeyman's bargaining position, led to successful combinations to improve conditions of work. Local craft unions joined together in 'city centrals' in Philadelphia, New York, Boston and elsewhere; and between 1834 and 1837 a short-lived National Trades' Union met annually in New York. But with hard

[1] John R. Commons and others, *History of Labour in the United States* (New York, 1918), vol. I, ch. I; Norman Ware, *The Industrial Worker 1840–60* (Boston, 1924), *passim.*

times after 1837 these associations disintegrated. Instead, in desperation, the workingmen turned to politics. With naïve faith in the boon of enfranchisement they joined the workingmen's parties which had become the radical wing of Jacksonian Democracy. The platforms of these parties with their long list of disparate aims—from the ten-hour day and the abolition of prison competition to popular education and the distribution of free land in the west—illustrate the social, as well as economic, *malaise* of workingmen who wished to recover their dignity as craftsmen.

The recognition of their new position as industrial wage-earners was delayed by this excursion into politics. Only in the 1850s did skilled tradesmen turn again to the more rewarding task of building up craft unions. But it remained uphill work, the gains in good times being dissipated in the depression of 1857. Americans were too restless, too easily wooed by the prospect of making a fortune in the west, to feel permanently committed to any trade or town, or to a manual status; and the growing influx of immigrants, prepared to establish a foothold by working for a pittance, made the task of protecting craft status a Herculean labour. If the English and some of the Germans were politically conscious enough to provide the unions with both file and rank, the Irish, and later the French Canadians, replaced New England girls at lower rates in the mills of Lowell and Chicopee, instilling in native workingmen a hostility to foreigners which played its part in the nativist movement of the 1850s.

Behind the Greek porticos of Chestnut Street, Philadelphia, in the bustling counting-houses of Wall Street, in the quiet of a mahogany-furnished sanctum lined with law reports on Boston's State Street, the mercantile fraternity transacted the business which governed America's growth. That fraternity consisted of many competing interests. Boston fought New York, New York outwitted Philadelphia, in the struggle for foreign business. Boston struggled to tap with a railway the vast hinterland which New York had acquired through the Erie Canal; the Baltimore and Ohio diverted to the Delaware port some of Philadelphia's trade with the trans-Allegheny West. The rise of textiles in New England and the coal and iron trade in Pennsylvania led to conflicts with importers over tariffs. The ironmasters won the day in Pennsylvania. In New England the forces were for some time nicely balanced; but that astute trimmer, Daniel Webster, Senator for Massachusetts, was converted to a protective tariff in 1828, as the balance shifted from overseas trade to domestic industry. In New York, too, there was conflict. But the overriding importance of Atlantic trade and of the cotton interests in the South kept the 'Cotton Whigs', an important interest, loyal to free trade and the Atlantic system up to 1860. As foreign trade declined, many listened to the beguiling voice of Henry Clay from Kentucky, who advocated an 'American system' whereby the manufactures of the north-east would be exchanged for the farm produce of the west behind a protective tariff wall.

But though there was rivalry over particulars, the mercantile community saw eye to eye on the broad issues of politics. These experienced merchants and bankers, these conservative lawyers and clergy, were at one in working for controlled, systematic development of the United States. They feared, as their English predecessors had feared, the pell-mell settlement of the West. They wanted the public lands of the United States to be sold in economic lots for good prices to attract men with capital who would farm commercially, and to repel the feckless good-for-nothings who were leaving their trades in the east, and were thus increasing the competition for labour and its cost. They advocated Federal and State aid for the construction of canals and railways to bind the west to eastern markets. They wished to counteract the speculative enthusiasm which exacerbated the wild swings of boom and depression. The men who managed the Suffolk Bank in Massachusetts understood the virtues of sound banking. They and their like gave support to Nicholas Biddle in his efforts to use the Second Bank of the United States to check the extravagant note issues of the rudimentary western banks. The mercantile fraternity lobbied for these policies in national affairs through the Whig Party which succeeded the Federalists as their spokesmen.

Atlantic in origin, the merchant community of the north-eastern seaboard had inherited metropolitan functions once performed for North America by Great Britain. As the American people moved into the heart of the continent, the division between the front and rear *échelons* of the operation became, not the Atlantic Ocean, but the Appalachian Mountains. The most important supply bases and control points were located on both sides of the Atlantic, and, in relation to the great westward thrust, Philadelphia and New York, Liverpool and London, New England and northern Old England, were partners in supplying the energy and confidence which alone ensured success. In that partnership Britain became increasingly a sleeping member. It was the mercantile community of the seaboard which took the strain of yoking continental expansion to the Atlantic world.

CHAPTER V

THE CONTINENTAL THRUST
1790-1850

'The West—not the East continually troubled with European visions—is ultimately destined to sway the country. The sea does not separate America from Europe; but behind the Alleghenies is springing up a new life and a people more nearly allied to the soil that nourishes them than the more refined and polished population of the seaboard.'

F. J. GRUND, *Aristocracy in America* (London, 1839).

THE upheaval of revolution hardly checked the westward thrust of the American people. The population doubled itself every twenty-four years: it was four million when Washington was inaugurated President in 1790, eight million at the close of the War of 1812, 16 million in the depression year 1839, and reached 32 million when the Confederates fired on Fort Sumter in 1861. Some of the increase swelled the port cities and a few inland towns; but even as late as 1850 over four-fifths of the population lived in communities of less than 2,500.[1] Americans were still thin on the ground; their larger numbers found elbow-room by moving west.

When, in 1803, Jefferson bought from Napoleon the unimaginably vast and remote Louisiana, he thought he had ensured enough space for Americans to expand for a thousand years; and when, in 1819, John Quincy Adams, in his Transcontinental Treaty with Spain, acquired Florida and a settlement of the Spanish-American boundary in the West, the continental security of the United States seemed indefinitely established. No one foresaw how quickly the American people would push into the heart of the continent.

By 1790 the stream of settlers had already broken through the Appalachian barrier south-westwards into Kentucky, west to the

[1] *Hist. Stat.*, Series B, 145–59.

forks of the Ohio and round the northern slopes into upper New York. By 1830, the frontier had leapt more than four hundred miles to the Mississippi and beyond, following the great river north from the old French town of New Orleans, north-westwards to take in the Missouri River settlements, and thence north-east across the Illinois prairie to the western shore of Lake Erie. There, for some time, it seemed likely to remain. School atlases wrote off Michigan as 'interminable swamp'; Black Hawk's War of 1832 was a reminder of the Indian menace north-west of the Mississippi; and, beyond the Missouri outposts, there stretched the Great American Desert, treeless, waterless, windswept and parched, which even sanguine pioneers deemed unfit for human life. Only the occasional missionary, or exploring party, and the corps of fur traders, making passage to their high secret empire in the Rockies, took the trail from Fort Leavenworth across the plains to South Pass. For twenty years the High Plains dammed the flow of migration, forcing it north into Wisconsin and Minnesota, and back to fill still unsettled tracts east of the Mississippi. It seemed as if the American people had reached their natural frontiers.

This penetration took place in a series of spurts stimulated by economic cycles in the Atlantic world: after the Revolutionary upheaval in 1783; after the War of 1812; during the great land and cotton boom of 1829–37; and, again, with the railway boom of the 1850s. In far-off coastal cities, merchants, bankers, real-estate promoters, engineers and politicians contributed to the development of America's first continental civilization in the Mississippi Valley; but the primary impulse came from the men of the back country, whose capital was a hatchet and a rifle, whose skill was woodcraft and whose temperament was that of the feckless drifter or the opportunist adventurer.

The first stage of migration was a continuation of the colonial movement. The men of the Appalachian wilderness, the Scotch-Irish, the Pennsylvania-Germans, the Virginian backwoodsmen, who had sojourned for perhaps a generation in the high mountain valleys, gradually moved west and south along the Wilderness and other trails, out through the gaps on to the western slopes and down the river valleys to the banks of the Ohio. Already at the turn of the century this backwoods community had been received into the Union, somewhat grandiloquently, as the States of Kentucky, Tennessee and Ohio, which in 1810 had a total population of some 900,000.

The advance guard, the frontiersmen proper, were a rare breed, indigenous to the forest; solitaries, shy of human contact; nomads for ever moving on, dressed in deer and coon skin, hunting game for food, trapping for barter, living much as the Indians whom they knew and hated like vermin in a game preserve. Their archetype, Daniel Boone, had already in 1810 abandoned the Kentucky he had surveyed for the Transylvania Company in the 1790s for the remoter haunts of the Missouri.

Their trails were followed and their bivouacs occupied by men more concerned to clear a patch of soil, raise some corn and subsist in a lean-to cabin. They, too, in the end, moved on, giving place to less transient 'settlers', often with families, intent on clearing tree stumps, building log houses, raising crops to make a living and to improve the value of the holding they had staked out. But even these often succumbed to the tempting offer of the stranger at the door to sell out and begin again farther west. Their claim to the land was sketchy, often non-existent; for they were ignorant of, or disregarded, the paper titles of land companies or the State. In the eyes of the pioneers, moral title was derived from the hazards of occupation. For they were exposed to the full rigours of the wilderness. The winter brought blizzards and the bitter cold of ten or twenty degrees below zero; the spring, floods and the frontier sickness from the foggy damps of river bottoms; the summer, a beating heat and mosquitoes. And always there were wild animals and Indians to be fended off. Human energies went largely into keeping alive; many went under, many were brutalized, and only the hardy endured, seasoned to a way of life whose values were inevitably transformed from those of the seaboard.

Lacking the capital and the hands to subdue the wilderness, the first settlers lived off the land as best they could: by hunting, trapping, clearing four or five acres for a crop of Indian corn, milking sorry, starved cows of unimproved breed, and salting pork from the lean razor-backed hogs which ran wild in the undergrowth.

Their craft was that of the woodsman; and, long after more advanced farming became possible, they clung to forest and wooded river bottom, to the primitive lore which taught that land without trees and scrub must be infertile.

The isolation of these early communities in southern Ohio and Kentucky limited them to a bare subsistence. The rough trails back east not only precluded the transport of bulky farm produce, but so restricted communications that for a generation there was danger of the western communities losing touch altogether with the seaboard. The Federal Government urgently prosecuted the building of a national road through the Maryland mountains to the west. This Great Cumberland Pike, which was ultimately pushed through to Vandalia, Illinois, carried in its hey-day, in addition to a throng of westward-moving settlers, an eastward traffic of drovers herding cattle on the hoof to eastern markets and pack-horses laden with light and valuable goods like pelts and whisky made from corn in a thousand backwood stills. Westwards along these primitive roads there also travelled another trader, indispensable to this rudimentary economy. The Yankee pedlar was a familiar figure in the western settlements. Suspect, but irresistible, he appeared unannounced at some isolated homestead, unloading from his pack, to the fast patter of his grotesque salesmanship, the scissors, needles, kitchenware, 'notions' and perhaps the legendary wooden nutmegs to delight the heart of the lonely settler's wife.[1]

But this trail-borne trade with the east was severely limited. It was far easier to move produce by water; and from earliest days there was a stirring of traffic down the rivers of the Ohio basin. Settlers floated their families and chattels downstream by raft, and the landings at which they fetched up on the Ohio and its tributaries—the Kanawha, the Kentucky, the Miami—became the centres of a river trade. As the surplus produce of the region grew, that trade found an outlet down the Ohio and the Mississippi. Even in 1800, New Orleans was the key to western trade, and to have it in American hands was the underlying motive of the Louisiana purchase. Farmers or storekeepers along the Ohio rivers floated their

[1] See Constance Rourke, *American Humor, A Study of the National Character* (New York, 1931), ch. 1; Richardson Wright, *Hawkers and Walkers in Early America* (Philadelphia, 1927), *passim*.

cargoes of potash, barrel staves, or grain on flatboats down the Ohio and Mississippi currents to New Orleans. Here, after a weary three-month voyage, both cargo and boat were sold, and the owner either made the tedious journey back overland or took a coastal schooner round to Philadelphia or Baltimore, where he bought store-goods which could be carried over the mountain roads back to the Ohio settlement. But the traffic was hazardous. The long journey down-river was fraught with danger from shifting currents, ice, snags and sandbars; the exigencies of the season brought the flatboats to New Orleans about the same time early in January, with the result that their produce was unloaded on to the market at the same moment, causing disastrous gluts; the immense labour of poling flat or keel boats upstream severely limited any return trade. To make full use of the great river network of the Mississippi Valley some means must be found of pushing boats easily upstream.

The problem was solved after 1812 by adapting the steamboat to western rivers. Successive improvements gave the Mississippi steamboat its unnautical but highly functional look: flatbottomed hull, stern wheel and immensely high superstructure enabled it to force a way against the strong current and to float in waters as shallow as a heavy dew, according to the boast. By 1860, steamboats penetrated into the remote reaches of the Mississippi system: from the head of Ohio navigation at Pittsburgh to the American Fur Company's post at Fort Union in the foothills of the Rockies, over a thousand miles up the Missouri from St Louis. On the lower Mississippi, the fast packets which competed for a growing traffic in passengers and freight were the romantic subjects for a new western folklore. Autocratic steamboat captains like the Mr Bixby immortalized by Mark Twain, with their uncanny memory for shifting channels and treacherous snags, and their nerve for the split-second decisions of navigation, risked wreck and explosion in wild races to St Louis or Cairo. Their life-and-death competition, which slashed freight rates, extended the benefits of the river trade and carried imports and immigrants from New Orleans into Missouri and Illinois.

The steamboat, with its two-way traffic, made the river network a single great trading system. By the 1830s, the quays of thriving river ports like Louisville and St Louis handled cotton bales, timber and farm produce from the remote interior. Pittsburgh, at the mouth of the Allegheny, already boasted ironworks producing nails and stoves, and engineering shops where steamboats were built. The Cincinnati of Mrs Trollope's bazaar was already an important meat-packing centre. These *entrepôts* did business with the local storekeepers who, in a hundred back-country settlements, bought the settler's surplus, sold or lent him implements, seeds and provisions, shipped his produce down-river and imported in turn the essential articles which the neighbourhood could not provide. Until long after the Civil War, the country store (at once post office, warehouse, shop and bank) carried on the essential functions of the western economy: with its warm stove in winter, its shady porch in summer and its cracker-barrel philosophers, the country store was the West's first drug-store counter—the gossip centre of the neighbourhood. Country store and river port were the nodal points of a trading area whose extremities were forest settlements, whose main channel was the Mississippi and whose outlets were the ports of the Gulf coast. Until the Civil War, the greater part of the West's trade drained south into the funnel of New Orleans, which increased steadily its annual turnover from 17 million dollars in 1819 to 185 million dollars in 1860.[1] It seemed as if the new West of the Mississippi Valley would be isolated by the Appalachian barrier from the eastern seaboard, and would be oriented by its great natural waterways southwards to the Gulf of Mexico.

By 1830, the advance guard of settlement was moving outwards from the Ohio basin north-west into southern Indiana and Illinois and south-west into Alabama and Mississippi. These two new frontier areas had each a population of about half a million; and, in each, more accessible markets encouraged a more specialized, though hardly less primitive, form of agriculture.

In the north-west, settlers at last emerged from the habitual protection of wooded watercourses into uncompromising, open country. 'Prairies', grassy openings in the woods, were at first shunned by hatchet-toting woodsmen with an eye for timber but not for

---

[1] E. R. Johnson and Others, *History of Domestic and Foreign Commerce of the United States* (Washington, 1915), vol. I, pp. 213 and 243.

tilth. By degrees, however, with the use of oxen and a new, heavy, metal plough, the tough prairie sod was scratched, if not turned, and in the fertile virgin soil there sprouted the frontier's first grain crop: wheat. Where rivers and the first canals gave access to markets, settlers on the prairies south of Lakes Erie and Michigan turned to wheat farming of an increasingly commercial character. The infant lake-settlement of Chicago sent its first grain-laden sloop along the Great Lakes to Buffalo in 1838. Maize, too, growing tall in the hot sun of Kentucky, southern Ohio and Indiana, was fed to cattle and hogs which were driven to Cincinnati for packing. By the 1840s, the north-west was on the threshold of its career as the purveyor of grains and hogs to eastern markets.

Further south, the rich country round Nashville, Tennessee, enabled the neighbours of General Andrew Jackson to keep up in a crude way the mixed-farming, tobacco-planting, horse-breeding, cockfighting existence which their forbears had known in the Virginia uplands. This planter tradition was quickened into new vitality by the revolutionary demand for cotton on the far-away Liverpool Exchange. From 1820 onwards, planters moved south from Tennessee into Mississippi and Alabama. Here, in the rich alluvial soils of the delta, and in a sub-tropical climate, it was possible to grow cotton in astonishing abundance, and to ship the crop downstream to the Gulf ports. The cotton boom of the 1820s drew to the deep South a new army of migrants from the Carolina seaboard, where the cultivation of cotton, as wasteful as tobacco planting had been, was already exhausting the soil.

This new Odyssey differed from the older backwoods movement. Overseers or younger sons were sent with a slave force to colonize a daughter plantation in the southern wilderness. Sometimes a whole planting family would migrate, like the Dabneys of Virginia —a cavalcade with slaves, equipment and household possessions, intent on resuming, in Mississippi, the decorous patriarchal life of the old South. The more unruly slaves of Virginia were sold for good prices 'down the river' into the more brutal conditions of a remote Alabama plantation. This movement brought capital and labour to the new frontier, and soon cotton bales from these plantations, as well as from small homesteads, had transformed the aspect of the quays at New Orleans. By 1840, planters had moved west into Louisiana, where sugar, as well as cotton, became an important staple crop. This southern migration did not stop at the Louisiana boundary of the United States. To the west lay the plains of the Texas Province of Mexico, where, by 1830, a group of American adventurers and scapegraces were cattle-ranching and intriguing for annexation by the United States. With the annexation of Texas in 1845 the American frontier was pushed farther to the south-west, and a new population, largely southern in origin and loyalties, was linked politically with the Mississippi Valley. This colonizing movement emphasized the southern outlook of the old West. The first settlers in Ohio and Missouri had looked south down the great rivers and had cherished family traditions deriving from the Appalachian uplands; and the newer colonists of the deep South, whose way of life became ever more self-conscious in their frontier isolation, were intensely loyal to the Carolina seaboard.

In the 1830s the old drift of settlement westward from the Valley of Virginia was supplemented by a flanking movement from the north-east which radically changed the character of the West and underlined contrasts between North and South in the Mississippi Valley.

In the early years of the century, settlers had moved up the Susquehanna Valley from Pennsylvania and along the Mohawk from the Hudson out into the fertile, rolling country south of Lake Ontario which had been the home of the Indian Confederation of the Six Nations.[1] The New Yorkers, anxious to prevent the produce of this region from being drained south via the Susquehanna to Philadelphia, embarked on the ambitious venture of digging a canal between the Hudson and Lake Erie. In October 1825 Governor Clinton, whose enterprise it was, was able to travel by the barge *Seneca Chief* the five hundred miles of his 'Big Ditch' from Buffalo to New York; and on 5 November he completed the opening festivities by pouring a keg of Lake Erie water into the Atlantic off Sandy Hook. The Great Western, or Erie, Canal was completed within eight years. A public works project of the State of New York, its success was a wonder of the western world and a dangerous

[1] From which New York derives its name of 'Empire State'.

example to the promoters of less well-sited canal schemes elsewhere. It transformed western New York from a primitive frontier area into a prosperous farming community which, for twenty years, was the wheat and milling centre of the United States.

The Erie Canal not only brought the rich farm surplus of western New York to the Hudson, but, by establishing a water link with Lake Erie, it made the whole vast region of the Great Lakes part of the hinterland of the port of New York. The cost of freight between Buffalo and New York fell from 100 to 8 dollars a ton. Between 1830 and 1850, canal shipments of flour grew from practically nothing to over three million barrels a year, a staggering index of the growth of the West.[1] In reverse, the canal was an easy route for migrants into the upper Mississippi Valley. Its wheat or timber barges, returning light from Albany, carried settlers to Buffalo whence they took sloop or steamboat to little ports farther along Lake Erie such as Cleveland or Toledo, and thence to new settlements in northern Ohio, Indiana and Illinois. The construction of the Erie Canal led to the digging of a network of canals linking Lake Erie with the Wabash and the Ohio, and Lake Michigan, at Chicago, with the Mississippi. These canals were a business failure for the States which undertook them; but they made possible the peopling of the mid-western prairies bordering on the Lakes. Unlike the earlier settlements farther south, which fronted on the Ohio, these communities had the Great Lakes for their front door. And, unlike those earlier settlers, their loyalties were not to a South of family tradition or childhood but to the North-east and even to the Europe whence, for the most part, they had come.

The barges of the Erie Canal carried westwards the main body of those immigrants who ventured from New York into the interior. An unknown but important number of Britishers, undeterred by Cobbett's propaganda against settling in the West, travelled by the Great Lakes route into the North-west. Some, like the Staffordshire potters of Wisconsin, the English community in Illinois, or the Cornish miners of Mineral Point, remain identifiable; but most travelled alone and were quickly assimilated into

[1] E. R. Johnson and Others, *op. cit.* vol. 1, p. 230.

Yankee settlements. In 1850, there were some 120,000 people of British origin in the North-west.[1] More striking, because of their greater numbers and solidarity, were the Germans, who travelled west by the boatload from the late 1840s, to form cohesive German-speaking, beer-drinking communities, particularly in the hardwood areas bordering Lake Michigan, where Milwaukee was, and remains, predominantly a German city. In 1850, there were 280,000 people of German birth in the North-west.[2] In large parts of Wisconsin and Minnesota, a third or more of the population was foreign-born in 1860.[3] But important as these immigrants were as minority groups, by far the greater part of the westward migrants were the sons and daughters of New England.

The reluctant soil and hostile climate of New England had never sustained her growing population. When the bumper yields of western New York eclipsed the meagre local produce in Boston market, up-country Yankees turned to sheep farming, sent their daughters into the Lowell mills, and their sons west to seek a fortune. Hill farmers of Vermont, weary of piling stones from fields on to walls, abandoned their mortgaged houses to bears and wild-cats, and set out for the Finger Lake country south of Ontario and beyond. Families migrated wholesale from New England along the Erie Canal route into western New York, where they stayed for perhaps a generation before moving on again to Indiana, Illinois or Michigan. Often a group of families migrated from the same neighbourhood, like those from East Poultney, Vt., who founded Vermontville, Michigan, in 1836.[4] These settlers travelled farther and faster than the earlier group from the southern uplands. They carried more baggage, both physical and mental. Wherever they went, they took with them the quality of New England.

Inured to northern winters, they were less indolent than their southern neighbours, and were determined to preserve in the wilderness the respectability of their Puritan inheritance. Free from back-

[1] F. J. Turner, *The United States 1830–50* (New York, 1935), p. 284.
[2] *Ibid.* p. 281.
[3] C. O. Paullin and J. K. Wright, *Atlas of the Historical Geography of the United States* (Washington, 1932), plate 71A.
[4] S. H. Holbrook, *The Yankee Exodus: An Account of Migration from New England* (New York, 1950), pp. 79–81.

woods prejudice, and knowledgeable about agriculture, they went in for arable farming on a commercial scale. They brought books and the habit of reading. They built schoolhouses where their wives and daughters taught the three Rs; and they established colleges. In communities where universal church membership was still the rule, they built Congregational churches in the style of the New England meeting-house. Here they listened on the Sabbath to interminable sermons from ministers fired with evangelical zeal to save souls, free slaves, put down drink and, in general, to herald that Millennium which some believed to be at hand for God's chosen in the wilderness. For people of Puritan stock, westward migration was but the hiving-off of another 'gathered community' dedicated to the pursuit of spiritual perfection in a promised land remote from the contagion of a sinful society. The New Englanders also brought the democratic habits of the town meeting and the homely philosophy of the social contract with its egalitarian twist reinforced by the conditions of the frontier. Disillusioned about the promise of the American Revolution by the prevailing seaboard evils of debt, absentee landlords, monopoly and unemployment, these up-country Yankees hoped to establish at last in the West that absolute democracy which was implied by the Declaration of Independence. Righteous, independent, shrewd and informed, the Yankee settlers provided the leadership for the development of the North-west. From their ranks were to come a remarkable number of the farmers, merchants, mechanics, railroadmen, who were to build an empire which, linked with the North-east, was to dominate the entire continent.

Fed by the arteries of the Great Lakes system the old North-west grew apace. Log cabins were replaced by frame houses; forest trails by dirt and plank roads. By 1860, the lakeside towns of Cleveland, Detroit and Milwaukee each boasted more than 40,000 people. Chicago, at the Michigan end of the Illinois Canal, which had been a mere cluster of cabins round Fort Dearborn in 1830, had a population of over 100,000 in 1860 and was shipping east the equivalent of 20 million bushels of grain. In 1850, the North Central States had a combined population of over four million—nearly a fifth of the total for the United States; and in the greater part of Ohio there were more than 45 persons per square mile.

These communities looked to the eastern seaboard for their markets, their manufactured goods, immigrants and capital. As they emerged from a frontier subsistence, the thrusting midwesterners called upon the merchants of Boston and New York for capital to develop their growing commercial empire, and began to vote for the Whig policy of a closed partnership between East and North-west embodied in 'The American system'. New York houses underwrote their crops and handled their marketing. In the 1850s, New York and Boston investors put up the capital and the brains to build the Midwest's growing network of railways. In 1853, a continuous line connected New York with Chicago, eleven hundred miles into the interior; and Erastus Corning was beginning to organize this into the trunk route of the New York Central. By 1860, the 'go-getting' Chicagoans, who could boast four trunk lines to the East as well as the Illinois Central route to the South, were on their way, with the help of their New York allies, to wrest the primacy of trade in the upper Mississippi Valley from St Louis. The merchants of the older and more conservative city, too complacent about the 'natural' flow of trade downstream, and too gentlemanly to tout for new business, mismanaged their railroading and lost ground to their upstart rivals in the North.[1]

The settlement of the Great Lakes region radically shifted the balance of forces in the West. An increasing proportion of trade in the upper Mississippi Valley was diverted east to New York and lost to the Great River. Although its annual turnover continued to increase throughout the 1850s, New Orleans had to rely more and more for its exports on the cotton and other produce of the lower valley. As frontier conditions gave place to more specialized occupations, the Mississippi Valley lost much of its homogeneity. The old North-west, with Yankee habits and loyalties, was distinguished from the South-west, with its plantation culture and allegiance to the old South. But for most of the period of this chapter that cleavage, which was fraught with such tragic consequences for the United States, was less apparent than the solidarity among most westerners against their supposed control and exploitation by an ultramontane seaboard.

[1] W. W. Belcher, *The Economic Rivalry Between St. Louis and Chicago, 1850–1880* (New York, 1947), *passim*.

The Continental Thrust, 1790–1850

Between 1790 and 1860, the cutting edge of the frontier had travelled from the Alleghenies beyond the bend of the Missouri; and
into the cleared area behind it there had surged a horde of Americans
intent on gathering the riches laid bare. In 1790, the statistical centre
of population was still on tide-water in Chesapeake Bay. By 1860,
it was in Central Ohio, still moving west as it continues to do today.[1] The lure of unlimited land enticed some 16 millions of
Americans to make a livelihood in the West rather than submit to
the painful process of adjusting themselves to the conditions of an
increasingly populous seaboard. Until the completion of a transport
system which could commercialize the West, its settlers, spread thin
over the vast expanse of the interior, had to be content with a primitive, semi-nomadic existence. As the frontier shifted, the horde of
speculators, settlers and dealers were on the move behind it, travelling light, risking disaster, picking up profits where these could be
easily made without heavy commitments. For the settler was more
in the habit of 'settling up' and moving on than of 'settling down'.
Until there was no longer a frontier, and Americans had to take
stock, they retained the instincts of the hunter: they were still, in a
measure, nomads, living off the land. They lacked the capital, the
labour and the knowledge to develop systematically the apparently
unlimited resources which beckoned to them; and in their westward
progress they exploited, in the narrow, destructive meaning of the
term, the natural wealth of the Mississippi Valley.

The fur traders had in colonial days exhausted the supply of
beaver in the Great Lakes region; and by the 1830s their successors,
the advance guard of American colonization, were engaged in the
far-away Rocky Mountains in an internecine competition among
themselves and with the Hudson's Bay Company which resulted in
the emergence of John Jacob Astor's monopolistic American Fur
Company.

Lumbermen, having depleted the white pine of Maine and New
Brunswick, New York and Pennsylvania, trekked west through
the virgin forests to the Michigan Peninsula, which they reached
about 1850, and thence to Wisconsin and Minnesota. Felling in the
hard winters, logging down the rivers in the spring thaws, these

[1] Paullin and Wright, *op. cit.* Plate 80A.

103

'Down-easters' from Maine, 'Bluenoses' from Nova Scotia, 'Canucks' from French Canada, together with Swedes and Germans destroyed the choice stands of white pine to provide frame houses and furniture for the West. They left behind a wilderness of stumps, and so upset the balance of nature that enormous tracts of the North-west remained derelict.

The prairie farmer, who had barely to scratch the surface of the virgin grassland to raise bumper crops of wheat, gave the soil no rest: he robbed it of its sweetness and left it exposed to the erosion of wind and flood. He was encouraged in his spendthrift habits by the knowledge that there was always more land to be had to the west. Indeed, he had no alternative. A British immigrant farmer like Morris Birkbeck learnt by humiliating experience that the sound agricultural practice of Surrey did not pay in Illinois.[1] The competition from virgin soils farther west proved too great. The moving frontier forced a continual adjustment in the practice of older farming areas. Wheat from western New York in Boston market soon drove the New Englander into sheep or dairy farming or market gardening; and when wheat from the Illinois prairies reached Buffalo, western New York, in turn, had to shift to mixed farming. Similarly, as the more southerly corn belt moved west, so did the chief centres of hog and cattle raising. This westward drift was perhaps most pronounced in cotton planting, where the special conditions of a slave labour force intensified the habit of exhausting the soil. During the half century before 1850, the cotton frontier shifted from South Carolina to Mississippi, and thence south-westwards into Texas.

Behind the crops came the processing industries. Rochester, New York, lost its pre-eminence as a milling centre to Chicago in the 1850s; and Chicago, in turn, gave place, shortly after the Civil War, to Minneapolis at the Falls of St Anthony on the upper Mississippi some four hundred miles to the north-west. Cincinnati, with a population of over 100,000 in 1850, remained an important meat-packing centre; but by the Civil War Chicago had become an important rival. It was the same story with farm machinery. Cyrus

---

[1] See the comments of Governor Edward Coles, in C. W. Alvord, *Governor Edward Coles* (Springfield, Ill., 1920), p. 373.

McCormick, a Scotch-Irishman who had migrated from Pennsylvania into the Shenandoah Valley of Virginia, experimented with a mechanical reaper which he began to manufacture in 1844 at Brockport in western New York's wheat country. Three years later he moved to Chicago where, by 1860, he was turning out some 4,000 machines a year in response to the crying shortage of harvesting labour on the prairies.

As the advance of the frontier was consolidated, western society became more like that of the seaboard. Farming became more specialized, commercial and dependent on eastern and, indeed, world markets. The problems of the Illinois wheat grower of the 1840s were nearer those of his competitor in Pennsylvania or New York than to those of the Alabama cotton planter, whose prosperity, like that of his Georgia cousins, was determined on the Liverpool Cotton Exchange. The affairs of Cincinnati, New Orleans or Chicago were in the hands of merchants, bankers, lawyers, clergy, who did business, pleaded, preached and even voted in much the same way as their kind in Albany or Baltimore; and tradesmen and mechanics in a town like Pittsburgh took their cue from the workingmen of Philadelphia. The citizens of Boston or Marietta, Ohio, Springfield, Ill., Montpelier, Ind., and a score of other scattered townships in the old North-west, modelled themselves on that New England of which they were outposts. They took their ministers from Andover or Cambridge, their schoolmarms from the Connecticut River Valley, listened respectfully in their Lyceums to lectures by Emerson or Dickens, read the poetry of Lowell and Longfellow, the speeches of John Quincy Adams, the novels of Hawthorne and George Eliot, the sermons of Theodore Parker. The German communities of southern Ohio preserved the traditions of their Pennsylvania 'Dutch' ancestry; the Germans of Wisconsin and St Louis, through their language, their Catholic or Lutheran churches, their *turnvereins* and beer gardens, indulged their nostalgia for the culture of the Rhineland or Switzerland. In the deep South, the exigencies of cotton planting and slavery drew upland farmer and planter alike into ever closer sympathy with the aristocratic culture of Carolina. The Mississippi planting family bore themselves in the autocratic and genteel style befitting the gentry of the old South, building elaborately pedimented mansions, laying out avenues and gardens in the unpromising wilderness, ordering their riding boots in London, and their wine from Madeira, reading the Charleston papers, the speeches of Calhoun, the novels of Scott and Thackeray and the poetry of Byron.

But although the westerner, both North and South, might feel nostalgia for his eastern origins, cherish a family tradition or cultivate metropolitan manners, the experience of migrating and settling profoundly, if subtly, altered his character.

The instinct to reject rather than submit which impelled emigrants to the New World and which was ever present in colonial society became markedly developed in the American moving west. As he travelled into the Mississippi Valley he turned his back on a seaboard community whose controls had become intolerable. By deciding to break with an interfering landlord or an overbearing master, to quit an outworn farm, to rid himself of the burden of debt, to escape from social disapproval or religious orthodoxy, or simply to make a fortune in the West, the migrant renounced the whole conception of a corporate, customary society into which he had been born to play a determined role. He ceased to think of society organically, and denied the need for continuing institutions which would mould all the transactions of everyday life to the traditions of the past. As he crossed the Alleghenies he turned his back on squire and parson, symbols of the vestigial society of status on the seaboard, and thought only of shaping his life for himself. He 'disestablished' not only the Church, but most of the institutions which formed the corporate societies of the Old World. Responsibility for law and order became direct and personal. Where firearms were a necessary personal protection, the army, with its harsh discipline and code of the gentleman, lost its exclusive authority. Where summary justice had to be done, the legal hierarchy of Bench and Bar lost its majesty. As the Churches colonized westwards, they had to countenance more independence in government; and they became increasingly fragmented with the splintering off of new and exotic sects proclaiming the immediacy of the relationship between God and the individual.

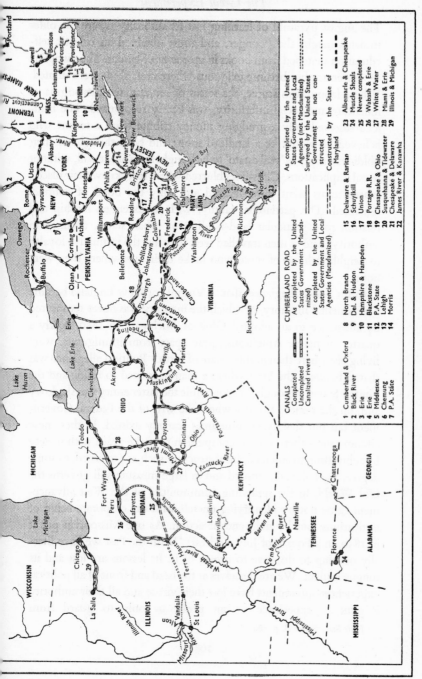

3. The North-eastern United States: Canals and Cumberland Road

The august pyramid of learning lost its authority where the older students taught the younger, and most obtained an eclectic self-education snatched from books in moments of leisure. The discipline of apprenticeship became exiguous where craft skills were diluted. Where labour was scarce, the status of servant, with its stigma of indenture and social inferiority, was barely recognized. The landlord received only a grudging money tribute from a tenant who believed he would be a landlord soon; and both thought of their holdings simply as 'real estate' to be bought and sold at will, without social implications. Class-lines blurred where few 'knew their place', where status went unrecognized and only the bond of contract remained. The patriarchal family, with its extended kinship and relation to a particular land-holding or urban status, declined in authority. And as men travelled west they lost the instinctive loyalty to neighbourhood of those who make their lives where they were born.

As for wider allegiance, that to Virginia or New England became a sentimental memory, of which the intensity was never recaptured by allegiance to an adopted Ohio or Michigan. In 1850, nearly a quarter of native Americans, quite apart from immigrants, were living elsewhere than in their State of birth.[1] Political allegiance was shared between the State where a man happened to reside and the United States, although for a long time the latter entity was shadowy and, on the remote frontier where the writ of the Federal Government ran but shakily, it sometimes scarcely existed. In these new circumstances there was no compulsion to make peace with society by submitting to an hierarchical structure such as governed, to some degree, the colonial seaboard and in large measure still governs the Old World. In the sprawling communities of the West advancement came not by identifying oneself with the corporate being of institutions, but by independent action. As one Missourian put it in 1850, in a Fourth of July Address: 'With the Past we have literally nothing to do, save to dream of it. Its lessons are lost and its tongue is silent. We are ourselves at the head and front of all political experience—precedents have lost their virtue and all their authority is gone . . . experience . . . can profit *us* only to guard from

[1] *Hist. Stat.*, Series B, p. 189.

antiquated delusions.'[1] Henceforward the American's loyalty to institutions rarely went beyond the tentative and the temporary.

On his western journey the American lost many habits of European origin; but the experience of pioneering, however much overlaid subsequently by conventions of settled life, fostered new social habits. Those who stayed on the seaboard adjusted to change by modifying their immediate circumstances within the given framework of township, farm and trade, as when Vermonters took to sheep farming and sent their daughters for a season to the mills or when the younger sons of Boston's China merchants turned to railroading along the New England shore. But for those who pulled up their roots, the line of least resistance to change lay in westward travel. Those Hoosiers[2] whose families had trekked west in stages from the Valley of Virginia, those men of Connecticut who sojourned in Western Reserve before sending their children on to Iowa, those British settlers in Illinois, those Rhinelanders in Wisconsin, those stylish Carolinians in Louisiana, were all members of a great caravan in spasmodic movement across the continent. Once they had suffered the wrench which separated them from an ancestral past, their way of life, their habits, conventions, taboos, were those of the caravanserai, and by living through the epic experience of migration they created a new form of social organization, strange and alien to the Old World: the mobile society.

Just as the pioneer developed new muscles, leaving older, habitual skills unexercised, so, too, the challenge of survival in a primitive settlement induced a new set of social responses.

The inexorable demand for physical labour broke down the old order of specialized skills and set a premium on adaptability and improvisation. Craftsmen, mechanics, lawyers, schoolteachers, clergy, doctors, found their *expertise* growing rusty as they learnt to handle an axe, drive a plough or set a roof-tree. On the other hand, isolated woodsmen or farmers were forced by the endless crises of daily life to turn their hands to repairing firearms, setting splints, arguing law cases, preaching sermons, keeping law and order; and their womenfolk to teaching, making clothes and

[1] B. Gratz Brown, journalist, Governor of Missouri and U.S. Senator.
[2] Citizens of Indiana.

delivering babies. As the migrant drifted west, he might become successively farmer, tavern-keeper, storekeeper, stage-driver or blacksmith in his effort to make a living in each new community. Inherited disciplines lost their force and professional standards became coarsened and vulgarized; even in agriculture, as we have seen, the moving frontier made nonsense of improved methods and encouraged the woodsman or settler to cling to his primitive and wasteful habits. The westerner became by force of circumstances newly adaptable and experimental. Unable to call on specialized services, he was forced to improvise, to work out by trial and error his own solutions to urgent problems. The immediate results might be disastrous; but in the long run the westerner benefited from this shedding of the skin of convention. Those who survived this hard school emerged with a new self-confidence in their ability to tackle successfully any problem to which they set their mind and with a cavalier disregard for the esoteric ritual of the craft tradition.

So it was with inherited status. In the caravanserai social origins mattered less than more personal qualities. In Sangamon County, Illinois or Boonville, Mo., influence came, not from letters of credit or connections, but from bringing labour to the land or wits to trade. In an undifferentiated economy, most began with the same sort of assets, and there was a career open to those with talents to survive the wilderness. Leadership went to forceful individuals, whatever the social circumstances they had left behind—and it was tactless to inquire too closely into these. Physical strength was at a premium. Large healthy families were the best solution to the labour problem. Big men acquired a natural ascendancy when so much depended on individual exertion. Abraham Lincoln owed not a little to his tall frame and legendary strength with an axe; and much of western folklore is concerned with the exploits of men of superhuman strength like Paul Bunyan, the giant lumberjack, whose footsteps made the lakes of Minnesota, or Davy Crockett, who could wrestle with bears and swing alligators by the tail. This emphasis on personal prowess exaggerated the individualism which the self-reliance of the pioneer had already made a cardinal article of faith. Status also came to have less to do with ethnic origins. Yankees, southerners, Scotch-Irish, Germans, British, Swedes might live apart in separate communities; but where all were new arrivals, it was difficult for any one group to maintain a special position, and all were allies in the struggle against natural forces.

The hopes of those who took part in the great trek lay exclusively in the future. The American people as a whole were remarkably young. In 1840 the median age of white Americans, that is the age dividing the population into two equal groups, was just under eighteen, as compared with twenty-nine for the United States in 1940; and in western communities most adults were still in their twenties. Although westerners, particularly women, aged fast, they were resilient and optimistic. Their image of the good life was not to inherit the customary trade, farm or house of their elders, but to build an idealized homestead for themselves in the golden west. The sordid reality of poverty, sickness and loneliness was felt to be only temporary, like the shelter of a particular homestead. Somewhere down the river, or over the next horizon, there would be found that perfect property, that idyllic way of life which all were seeking. This will-o'-the-wisp led many a family to sell out an improvement and to start again farther west the back-breaking work of clearing a new holding. One pioneer from Virginia, who moved to Ohio in 1819, thence to Indiana in 1825, and ten years later to Wisconsin, wrote in 1849: 'I reached the Pacific and yet the sun sets west of me and my wife positively refuses to go to the Sandwich Islands and the bark is starting off my rails and that is longer than I ever allowed myself to remain on one farm.' An almost demonic search for 'God's Country' possessed the western spirit; only when the great migration was at an end did it become clear that this impulsive yearning was but the pioneer's primitive response to the Romantic Age. As one who experienced the last frontier in Oklahoma put it: 'We learned that God's Country isn't in the country. It is in the mind. As we looked back we knew all the time we was hunting for God's Country we had it. We worked hard. We was loyal, honest. We was happy. For forty-eight years we lived together in God's Country.'[1] The search for Utopia united all who felt the lure of the great continent: the roistering back-woodsman, the God-fearing Yankee farmer, the drifting remittance

[1] B. A. Botkin, *A Treasury of American Folklore* (New York, 1944), p. 279.

man no less than the preacher of a messianic faith and the eccentric who hoped to establish an ideal community in the wilderness.

The American backwoods attracted many reformers, secular and religious, from both sides of the Atlantic, who chose to practise their ideas in a model community withdrawn from the corruption of the world, rather than to combat the evils of an existing order. By 1860, nearly ninety different communities, dedicated to some form of communal life,[1] had been established west of the Appalachians. Many were religious, like the German-speaking Rappite and Herrnhuter sects, the Shakers, the Perfectionists and the Mormons. Many were secular and socialistic. The possibility of asylum, which had brought so many English and German religious bodies to North America in the seventeenth and eighteenth centuries, attracted also those oppressed by the social upheavals of nineteenth-century Europe. German hearts responded to accounts of Rappite success; from France Etienne Cabet took his followers to found the Icarite communities of Illinois and Iowa. From the 1790s, when Coleridge planned his pantisocracy on the Susquehanna, Englishmen thought of emigrating with a choice band to the American backwoods. English emigrants such as Frederick Evans became leaders in the Shaker community, the origins of which went back to Mother Anne Lee and her disciples, who emigrated from Manchester at the time of the Revolution. The impulsive Frances Wright, inspired by Bentham and Lafayette, established an ill-starred little colony at Nashoba, Tennessee, to help slaves to buy their freedom by putting them to work on the land.

But the most important example, in scale, imagination and influence, was Robert Owen's community at New Harmony, Indiana. Losing heart over the possibility of making industrial capitalism serve a social purpose in Britain, Owen in 1824 emigrated to Indiana, where he consumed the greater part of his fortune in establishing a socialistic community whose members were to be weaned from acquisitive habits by an education based on the best rational principles.

Some of these communities, Owenite, Fourierite and sectarian,

---

[1] A. E. Bestor, Jr, *Backwoods Utopias: The Sectarian and Owenite Phases of Communitarian Socialism in America: 1663-1829* (Philadelphia, 1950), Appendix.

were initially successful. Isolated in the wilderness, they benefited from pooled labour and a planned use of skill. But as the early enthusiasm waned, and they began to have intercourse with a wider world, they tended to break into factions and resume the practice of individual ownership. In the end, their farming, handicraft economy capitulated before America's industrial revolution; and by the 1880s, the Oneida and the Shaker communities survived only by marketing such articles as bear traps, plated silverware and hand-made furniture. But before the Civil War, while there was elbow-room for all, such communities were characteristic, if idiosyncratic, manifestations of the common Utopian ideal.

In the continental interior Americans had this forward-looking mentality whether they continued to trek westwards into Iowa or Kansas or lived out their lives in western New York or Ohio. For while the former became inured to new places, the latter under-went the strain of adjustment to a neighbourhood which might change its character radically every few years. In 1820, a young man making his way in western New York lived in a log cabin, wore homespun and obtained essential provisions by selling the potash made by burning timber felled in clearing his land. Thirty years later he might be selling his wheat crop to a miller in Rochester, a town of 40,000 with Greek Revival houses, sidewalks, banks, stores (with plate-glass windows), hotels, a railway station and a theatre.[1] A storekeeper at Fort Dearborn, dealing in furs and timber in 1830, might find himself only twenty years later a prosperous merchant of Chicago, a city of some 100,000, following the price of wheat in New York and New Orleans, investing in hogs or corn, ware-houses or railways. Such was the pace of change that all the land-marks of a man's youth might be wiped out by the time he reached middle age: forests, paths, cabins, even whole settlements, might disappear, to be replaced by an open, tilled countryside, or a town of frame houses or even brick and stone, a canal, a railroad track, a row of grain elevators against the sky. Youthful occupations—lumbering, trapping, railsplitting—were a dim memory to a whole-sale merchant, an agricultural engineer or a railroad dispatcher.

[1] B. McKelvey, *Rochester the Water-Power City, 1812–1854* (Cambridge, Mass., 1945), *passim*.

This dynamic pace of change forced those who responded to it to readjust themselves perpetually to new conditions, to acquire new techniques, to gamble on new enterprise. Those who 'grew up with the country', and survived the struggle, were tough, resilient, versatile, adaptable and open to ideas. Their past was quickly obliterated; their efforts were concentrated on keeping up with the rate of change, on anticipating the future.

The new conditions had a marked effect on attitudes to getting and spending. Most westerners depended on farming for a livelihood; and their view of economic problems was essentially agrarian. They not only needed enormous draughts of credit to enable them to raise and market their crops, but they demanded it as their privilege for the back-breaking toil of subduing the wilderness. Easily tempted to gamble on the future, western farmers were chronically burdened by debt. Homesteads were quickly mortgaged to storekeepers or bankers (sometimes the same person), and the Jeffersonian ideal of a universal freehold faded with bankruptcy, the consolidation of landholdings in capitalist hands, and the growth of tenant farming. The farmer resented capitalist enjoyment of unearned increment from the soil, and especially the machinations of eastern capitalists who appeared to prey on his well-being.

But the westerner was not a peasant, and his outlook was not fundamentally anti-capitalist. The settler's ambition did not normally run to striking roots and developing his homestead as a permanent residence and livelihood for his children. His attitude to land holding was not primarily social but speculative and commercial. As Alexis de Tocqueville observed, 'he brings land into tillage in order to sell it again, and not to farm it'.[1] He traded not only in land but in any commodity or service he could turn to good use. Even the earliest frontiersman had lived as much by swapping pelts and 'moonshine' as by the produce of his corn patch; and the versatile westerner developed a keen sense of the main chance. He traded in horses and cattle, skins and furs, guns and knives, in hay, corn, even manure. He hired out his services as carpenter, blacksmith or water diviner. He speculated by starting a crossroads tavern, grist mill or country store; by buying land where it was

[1] Alexis de Tocqueville, *Democracy in America*, vol. II, bk. II, ch. xix.

rumoured a railway would run. He bought always for a rise, trying to persuade himself, neighbours and strangers that his tiny settlement would soon be a city in the wilderness. He subscribed credulously to the stock of canal companies in the '30s, and railways in the '50s; he pestered his State legislature for transport subsidies and his Congressman for Federal aid for 'internal improvements'. As another French visitor put it in 1835, 'everyone is speculating and everything has become an object of speculation . . . cotton, land, city and town lots, banks, railroads . . .'[1]

Sometimes this gambling on the future paid off with spectacular results; more often it left the gambler where he started, like Colonel Sellers in Mark Twain's *The Gilded Age*, still spending generously whatever came his way. For, 'One could always begin again in America; bankruptcy, which in the fixed society of Europe was the tragic end of a career, might be merely a step in personal education.'[2]

In short, the westerner, whatever his occupation, was fundamentally concerned to make money, and where so much around him was uncertain, so much awaited exploitation and men felt free of the restraining hand of custom, the cash nexus increasingly governed his social transactions and capitalism found a uniquely fair field to grow in.

The exigencies of western living encouraged new forms of social action to replace the formal, institutionalized relations which had not survived the conditions of the caravan.

The earliest denizens of the backwoods, the frontiersmen proper, were solitaries, shy of human contact, owing nothing to any man, suspicious of strangers. The *Crockett Almanac* of 1838 described them thus: 'The backwoodsman is a singular being, always wanting to move westwards like a buffalo before the tide of civilization. He does not want a neighbour nearer than ten miles; and when he cannot cut down a tree that will fall within ten rods of his log house he thinks it is time to sell out his betterment and be off.' When in 1799 Daniel Boone, at the age of 65, was asked why he was leaving

---

[1] M. Chevalier, *Society, Manners & Politics in the United States* (Boston, 1939), p. 305.
[2] John Krout and D. R. Fox, *The Completion of Independence, 1790–1830* (New York, 1944), p. 3.

Kentucky for frontier Missouri he is said to have replied: 'Too many people; too crowded; too crowded! I want more elbow-room.' Such addicts to the solitude of the wilderness were a rare breed who quickly passed on their way. But their less flighty successors, the settlers proper, were equally, if more involuntarily, bound by the wilderness to a lonely existence. Most westerners lived not in compact settlements, like those left behind perhaps in New England or Pennsylvania, but in scattered homesteads often separated by many miles of rough tracks from the nearest neighbour. There was no village life west of the Alleghenies, and the dispersed settlements had no focus sharper than the vague unit of the county. For months, sometimes years, on end the isolated family was thrown back on its own resources for livelihood and companionship. As Harriet Martineau observed in her travels through the West in 1836: 'Among the most interesting personages . . . are the Solitaries—solitary families, not individuals. Europeans, who think it much to lodge in a country cottage for six weeks in the summer, can form little idea of the life of a solitary family in the wilds. I did not see the most sequestered . . .; but I witnessed some modes of life which realized all I had conceived of the romantic or of the dismal.'[1] In the infancy of the West the settler's family was the only social unit, and the pattern of western culture was formed almost entirely on this single *motif*.[2]

Migration altered the character of the American family. It became a truncated affair without associations of place, without any marked sense of kinship and with decreasing loyalty to a single ethnic stock. Families whose ancestors had lived at the mouth of the Connecticut River since the 1630s might be in Ohio or Minnesota in one generation and on the Pacific coast in the next. Children brought up in the West might never have known grandparents, uncles, aunts or cousins and, far from having seen their parents' birthplace, might have only the vaguest tradition as to its whereabouts. In turn, when children grew up, they normally left home to carve out a homestead of their own or live by their wits. And when they married, although most sought out their own kind—Scotch-Irish, English or German—

[1] Harriet Martineau, *Society in America* (London, 1837), vol. I, pp. 162–3.
[2] A. W. Calhoun, ' The Early American Family', *Annals of the American Academy*, 1932.

an increasing number happened to choose girls of a different stock. The family which settled the American interior was a single-generation group appropriate to a mobile society.

But the family acquired a new loyalty from its isolated circumstances. All its members worked to support its self-sufficient economy. Children were an economic asset, and, despite a staggering mortality rate, large families were the rule. The average size of the western family in 1850 was over five persons. On more established farms, single relations or 'hired hands' lived as part of the family and shared its fortunes. In addition to making a living the family had to rely on its own resources for defence against marauders, for building house and barns, making furniture and clothing, for school and religious worship, and for high days and holidays. Homestead children knew only the few intense personal relationships of the family; for them the family board was the whole of social life.

The value of women to this family society enhanced their status. In the migrating stream, whether from Europe or from the eastern seaboard, young unmarried men predominated. The population of the United States in 1850 contained half a million more men than women, and the predominance of men was even more marked in the western States, which contained 529 men per thousand population compared with 504 for the eastern seaboard.[1] Women were scarce. They were also invaluable economic assets. Although women habitually worked in the field in German or Scandinavian communities only, where the habits of peasant culture persisted, settlers' wives were full partners in the homestead, performing the duties not only of farmers' wives but of household industry, in addition to bearing and bringing up children. These responsibilities made them independent and self-confident. Free from the conventions of the seaboard, women in the West were almost the equals of men. They could handle horses and, at a pinch, firearms; they could hold their own in business; and they could talk politics or religion, for they were at least as well educated as their fathers and brothers. When the progress of settlement at last provided some leisure, they took the lead in demanding formal rights for their sex. The first

[1] U.S. Bureau of the Census, *A Century of Population Growth* (Washington, 1909), p. 93.

co-educational college was founded at Oberlin, Ohio, in 1833, and from it there graduated women dedicated to such causes as anti-slavery, women's rights and temperance, one of whom, Antoinette Brown, became the first woman Congregationalist minister. Catherine Beecher, daughter of the Principal of the Lane Seminary, Ohio, became the leading advocate of equal educational opportunities for women. Elizabeth Blackwell, who was Bristol-born but spent her formative years in Ohio, was the first woman to force an entry into the medical profession. Jane Grey Swisshelm of Pittsburgh, and later of Minnesota, was a powerful crusading journalist. Susan B. Anthony of western New York became the leader of the women's temperance movement.

The demand for woman suffrage was first voiced in 1848 at Seneca Falls, western New York, and a remarkable number of its most earnest women advocates, like Elizabeth Cady Stanton herself, were brought up in that district which the Erie Canal, within their own memory, had transformed from a wilderness to a prosperous community.[1] Woman suffrage societies flourished throughout the Mississippi Valley, and it was no accident that Wyoming was the first State to grant women the vote.

Although the westerner looked to the family as the one stable social unit, he developed a special sense of loyalty towards those who were for the time being his neighbours. This was not institutionalized like the ordered relationship of an English village. It was rather the spontaneous instinct for mutual aid and companionship in a hostile wilderness, where life was a continuing emergency. Newcomers would be given shelter and supplies. When extra labour was needed, after a tornado or an ice storm or at harvest time, the neighbourhood would be mobilized to assist. There were customary occasions for junketing: a house-raising, when the setting of the roof-tree required the most skilled hand in the county; a corn-husking; a quilting party; or a 'shower', when a bride would be presented with the precious nucleus of kitchen stuff and linen. Such 'get-togethers' were welcome relief from tedium and loneliness. For where human beings were so thin on the ground, neighbours

---

[1] See biographies of early American suffragettes in S. B. Anthony and E. C. Stanton, *History of Woman Suffrage* (New York, 1881).

and strangers, far from trespassing on privacy, were welcome diversions. Out of frontier conditions came the American's indiscriminate
curiosity about people, his habit of generous hospitality, his strong
gregarious instinct, and his tradition of group effort.

The westerner was content with the largely self-made amuse-
ments of country life; horse-racing, wrestling, fiddling and dancing;
and, in more settled times, the annual excitement of the county or
State fair. But people travelled long distances to St Louis or Cincinnati to see waxworks or puppet shows, to see the Booth family
in Shakespeare, to hear Jenny Lind or Adelina Patti, or even occasionally some fustian company in German or Italian opera. And,
on the long river-boat journeys, wits were sharpened in interminable
talk on religion, politics and the future of the West, with chance
companions, including immigrants or even the occasional European
traveller.

Book-learning was a cherished talisman. Western communities
were quick to organize schools, and in the old North-west where,
under the North-west Ordinance of 1787, public land was set aside
for the support of education, a public school system grew up with
settlement itself. The services of New England schoolmarms, of
even eccentric Scots and English schoolmasters, were eagerly sought.
The first glimmering of higher education was brought to the West
by the earliest Virginia migrants, who established Transylvania
University at Lexington, Kentucky, in 1799. The eastern churches
established denominational colleges and seminaries like the Episcopal Kenyon College, or the Congregational Lane Seminary, both
in Ohio. Primitive 'State universities' grew up with the support of
State land appropriations. Although the curriculum gave precedence
to classics, mathematics and 'moral philosophy', it also included
manual and agricultural arts, useful for exercise, for a training in
western living and often as a means of making a college pay its way.
The habit of working one's way through school was an early feature
of education in the West. So, too, was co-education. Both were
prominent at Oberlin, and at Antioch, where the New England
reformer, Horace Mann, put into practice his experimental ideas
in the '50s.

The isolation of rural life encouraged reading. Subscription libraries, composed of classics such as Locke, Hume, Gibbon and Jefferson's *Practical Farmer*, flourished from earliest times, and Cincinnati became the centre for a prosperous book trade in magazines and romantic novels.[1] Although much of this literature was imported from the East, the writings of such men as James Hall and Timothy Flint were genuine attempts to capture the western spirit, which was still reflected, for the most part, only in a primitive folk culture. There was a new kind of humour in the tall talk of the backwoodsman, that 'gamecock of the wilderness' who rhapsodized himself as: 'A regular tornado, tough as hickory and long-winded as a nor'wester. I can strike a blow like a falling tree and every lick makes a gap in the crowd that lets in an acre of sunshine';[2] or in the terms of a whole new bestiary: 'half horse, half alligator, the sea-horse of the mountain, a flying whale, a bear with a sore head'.[3] There were the ballads of longboatmen and lumbermen. There was the dry anecdotage of an Abraham Lincoln. There were the primitive landscapes of travelling 'limners', the quilts and wood-carvings of backwood homes, the severe functional lines of Shaker furniture. Much of this folk experience was caught and remembered by the young Samuel Clemens growing up in Hannibal, Missouri; and through him and others it was absorbed into the main stream of American consciousness.

The harsh wilderness brutalized some and induced nervous breakdown in others; but many were sustained, at any rate temporarily, by a religious experience of a more personal and violent quality, in keeping with frontier conditions. The evangelism of colonial times, with its emphasis on sin and conversion, developed its most extreme forms in the trans-Appalachian West. Circuit-riding preachers like the indefatigable Peter Cartwright conducted revivals in back country districts. The settlers who flocked to these open air congregations, often from great distances, yearned for spiritual companionship, and their highly charged tensions were released in a peculiarly violent way. The camp meeting, with its several days' session, its repentance-seat, its hymn-singing and the violent exhortation of its ministers, induced a state of ecstatic trance in which

[1] B. W. Bond, Jr, *The Civilization of the Old Northwest* (New York, 1934), p. 431.
[2] Rourke, *op. cit.* p. 36.
[3] *Ibid.*

the more susceptible barked like dogs or suffered paroxysms of 'jerks' and hysterical laughter. Such mass hysteria was an invitation to the charlatan and the hypocrite, and some camp meetings degenerated into orgiastic excesses; but they were a genuine religious manifestation of the early West, and the tradition persists. In the more settled '40s and '50s, the revival gave place to more orthodox practices. People looked to the Sunday sermon for intellectual exercise and a rhetorical treat; and argument about religion became a favourite pastime for disputatious country folk. The most effective colonizing Churches were those with the simpler theology and the most free Church government, particularly the Methodists and the Baptists. But the westerner, wont to determine his own beliefs, sampled different doctrines to suit his eclectic taste. He was attracted especially to the simplified beliefs and lay leadership of the Disciples of Christ, or 'Christians', followers of the Scotch-Irish immigrant and Presbyterian renegade Alexander Campbell. The West also provided a haven for more exotic sects claiming some special Revelation or preaching some esoteric discipline. The messianic belief which was the religious aspect of the westerner's Utopian yearnings, deluded the followers of William Miller, a western New Yorker, who not only preached, but made practical preparations for a Second Coming in 1843. Joseph Smith claimed to have received the golden plates which he incorporated in the Book of Mormon as a result of a divine visitation under a tree near Palmyra in upper New York in 1830, and his disciples, the Church of Latter Day Saints, moved west with the migrating stream to Illinois and then to Utah in their search for a Promised Land for the lost tribes of Israel. Their practice of polygamy was only one of several experiments in sex carried out in the seclusion of a backwoods community. The Shakers practised total continence, combined with elaborate, formal dancing; the Perfectionists, followers of John Humphrey Noyes, in their community at Oneida in upper New York indulged an elaborately eugenical promiscuity under the guise of 'spiritual affinity'.

Upper New York was, indeed, not only a nursery for westward migration but a forcing ground for religious ideas which took root all over the old North-west. Perhaps the most important of these rippled outwards from the turbulent revival of 1826. The ministrations of the Rev. Charles G. Finney and his band of brothers started a forest fire of conversion in that lately settled area which left few untouched, and such spiritual exhaustion that western New York became known as the 'burnt-over' area. The zeal for moral improvement due to the revival induced many western New Yorkers to become workers in the great empire of humanitarian endeavour.[1] Anti-slavery owes much to western New York. One of Finney's Brothers, Theodore Weld, led the students' revolt from the Lane Seminary at Cincinnati in 1833 over this issue; and later he and his lieutenants were responsible for the rapid growth of anti-slavery societies through the North-west in the 1830s. The cause of women's rights owes much to the generation of women brought up in anti-slavery households, especially in western New York, for whom the emancipation of their sex was a logical and passionately held corollary to the emancipation of the slave. Temperance, also, owes one line of descent from the frontier, where men drank heavily to dull the pain of hardship and loneliness, and especially from western New York, where the great revival created numerous temperance societies. The connection between temperance and feminism was close in a society where long-suffering wives in desperation 'visited grog shops and demolished decanters and stove in barrels'.[2] Thus a characteristic western religious revival, by preaching that human life was a process of moral betterment through personal conversion, gave to a whole generation the conviction that personal values were bound up with social reform.[3] And as those who had sojourned in western New York moved on, they carried with them into the old North-west a set pattern of living which did not easily accommodate itself to the more easy-going pattern brought by earlier settlers from the Valley of Virginia.

The conditions of western life fostered new attitudes towards law, order and politics. There was no police. Authority was vested in a sheriff who relied for force on a *posse* of citizens. In the last resort, the law was in a man's own hands. Outlying homesteads

---

[1] See G. H. Barnes, *The Anti-Slavery Impulse, 1830–44* (New York, 1933), *passim*.
[2] *The Genius of the West* (Cincinnati, 1856), p. 224; quoted in H. C. Hubbart, *The Older Middle West, 1840–1880* (New York, 1936), p. 37.
[3] See ch. vi.

were menaced by cattle- and horse-thieves, or by gangs of toughs. Self-defence led to vengeance and feuds, and 'crime was more an offence against the victim than a violation of the law of the land'.[1] Murder went unpunished, and was condoned if committed in hot blood, while the penalty for horse stealing was lynching. Bands of citizens took it upon themselves to maintain order, like the 'Regulators' of southern Illinois in 1846, who became more embarrassing to the Governor than the rowdies themselves, or the pro-slavery men who enforced black codes, destroyed abolitionist presses and murdered Elijah Lovejoy at Alton, Illinois, in 1837. Frontier conditions gave rise to an evil tradition of amateur law enforcement, from the Regulators and the Iowa Claims Association to the vigilantes of the Pacific coast. Access to the courts had always been a problem for the back country. The holding of district courts involved continuous and exhausting travel for judges and Bar. Judges and leading counsel shared beds, while juniors and clerks made do with bare boards. The forensic level matched that of comfort. Most lawyers had taught themselves whatever law they knew from dog-eared volumes of Blackstone. Cases were often argued by laymen, and decided on the rough and ready method of common sense by elected judges who knew less law than the attorneys. But in spite of this lack of learning, westerners were chronically litigious. They relished argument, enjoyed the drama of trial and made the holding of an assize the excuse for a party.

Politics were based on the assumptions of direct democracy. A say in politics was every man's prerogative. Where most held land, and rich men were rare, the vote was a natural right. There existed in the West no class brought up to manage political affairs as they managed estates and counting-houses. Men used to turning their hands to anything did not admit the need for special training in the office of sheriff or judge, State Senator or even Federal Congressman. They were ready at the drop of a hat to take on any job themselves, or to choose their candidates from neighbours and acquaintances who saw things the same way and could be expected to watch over local interests. Without reverence for authority, they were on

[1] F. J. Turner, 'The Problem of the West', in *The Frontier in American History* (New York, 1920), p. 212.

guard against 'the never-ending audacity of elected persons', believing rotation in office an essential safeguard against corruption. On the other hand, since they had no means or leisure to act without compensation they turned an indulgent eye on those who made money out of office. The cry 'to the victors belong the spoils' had a predatory ring, but also an air of rough justice. Their fear of authority made them hostile to external control, whether by the county town, the State capital or Washington, a hostility which increased in intensity with distance. Elected representatives were expected to concern themselves almost exclusively with promoting parochial interests. Delegates rather than true representatives, they were ridden with a short rein by citizens who did not consider their duty at an end after the elections, but on the contrary kept up a barrage of comment and criticism on current issues both local and national. Westerners were as happy to criticize the intricacies of a Webster-Ashburton Treaty as they were to protest against the failure of their State assemblyman to arrange for a railway to be run through the home county.

Politics were conducted in a spirit of rhetoric, horseplay and carnival. Voters were best influenced by open-air meetings, another welcome relief from the tedium of rural life. Rival candidates went 'on the stump', and their electioneering took the form of contests in drollery and bombast, to the enjoyment of crowds who had come more to be entertained than instructed. The campaign was inevitably pitched at a demagogic level. The voter was edified, not only by the violent ranting of the candidate, but by a liberal provision of hard cider or rum, the spectacle of torchlight processions, the music of bands and choirs, and the extravagant controversy of crudely printed newspapers. Candidates were presented as folk heroes. Indian fighters such as General Andrew Jackson, Colonel Richard Johnson or even Abraham Lincoln, who had taken part in Black Hawk's War, were 'natural' figures for politics; and the gentlemanly and mild General Harrison was swept into the White House in 1840 in the Whig interest after the constant advertisement of the legend of his victory at Tippecanoe and his birth in a log cabin. Such methods were the inevitable outcome of the new mass electorate which was not susceptible to more traditional practices.

In an electorate restricted to substantial property owners, such as dominated the seaboard until the 1830s, politics remained a matter of influence. Candidates were arranged and votes marshalled during the course of business or over the wine; and party cohesion was ensured by the gentlemanly caucuses of State and Federal legislatures. Such methods were not relevant in the new West where votes must be canvassed, cap in hand, of widely scattered communities whose only relation with the candidate was political. This situation affected not only the immediate campaign but the organization of the party. Party cohesion was secured by the development of a new structure of loyalties. This began with the individual voter at the 'grass roots',[1] who had his say in the nomination of candidates for county office. The county convention sent delegates to district and State conventions for the nomination of Congressional and State candidates. Once every four years the State conventions, in turn, sent delegates to a national convention charged with nominating the party's Presidential candidate. With the multiplication of offices, both elective and appointive, at all three levels of the political structure, the loyalties of an increasing number of party workers were bound up with the party's campaigns in the counties, the States and in the nation. Patronage, 'spoils of office', lubricated the workings of this elaborate party machine which depended so largely on the efforts of humble amateurs without means. Since the purpose of the new kind of party was to build up a system of loyalties from parochial foundations, the party's policies were an amalgam of local interests; and since many of these local interests inevitably conflicted with one another, policy was a matter for bargaining and compromise, rather than any clear-cut statement of principle.

Such, in brief, was the American party, as it emerged with the Jacksonian Democrats and the Harrisonian Whigs, and as it has remained, in very large measure, until today. Many of its techniques derive from the East and especially from the city machines of New York and Philadelphia. But its early growth as a national system was forced by the urgent need to impose a political discipline upon the sprawling communities of the Mississippi Valley.

[1] The phrase itself, used in this sense, appears only to have come into use in the 1880s; see the *Oxford Dictionary of Americanisms*.

CHAPTER VI

THE EMERGENCE OF THE DEMOCRATIC IDEA

1820-50

> When the Muses nine
> With the Virtues meet,
> Find to their design
> An Atlantic seat,
> By green orchard boughs
> Fended from the heat,
> Where the statesman ploughs
> Furrow for the wheat;
> When the Church is social worth,
> When the state-house is the hearth,
> Then the perfect State is come,
> The republican at home.
>
> RALPH WALDO EMERSON.

WHEN on 4 March 1829 a jostling crowd of clod-hoppers and mechanics, come to town to enjoy the triumphant inauguration of their heroic General Jackson as President, tramped the public rooms of the White House in search of punch to drink his health, the fastidious ladies of Washington society shuddered behind drawn blinds. For them, and for many an established man of property up and down the seaboard, the spectre of revolution stalked the yet unpaved streets of the nation's capital that day. There was good reason, for, although there were to be no barricades, the election of Jackson was the writing on the wall for the easy ascendancy of their kind. As George Bancroft, historian and Jacksonian politician, put it in 1836: 'It is now for the yeomanry and the mechanics to march at the head of civilization. The merchants and the lawyers, that is, the moneyed interest, broke up feudalism. The day for the multitude has now dawned.'[1] The twin influences of levelling and geographic spreading had broken the hold of oligarchy on the destinies of the American people. It was the beginning of a new, democratic age.

The lure of the West proved too powerful for the restraining disciplines of the seaboard. Just as British imperial power had failed to hold in check the centrifugal forces of the colonial back country, so the mercantile oligarchy lost control of the peripheral West beyond the Appalachian Mountains. The whole nationalist programme of ordered advance went by the board. The restricted sale of public lands to men with capital to develop them; the building of a transport system at Federal Government expense which would create markets *pari passu* with settlement; the safeguarding of property values from inflationary pressure by means of a hard currency and sound banking practices, including a national bank; the preservation of the eastern labour force against seepage to the West; the development of industry by means of the mercantilist apparatus of private monopoly, State enterprise and a protective tariff—one by one these controls were swept away in the turbulent wake of migration; and power to determine American affairs passed from gentlemen in cravats to a new generation of small men—farmers, middlemen and manufacturers—to whom the spreading of American resources brought new opportunities.

What most astonished de Tocqueville in 1833 was 'the innumerable multitude of small undertakings'[2]: of woodland homesteads, prairie farms, country stores, gristmills, tanneries, ironworks, and livery stables. The farmer, who became the American archetype, demanded the land as his birthright. Federal and State governments were forced to relax the terms of sale for public land. In 1804, a settler could buy as little as a quarter section (160 acres), and in 1830 could pre-empt the land on which he was squatting; he could get land for as little as $1.25 an acre in 1820, and finally for nothing after the Homestead Act of 1862. Western farmers and their

---

[1] George Bancroft to O. A. Brownson, 21 September 1836; H. F. Brownson, *Brownson's Early Life*, pp. 180-1; quoted in A. M. Schlesinger, Jr, *The Age of Jackson* (London, 1946), p. 319.
[2] de Tocqueville, *op. cit.* vol. II, bk. II, ch. xix.

middlemen allies, in need of easy credit terms to develop their enterprises, encouraged the growth of inflationary banking practices, to
the detriment of eastern creditors, and resisted the efforts of the Bank
of the United States and the eastern banking fraternity to curb their
excesses. Suspicion of seaboard capital led westerners to prefer State
to Federal support for transport schemes, and to join with southern
planters in opposing an industrial tariff. Small business men everywhere chafed at the mercantilist policies of the seaboard merchant
class. In Massachusetts and Pennsylvania, they attacked monopolistic
privileges granted to exclusive syndicates to build turnpikes and
railways, and State-owned public works which competed with
private enterprise; and they demanded general incorporation laws
to put small manufacturers and business men on even terms with
old family connections in attracting new capital. In their demand for
elbow-room the incipient manufacturing class, which was to
determine America's destiny in the coming generation, succeeded
in demolishing the structure and the theory of mercantilism in the
older States. By 1850, hostility to State authority had gone so far
that *laissez-faire* in economic matters was accepted as the only
healthy order for the American Republic. Even journeymen workers in the ports and inland towns attributed their depressed status
to the baleful influence of the mercantile oligarchy, and welcoming
both farmers and manufacturers to their workingmen's parties,
sought through a political programme which included rights to
education and land as well as to industrial combination, the restoration of their independent craft status. Theirs, they felt, was a temporary discomfort which the intelligent use of their new vote would
rectify. In no sense a working class, they still had the instincts of
self-employed persons, assumed a social equality with their 'betters'
and were sustained by the hope that, in the last resort, they could
better themselves by moving west.

The great mass of petty enterprisers were the leaven for this
society in ferment. Their outlook gave the age its special ethos.
Without the social inhibitions of a customary community, their
values were 'commuted' into monetary terms. They were capitalists, and speculative capitalists at that. Their professed hostility to
'capitalism', when it was not agrarian resentment at middlemen's

profits, was, in reality, a chafing against special privilege. Where there was so much new growth of small business the appearance of equality and competition obscured latent inequalities and the pull towards monopoly. Men felt themselves to be acting fully and responsibly alone in their own interests in a society whose moral purpose, governed by the unseen hand of Providence, emerged as the result of free competition. The great mass of Americans assumed as self-evident the postulates of 'liberal' economic theory which Henry Carey and other economists were preaching to a more sophisticated reading public. Fearing authority, they distrusted all forms of economic concentration, especially when these involved special favours from government. They believed the State should abdicate in the economic sphere in favour of the rule of *laissez-faire*.

In this society, broken down into individual units, political forms took a democratic shape. The new electorate believed in the principle of dispersal in politics as instinctively as in economics. Their village-store economics were matched with parish-pump politics. Self-government was inescapable in a frontier community; and the Founding Fathers did well when they profited from the mistakes of British colonial policy by arranging for the automatic admission of western communities to full rights within the Union. The shift from political power as the privilege of property to political power as the inalienable right of the individual was imperceptible. Western society for a time approximated to the Jeffersonian ideal of a yeoman republic where property owning, in the form of land, was almost universal, and all could be regarded as having a stake in the country. Many of the trans-Appalachian territories granted universal male franchise when they became States. By 1830, only Ohio of the north-western States retained a light tax-paying qualification. In the South where the implications of Jeffersonian democracy were modified to fit the hard facts of slavery and where apologists took refuge in the dream of a Greek democracy of white, free men resting on the manual labour of black slaves, tax-paying or property qualifications were retained. But the example of the West encouraged back-country areas in seaboard States to combine with the towns to achieve universal franchise, like New York, or only a light property qualification, like Pennsylvania, and a more equable arrangement of constituencies. After 1830, the seaboard oligarchy had to seek new methods of control. The promise implicit in the Declaration of Independence had at last been written into State, and so into the Federal, constitutional practice.

The new electorate, fearing institutional authority as the instrument of vested interest, believed that political power should be widely and equally distributed in individual hands. Power should not be imparted from above, but should be built up from the ground as a result of the *ad hoc* co-operation of individuals in the pursuit of enlightened self-interest. This building-up process became the outstanding characteristic of politics in the new age. Parochial groups coalesced to control State and regional politics; and regional interests in turn formed alliances aimed at exercising national power. Some of these combinations survived over the years; but most were temporary and easily broke down into their constituent parts. With a population widely dispersed over half a continent—the essential condition for which the Federal framework was designed—these interests were geographic rather than functional. Their cohesion was the result of innumerable compromises at all levels. Just as the whole structure of interest-groups rested ultimately on the individual, so the only general policies which were national in effect were those simple slogans like 'Down with the Bank' or 'War with Mexico' which, on the lips of a President with a flair for the dramatic, could touch the imagination of the innumerable individuals to whom, in the last resort, political power returned.

This revolt from authority, this political atomism, also characterized social relations. Americans, responding to westward pulls, not only abolished the whole apparatus of mercantilist and oligarchic control, but, as was shown in Chapter V, disestablished authority in all its institutional forms: church, law, learning, craft, landlord, class and family. Instead, authority rested on the isolated individual who, owing no obligations to any wider corporate unity, carried so much of the responsibility for ordering his life. It was recognition of this fact which led de Tocqueville to invent the term *individualisme* to describe the dominant characteristic of the America he visited in the 1830s.

This psychological release from the inhibitions of an authoritarian society gave the new generation an intoxicating sense of the potential of life in America. The individual was raised to a higher power. Democracy, not simply as a political system, but as an ethos, promised the complete fulfilment of individual aspirations. Within its expanding orbit men were perfectible, moral progress was a fact and Utopia not an ideal but a practical plan. The dynamic pace of change intensified the conviction that the United States had been singled out for a special role in the regeneration of mankind. Americans believed in their 'manifest destiny' to people the New World with free men; and some of them in a messianic role to herald the Kingdom of God on American earth. Europeans caught the contagion and flocked across the Atlantic not only to make a better living but to free themselves of social constraints, to experiment in new forms of social action or to practise a messianic faith.

This buoyancy sustained Americans in their response to the pressure of change, which was often gruelling and demoralizing. American society suffered from acute growing pains. The unplanned, haphazard expansion into the Mississippi Valley went ahead too fast. The great boom before 1837 culminated in the disastrous collapse and exhaustion of 1839–42 and the slow recovery or the 1840s. Many of this literally dislocated generation, without familiar landmarks, lost the senses of identity and direction. Financial bankruptcy might be only an episode for the tough and thrusting; but those with less adaptable resources suffered a more personal disintegration. Many succumbed to the violence and solitude of the frontier which abounded with shiftless drifters and strange, broken characters, flotsam on the turbulent flood of change. Artisans lost their pride of craft. Immigrants suffered an intolerable nostalgia for home. Many were sustained only by the promise of the future, and in their dismay pinned their hopes on some beguiling panacea.

This, America's age of ferment, was also her age of reform. This exuberant individualism produced a hundred and one home-made solutions to the problems created by America's growth.

Men organized political parties to remedy particular grievances which were regarded as single obstacles to a general betterment. The disappearance in 1826 of one William Morgan, who had exposed the secrets of Freemasonry, gave rise in New York State and elsewhere to an obsession that this secret order played a sinister part in the oligarchic control of politics and office holding. An anti-Masonic party had considerable success in the rural politics of New York, Pennsylvania and New England in the 1830s. Fear of the Irish as an alien immigrant group created a wave of hysteria against Roman Catholicism which, beginning with the burning by a mob of the Ursuline Convent in Boston in 1834, developed into the Nativist Party of the '30s and the Know-Nothing or American Party of the '50s. The anti-Sabbatarianism of workingmen's parties was an attack on the clerical wing of the 'banking' oligarchy. Most of these parties were used by professional politicians to canalize local interests into the great national parties. Only the Free Soil Party, born of anti-slavery sentiment in New York State in 1840, was destined to transcend the narrow appeal of the one-idea party and to impose its platform on the nation.

In the religious mode, this impatience with the present, and confidence in a future perfection, brought forth a lunatic fringe of prophets, like Joseph Smith and William Miller, each claiming a special, individual revelation. In the same neighbourhood as Smith and Miller, John Humphrey Noyes, a Yankee Fifth Monarchy man, was drawing up the creed for his Oneida community: 'As a believer in the Bible I know that the territory of the United States belongs to God and is promised . . . to Jesus Christ and his followers. . . . The Son of God has manifestly to me chosen this country for the theatre of such an assault . . . God has moved me to nominate Jesus Christ for the Presidency not only of the United States, but of the world.'[1] And without an orthodox authority to cry heresy, simple people were attracted to such elementary messianic faiths. 'Come-Outers' who had suffered such rapid changes felt nothing implausible in an immediate and final *dénouement*.

Such doctrines were strong medicine for credulous and bewildered souls. But the more educated and conventionally balanced were equally taken up with practical programmes of moral reform. Although the fever of evangelical revival passed, the habit of conversion left a disposition towards humanitarian endeavour. A stage

[1] J. H. Noyes to W. L. Garrison, 22 March 1837; W. P. and F. J. Garrison, *William Lloyd Garrison* (London, 1885), vol. II, pp. 146–7.

army of philanthropists under such leaders as the Tappan Brothers of New York or Gerrit Smith of Syracuse or the elders of the Society of Friends embraced first one and then another 'cause' in a congeries of reforms the purpose of which was the regeneration of mankind, beginning with North America. The distribution of Bibles and tracts, prison reform, missions to Indians, to New York prostitutes, were followed by ever more ambitious crusades. The movement for total prohibition had its first great flowering in the 1840s with the American Temperance Society and the Washingtonians, precursors of 'Alcoholics Anonymous'. William Ladd founded the American Peace Society in 1828. In 1831 William Lloyd Garrison sounded in *The Liberator* a bugle call for a radical attack on slavery which was heard in hundreds of communities in the North and West. By 1837, the American Anti-Slavery Society was supported by over a thousand local societies dedicated to the extirpation of slavery in the interest of the souls of the blacks and the moral well-being of American society as a whole. And out of this generation of anti-slavery enthusiasts were bred the first women leaders and male sympathisers in the movement for feminine emancipation. Men and women also sought to improve their minds by the discipline of physical cults. Grahamites preached the virtues of whole-wheat bread; vegetarians shunned meats; hydropathists gladly suffered the rigours of cold plunges and wet-blanket baths; fresh-air maniacs opened parlour windows on principle; women abandoned stays and layers of petticoats, and the more daring adopted the freedom of Mrs Amelia Bloomer's pantaloons; phrenologists followed the Scotsman George Combe and the Swiss Spurzheim in a search for the key to human personality through cranial formation; spiritualists sought the key to the hereafter in the spirit rappings of the mysterious Fox Sisters of Rochester, New York.

The aim of these movements, which, as we have seen, transcended national frontiers,[1] was the regeneration of the 'universal' man. As a writer in *The Dial* put it in 1841: 'A true community can be founded on nothing short of faith in the universal man, as he comes from the hands of the Creator, with no law over his liberty but the eternal ideas that lie at the foundation of his being . . . The final

[1] See ch. iv, pp. 81–82.

cause of human society is the unfolding of the individual man into every form of perfection, without let or hindrance, according to the inward nature of each.'[1] The method was universal reform (the first anti-slavery newspaper was fittingly called 'The Genius of Universal Emancipation'). Devotees of individual cults came together in conventions to advocate their panaceas in combination. Emerson described one such famous occasion, the Chardon Street Convention, which met in Boston in 1840. 'Madmen, madwomen, men with beards, Dunkers, Muggletonians, Come-Outers, Groaners, Agrarians, Seventh-Day Adventists, Baptists, Quakers, Abolitionists, Calvinists, Unitarians and Philosophers: all came successively to the top and seized their moment, if not their hour, wherein to chide, or pray, or preach, or protest.'[2] The more extreme embraced all reforms with a catholic enthusiasm. William Lloyd Garrison split the anti-slavery movement by his insistence on dragging in temperance, pacifism, woman's rights and a universalist position in religion. For thirty years he carried on a violent and indiscriminate agitation against such institutions as slavery, the subordination of women, the Sabbath, orthodox theology and even the authority of the State itself. In 1838, he organized a Non-Resistance Society which declared itself in the following terms: 'We cannot acknowledge allegiance to any human government; neither can we oppose any such government by a resort to physical force. We recognize but one KING and LAWGIVER, one JUDGE and RULER of mankind . . . Our country is the world, our countrymen are all mankind . . . The interests, rights and liberties of American citizens are no more dear to us than those of the whole human race.'[3] When in 1854 Garrison publicly burned a copy of the U.S. Constitution, denouncing it as 'a covenant with death and an agreement with hell', the moral anarchism of universal reform could go no further.

Others, sceptical of the efficacy of universal reform, sought salvation in the practice of special disciplines in communities withdrawn from the unreformed world. Some of these Utopians were

[1] L. V. Parrington, *Main Currents in American Thought* (New York, 1930), vol. II, p. 348.
[2] R. W. Emerson, *Works* (Riverside Edition), vol. X, p. 374.
[3] Garrison, W. P. and F. J., *op. cit.* vol. II, p. 230.

religious like the Shakers, the German Rappites or the Perfectionists; but the greatest number of 'communitarian'[1] experiments in the 1840s and '50s were secular attempts to provide an alternative to an acquisitive, capitalist society, the evils of which were becoming manifest in the 'dark satanic mills' not only of Old, but of New, England. Both the Owenite communities and the larger number of Fourierite 'phalanxes' which dotted the map of the North-east and North-west were essays in an agrarian and handicraft economy based on common ownership. But even their socialism was individualistic. They held together on the principle of voluntary association and they fell apart as the enthusiasm of leaders declined and the treasure chest emptied. Their revolutionary fervour was no more radical than that of the short-lived but better-known Utopia of New England intellectuals at Brook Farm, West Roxbury, Massachusetts, which L. V. Parrington describes as: 'a homely Yankee pastoral, a sort of May Day adventure in brown holland tunics, an inspiring quest of the ideal amongst furrows and manures. It is a social poem fashioned out of Yankee homespun. No hint of rude social levelling is associated with its aims; even its communism suggests no stigma.'[2]

Brook Farm was the *jeu d'esprit* of that circle of New England Transcendentalists who provided America's age of ferment with its most distinguished intellectual leadership. Transcendentalism was the reaction of Puritanism to the Utopian individualism of the age. The New England theocracy had fought to the last pulpit to defend the whole dry Calvinistic corpus of depravity, election and predetermination. But the merchant families who rented pews began to find such theological disputation, however subtle, increasingly irrelevant to the comforting facts of their ledgers and larders. If his works were good, man could not be depraved; if by hard work one could acquire graceful manners and firm character, predestination seemed a denial of virtue. He who was born in Boston, went the wisecrack, had no need to be born again. And so the very classes who had shunned the French Enlightenment as the work of the devil were happy to pay the stipends of younger ministers who went behind the Calvinistic *rationale* to preach a religion of love flowing

---

[1] The term is used by A. E. Bestor, *op. cit. passim.*
[2] Parrington, *op. cit.* vol. II, p. 346.

from the goodness of the human heart. The bloodless revolution of Unitarianism at last brought eighteenth-century rationalism to New England. With the capture of Harvard College by the Unitarians in 1805–6 the intellectual *élite* of New England broke for good with the narrow pessimism of Calvinistic authority. But the Unitarian creed, generous and open-minded as expounded by William Ellery Channing, was a pallid negation, not a constructive force. The uncompromising ethics, the marked sense of individual responsibility, which were the root of Puritanism, needed to draw upon the deeper well-springs of emotional belief. Puritanism found a new faith in the Transcendentalist philosophy of the Romantic Age. Where the Calvinists had seen depravity and the Unitarians goodness, the Transcendentalists saw divinity: the secret intimations of the human soul were the manifestations of a God who was immanent in man and nature. Theodore Parker, who remained, as most Transcendentalists began, a Unitarian minister, preached to fashionable congregations the immanence of God, the transcendence of man, the negative nature of evil and, before Darwin provided a text, the 'progressive development' of man towards 'the unity of life of the human race'. Ralph Waldo Emerson abandoned the Unitarian ministry at twenty-eight to communicate, by means of the lecture and the aphoristic essay, his mystical sense of 'the divine sufficiency of the individual' and the unity of the microcosmic soul in the divine 'Over-Soul' of the universe.[1] Henry Thoreau, in his hermitage by Walden Pond, practised a political economy based on the rigidly simplified values of an anarchistic individual in direct communion with nature. The Transcendentalists were mystics; but they were also *engagés* in the crusade for universal reform; for their search for personal values was prompted not only by the possibilities of life in America, but by the crass philistinism of the middle class and the patent injustices of industrialism. Parker preached abolition, Emerson denounced business morality and praised democracy, and Thoreau went to gaol rather than pay taxes to a State guilty of military aggression against Mexico. Their lives were devoted to the urgent duty of providing the materialist individualism of the age with spiritual values.

[1] Parrington, *op. cit.* vol. II, p. 390.

The Emergence of the Democratic Idea, 1820–50

The New England Renaissance, of which these men and others were the embodiment, was predominantly the product of Atlantic influences. It was the delayed flowering of colonial civilization. Its culture bed was the seaboard trading community; its intellectual tradition and literary style were English; it acquired metaphysical forms from English Romantic writers and poets, especially Coleridge and Carlyle, and from Kant, Fichte and Goethe, to whose fatherland a new generation of Harvard scholars flocked for instruction. But the New England Renaissance drew nourishment from continental America. It was the spontaneous impulse of minds freed from the shackles of Calvinism to range the infinite expanse of human possibility in North America. Even Thoreau, bound as he was to the village of Concord, confessed that when he started to walk his footsteps turned instinctively westwards; and Emerson, in his famous Addresses on 'The American Scholar' and 'The Young American', preached the cultivation of a genius and character peculiarly American: 'Another sign of the times . . . is the new importance given to the single person. Everything that tends to insulate the individual—to surround him with barriers of natural respect, so that each man shall feel the world is his, and man shall treat with man as a sovereign state with a sovereign state—tends to true union as well as greatness. . . . A nation of men will for the first time exist because each believes himself inspired by the Divine Soul which also inspires all men.'[1] And to the young American: 'I call upon you, young men, to obey your heart and be the nobility of this land. In every age of the world there has been a leading nation, one of a more generous sentiment, whose eminent citizens were willing to stand for the interests of general justice and humanity, at the risk of being called, by the men of the moment, chimerical and fantastic. Which should be that nation but these States?'[2] In comparison with the nation nearest to him in sympathy: 'The English have many virtues, many advantages, and the proudest history of the world; but they need all and more than the resources of the past to indemnify a heroic gentleman in that country for the mortifications prepared for him by the system of

[1] Emerson, *Works*, vol. I, p. 112.
[2] *Ibid.* vol. I, p. 365.

society, and which seem to impose the alternative to resist or to avoid it. . . . It is for Englishmen to consider, not for us; we only say, Let us live in America, too thankful for our want of feudal institutions.'[1]

Not all the writers of this generation shared the Transcendentalist's confidence in human perfectibility. Nathaniel Hawthorne, conscious that the cultural stream which bore him was running into the sands, looked out from his Salem attic, not on to the bustling wharves but into New England's past in which he traced, with fatalistic scepticism, the inexorable course of evil in human affairs. Another customs officer, Herman Melville, gazed with the narrowed eyes of a seaman beyond New York Bay to an ocean world which was the symbol of man's quest for his inscrutable fate. Each was obsessed with the lonely responsibility of the individual soul; and with Melville that obsession brought forth the most profound study of man's defiance of the universe. These men were the 'sports' of their generations; but, equally with Emerson, they represent the apotheosis of individualism.

But the message of New England was transmitted in the language of Old England, as no one knew better than Emerson. The authentic speech rhythms of America still lay sleeping: 'in some western idiom or native Michigan or Tennessee repartee, or stump speech . . . or in Kentucky or Georgia, or the Carolinas . . . or in some slang or local song or allusion of the Manhattan, Boston, Philadelphia or Baltimore mechanic . . . or up in the Maine woods . . . or in the breasts of the young farmers of the Northwest, or Canada, or boatmen of the lakes. Rude and coarse nursing-sheds, these; but only from such beginnings and stocks, indigenous here, may haply arrive, be grafted and sprout, in time, flowers of genuine American aroma, and fruits truly and fully our own.'[2] The writer of this passage, Walt Whitman, the printer-journalist of Brooklyn, and Camden, thought in a new American idiom. His prose and poetry alike were mosaics built up from the multitudinous images of individual American men and women, place-names and places, sounds, sights and smells, cranks, heroes, failures, slangs, pro-

[1] Emerson, *Works*, vol. I, p. 371.
[2] Walt Whitman, 'Democratic Vistas', *Complete Poetry and Selected Prose and Letters* (London, 1938), p. 708.

grammes and religions; his rhetoric expressed his exuberant and boundless acceptance of the sum of American experience. For he was the prophet, not only of an American language but of a universal democracy. Whitman went beyond individualism; seeking 'not only to individualize but to universalize'. He accepted the teeming whole of America—the Devil as well as God, graft, corruption, the genteel, the southern secessionist—for America was 'in a sort of geological formation state, trying continually new experiments'.[1] He exulted in the great westward march, in the exploitation of the continental riches which would bring 'a more universal ownership of property, general homesteads, general comfort—a vast, intertwining, reticulation of wealth'.[2] American democracy had a 'manifest destiny' to expand indefinitely: north to Canada, westwards to the Pacific islands and eastwards to blow the fertile pollen 'over to European lands by every western breeze'. For the purpose of democracy, 'supplanting old belief in the necessary absoluteness of established dynastic rulership, temporal, ecclesiastical and scholastic, as furnishing the only security against chaos, crime and ignorance, is', he said, 'to illustrate . . . this doctrine or theory that man, properly trained in sanest, highest freedom, may and must become a law, and a series of laws, to himself, surrounding and providing for, not only his own personal control, but all his relations to other individuals and to the State'.[3] Americans were thus entrusted with a high, universal purpose.

Although the democratic spirit in politics affected all parties, it is associated chiefly with the name and character of Andrew Jackson. Jackson's predecessor in the White House, John Quincy Adams, the second of the Adams dynasty, was the last President of the old order. Although by family loyalty a Federalist, he had been drawn, during that decade of 'good feelings' following the War of 1812, into the service of the National Republican Party which, under the leadership of Virginia, for the time being held the forces of American politics in balance. But not even the talents of Madison, Monroe

[1] Walt Whitman, *op. cit.* p. 678.
[2] *Ibid.* p. 682.
[3] *Ibid.* p. 671.

and Chief Justice Marshall could hold in check the dynamism of westward movement. Adams was allowed his single term as President, from 1825–9, on the sufferance of Henry Clay of Kentucky; and at its close no amount of caucus manoeuvre could any longer control the welling tide of democratic aspiration. Jackson was elected in 1828 by the combined votes of back-country farmers, mechanics and shopkeepers and enough southern planters to turn the scale. The southerners' misgivings were soothed by the fact that Jackson was himself a planter and a gentleman; but the farmers and mechanics were united in their enthusiasm for 'Old Hickory', this national hero, this conqueror of Indians and British invaders, this white-maned, choleric figure with his trigger-happy sense of honour, untainted by corruption in elegant places, who would break the hold of propertied men on government.

Once in office, Jackson's problem was to transform the inchoate enthusiasm which had placed him there into a manageable political following. The old caucus methods were largely irrelevant to the new, mass electorate composed of millions of individual voters. The President's greatest asset was the name of General Jackson, which his flair for flamboyant leadership had made a household image. But his novel bearing as a tribune of the people, although enhancing the office of President, was not enough in itself to galvanize support. He and his lieutenants were faced with the job of constructing a new kind of political party articulated to the anonymous individuals in remote rural counties and in the precincts of the cities. Jackson's chief satrap, Van Buren, had managed the Albany Regency, New York's first experiment in machine politics; and the Democratic Party under Jackson combined Tammany Hall methods with political habits of 'grass roots' democracy. The resultant linking together of local interests into a loose, national federation, formalized through a chain of local, State and national conventions, provided a continuing basis for a Federal administration and the instrument for fighting elections. The creation of the mass, democratic party was perhaps the most enduring achievement of the Jacksonian revolution. Henceforward the techniques of the Democratic Party, largely unchanged to the present day, became the pattern for American political life. When the opponents of the Jacksonian alliance combined to oust it from power they were forced to copy its methods. The new Whig Party, which rose like a phoenix from the ashes of New England Federalism and National Republicanism, abandoned the gentlemanly modes of the caucus in favour of the democratic chain of responsibility and won the 1840 election by presenting the mild General Harrison to the mass of voters as another paragon of backwoods virtue. 'Log cabin and hard cider', 'Tippecanoe and Tyler too' were the slogans which brought the moneyed and seaboard conservative Whigs back into office.

Jackson's success in office depended not only on the formation of such alliance, but on a choice of policies most likely to sustain general enthusiasm and least likely to alienate particular interests. Jacksonian insurgency succeeded only so long as enough supporters throughout the continent were prepared to ignore mutual differences in the pursuit of a common programme; it failed where sectional interests resumed the upper hand. That programme consisted of an attack on the authority of the mercantile oligarchy which temporarily united the westerner who chafed against seaboard restraints on western development, the southern planter who resented the exploitation by northern capital of cotton, and the small business man and artisan of the North-east in revolt against the entrenched power of the merchant class. This attack took the form of a multiple drive against mercantilist controls. A campaign by Senator Benton of Missouri liberalized the laws relating to the disposition of the public lands in favour of the poor settler and squatter, and against the interests of the large investor. By vetoing a scheme for building a trunk road in Kentucky at Federal expense in 1830, Jackson put a stop for a generation to the subsidizing by the Federal Government of private enterprise in the field of transport. But the most important step, politically, by far was Jackson's refusal to renew the charter of the Second Bank of the United States. This decision, upheld in the election of 1832, to sever the connection between banking and government, symbolized the attack on the entrenched privileges of the mercantile class. For the urban artisan and the western settler alike the defeat of Nicholas Biddle, the elegant President of the Bank, was a signal blow at the money power, and in their joy they recked little of what this might mean for America's financial stability.

But Jackson's adroit conduct of affairs could not indefinitely mask sectional divisions. Any move he made was liable to offend some interest and it was not long before important defections occurred. The rapidly growing West began to split up into more specialized interests; the cotton growers of the South-west drew closer to the old South; the commercial farmers of the Great Lakes basin looked increasingly to the seaboard North, and the old homogeneous West, which only ten years previously had brought Jackson to power, was already a thing of the past.

The high tariff of 1828, which had the support of parts of the West and the eastern workingmen, alienated the southern planters who regarded it as a further tax by northern capitalists on the hard-earned labour of the fields. Increasingly committed to a cotton slave-culture, the South, seaboard and interior alike, had come to feel an isolated minority in the Union. This sectional feeling over-rode their loyalty to the Union, and South Carolina threatened to secede from the Union in the Nullification Ordinance of 1832. Jackson's firm handling of this crisis alienated the southern leader Calhoun, and large parts of the southern States turned for support to the Whigs in the election of 1836. For, as was said in Virginia, 'Whigs know each other by the instinct of gentlemen.'[1]

After 1832, the Jacksonian lines were redrawn; and it was a more robust coalition of western farmers and eastern artisans which fought the Bank War to its triumphant conclusion. But even this axis was shaky. Although farmers and workingmen might see eye to eye on land policy and on curbing mercantilist control, their economic motives in attacking the Bank were fundamentally different. The wage-earner was venting his hatred against banks as such, symbols of that moneyed order which was responsible for his loss of status and respect, engines for manufacturing credit which appeared to raise prices, and thereby to rob his pay packet of some of its value. The westerner disliked the Bank, not because of the inflationary effects of banking in general; on the contrary, as a borrower, his thirst for cheap credit was insatiable. What he

[1] J. G. Randall, *Civil War and Reconstruction* (New York, 1937), p. 35.

wanted was more banks, not fewer. He hated Biddle's Bank because it was an eastern organ, specially privileged by its monopolistic relation to the Federal Government, and one which acted to curb the bullish optimism of western land speculation. More and more inhabitants of Kentucky, Ohio or Indiana were demanding capital for commercial expansion, for canals or railways to connect with seaboard markets; and as a result were attracted by the programme of Jackson's Whig opponent, Henry Clay, which offered a partnership between North-west and North-east for the capitalistic development of both. The influence of Jackson's personality was still sufficient, in 1836, to ensure a third term for the Jacksonian Party under the Presidency of Van Buren; but, with the master himself in the retirement of his Tennessee hermitage, it was clear that the *élan* of insurgency was spent. The Jacksonian party was reduced to a rump consisting of Van Buren's own empire, the urban radicals of New York and Pennsylvania; and in 1840 it was ejected from office by a new combination of hostile interests, the Whig Party.

The Jackson regime marks the high-water mark of insurgency against seaboard, mercantilist control of continental expansion. After 1840, the first great boom period of western growth was at an end. The speculative prosperity of the 1830s, which buoyed up the Jackson party, resulted in an over-extension of American resources which, in turn, brought about the inevitable collapse of 1839. The decade of the 1840s was characterized by a nervous exhaustion which had much to do with the hysteria of the age of ferment. When the American people had gathered enough strength for a second burst of expansion, the resumed westward thrust took a new form which radically affected the alignment of continental politics. The Mississippi Valley had grown up; and with economic specialization its homogeneity was at an end. The North-west looked for a renewal of its strength to new injections of capital, trade and ideas from the North-east. The South-west, which had become the economic centre of the slave empire, formed a solid and increasingly separate block of interests with the seaboard South. Henceforward the old tensions between continental expansion and seaboard control gave place to new tensions between North and South. A Greater

New England and a Greater South struggled to dominate the new phase of westward expansion. That struggle, which became increasingly bitter and unaccommodating, placed in jeopardy the whole system of sectional compromises which alone kept the American Union in equilibrium. The root cause of that conflict was the institution of slavery. The Age of Jackson signalized the emergence of the spirit and the practice of democracy as the dominant force in American society. But the victory of the democratic idea was not complete. Across the path of a dynamic individualism there lay, in the South, a society founded on slavery which was static, conservative and wholly committed to the principle of inequality.

CHAPTER VII

THE DEMOCRATIC IDEA AND THE PROBLEM OF CASTE: THE TEST-ING TIME OF CIVIL WAR

1850-75

'In all social systems there must be a class to do the menial duties, to perform the drudgery of life . . . requiring but a low order of intellect and but little skill. Its requisites are vigor, docility, fidelity. Such a class you must have or you would not have that other class which leads progress, civiliza-tion, and refinement. It constitutes the very mud-sill of society and of political government; and you might as well attempt to build a house in the air, as to build either the one or the other, except on this mud-sill. Fortunately for the South, she found a race adapted to the purpose of her hand . . . We use them for our purpose and call them slaves.'

GOVERNOR J. H. HAMMOND of South Carolina.

'ABOUT the last of August came in a Dutch man of warre that sold us twenty Negars.' John Rolfe, of Virginia, husband of Pocahontas, wrote these words in 1619, a year before the *Mayflower* landed her Puritan ship's company on Cape Cod Bay. The Negro thus arrived earlier than the Yankee on American shores. From the first bridgehead onwards he has played an integral role in the conquest of North America: the role of a forced labourer. Where labour was scarce and capital brought such slow returns, well-being had to be sacrificed in the task of subduing the wilder-ness. Forced labour is a scarlet thread in the pattern of American settlement. It is discernible in the broken lives of successive waves of pioneers and construction workers, expendable in the inexorable advance of migration, no less than in the institutionalized bondage of indentured servants, convicts and slaves. The Negro's servitude differed from the indentured servant's in being involuntary and for life; it differed from the convict's in being not only for life but in being transmitted to his children. But these were differences of degree within a common legal framework. What made the Negro a marked man was his colour. The white servant had his origins in the common kindred of his colonial masters. The origins of the Negro slave were lost in the impenetrable obscurity of tribal Africa. His primitive culture and the nameless fears of racial prejudice set him apart from other Americans. Behind the problem of the slave lurked the even more formidable problem of the Negro. Caste based on colour fastened slavery on the American people so firmly that when slavery became both an anomaly and an offence to democratic aspirations, its hold could be loosened only by a bloody civil war; and even when the victory had been won the abolition of slavery merely revealed the institution of caste to bedevil in a more naked and inhumane form the ethics of American democracy.[1]

The problem of caste would never have disrupted American society had not slavery concentrated the Negro population in the South in such numbers as to threaten the supremacy of the whites.

In the early years of the Republic, men expected that slavery would die out as indentured service had done. The long decline of tobacco and indigo planting encouraged a shift to mixed farming for which slaves were less profitable. Men of affairs in the South, as in the North, pinned their hopes, not only on the cultivation of varied agricultural arts, but on trade, transport and the establishment of industry. John C. Calhoun voted for the tariff of 1816 and advocated the mercantile expansion of southern Appalachia. Under pressure from Britain the slave trade was abolished in 1807. Humane planters, in the golden afterglow of the Enlightenment, followed Jefferson in manumitting slaves in their wills, and supported the American Colonization Society in its efforts to establish a colony of free Negroes in Liberia.

The advent of King Cotton put an end to such hopes. The cry for raw cotton in Lancashire mills was heard in Carolina; and when in 1793 Whitney's ingenious cotton gin made it possible to separate

[1] See Gunnar Myrdal, *An American Dilemma* (New York, 1944), p. 88.

seed from lint in the short-staple plants which could be grown inland, southerners turned thankfully to this new, bonanza crop to solve their economic ills. After the War of 1812, cotton eclipsed rice, tobacco and sugar as the chief concern of a South which, under this stimulant, spread westwards to Louisiana and beyond to Texas wherever the long, warm growing season permitted. The crop doubled in size each decade, from some seventy thousand bales in 1800 to nearly four million in 1860.[1] Lancashire's insatiable appetite for cotton fastened slavery ever more firmly on the South. Negro slaves provided the best, indeed the only, labour force whereby Europe's need for cotton could be made good from the rich, virgin soils of the interior. Cotton was a simple crop to raise, well suited to Negroes who could endure the heat and heavy toil, and to slave gangs who were most economically employed in the slow, steady rhythm of an unskilled field job. Ploughing, planting, hoeing and repeated pickings kept all ages busy from February to November, year in, year out. In the warm climate slaves were cheaply fed on bacon and hominy grits, clothed in burlap and housed in rude cabins. As a result, the demand for slaves reversed the tendency to emancipation. The Negroes, who multiplied from about a million in 1800 to nearly four and a half million in 1860, remained overwhelmingly a slave population concentrated in the South, and especially in the new, black belt of the South-west, where they were more numerous than the whites.

Once started on this path the South was committed ever more deeply by the existence of slavery to a plantation culture which preserved in an exaggerated form all the features of a primitive, colonial agriculture, tributary to the mercantile empire of the northern seaboard. The planter's capital was his slaves. This fact governed his operations and seriously restricted his freedom of movement. In order to obtain a return on his investment, he must work his slaves to raise those single, staple crops in which they were most efficiently employed, and raise the same crop, year in, year out, in the primitive routine of an extensive agriculture which exhausted the soil and demanded an unceasing supply of new land. The unloading on to the market of abundant crops from newer, fertile soils

[1] *Hist. Stats.*, Series E, 218.

depressed prices and forced the planter to a hand-to-mouth existence, buoyed up by hopes of a good year which, when it came, only
encouraged him to buy more slaves and clear more ground. With
capital in slaves and fortunes bound up with cultivating one crop
the planter was increasingly at the mercy of northern merchants
who supplied him with northern and British manufactures on credit
secured by the only negotiable asset he had: cotton.[1] With future
crops mortgaged, he had no alternative but to perpetuate his wasteful system of single crop husbandry. Thus he was beguiled by an
inexorable set of economic circumstances into accepting cotton
culture as an ordained way of life. The dependency of an agrarian
economy on merchants and markets was exaggerated by the
peculiar rigidity of the planter's labour force.

The dangers of this position were not at first apparent. The
European cotton market, and that of New England, absorbed ever
larger crops. In ideal circumstances, the slave plantation was not
inefficient, and good years brought handsome profits to the large
well-balanced plantations of Mississippi and Alabama. But the
rigidities of slavery made the system increasingly uneconomic. The
inevitable tendency to over-production depressed the price of cotton from an average of 15 cents a pound on the world market in
the early '20s to 9 cents in the early '50s.[2] Meanwhile, costs at home
had been mounting, and it was out of the planter's power to reduce
them. The supply of suitable new land was not inexhaustible. By
the 1850s, cotton culture, well established in Arkansas and Texas,
was no longer practicable in the new frontier region to the north
in Kansas; and in existing areas new land had to be brought into
cultivation so remote from the market that transport costs became
a burden. Marketing costs in general mounted. The routeing of the
crop through New York, Boston and Philadelphia on its way to
Europe increased the charges for freight, commissions, credit and
bills of exchange, tied the cotton economy to the speculative
vagaries of the New York money market and forced the South to
compete for capital on unfavourable terms with northern railways

[1] For the dependence of the southern economy on the North, see H. R. Helper,
The Impending Crisis of the South (New York, 1860), pp. 22–3.
[2] L. C. Gray, *History of Agriculture in the Southern United States to 1860* (Washington,
1933), vol. II, Appendix, Table 41.

and industry. The general rise in prices after the production of California gold increased the cost of the planter's supplies and fanned his suspicion that the tariff discriminated against him and in favour of the northern manufacturers.

But the most significant cost-increase was that of slaves. Despite the growing Negro population and the internal trade which supplied slaves for the cotton belt from older and less profitable regions like Virginia, the price of prime field hands mounted in response to the demand for slave labour from about 350 dollars at the end of the eighteenth century to more than 1,500 in 1860.[1] This increase affected least the large planter who bred his own slaves, and most the small farmer who had to replace superannuated field hands in the open market.

Planting became increasingly unprofitable. In the 1850s even large, well-stocked, well-managed plantations in the deep South only showed a profit because their accounts failed to include a reasonable sum for depreciation.[2] The South was living on its capital and its economy was slowly running down. The ultimate cause of its decline was slavery, which restricted so much southern effort to producing a single staple for a world market, prevented a shift to more profitable forms of enterprise, wasted the soil by its primitive culture, starved the planter of working capital and, ultimately, because of the restricted supply of slaves, made that peculiar form of labour too expensive for profit.

Southern leaders, aware at last of the dangers ahead, attempted to reverse the engine which was bucketing them along their ramshackle, single-track economy. Progressive planters like John Taylor 'of Caroline', or Edmund Ruffin, preached the need for a more scientific and balanced agriculture to spread risks and conserve the soil. Attempts were made to break the hold of the North by opening direct connections between the South and its great transatlantic customer; shipping lines were started direct to Liverpool from Savannah; and southern merchants paid court to British capitalists.

[1] U. B. Phillips, *American Negro Slavery* (New York, 1918), pp. 370–4.
[2] See plantation accounts analysed by R. B. Flanders, *Plantation Slavery in Georgia* (Chapel Hill, 1933), pp. 221–3, and C. S. Sydnor, *Slavery in Mississippi* (New York. 1933), quoted in L. M. Hacker, *The Triumph of American Capitalism* (New York, 1940), pp. 318–20.

Southern politicians struggled to reduce the already low tariff to a virtual free trade in the interests of the transatlantic cotton kingdom. Railways were promoted to bring cheaper transport to the remote southern interior. Enterprising southerners began, with the use of slave labour, to exploit the coal and iron deposits of West Virginia and Alabama. And in the '50s, convention after convention met to establish industries and promote commerce. But these efforts were either impracticable or too late. Southern men of affairs were by temperament landed gentry, despising the niggling margins and aggressiveness of the business man. The slave was not only unwilling, but lacked the skill and independence of the artisan. For building railways and levees Irishmen were preferred; and even navvies, let alone other, more skilled, immigrants, were too much repelled by local conditions to enter the South in any numbers. British capital preferred the dynamic conditions of the North-west railway boom of the 1850s. And so, in the clamour of policies there were heard increasingly the strident voices of extreme slavery advocates demanding the reopening of the African slave trade and claiming a 'manifest destiny' for the slave-ocracy to expand south into the Caribbean islands and the shores of the Gulf of Mexico. These were the desperate remedies of a lunatic fringe. But they were born of the logic of the slave empire which must expand or go under.

The true remedy for the southern economy was the gradual elimination of slavery. Slavery alone insulated the South from the dynamic growth of the continent. There was no geographical frontier to separate the South from the rest of the American people, to prevent the ultimate dovetailing of southern with Yankee and western ways of getting and spending. Only a small minority of southerners were slave-owners, and the economic interests of the great mass of yeoman-farmers differed little from those of their kind farther north. There was only the artificial frontier of slavery, the Mason-Dixon Line, to separate North from South in the Mississippi Valley. To eliminate slavery would have been a long, complex process dependent on the good will of North and South. That good will was not present on either side. Southerners especially were not prepared to give up slavery even to ensure their future.

For, *au fond*, the sanction of the institution was not economic but social.

Slavery gave its peculiar caste to the planting classes. Four million slaves formed the broad base of a social pyramid, the apex of which consisted of some three hundred great planters each owning more than two hundred slaves. Immediately below the planting princes were some two thousand aristocratic families, each supported by more than a hundred slaves in a life of comfort and elegance on their sequestered plantations. Below them were about one hundred thousand gentry with at least ten slaves each who, along with merchants and professional men, formed the southern middle class; and below them again were some quarter of a million slave-owning yeomen with less than ten slaves each, of whom some 77,000 owned but a single slave.[1] Although not all the socially elect were slaveholders, slaves supplied a simple index of social prestige. The planting aristocracy, in setting the tone of manners, was followed by smaller planting and professional families whose status tended to be fixed by numbers of slaves and whose social ambitions were centred on acquiring more. The rising cost of Negroes concentrated slave ownership in fewer hands, so that the planting aristocracy became an increasingly exclusive congeries of inter-married families, while the slave-owning yeomanry, for social as well as economic reasons, became the most radical advocates of a re-opened slave trade. The fact that wealth lay in slaves restricted the occupations open to the southern 'gentleman' and inhibited the growth of a class of artisans.

But large slave-holders were only a tiny fraction of the southern white population. Only one southerner in four was either directly or indirectly connected with slave-holding, and only 46,000 individuals out of eight million owned the twenty slaves which made planting profitable. The great mass of southerners were yeomen, living a life which differed little from that of their kind to the north. These small farmers, with or without the help of a slave or two, raised corn, hogs and a little cotton or tobacco from the Appalachian slopes to the upland fringes of the black belt. And socially

[1] *Agriculture of the United States in 1860* (U.S. Eighth Census), table p. 247; A. C. Cole, *The Irrepressible Conflict* (New York, 1934), p. 34.

beneath the yeoman were the 'poor whites', who, without the hope of ever owning a single slave, led a shiftless existence in the Appalachian back country, the Arkansas highlands, and the sand barrens of Georgia and Mississippi. These hill-billies, the degenerate remnant of the original pioneer stock, were the slum population of the rural South: 'At their best, with simple piety and frugality, they eked out a precarious livelihood by tilling a scrubby farm . . . at their worst they ate clay, chewed resin and snuff, drank fiery "rot-gut" whisky and dreamed on in blissful ignorance of the contempt with which the outside world regarded them.'[1] Yet even the 'poor white trash' were princes compared with the Negroes on the other side of the caste barrier, although a quarter of a million of these were free, a few comfortably off, and, in rare cases, slave-owners themselves.

For although the fortunes of only a small minority of southerners were dependent on slaves and on the plantation system, although the husbandry of the yeoman differed little from that of the Yankee settler to the north, and although he might work alongside his slaves in the fields, although poor whites might be indifferent to planting and hate the planting class with a bitter hatred, nevertheless most southerners felt committed by their deepest instincts to slavery. It was not merely that artisans and poor whites in mine, workshop and field feared Negro competition. All southern whites felt that their self-respect, indeed their very personal identity, depended on maintaining the institution. The poorest 'white trash', whom want, disease and ignorance had pushed to the edge of survival, clung, as to life itself, to the dignity of their white blood. However indigent, they could hold up their heads in pride at their English or Scotch-Irish ancestry which made them kindred to the great families and fixed an impassable gulf between them and the most cultivated houseman or their most prosperous free Negro neighbour. For them, as for all white southerners, the Negroes were a separate caste, an inferior race of mankind. And they believed that, in a society where the two races had to exist side by side, and especially where, as in the deep South, the Negro was in a majority, only the institution of slavery could prevent

1 A. C. Cole, *op. cit*, p. 39.

the identity of the whites from being engulfed in a rising sea of colour. And so, when it came to the sticking-point, even those whites who had least to gain materially from slavery and had most to lose from the maintenance of the plantation economy, ranged themselves in its defence in serried ranks of grey behind their planter-officers. For these men slavery must be defended, not as an economic system, but as a device for ensuring white supremacy. 'We have among us but one great class, and all who belong to it have a necessary sympathy with one another; we have but one great interest, and all who possess it are equally ready to maintain and protect it.'[1] On the basis of slavery the South developed a culture so individual as to acquire most of the characteristics of nationality.

Plantation and social structure determined that the southern ethos should be that of the country gentleman. Two thousand plantation families placed their stamp upon the mind of the South. Some, like the Carters of Nomini Hall, Virginia, descendants of the seventeenth-century 'King' Carter, the Joneses of Tallahassee, Georgia, descendants of one of Oglethorpe's lieutenants, the Huguenot Manigaults of Gowrie, S.C., or the Dabneys, of Virginia and Mississippi, boasted distinction in colonial times, although few went as far back as the Carters or the Byrds and hardly any could lay claim to that Cavalier ancestry which snobbery and romanticism imputed to the best nineteenth-century southern families. More stemmed from the lesser gentry and yeomanry whose scions had risen as overseers or married money or made a lucky speculation in the rich soils of the cotton belt. Of such were the Taits of Alabama or John Palfrey, a Yankee adventurer from the West Indies.[2] Some faded into obscurity after bankruptcy in 1829, 1838, or 1857; but most survived and, as they persisted, intermarriage and economic advantage established them as the dominant families of the ante-bellum South. Although their seeming prosperity might be based on wasting assets they governed southern society with brilliance and assurance for a generation.

Running a plantation was not the occupation for an idler; and

---

[1] Judge Upshur, quoted by W. S. Jenkins, *Pro-Slavery Thought in the Old South* (Chapel Hill, 1935), p. 288.
[2] U. B. Phillips, *Life and Labour in the Old South* (Boston, 1937), ch. xii–xiv.

southern planters were a hard-worked—indeed, harassed—class. The annual negotiation with the factor for marketing the crop, for the purchase of supplies and for raising future loans was only the culmination of a routine which gave no rest from the daily minutiae of administration. The sequence of cultivation and the discipline, physical care and *morale* of the slaves demanded the constant attention, not only of the master in his office, on horseback, even at meal times, but equally of the mistress who looked after the womenfolk and house-servants and saw to education and religious instruction. In a well-run plantation the slaves were cared for in patriarchal fashion with humanity, affection and humour mixed with a shrewd awareness of the economic importance of a happy slave community. Where the planter's family were resident, indeed, despite adverse testimony like that of Fanny Kemble,[1] slaves were well cared for, not only in their prime, but in childbirth, sickness and old age. But standards tended to degenerate where affairs were in the hands of overseers who, drawn mostly from the yeomanry, lacked the personal concern of the planter and took only a short-term, commercial interest in the plantation; and it was the same in the newer region of the deep South where the patriarchal tradition wore thin. The most humane master might not be able to avoid the misery of parting families through selling slaves; and against a corrupt or sadistic master the slave had no defence. But these were evils inherent in a system which, however indefensible in theory, was mitigated in practice by the code of *noblesse oblige* to which the planting gentry subscribed.

Although the planter was hard-worked, the atmosphere of the plantation was one of comfort and leisure. Supported by a troop of house-servants his family lived in style, pursuing in the leisurely tempo of southern days the diversions of the country house according to the code of the gentleman. That code emphasised courtesy, honour and chivalry. The plantation preserved the old tradition of the open house which relieved the tedium of a sequestered life. Strangers were welcomed and protected; neighbours were entertained to the generous hospitality of barbecues, balls and a lavish

[1] The English actress who married Pierce Butler, the planter, and published a 'diary of her sojourn on his sea island plantation in Carolina'.

table, and distant relations were received on visits for months at a time. The men, bred to handle horses and firearms since infancy, incessantly in the saddle, riding to hounds, shooting the plentiful game of the southern wilderness and used to heavy drinking, provided the United States Army with the nearest America has ever come to an officer class. Pride in family blood and social leadership encouraged an aristocratic integrity expressed in terms of a sensitive personal honour. Offence, easily given and taken, found arrogant satisfaction in ostracism and the duel. This code also encouraged a protective attitude towards women who, although equally nerved to handle horses and dogs, were brought up to the artificialities of the 'clinging vine' convention; they read memoirs and novels, practised music and embroidery and were trained in good works in preparation for marriage and the exacting life of a plantation mistress.

Southern culture was that of a finishing school. The planter's children were educated mostly by tutors or in local, private schools. The South had no system of public education like that developing in the North. Most southerners picked up an exiguous book-learning by casual reading, and the increasing pressure of the slave code denied the Negro the barest literacy. The University of Virginia and William and Mary College were too limited to serve the needs of the planter class who, if they could afford it, sent their sons north to Princeton or Harvard. The only city worth the name was Charleston and the South consequently lacked that urbanity which distinguished the intellectual life of Boston or even New York. Literary taste was 'genteel', formed on shaded porches by southern belles whose taste ran to the romances of Scott, Thackeray's novels of manners, and the poetry of Byron and William Gilmore Simms.

But though literature in the formal sense was provincial and derivative, southern talent found characteristic expression in politics. Apart from the Church, the Bar was the most respectable profession for younger sons; and the discipline of the law not only produced learned lawyers but gave to politics a classic style in rhetoric and argument. The Law School of William and Mary College under its great teacher George Wythe had been the nursery for that able group of lawyer-statesmen, including Jefferson, Madison and

Marshall, who had brought so much distinction to the early years of the Republic; and although the liberalism of the Enlightenment and the nationalism of the Era of Good Feelings gave place to a more sophisticated and a more narrowly sectional outlook in politics, the tradition of the Virginia School endowed a new generation with talents which enabled them to dominate the arena of law and politics at Washington. The greatest son of the South, John C. Calhoun, not only scaled the heights of statesmanship in a career devoted to safeguarding the interests of the South in the nation but justified his position in two classics of political thought, the *Disquisition on Government* and the *Discourse on the Constitution*. Characteristic of southern letters was also the work of John Taylor 'of Caroline' who made notable contributions to American political theory in his *Constitution Construed and Constitutions Vindicated*, and to agrarian political economy in his *Tyranny Unmasked*.

The conservative and institutionalized character of southern life was also reflected in religion. Although the older 'enthusiasm' had left its mark and revivalism continued to agitate poor whites in the back country, the planting class adhered to the more traditional and hierarchical forms of Church discipline—to the Methodism, Presbyterianism, Anglicanism and even Catholicism which consorted with their position as the social leaders of the community. The southern clergy, of whom many belonged to the planting class and some owned slaves, had no alternative but to accept the fact of slavery, justifying their stand by appealing to the Old Testament. This led to severe friction with their northern brethren in many denominations and, in the Baptist and Methodist Churches, to actual schism in 1843-4.

Slavery determined the South's attitude to politics. The generous aspiration towards democracy which characterized Jefferson evaporated in his own native region, leaving a hard precipitate of conservative republicanism based upon legal rights narrowly interpreted. The existence of slavery not only caused the frank abandonment of the theory of natural rights in favour of a theory of biological inferiority, but led to the belief that political responsibility belonged exclusively to that small *élite* with the leisure and breeding to assume leadership. Democracy in the South meant equality for a small ruling class, justified by reference to ancient Greece, in particular to the Aristotelian view of slavery, and to the Old Testament. Politics were the preserve of the slave-owners. Although some western States in the South had manhood suffrage from frontier days, most States preserved a property or tax-paying qualification for office-holders, and the apportionment of constituencies often guaranteed power, as in South Carolina, to the wealthiest planting districts. Like the squires of eighteenth-century England, the southern gentry saw eye to eye on fundamentals and were united in preserving the existing social order. And although the planters of South Carolina or Tennessee might have difficulty with the men of the back country in those States, they could rely, when it came to a show-down, upon the support of the bulk of the southern whites in defence of a social order which guaranteed white supremacy.

That social order represented the greatest interest of all, to be promoted and defended at all costs in national politics. The South, insulated from the nation at large by her economy, her social system and her values, came to regard the protection of her peculiar interests as the sole object of Federal representation. In opposing internal improvements which would bind the West to the North-east, in advocating a strict land policy which would benefit planters at the expense of the horde of settlers and immigrants, in attacking the tariff and a National Bank which benefited northern capitalists, the South pursued her interests with single-minded persistence. Above all slavery must be protected, not merely where it existed but in Missouri, in Texas, in Kansas, and the right to own property in slaves must be upheld by a Fugitive Slave Act and the Supreme Court. And as the South began to feel not only isolated but encircled —a diminishing minority in the nation—she moved to the defensive, taking her stand in national politics, not on moral right but on legal rights. Like the Federalist North-east of 1812 before her, the South countered what she felt to be discrimination against her in Washington by falling back on the doctrine of States' rights which, with Calhoun, became a sophisticated constitutional theory. Calhoun argued that the essence of the Federal Constitution was a balance of limited powers, that the tyranny of an absolute, central government based on a numerical majority was held in check by the preponderance of 'interests', largely regional, which the Constitution intended to be paramount. Federal policies, to be valid, must have the support, not merely of a numerical majority but of a *concurrent majority* representing *all* interests concerned. Where policies ran counter to the basic interests of important minorities, they could be legitimately resisted. In particular, since the Constitution had come into being as a compact among pre-existing States, any State which considered its interests threatened by irresponsible Federal action had the right to dissociate itself, if necessary by secession. This was the argument which justified South Carolina's Nullification Ordinance of 1832 in protest against a high tariff, and which remained at the back of the minds of a legally-minded generation increasingly occupied by northern attacks on slavery.

Plantation culture gave the South a well defined and consistent set of values, felt at all levels of experience. The most basic of these values was agrarian: the passionate conviction that there was a special virtue in a life devoted to the soil. This Jeffersonian *mystique* was intensified as the South, committed to plantation culture, found herself increasingly at the mercy of a capitalistic North. Southerners as gentry despised trade, as countrymen they hated towns, as farmers they feared industrialism. Their prejudice was reinforced by the discovery that northern capitalism not only levied tribute on the southern economy, but bade fair to encircle the South in its drive westwards. John Taylor was only the ablest of an array of southern publicists who attacked the baleful influence of capitalism with arguments which, in some cases, anticipated Marx. Upon this agrarian base was built a whole structure of values. The existence of slavery coloured the southern attitude to physical labour and perpetuated a class society whose values were bound up with status. The whites as a whole, deriving as they did from the older Anglo-Saxon stocks, and without that sense of relativism which came from the juxtaposition of newer, immigrant groups, felt a sense of solidarity against the Negro. The upper classes were bound by a strong class loyalty based on the family connection which kept within bounds the individualism of an expanding society. The family preserved much of its traditional character, identified with plantation or neighbourhood, conscious of forbears and of the need to provide for posterity, conforming to the code of *noblesse oblige*. While culture suffered from the complacency of the genteel, and religion preached the acceptance of an imperfect world, politics concentrated on the defence of the *status quo*.

The South was too rigid to adjust itself to the changes transforming the rest of American society. Plantation culture could expand only geographically. Southerners who colonized westwards, unlike northern migrants, transplanted the whole apparatus of cultivated life to a frontier location so that much of the new South-west never knew rough living nor was psychologically influenced by that revolt from authority which was so typical of the upper West. The southerner conceived of the future in terms of an indefinite extension of planting. He had none of the northerner's passionate belief in the dynamics of progress. Conscious of overriding obligations to family, class, Church and, above all, slavery, he disciplined his individualism into a strongly defined social ethic. And with the necessity of force so peculiarly evident, with the evils of slavery so patently manifest, the southerner was restrained by a strong sense of original sin from accepting what he regarded as the specious doctrine of human perfectibility. In an optimistic nineteenth century he remained pessimistic. He therefore looked for his ideal, not forwards, but back to some golden age, to colonial Virginia, seventeenth-century England, medieval Christendom or even ancient Greece. He belonged to a tradition-directed society.

The ethos of the South contrasted ever more sharply with that of America as a whole. By 1850, the northern drive to conquer the continent had swept along with it the struggling communities of the upper Mississippi Valley into one great swirling tide of settlement and empire. The North-west, no longer estranged from the seaboard, was only the most exuberant, aggressive and, indeed, nationalistic manifestation of a single culture which stretched back from the wooded lakes of Minnesota to the rocky coast of Maine and beyond, across the Atlantic Ocean to north-west Europe where it struck a sympathetic response among the dislocated. The

North-west, where the elements of the new democratic culture crystallized out, provides the key to the conflict between North and South.

The men of the North-west were confident of a rich future when, criss-crossed by railways, the land of the prairies and lakes would reach out to the industrial East to form a dominion of iron, steam, timber, hogs and wheat. Bankers of New York and Boston joined hands with the thrusting business men of Chicago to build ambitious trunk lines to bind the North-west to the East and establish a great continental market for New England textiles, Pennsylvania iron-ware, the timber of Minnesota, the ores of Michigan and the farm produce of Illinois. The Chicago merchant, no less than the Pennsylvania ironmaster, clamoured for capital for a hundred and one varied enterprises. The prairie farmer pledged his credit to buy the ploughs, hoes and mechanical reapers, which emancipated his family from the grinding poverty of a frontier subsistence by enabling them to cultivate, unaided, that homestead of 640 acres which he demanded as his birthright and which he was to obtain with the Homestead Act of 1862. Machinery and cheap transport were integrating the frontier family into the expanding, capitalistic economy.

For cultural values the people of the North-west looked back to their origins: the nostalgic Germans to a peasant life or the liberalism of '48, the Scotch-Irish to an eighteenth-century presbytery in New Jersey, the English to Surrey or Stafford and the radicalism of the '30s; but above all it was to that New England whence so many of their families had come that most north-westerners looked for moral and intellectual leadership. From the infant St Paul, high on its Mississippi bluff, to the lakeside ports of Erie, the North-west was dotted with communities whose values were sharpened by an inherited Puritanism. The individualism natural to the West was given ethical stiffening by the Calvinistic emphasis on the responsibility of the lonely soul. This temper of mind gave form and purpose to self-improvement and to democratic practice in social relations, education and politics. It was given emotional depth by those spasms of religious experience which, radiating westwards with migration from the centre of nervous disturbance in western New

York, affected profoundly the religious beliefs of the North-west. The emotional effects of a violent conversion might wear off, but they left behind, if not a sustained conviction that the Second Coming was at hand, at any rate an habitual belief in the possibility of spiritual regeneration. It was this frame of mind which induced so many people in the North-west to take part in those movements of humanitarian endeavour to which reference has already been made.[1] But it was the anti-slavery movement which provided the most spectacular theatre for exercising the passion for moral crusading. Here was the most clear-cut, the most urgent, the most conspicuous evil degrading the souls of men; and, moreover, it was an evil which lay in the midst, a badge of shame for an America whose moral purpose it was to lead the world to a higher order of being. Little wonder that evangelicals concentrated their reforming zeal on this anachronistic institution.

In the North-west Americans were developing a way of life which was democratic in spirit as well as in political forms. Conditioned by the great westward trek, travelling light, mobile, adaptable, self-reliant, without loyalty to place, or ancestor, or occupation, the rural family of the North-west proved an ideal instrument for northern expansion. Here were few institutional barriers to the free flow of enterprise. Family board and pew, court room and polling booth were the only institutional symbols demanding full allegiance. The rest was a wide field for conflict, competition and for voluntary co-operation among those for the time being thrown together. Even ethnic loyalties ceased to be absolutes where New England, Scotch-Irish, English and German communities lived cheek by jowl, and new immigrant strains, direct from Germany and Scandinavia, added their distinctive elements to this plural society. Where frontiers expanded fast, the contradictions between liberty and equality were not in evidence. Where social relations were so fluid, the individual was raised to a new power. *Laissez-faire* ruled, not only in economics but in all aspects of life. Physically on the move, men adopted a dynamic attitude to change. With their backs to the traditions of the past, straining with narrowed eyes towards a hopeful horizon, they believed not merely in progress but in Utopia: in that

[1] See ch. v, pp. 121–122, and ch. vi, p. 133.

physical Utopia of God's Country, that moral Utopia where reformed Man made the State no longer necessary, that spiritual Utopia of the Promised Land or the Second Coming.

This ethos was at odds on almost every point with that of the South. The first Yankee settler to penetrate into the fertile river bottoms of the Ohio Valley had been suspicious of the Virginian backwoodsman he found there; and friction between the two became ever more heated as the North-west grew in power and confidence. The Hoosier or the Chicagoan built out of prejudice a southern stereotype which he regarded with increasing mistrust. He came to look on the South as something alien from the true spirit of America, something akin to the spirit of Europe which in all other respects Americans had thrown off—reactionary, ignorant and proud. Excited by the prospect of conquering a continent with the aid of steam, iron and machinery, he scorned the primitive culture of the plantation, which bound the southerner to an ageless past. Unimpeded by social distinction, he despised the southerner's class-consciousness, and, although not unmindful of his New England or Pennsylvania background, he regarded as pretentious the southerner's exaggerated pride in English ancestry and family breeding. He hated the tradition of the gentleman, and as like as not believed duelling, cockfighting and heavy drinking to be signs of wickedness. Brought up to hard and often manual work he despised the southern pose of idleness; and, sharing his table with his 'hired help', he revolted against the idea of being waited on by servants. Accustomed to womenfolk of independent spirit, he disliked the simpering ways of the southern belle; and when he considered the opportunities for sexual indulgence offered by Negro slavery, he thought the worst. For it was slavery above all that he hated: slavery for its primitiveness as labour, slavery for its cruelty, slavery as a moral evil in itself, slavery as the cause of all the moral distortions, as he saw them, of the people who lived to the south athwart the passage of the great Mississippi.

By 1850, a Greater North and a Greater South had emerged as two distinct cultures within the American Union, the one democratic, capitalistic, ambitious and morally cocksure, growing fast in people and empire, and on the threshold of industrialism, the other lagging in growth, agrarian, tradition-minded, caste-conscious and proud; the one representing a new, modern world coming into being, the other an older order destined to be overwhelmed. It was inevitable that the South should, in the end, come to terms with the dynamic forces transforming the rest of America. The question was whether the South could take the strain of a gradual adjustment or whether her rigid social structure would necessitate a violent dislocation. It was the tragedy of the American people that the second alternative prevailed—in the form most to be dreaded, that of civil war. The reason is not far to seek: slavery not only hobbled the South but set up a polarization of values, South and North, so intense as to require a forcible discharge.

Slavery had been protected in the Union by that habitual practice of compromise which alone held the Federal System in equilibrium. It was recognized in the Constitution, and no one had thought of interfering with it in the States where it had taken root. The problem arose in relation to new States and was a product of continental expansion. The need to protect the slave-interest by preserving the balance between slave and free States became acute as early as 1821 with the admission of frontier Missouri. Constitutional conflict was averted by a compromise whereby Maine was carved out of Massachusetts as a separate free State to counterbalance a slave Missouri, and in future that part of the Louisiana territory north of latitude 36°.30′ was to be regarded as free. The issue was deferred for over twenty years by the check to the frontier at the High Plains; but when it was posed again by the territory wrested from Mexico in 1848 and by the clamour of the Californians to be admitted as a free State in 1849, the slavery issue had so raised the political temperature that the Missouri compromise no longer commanded acceptance. Slavery now drew the fire of such powerful forces in the North that southerners felt impelled not only to defend it in practice but to promote it in principle in order to preserve the sectional balance.

During the years 1832–3, when South Carolina attempted to withdraw from the Union in protest on behalf of the South against a high tariff, slavery was abolished in the British West Indies, the American Anti-Slavery Society was founded, and there began a decade of violent abolitionist propaganda by northern zealots like Garrison and Birney, who, although unimportant in numbers and impractical in programme, contrived by speeches, conventions, pamphleteering and petitions to Congress,[1] to make the American public slavery-conscious and to keep the issue to the fore in national politics. Northern railway promoters who chafed at southern opposition to Federal aid for ambitious schemes to the West, northern settlers and land speculators who resented southern resistance to a cheap land policy in the expanding North-west—indeed all those northern interests impatient for a rapid advance across the continent—came to regard slavery as the stubborn obstacle to their ambitions. On the other hand, southerners, who detested anti-slavery propaganda as the interference of busybodies with established institutions, became increasingly sensitive to any opposition whatsoever, not only to slavery but to its territorial extension.

In 1849, the demand for admission to Statehood by California, which straddled the Missouri latitude, created a new and more bitter crisis. Only after a protracted congressional deadlock was a new compromise arranged whereby California was to become a free State in return for the passing by Congress of a Fugitive Slave Law which would protect southern rights to slave property from the drain of slaves escaping North by means of the abolitionist-organized 'underground railway'. In this compromise, Calhoun abandoned the territorial guarantee of the Missouri doctrine for the purely legal guarantee of slave property in the Constitution; and, shaky and limited as it was, the new arrangement was only brought about by that older generation of statesmen, especially Calhoun, Clay and Webster, who still thought of the issue in terms of sectional compromise within the framework of the Constitution. Henceforward emphasis by the North on moral justice and by the South on legal rights prevented any further effective compromise. With Calhoun's death southern leadership passed to extremists like Rhett and Yancey—unashamed southern nationalists prepared to play the last, trump card of secession in order to preserve the southern way of life.

[1] The petitions were used in Congress with masterly skill by the aged John Quincy Adams.

The Democratic Idea and the Problem of Caste

When the renewed land and railway boom of the early 1850s led to the rapid settlement of Nebraska territory, both interests worked hard to create settler communities after their own images in the hope that a *fait accompli* would determine the status of slavery. Southerners, moving hopefully with their slaves up from Missouri to cultivate hemp and tobacco, clashed with settlers moving down from the North-west to grow corn. The result was a new slavery crisis, solved this time, in the Kansas-Nebraska Act of 1854, by dividing the territory into two parts, of which the southern, Kansas, was expected to become a slave State and the northern, Nebraska, a free one; and by leaving it to the people in each territory to decide the issue of slavery for themselves. But this new compromise also failed. For northern sympathizers, including a contingent of settlers armed by the abolitionists not with pamphlets but rifles, infiltrated Kansas to swing opinion in favour of a free constitution. Out of the resulting bloodshed and the confusion of rival conventions and draft constitutions Kansas emerged as a free State.

This last attempt to find a basis for compromise was doomed. The doctrine of 'popular sovereignty' which failed to secure a southern Kansas in compensation for a northern Nebraska proved unacceptable to the South. Southerners, aware of the geographical limits to slave culture, could not hope to counter with southern sympathizers the flood of northern and immigrant settlers pouring into the new territories. Their only hope was to force the protection of slavery wherever it existed by cast-iron constitutional guarantees; and in this they were encouraged by the decision of the southern-dominated Supreme Court in the Dred Scott Case of 1857 which laid down that Congress had no power to forbid slavery as a form of property in the territories.

Thus the South took her stand on legal rights guaranteed by a Constitution not subject to reinterpretation while the North insisted on the moral right of the majority of the American people to determine the kind of society which should dominate the whole. There was no longer any common ground for compromise; and since compromise was the cement which kept the Union together the national structure of party politics began to disintegrate.

The history of party politics after the triumph of Jacksonian democracy is the story of a realignment of forces round the issue of slavery. The Whig triumph of 1840 proved short-lived. It was not merely that Tyler, who became President on Harrison's death, proved to be a southern Democrat in disguise, but that the whole temper of agrarian imperialism, of 'manifest destiny', which dominated the '40s, with the acquisition of slave-holding Texas, the Oregon Controversy, the Mexican War and the mushrooming of California, played into the hands of the Democratic Party which, except for one Whig interlude, remained in power until 1860. That party was led by southerners who, with their greater talent, their exceptional power in the Senate and the discipline which came from the defence of slavery, made the running of policy. Both parties were split with internal divisions over slavery, as was shown by the voting on the Wilmot Proviso of 1846 which attempted to ban slavery from the Mexican annexation; but the persistence of the slavery motive in the Democratic Party in the long run forced the growth of an opposition predominantly northern and 'free soil' in tone.

The Whigs were weakened by their division into conscience—or 'free soil'—Whigs and cotton Whigs, among whom were the New York interests committed to the cotton trade. In addition to the rump of conscience Whigs, the Democrats were faced, in the decade after 1846, with the rise in the North of several of those characteristically American single-idea parties which strengthened the opposition to Democratic hegemony. There were the Barnburners. These 'Methodists of Democracy', strongly entrenched in the 'burnt-over' region of western New York, heirs to the Jacksonian Loco-Focos, left the Democrats in answer to the Higher Law at the time of the Mexican cession. New York, too, gave the conscience Whigs the remnants of the old, and rabidly evangelical, Anti-Masonic Party. The Know-Nothing Party of the '50s exploited the nativist hysteria against immigrants in the eastern cities by uniting those who feared immigrant labour competition, German labour radicals and the influence of the largely Irish Roman Catholic Church. By trading votes with minor groups like the Prohibitionists, the Know-Nothing Party became a powerful factor in the election of 1854. But the most significant was James G. Birney's radical anti-slavery group, the Liberty Party, which, allying with the Barnburners to form the more broadly based Free Soil Party, ensured the election of the Whig President Taylor in 1848. The coalescence of elements from all these groups, under the pressure of the slavery issue, brought into being a new, continent-wide party strong enough, in the election of 1856, to challenge the Democrats.

The Republican Party which replaced the old Whigs as the effective opposition to the Democrats was, like all American national parties, an amalgam of many, sometimes conflicting, interests. The platform drawn up in Chicago at the portentous Wigwam Convention of 1859 included the protective tariff for east coast manufacturers, especially Pennsylvania ironmasters, a homestead law for western settlers, a Pacific railway for New York bankers and Chicago business men and protection for the existing immigration law which permitted thousands of immigrants to stream yearly into the North and North-west. Above all, it included a 'free soil' plank to give unity and moral force to the other disparate interests. It was an accurate political summary of the aspirations of the new, dynamic, thrusting, capitalistic, democratic America which was ambitious to dominate the continent; it was a northern programme challenging directly not merely Democrats but southerners.

The fate of the Union depended on whether the Democratic Party could hold firm across the continent in the face of this purely sectional threat. Democratic politicians worked desperately to bring yet one more compromise out of the hat in order to keep free soilers and southern extremists within the party. Among a generation of politicians conspicuous for their mediocrity in all parties, Stephen A. Douglas, Democratic Senator for Illinois, stands out. Douglas's constituency itself made him a key figure. The North-west was not merely the stronghold of the Republican Party; it was the fount and origin of its being. Its birth dates from a mass meeting of Nebraska fusionists under an oak in Jackson, Michigan, in 1854, and it derived its *élan* from the aggressive, uncompromising spirit of that brash countryside. Much more than the Senator's own seat depended upon preventing Democrats in the North-west from drifting into the Republican fold. Douglas, who was involved in railway promotion west from Chicago, pinned his hopes for peace over the Great Plains on the popular sovereignty doctrine which he made his own. From 1854 onwards, with all the professional dexterity at his command, he tried to foster Democratic support for his formula. But although astute and public spirited, he was too limited to realize that the day for formulae was past. It needed a statesman to see beyond the day-by-day practices of politics and to realize that the issue of the extension of slavery must be settled once and for all.

The statesman whom, as so often in time of crisis, the American people thrust forward was significantly a contestant, against Douglas, for the support of the people of Illinois. Abraham Lincoln personified, in his tall gaunt rough-hewn frame, the essential Northwest. Born in a lean-to cabin in Kentucky, son of a feckless Virginia migrant, bred to the catch-as-catch-can existence of the frontier, he had grown into a youth whose moody, introspective temperament was redeemed for his neighbours by his prowess at splitting rails, wrestling and telling dryly humorous and often wildly improper stories. After an absent-minded spell at storekeeping, his bookish nature and gift for argument turned him to the law. Something about his bearing, perception and ambition distinguished him from the other draggle-tailed, Blackstone-toting, circuit-riding attorneys of the backwoods, and over the years he acquired increasingly important briefs, becoming one of the outstanding corporation lawyers of Illinois. He entered politics as a Whig and an admirer of Henry Clay; but although he served in the Illinois Legislature and for a short spell in Congress, he was almost unknown outside his State when, in 1858, he received the nomination of the infant Republican organization to oppose Douglas for re-election to the Senate. In this typically western campaign, the two candidates debated against each other to the delight of remote rural audiences come to get the most out of the sport of politics. But because of the quality of the men and the urgency of the issue the debate has gone down to history as one of the turning-points of the slavery struggle.

Like most north-western Republicans, Lincoln was at heart a Jeffersonian democrat, believing that Negro emancipation, like manhood suffrage and rights for women, was a moral corollary to the Declaration of Independence. He was, however, no abolitionist.

He confessed that he had no solution for the slavery problem, and he was even prepared to tolerate the extension of slavery if this would preserve the Union. But after years of brooding and shrewd political speculation, he had slowly arrived at the deeply held conviction that the North would become alienated from a Union which promoted slavery, that the Union could no longer be preserved by compromise: 'A house divided against itself cannot stand. I believe this government cannot endure permanently half slave and half free. . . . Either the opponents of slavery will arrest the further spread of it and place it where the public mind shall rest in the belief that it is in the course of ultimate extinction, or its advocates will push it forward till it shall become alike lawful in all the States, old as well as new, North as well as South.'[1] The time had come for a showdown; and in his debates with Douglas he exposed the unreality of Democratic hopes for compromise by probing into the Senator's convictions about popular sovereignty. He made Douglas admit that he had no moral scruples against slavery and, on a hot July afternoon at the little town of Freeport, he forced him to assert that, despite the Dred Scott decision, a territory could still exclude slavery by refusing to give it police protection. Although Douglas was re-elected, the debate, which showed up the bankruptcy of his statesmanship and brought Lincoln national publicity, hardened opinion on both sides against compromise.

As the Presidential Election of 1860 approached, political tension mounted. The raid of the half-crazed John Brown upon Harper's Ferry, Virginia, with intent to start a slave insurrection whipped southern hysteria to a point where moderation was impossible. At last what thinking persons had long feared happened. The Democratic Convention, which met at Baltimore, failed to agree on a Presidential candidate. Breckinridge took the field for the southern fire-eaters, Douglas for the northern Democrats: the one remaining national party had split over the slavery issue. This left the way open for the Republicans. Lincoln, who at Chicago had been nominated as a 'dark horse' candidate to make sure of the all-important North-west, secured a majority of electoral votes over all the other

---

[1] Speech delivered at Springfield, Ill., 16 June 1858; R. P. Basler, *Abraham Lincoln : His Speeches and Writings* (New York, 1946), p. 372.

candidates combined. Thus, although the Republicans had control of neither house of Congress, a sectional party had at last seized the national administration.

The election of Lincoln was the signal for revolt in the South. Following the lead of South Carolina, the ten States of the cotton South one by one seceded from the Union and joined together in a new confederacy the cornerstone of which, in the words of Alexander Stephens, rested 'upon the great truth that the Negro is not equal to the white man; that slavery—subordination to the superior race—is his natural and normal condition'.[1]

The only remaining issue was whether the North, in the words of William Seward, Lincoln's Secretary of State, should allow the 'erring sisters to depart in peace', or should enforce the view that the Union was 'indissoluble' by regarding secession as a rebellion to be put down by force. But the question was unreal. The North was too aggressively nationalistic to allow an aridly constitutional doctrine of States' rights to stand in the way of her ambitions and her moral convictions. When Lincoln did his constitutional duty by ordering the defence of Federal forts in southern territory, northern opinion stood firm. On 12 April 1861, Confederate artillery, on learning that a Federal relief expedition was on the way, fired on the besieged Fort Sumter in Charleston harbour and the issue was joined. The North went to war not only to keep the southern States within the Union but to force southerners to adjust their manner of life to that of the American people as a whole.

The character and outcome of the fighting show that it was simply a military extension of that social conflict which had been gathering for over a generation.

The American Civil War was not characterized merely by the desperation, bitterness and horror peculiar to civil conflict; it was in many respects the first 'modern' war. During the long four years the resources of both sides were mobilized and consumed in the way we have come to expect of 'total' war. Great armies took the field; perhaps as many as two million served in the Union forces and

[1] Alexander Stephens, speech at Savannah, 21 March 1862; Henry Cleveland, *Alexander H. Stephens in Public and Private* (1866), p. 726.

something under a million in the Confederate; and conscription was introduced on both sides, although, in that land of unruly individualism, it was only partially effective. Manpower was drained from the fields; transport was commandeered wholesale; and industry was converted to a war footing. In the closing stages the Union prosecuted a 'scorched earth' policy against soldiers and civilians alike to destroy the spirit of the South and its capacity to make war. Constitutional forms were distorted by military expediency and politics were reduced to propaganda. Military techniques took a recognizably modern form. Large, heavily-armed forces were deployed by rail. Ironclads, even submarines, were built to enforce or break the blockade. The rifle replaced the musket, the telegraph revolutionized signalling, wire entanglements and balloon reconnaissance aided the trench warfare in which, during 1864, wave upon wave of serried blue ranks were thrown against the opposing grey to force an advance by weight of numbers and fire-power in a manner not seen again until 1915. Medical services were organized on a modern scale to handle casualties estimated at about a million, either dead from wounds or disease, or permanently disabled. General staffs were built up to plan a continental strategy. In these new circumstances the advantage lay, in the long run, overwhelmingly with the Union, which could mobilize resources of manpower and material unmatched by the Confederacy. The defeat of the South was the collapse of an outmoded, agrarian order before the onslaught of modern industrial society.

Southerners dared to put the issue to the challenge of war in 1860 not merely because they saw no alternative to defending their way of life, nor because with a population of only six million whites against the North's twenty-two—a discrepancy which natural increase and immigration were rapidly increasing—the longer they delayed the greater would be their disadvantage, but because the conception of total war was beyond the reach of their imaginations. Insulated by their way of life from the impulses which were transforming the world outside, southerners still thought of war in terms of the code of chivalry. Southern boys, bred to feel a horse between their knees, to take aim along a rifle's sights and to satisfy an affront by drawing blood, showed the temper of soldiers; and from their ranks were drawn a splendid corps of officers and the finest group of generals on either side. But that very pride of bearing and breeding which produced the peerless Robert E. Lee made them ill-disciplined and wildly over-confident. Ignorant and provincial, they were the victims of their own propaganda in believing that any southerner could lick five money-grubbing, town-dwelling Yankee artisans. And for them the war was to be quickly won after pitting man against man in a series of glorified cavalry skirmishes. As an old soldier from the South put it: 'we have courage, wood-craft, consummate horsemanship and endurance of pain equal to the Indians but that we will not submit to discipline. We will not take care of things, or husband our resources. Where we are, there is waste and destruction. If it could be done by one wild, desperate dash, we would do it.'[1] Few paid heed to the logistics of transport, supply and industrial potential. Instead, most believed that if things went ill the threat to King Cotton would create revolution in northern mill towns and quickly bring British intervention on their behalf. The reality of war broke the spell of the southern enchant-ment; and the result was not merely military defeat but the utter collapse of the old southern society.

Hopes of a quick victory faded. Hastily formed Union forces, although thrown into confusion at Bull Run and elsewhere, managed somehow to stave off a series of brilliant offensives by the Confederate army thrusting from Virginia at Washington and Penn-sylvania and gave time to General McClellan to make the Army of the Potomac a true fighting force and to the Union Government to mobilize the war-making capacity of the North.

The expectation of British intervention also proved unfounded. The Confederacy deliberately withheld the 1861 cotton crop from the market partly in the hope that a cotton famine would bring Britain to her rescue. But neither this, nor the U.S. Navy's blockade of southern ports, produced the desired result. There was great sympathy in Britain for the southern cause among those sportsmen who saw the South as an underdog rebelling against intolerable

[1] General Winfield Scott, General-in-Chief of the U.S. Army at the opening of the Civil War, quoted by a contemporary diarist; Mary Boykin Chesnut, *Diary from Dixie*, ed. by I. D. Martin and M. L. Avery (New York, 1929), p. 182.

conditions, among those who were beginning to fear the newly aggressive power of the United States in Atlantic affairs, and among the upper classes who felt akin to the southern gentry and scorned democracy. But although Lord John Russell not only recognized southern belligerency, as was right and proper, but for a time turned a blind eye to the fitting out of Confederate warships in British ports, diplomatic relations with the Union Government, though strained, were never broken. In October 1862 a speech by Gladstone, implying that the Cabinet were blandly considering mediation with a view to southern independence, drew forth the effective protests of Cobden, Bright, W. E. Forster and others on behalf of radical and nonconformist opinion. The British governing classes, in their American policy, overlooked the powerful sentiment which bound the middle and artisan classes to American democracy. The North shared that common outlook which, in a measure, bound all those affected by Atlantic expansion,[1] whether in Britain or America, into one community. The Emancipation Proclamation of 22 September 1862, which made explicit at last the intention of the North to abolish slavery, rallied these elements in British opinion to the northern cause as fervently as Nebraska had rallied the same elements in America to the Republican Party. The Manchester School, hostile to slavery, welcomed a shift in imports from the slave cotton shut off by the northern blockade to the free corn which came to the rescue after bad harvests in 1861 and 1862; and Lancashire cotton operatives, proudly bearing the hardships of unemployment, sent their good wishes to the great American President who expressed their own aspirations in such simple, arresting language. The South miscalculated in this, as in so much else. The Atlantic partnership still held firm; but although built upon the cotton trade it had transcended its origins. By their action in keeping Britain neutral the men who depended most on cotton passed a vote of no confidence in the society which provided their raw material.

With the door shut on foreign recognition, the Confederacy was left to fight it out with its own resources. As 1863 drew on, it became clear that interior lines, good generalship and fighting spirit were not enough to withstand northern pressure indefinitely. The

[1] See ch. iv.

remaining reserves of men dwindled. Cut off by the blockade from foreign supplies, the armies of the South ran short not only of the munitions, boots and clothing which her rudimentary industry was so pitifully ill-equipped to provide, but, with every available white man in the forces, of food itself. Southern railways were so 'cannibalized' for urgent military purposes that they disintegrated, leaving the army dependent on an ever-diminishing supply of mules. Meanwhile the North, in spite of a slow, fumbling start, of languishing public opinion, mass desertions, the scandals of bounty-jumping recruits and swindling contractors, had built up a powerful war potential. With her superior manpower—she had 900,000 men under arms at the armistice in comparison with the South's 200,000 —and with the use of agricultural machinery she provided food for home and export. The iron foundries of Pennsylvania, the mass-producing small arms factories of Connecticut, the new machine-operated boot factories of Massachusetts provided ample sinews of war. The railways, which had been welded into a great east-west system during the 1850s, handled an immense military traffic, and with branches thrusting southwards provided the supply-lines for the grand, encircling strategy of the Union command. For the Federal military purpose, like the more peaceful purpose of northern politics before it, was the encirclement of the South. After almost two years of attempts to dislodge the Confederate Army from the main cockpit in northern Virginia, the Union succeeded in 1863 in thrusting a western army down the Mississippi River. The following year, this army joined up with forces moving north, after the capture of New Orleans from the sea, to seal off the South's corridor to Texas. Meanwhile, Lee's dangerous offensive into Pennsylvania had been stopped, at heavy cost, at Gettysburg in July 1863, and a central Union army under Sherman thrust south through Tennessee to capture Atlanta a year later. Sherman's subsequent drive to the Atlantic, which laid waste a great swathe of Georgia countryside, cut the South in two, and dealt a body blow to a Confederacy already reeling from Grant's sledge-hammer attacks on the Potomac towards Richmond. By the spring of 1865 this war of attrition had brought the South to a standstill. When on 9 April Lee presented his sword in surrender to Grant at Appomatox Courthouse, the springs of southern life had sunk so low that the Confederate troops were allowed to return home with their horses and mules 'to work their little farms' in order to stave off the famine which stalked through the countryside.

The South was prostrate. A few blackened chimneys pointing skeleton fingers to the sky marked the sites of whole towns; railways, roads, navigable waterways, even the very fields were engulfed by the insurgent wilderness. Ex-generals, their mansions ruined, their money worthless, their slaves dispersed, worked a corn patch, kept alive by roots and hopes of what the quickening life of the soil might once again bear. Northern democracy had achieved a total victory over southern autocracy; but the violence of the struggle bred a litter of evils to bedevil American life, South and North, in the years of reconstruction.

Human wilfulness destroyed the innocence of the democratic creed. In the *élan* of victory, the North refused to tolerate Lincoln's magnanimous arrangements for the restoration of the southern States to their rights within the Union once secession had been renounced and slaves freed. After Lincoln's assassination the radical Republicans who controlled Union politics blocked the well-meant efforts of his successor, Andrew Johnson, to carry out his policy and embarked instead on a doctrinaire programme designed to reconstruct the entire South by force according to the blue-prints of northern democracy. 'Radical Reconstruction' was a disaster, not only because much of it was irrelevant to the predicament of the South, but because its constructive element was quickly overwhelmed by predatory forces intent on exploiting southern weakness.

Many radical leaders were well-intentioned according to their lights. A Thaddeus Stevens or a Charles Sumner, although narrow-minded, self-righteous and poisoned by hate for the old South, fervently desired to put something better in its place. The Thirteenth Amendment, which confirmed Lincoln's Emancipation Proclamation, swept away slavery for ever; the Fourteenth and Fifteenth Amendments which guaranteed civil and political rights to the Negro, the Freedman's Bureau which brought him relief and rehabilitation, the unsuccessful efforts to give him the freehold, all were part of a programme designed to break up the old planting order and to foster a 'free' society in which the Negro as well as the poor white would find a place. At radical dictation, State constitutions were democratized, State laws reformed, and systems of State education and poor relief introduced. Northern capitalists were given every encouragement to rebuild railways, establish industry and foster commerce in the South.

But good intentions became cant when exposed to the evils ot unbridled authority. For the Union's victory had given a monopoly of power to an unholy alliance of politicians and business men. The Republican victory in 1860 had introduced the business man to the inner sanctum of political control. When peace came contractors and manufacturers had vast capital to invest and an unquenchable thirst for power. These men, accustomed by now to getting their way with politicians, looked forward to an era of unbridled advance, aided and abetted by government in a grotesque travesty of the Hamiltonian ideal. To these, Reconstruction gave the opportunity to pick up bargains in southern timber, iron, coal, railways.

The radical politicians for their part were equally determined to treat the South as a conquered province. Should the southern States be restored to play their full part in the Union and in Democratic politics, Republican ascendancy would be undermined. And that ascendancy the radicals were determined to preserve. To keep the South a Republican tool, Congress passed a series of Reconstruction Acts which, enforced by military authority, prevented southern States from being readmitted to Congress until they were safely in the hands of northern-directed 'carpet-bagger' regimes based on the Negro vote. Not content with establishing puppet governments in the South, the Radical Party in Congress were determined to snuff out opposition to the sovereign power of the Republican Party wherever it might flicker. This involved riding roughshod not merely over States' rights but over all those safeguards which had been written into the Constitution to prevent the rise of precisely this kind of one-party tyranny. Andrew Johnson, who did his Presidential duty by vetoing, in the interests of the American people as a whole, the more extreme Reconstruction bills, came within one vote of being impeached after a Congressional trial which was no more than a piece of political hi-jacking; and the Supreme Court was browbeaten into acquiescing in the more constitutionally questionable features of the radical programme. The Government of the United States was entirely in the grasp of a Congressional Committee of Fifteen who, under the premiership of Thaddeus Stevens, subverted the Constitution into a kind of improvised parliamentary government of the English pattern without the safeguard of a parliamentary opposition. The unscrupulous rule of the radical minority was the apotheosis of those disruptive forces which, by denying the conventions of balance and compromise in the Constitution, had brought about the Civil War. With legality at a discount, with the collapse of morals following in the train of war, and with the temptations of untold wealth, the conditions were set for that notorious Gilded Age when politicians and business men conspired to make a Roman holiday with the fabulous riches of the American continent.

The distemper which afflicted the triumphant North also infected the South. Southerners, who still persisted in thinking of the war in narrowly military terms, were embittered, not by their defeat in the field, but by the attempt of the North to destroy the whole basis and values of their society. Southerners might accept the doom of slavery and admit the error of secession; some might welcome northern capital and enterprise for a new start; yeomanry and poor whites might be tempted to co-operate with carpet-baggers in order to get back at the hated planting class. But the iron-fisted determination of the North to keep the South in permanent subjection by enlisting the Negro united most southern whites in implacable resistance to what they felt in the marrow of their bones to be a threat to their personal identity. For the abolition of slavery had left southerners face to face with the problem of the Negro in a more naked and urgent form. Southerners hoped to solve that problem in their own way; they were not prepared to accept the doctrinaire solution of the North which would perpetuate social chaos.

A solution to the economic problem of the Negro was quickly found. Planters, to whom after a liberation spree many helpless ex-slaves returned, put the Negro to work by leasing him land and providing him with seeds, tools and provisions in return for half the crop raised. This 'share-cropping' tenancy, although subject to grave abuses because it kept the tenant bound to the land by what was almost forced labour, was admirably suited to the employment of ignorant, dependent and shiftless freedmen, and to safeguarding the interests of landowners and therefore of the old social order. Once the northern idealist had been defeated in his attempt to give the Negro the freehold, the southern white felt that an economic framework which would preserve the equilibrium between the superior and the inferior race was secure. But so long as the Negro was protected by Federal bayonets in the enjoyment of the full rights of citizenship, including the champagne splendours of office, he remained unamenable to discipline and his master was denied his political birthright. Some means had to be found of teaching the Negro his place as a member of a backward race in a society whose natural governors were the civilized whites. The net result of the grotesque tragi-comedy of carpet-bagger government was the rise of a virulent racialism on the part, not merely of the planting class, but of most southerners, including the poor whites who were faced with Negro competition. The shackles of slavery were replaced by cruel intimidation from hooded, night-riding ghouls of the Ku Klux Klan who threatened 'uppity niggers' with lynch law, and carried out their threats without compunction. In the end, such methods were denounced as criminal even by a desperate southern opinion, and the Klan was officially dissolved in 1869. But it had done its work, and the persistence of occasional lynchings reminded coloured folk of the naked weapon of violence held in reserve to keep them in their place. Instead of the Klan, southern politicians developed that armoury of chicanery—poll taxes, literacy tests, moral and physical intimidation—which, below the Mason-Dixon Line, was to prevent the Negro from exercising his full rights of citizenship well into the present day.

Such tactics ultimately enabled the southern Democrats to re-capture power in State after State, so that in 1876 only disputed election returns, the result of a final battle with the Republican machines of the South, prevented the election of a Democratic

President; and the compromise, which ensured victory for the Republican, Hayes, by stipulating the withdrawal of the last Federal troops, brought to an end Republican rule in the South. The *élan* of Union victory was spent; and with the inevitable break-away of incompatible interests—especially those agrarian interests hostile to the new power of capital—the hegemony of radical Republicanism was over. Although the Democrats were to remain a minority party for another generation, they had returned to play their essential political role in the nation. And powerful in their counsels were the satraps of the 'solid South'. For the logic of Civil War and Reconstruction made membership of the Democratic Party a fundamental tenet of the South's political creed. This was not due simply to the bitter knowledge that Republicans had worn Union blue; nor to that magnolia-sweet memory of romantic chivalry which was to be cherished by southern pride—the fantasy induced by the traumatic experience of defeat. The reason was that southern whites, whether or not they belonged to the 'Bourbon' upper class—so-called because, like the French dynasty, they were accused of having learnt nothing and forgotten nothing—were united in one party to preserve the whole structure of white supremacy. So long as the Negro remained concentrated in the South in such numbers as to constitute a problem of caste, southerners felt impelled to practise all the arts of segregation and subordination from 'jim-crow cars' to Negro schools. And to protect their social system southerners had to preserve a united front against the party which had given the Negro his freedom and which still drew his allegiance. The Civil War had given the Negro his technical freedom. But the intractable problem of race relations persisted to create a great monolithic party in the South and to trouble the conscience of American democracy.

CHAPTER VIII

THE
CONQUEST OF A GREATER WEST
1845-1907

'Already the advance guard of the irresistible army of
Anglo-Saxon emigration has begun to pour down upon
(California), armed with the plough and the rifle, and mark-
ing its trail with schools and colleges, courts and representative
halls, mills and meeting-houses . . . Away then with all idle
French talk of *balance of power* on the American continent!
Though they should cast into the opposite scale all the
bayonets and cannon of Europe entire, how would it kick
the beam against the simple, solid weight of the two
hundred and fifty or three hundred millions destined to
gather beneath the flutter of the stripes and stars in the fast
hastening year of the Lord 1945?'

J. L. SULLIVAN, *The United States Magazine and
Democratic Review*, July and August 1845.

WHEN in 1854 Yankees and southerners were jostling for
position on the Kansas border, American settlement reached
hardly farther west than the 95th Meridian from Texas north
to Minnesota, only half-way across the continent; but the citizens of
the United States, with the experience of a generation of rapid
continental advance behind them, confidently assumed it to be their
'manifest destiny' to inherit the vast and still mysterious domain
which stretched westwards nearly two thousand miles to the Pacific
Ocean. American settlers, streaming into Texas from the Mississippi
Valley, had already wrested that outlying province from the flaccid
hold of Mexico. A handful of Americans far away in another
ancient Mexican province on the Californian coast had in 1845
started the intrigue which prompted the United States to seize by

force of arms the remaining Mexican territory north of the Rio Grande and the Gulf of California. A thousand miles to the north, on the Pacific coast, a colony of American fur traders, settlers and missionaries had staked a claim to the fertile and temperate Willamette Valley and to the majestic, forest-bound waters of Puget Sound, a claim which held firm against shadowy Russian pretensions and more plausible British claims to Oregon. But between Oregon territory and the new State of California on the one hand, and Nebraska territory on the other, lay a formidable terrain of peaks, plateaux, alkali deserts and plains—the silent and lonely dominion of Indian and buffalo, of mountain lion and bear—discouraging settlement. West of the 98th Meridian, of the three staples of settlement—land, wood and water—only land remained[1]; and settlers trained to woodcraft faltered, at a loss, in the face of this new intractable line of country.

Beyond the Missouri, life took on the character of a military operation. The bustling throng who, in the spring, loaded their prairie schooners at the frontier outposts of Council Bluffs and Fort Leavenworth consisted of fur traders bound for the Rockies, missionaries for the mountain Indians, adventurers for California or settlers for the Oregon country; and their object was to get across the menacing High Plains as expeditiously as possible with the minimum loss of life from Indians, fatigue, thirst and exposure. The wagon companies which took the three months' trek along the California, Oregon or Sante Fé trails had to be expertly guided and disciplined to repel Indian attack, to hunt buffalo and to conserve water, provisions and faltering *morale*. The Pony Express, which carried the United States mail from St Joseph, Missouri, to Sacramento in ten days, and the Overland Mail coaches from St Louis to San Francisco were remarkable achievements in riding and staging enterprise. And in the background the United States dragoons conducted a series of full-scale operations against the savage and desperate plains Indians who, from the First Sioux War in Minnesota in 1862 to the death of Sitting Bull in the Fourth Sioux War in 1890, fought against white encroachments on their country all over the High Plains and North-west.

[1] Walter Prescott Webb, *The Great Plains* (Boston, 1931), p. 9.

The Great Experiment

Even the first settlement was the achievement of an expeditionary force. Not all the wagon trains had the Pacific as their destination. The first to face the problem of settling in this forbidding country were driven to it by desperation, and by faith that somewhere in its secret wastes they would find a divinely promised land. In 1847, Brigham Young had led a shattered remnant of the persecuted Mormon community of Nauvoo, Illinois, nearly a thousand miles across the Great Plains and through the eastern range of the Rockies to the shore of the Great Salt Lake where, walled in by arid mountains, the Latter Day Saints began the task of creating a land of milk and honey out of their barren Deseret. With purposeful leadership and iron discipline they established in their isolation a theocratic community in which the Church owned capital, land, and water rights, pioneered irrigation, and conducted all relations, including trade, with the outside world. An ambitious missionary and immigration campaign brought tens of thousands of Mormon converts to Utah, especially from north-west Europe where the artisans of England were particularly sought after for their skills. The story of Mormon migration from Liverpool by boat, railway, wagon train and, in one disastrous experiment, by handcart across the Great Plains, is an epic of courage, discipline and organization. Its significance for Utah is indicated by the fact that in 1880 over seventeen per cent of the population were British born.[1] But until the 1880s, when Mormon theocracy capitulated before the outside pressures of rail-borne trade and the political conditions prescribed for entry into the Union, Utah remained an isolated experiment in permanent settlement. Elsewhere in this wild west, Americans were still nomads: trappers, miners, lumbermen, cattlemen.

The discovery of gold in Sutter's mill-race on the American River in January 1848 drew to the Pacific slope a motley crowd of adventurers—who transformed California almost overnight into a new, populous State within the Union—and sent prospectors on a quest first for precious and then for industrial metals into the lofty interior of the Sierras and the Rockies. Ten years later, the discovery of the fabulously rich Comstock silver lode in the Sierras created Virginia

[1] Not counting the Irish; *Compendium of the 10th Census of the United States*, Table XXX.

City and the beginnings of the silver State of Nevada; and in the same year a strike far to the east at Pike's Peak was followed by a new gold rush which set its cluster of mining camps on the eastern foothills of the Colorado Rockies. Then the familiar process was repeated with gold strikes from Arizona in the south to Helena, Montana, and the remote fastness of Idaho in the north. For a few these bonanzas brought fortunes, often as quickly lost as won; and profits from the mines financed San Francisco's shipping, commerce and machine shops and California's agriculture. But for most, mining, in its early, roaring days, was a sorry story of the vain search after a glittering image of wealth pursued on mule-back with prospector's tools and placer's sieve. For like other kinds of frontiersmen the miner had neither resources nor patience to do more than scratch the surface of these rich layers of mineral deposit. The early miners and their camp followers were nomads. As they and their successors followed the mining frontier from strike to strike north to faraway Alaska and the Yukon, they left behind not only abandoned diggings but ghost towns like Central City, Colorado. Here, 8,000 feet up in the Rockies, stand an opera house, saloons and hotels, preserved in the dry mountain air as a historical memorial to those roughneck communities, in state of siege against the wilderness, whose code of summary justice, fancy prices, fabulous stakes, rococo bars and flamboyant women have been recorded by Bret Harte and Mark Twain. Permanent, commercial mining had, however, to wait until the 1880s and '90s when the railway brought heavy mining and tunnelling machinery and carried away, in addition to precious metals, copper, lead and tin ores for industrial use. With the coming of the railway, western States like Montana, with its mountain of copper at Helena, or Nevada, whose Senators were to help to make silver an issue in national politics, entered the Union as dependencies of great, absentee mining corporations.

The California gold rush called the attention of lumberjacks to the thick stands of pine on the slopes of the Sierras, to the redwood north of San Francisco and the Douglas fir of the Pacific North-west. Here the first 'cruisers', having travelled, it seemed, with the seven-league boots of their legendary giant Paul Bunyan, were already at work on forests with trees, some as high as three hundred feet, and five times as thick to the acre as in eastern forests; and lumber barons like Frederick Weyerhaeuser were soon to carve great logging empires for themselves out of public and railway land. Assuming the forests to be inexhaustible, they cut recklessly, without thought for replanting, in response to America's urgent demand for building materials, until in 1906 American production reached an all-time peak of 46 billion feet of sawn timber.[1] Out of their profits grew Seattle, Portland, Spokane—cities which quickly acquired an air of cultivation from the established families, some proud of New England origin, who had moved west from St Paul behind the timber frontier.

The news that California miners paid good money for rations was heard as far away to the south-east as Texas, where American settlers had taken to raising the rangy, long-horned Spanish cattle. So profitable were these early drives to the mining camps that Texas cattlemen began to venture north-east along the Chisholm and other trails to the frontier markets of the Midwest. The pushing of railway spurs to the edge of the High Plains enabled Texans to take full advantage of the rising demand for beeves from mushrooming eastern cities and from Britain where, in the '70s, American dressed beef appeared on English tables. A herd of steers, fed during the long drive from Texas or New Mexico on the rich grasses of the plains, sold at railhead in Kansas at anything up to 700 per cent profit. No wonder that by 1885 five and a half million head of cattle had been driven north from Texas. The resulting boom in cattle ranching attracted venturesome spirits and funds from the east and from across the Atlantic. In Britain especially where the mining bonanza had already called the attention of investors to the new West, sporting landlords had begun by 1880 to buy an interest in western ranches. 'Drawing-rooms buzzed with the stories of this last of bonanzas; staid old gentlemen, who scarcely knew the difference between a steer and a heifer, discussed it over their port and nuts.'[2]

In the next twenty years British, and particularly Scottish,

---

[1] *Hist. Stats.*, Series F, 109.
[2] John Clay, *My Life on the Range*, quoted in E. S. Osgood, *The Day of the Cattleman* (Minneapolis, 1929), p. 101.

syndicates promoted some thirty-seven cattle companies with initial capital of more than thirty-four million dollars[1]; and many a ranch in Wyoming or Texas was managed by a Scot and governed from board-rooms in Edinburgh, Dundee or Aberdeen. The Great Plains provided 'free air', as their boundless pasturage was called; but, far from being easy money, the long drive, with its risks of attack from Indians, rustlers and buffalo, of blizzards and of drought which sent herds of crazed steers stampeding to death, was a dangerous adventure. The cowhands, herding their cattle over the endless prairie, rounding them up for branding in the spring and fall, and relaxing the arduous discipline of the trail in wild orgies at Abilene or Dodge City—that 'bibulous babylon of the frontier' whose Boot Hill Cemetery was so-called because of its 'stiffs' buried there in boots and spurs—formed another distinct, nomadic, masculine society of the Great West immortalized by Owen Wister and Theodore Roosevelt. Tough, quick-tempered, wildly independent, the cowboys had also a graceful style and a moral code, inherited from the old South and tempered by the allegiance of the trail and the solitude of a limitless horizon.

But the long drive, like the citadel of the Saints or the mining and logging camps, was only a transient episode in the conquest of the Great West. The iron rails, which carried Texas longhorns to the slaughterhouses of Chicago, brought in return, packed almost like cattle themselves, a freight of settlers. And as the rails were built westwards, so, too, a scattering of homesteaders ploughed up the range and fenced it off with barbed wire. The cattlemen fought back, often with firearms; but even powerful organizations like the Wyoming Stock Growers' Association, which in its time was the *de facto* government of that territory, failed to withstand the infiltering settlers. Henceforward the closed ranch replaced the open range[2]; the breeding of Herefords and Black Angus replaced the casual raising of longhorns; and the day of the long drive, when guts and a stocking full of dollars could bring a fortune, was gone for ever. Instead of the herdsman, the corn farmer;

---

[1] H. O. Brayer, 'The Influence of British Capital on the Western Range-Cattle Industry', *Journal of Econ. Hist.*, Supplement IX, 1949.

[2] Although, like the Bell Ranch in Texas, it might be as large as forty square miles.

instead of the cowboy who bedded down where he drew rein under the stars, the homesteader with a wife and a cabin full of children.

The railway gave a new mobility to settled society, pushing back once again the nomadic fringe of American life. Without the railway, the development of not only the High Plains and the Rockies but of the Pacific coast would have languished. Between the Civil War and the Great War, the railway was the one paramount agency for colonizing the Far West; and the opportunities it afforded determined the thrust of American life.

When the railway builders tackled the Great Plains the character of railway enterprise had been established. Local lines were being knit together into trunk routes reaching out towards the Mississippi; and the process of consolidation gave ruthless operators unlimited opportunity to make fortunes, not from railroading, but from promotion. In addition to construction contracts, ransom exacted by control of key routes and stock manipulation, there were the profits from land. The early lines did not pioneer new country. But in those buoyant days, men were tempted to build, not merely where settlement guaranteed immediate business, but through sparsely settled regions where profits from freight must await the settlement which the railway itself would bring. In such schemes money was to be made from the sharply rising value of land adjacent to the tracks. The new railway boom was but the old land boom writ large. Capital for ventures like the Chicago, Burlington and Quincy, or the Illinois Central, was subscribed by local boosters who anticipated not only new markets for their produce but rich capital gains from their land; and many were the intrigues to divert the planned course of the tracks through a favoured vicinity. But local resources fell far short of what was required for an ambitious engineering undertaking. In order to attract outside capital, promoters turned for subsidy to the State and then to the Federal Government which in 1850 handed over to the Illinois Central large grants of public lands under and adjacent to the proposed tracks. Land grants gave railways a new attraction to outside investors who regarded their bonds as mortgages on valuable real estate and were comforted in the prospect of an income from the sale of railway land to settlers being gradually replaced by one earned from carrying the settlers' produce to market.

Thus, although in the renewed railway boom after the Civil War, some companies, notably Boston concerns like the Michigan Central, were soundly built to show an operating profit, many were the result of foolish optimism about the country's rate of growth and some were frankly devices to enable the promoters to make a killing in promotion activities. The possibilities for corruption in government charters involving land or money grants, in a gullible public eager to be in on the ground floor and in the eclipse after the war of the older patrician code of business ethics by a dizzy, good-time spirit, brought to the top a group of railway buccaneers solely interested in getting rich quick at the expense of both stockholders and travelling public. Men like Daniel Drew, who so weakened the Erie by successive stock watering that the trains hardly ran, or Jay Gould and Jim Fisk, who conducted their affairs from an opera house and once tried literally to capture the Albany and Susquehanna with an armed, train-borne force,[1] were only the most flamboyant figures in a generation which thought more of speculation than of engineering or operation.

Such was railroading experience when Americans began seriously to consider a railway from the Mississippi Valley network clear across the unsettled expanse of plain and mountain to the Pacific slope. The idea of a transcontinental railway, which had been a shuttlecock for the western ambitions of North and South in the '50s, became a national plan with the Republicans' Pacific Railway Act of 1862 and a practical undertaking immediately after the Civil War. To build a railway a thousand miles across uninhabited and hostile territory was a project of which the immediate purpose was national and strategic—the carriage of troops and mails to bind California to the Union. The Federal Government, therefore, following the precedent of the Illinois Central, subsidized two private companies, by the grant out of the national domain of alternate blocks of land thirty-six square miles on either side of the track and

[1] The story, which was climaxed by a head-on collision between two locomotives, is told by C. F. Adams, 'An Erie Raid', in C. F. and H. Adams' *Chapters of Erie and other Essays* (Boston, 1871).

by a money grant of from $16,000 to $48,000 a mile, according to the terrain. With this backing the Central and Union Pacific companies secured enough capital to begin construction west from Council Bluffs, and east from Sacramento. Three years later, on 10 May 1869, the telegraph flashed the news to an admiring nation that a golden spike had fixed the last sleeper under the converging rails at Promontory Point, Utah. The Union Pacific was a characteristic result of western hustle, big thinking and military discipline. Whole shanty towns moved on wheels behind the track-laying gangs of specially imported Chinese coolies, or Civil War ex-servicemen who could be deployed against Indians or buffalo. Formidable engineering hazards such as shifting sands, rail-buckling heat, mountain gradients and landslides, had to be overcome. But though the western section stood the test of time, the shoddy eastern section, which soon had to be re-made, bore witness to an impatience for results. It was also a symptom of that buccaneering spirit which tempted Collis P. Huntington and his fellow-directors, with the connivance of heavily bribed Senators and Congressmen, to capture fabulous riches for themselves at the expense of the company and its public assets. The scandal of the Credit Mobilier Construction Company, a device for enabling Union Pacific directors to grant outrageously favourable construction contracts to themselves, proved too much even for President Grant's Washington, and the exposure contributed to the loss of railway credit which ended in the panic of 1873.

Despite these frauds, the Federal Government persisted in the Union Pacific pattern of transcontinental railway building. During the '70s and '80s, the Southern Pacific, the Kansas and Pacific, and the Northern Pacific crossed or skirted the Rockies to the coast, and other companies built less ambitious lines, all with the aid of Federal and State land grants. Altogether, some 155 million acres of public domain—an area almost as large as Texas—was handed over by the Federal Government alone in fee simple to railway companies which became, in many parts of the Far West, almost despotic sovereignties in the territories and States. In spite of such princely aid, mammoth empires like the Union Pacific never wholly recovered from the unsound planning and rascally finance which brought them into being. However, in the 1880s and '90s younger railway men like Harriman of the Southern Pacific and the Canadian James Hill of the Great Northern—the last of the transcontinentals, built without benefit of land grant—concentrated their talents not on promotion but on railroading, rationalizing operation and consolidating the haphazard growth of lines into a few great empires.

The American railway network was built only at the expense of corruption, injustice, waste and misdirected effort. The old doctrine of 'internal improvements' was stood on its head. Whereas east of the Mississippi private enterprise had refused to be hobbled by government direction of a mercantilist kind, in the Far West, where private capital proved inadequate to open up the land, private enterprise obtained from government public resources with virtually no strings attached. Yet the national mood made this inevitable. Americans, impatient as ever to develop their continent, demanded that railways should be built at all costs; even at the cost, material and moral, of tolerating the fancy gamblers who had the audacity to play the high numbers on a rigged wheel; and at the cost of depleting the national domain, much of which, it must be remembered, would have remained valueless without the railway to fertilize it. Whatever the waste involved—and it is doubtful whether a publicly planned operation would have proved more efficient— the fact remains that by 1900 under the stimulus of this public aid to private enterprise American and European resources had built some 190,000 miles of railway—about 40 per cent of that of the entire world.[1] This signal achievement marks at once the last chapter in the territorial expansion of the American people and the first chapter in the emergence of modern America. For without a continental railway network there could be no single continental market. Little wonder that Americans invested their railways with an aura of romance like that with which Englishmen have invested the sea. Not sea shanties but 'Casey Jones', 'John Henry' and the honky-tonk tunes hammered out in railway towns like Kansas City or Chicago are the true folksong of a people for whom the railroad depot, with its bustling trains departing for distant and exotic points, was the one magical link with a wide, continental world.

The railway most directly shaped the lives of Americans beyond

[1] U.S. Census, 1900.

the Mississippi River. West of the 98th Meridian especially, the rails themselves were the pioneers, carrying trains of men and women intent on settling the rolling lands of the cowboy, the trapper and the Indian. The Homestead Act, with its grant of a quarter section to any *bona fide* settler, had fashioned the classic pattern of settlement out of the experience of the Mississippi Valley. But it was the railway companies, anxious to create freight-earning communities on their own land-grants alongside the track, which stimulated the greatest settlement. Although they retained important timber- and mineral-bearing tracts for future profit, it was their policy to dispose of as much land as possible in small lots to would-be settlers. From the time of the Illinois Central onwards, railway land settlement agencies recruited settlers, transporting them and their families on special terms by rail across the continent direct to some lonely stretch of prairie. Such was the need for settlement that these agencies reached out across the Atlantic to Liverpool, Havre, Hamburg and even further afield into Scandinavia and Central Europe. Most of the English, Swedes, Norwegians, Germans and 'Bohemians' who left their farms and workshops for Europe's new frontier in the golden West did so as a result of ambitious advertising campaigns in their local press by American railway and steamship agencies which conveyed many of them, in crowded steamers and special trains, to distant Dakota or Kansas. Indeed, the revolutionary speed and smoothness of their Odyssey hardly prepared the bewildered travellers for that new start which must be made once the immigrant train had dumped them down at their prairie terminus. So great was this movement that whole regions of the trans-Mississippi West took their character from distinct immigrant communities like the Czechs of Nebraska among whom Willa Cather grew up, or those conservative Lutheran farmers, brought from Sweden and Norway by 'Yim' Hill's Great Northern Railway, who have given so marked a stamp to the Dakotas and Minnesota.[1] Largely owing to this railway colonization the population of the trans-Mississippi West grew from 175,000 in 1860 to 1,675,000 in 1900.[2]

[1] See Willa Cather's novel, *O Pioneers!* and Ole Rolvaag's novel, *Giants of the Earth.*
[2] *Statistical Abstract of the United States.*

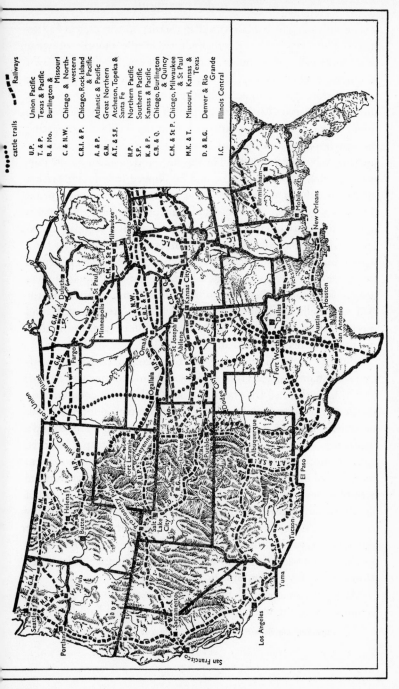

4. Principal Western Railways of the United States

The railway which transported the settler to the prairie had to sustain him. Unlike his Kentucky forbear, the pioneer of what came to be called the Middle Border could not subsist on his own resources. Lacking wood, he had to take shelter from the bitter winter before fires of buffalo dung in dug-outs made of the very sod of the prairie. With lack of timber went lack of game and, often, water. The settler's only asset was the fertile, virgin earth; his only hope, to survive until a crop of wheat or maize could be sold for cash to buy supplies. For this he was dependent on the railway by which alone his crop could be shipped to a distant market in Minneapolis or Kansas City. And he was equally dependent on the rails for clothing, provisions and household stuff and implements to transform his holding operation into effective occupation. As return freight, the railway brought timber for barns and later for a stout frame house, and a variety of newly perfected devices essential to subdue the plains to farming: the heavy, cast-steel plough to bite deep into the soil, barbed wire to serve for fencing, cheap, standardized windmills to pump water for stock from artesian wells, and mechanical reapers, binders and steam traction engines to multiply the power of his family's manual labour.

From the beginning, farming had to be commercial and specialized—an affair of single crops sold for cash in a continental, indeed, a world, market; and it was machinery, which, by counteracting the perennial shortage of labour on the frontier, alone made this possible. A man could reap by sickle and flail only about seven and a half acres, but with a mechanical reaper he could reap a hundred acres or more. Machinery had been used to take the place of farm hands called to the colours in the War, and this example encouraged a rush of new settlement from the Texan to the Canadian border in which small men mortgaged themselves to the ears to buy reapers, and men of means operated vast 'bonanza' farms of many thousands of acres with the aid of batteries of multiple harvesting machines. Between 1866 and 1898 the production of wheat increased from 152 to 675 million bushels.[1]

Machinery exaggerated the frontier practice of cropping continuously until the soil became exhausted and new land had to be

[1] F. A. Shannon, *The Farmer's Last Frontier* (New York, 1945), Appendix.

taken up. The bumper yields came, not from more intensive use of the soil, but from an increase in the area under cultivation, from 15 million acres in 1866 to 44 million in 1898.[1] Agriculture remained extensive and cheap land encouraged a rapid movement of the frontier. The science of agronomy came to the aid of the wheat farmer. The Morrill Act, part of that corpus of Republican legislation which gave the West its homesteads and railways, set aside public land to support mining and farm schools. Out of the laboratories thus established came hardier wheat strains which pushed the spring wheat belt not only west but north into Minnesota and the Dakotas. In the late '90s it was moving up the Red River Valley into Manitoba on its way to the Arctic Circle, and the pace of competition was coming to be set, not by the United States, but by the frontier soils of western Canada. In twenty years the centre of the maize belt moved west from southern Indiana into Iowa and Kansas, and with it went the hog-raising industry. South of the maize belt new strains of winter wheat spread into Missouri, Kansas and Oklahoma, and, farther south still, the cotton belt travelled into New Mexico and California. As a result of this advance, settlement spread thinly outwards from the Middle Border and from the Pacific coast so that although much new land remained to be taken up in the twentieth century—the peak of Homestead entries came only in 1913—the census-takers of 1890 felt justified, on their statistical basis, in declaring that 'there can hardly be said to be a frontier line'. Such was the accelerating rate of growth that, less than ninety years after Louisiana was bought, the American people had spread themselves over a continental area which Jefferson had believed good for a thousand years of expansion; and in Wisconsin a young assistant professor of history, Frederick Jackson Turner, was already beginning his revolutionary study of the frontier as a thing of the past.

This spectacular conquest of the plains was not made without an incalculable toll in waste and human suffering. A success story for the exceptional few, it was for more a tragedy of aspiration and defeat. For plains farming was subject to hazards not mentioned in the glowing propaganda of the railway companies.

[1] F. A. Shannon, *op. cit.* Appendix.

In winter, blizzards froze stock to death and marooned families. In the spring, melting snows, no longer absorbed by surface vegetation where plough had broken sod and axe destroyed timber, carried away the crumbling soil down swollen rivers which transformed the Missouri and Mississippi into seas of devastating, chocolate-coloured floodwater. Summer might bring an unlucky 'twister' to scatter stacks, buildings and animals through the air like toys; or a plague of grasshoppers to devour, in an hour or two, the sprouting grain. But the worst of these terrible visitations, which confirmed the gaunt, horny-handed pioneer in his Old Testament fundamentalism, was drought. Farmers in parts of western Kansas, Nebraska and South Dakota, where there is sometimes less than fifteen inches of rain in a year, saw the beating sun shrivel their crops and the parched soil blown away into dust storms by the hot wind. German-Russian immigrants from the Volga introduced the practice of sprinkling the soil with a covering of dust to keep in the dew. But after droughts, in spite of such shifts, much land had to be abandoned to the winds which made of the wasted soil a dust-bowl as a legacy for future generations.

The pioneer family had also to nerve themselves against monotony and loneliness. Railway colonization was a large-scale operation. The traffic of commerce was carried hundreds of miles along disappearing vistas of straight rails to unknown cities. On these iron-bound prairies there was no place for the small market town with its churches, banks and friendly general stores which had so quickly grown to be natural neighbourhood centres further east. Just as the village failed to survive west of the Appalachians, the market town disappeared as the frontier moved over the plains. The plains farmer knew no social intercourse beyond the occasional buggy trip to the railway depot or to a neighbour's distant frame house standing, identical with his own, uncompromising and unprotected on its rectangular tract of prairie.

The absence of social intercourse exaggerated the farmer's feeling of defencelessness against what he regarded as victimization by the remote, impersonal and all-powerful forces of capital which appeared increasingly to restrain his freedom of action.

Sometimes an unscrupulous railway or land company sold him a tract of what turned out to be marsh or sand. Even sound land was worthless without water, the right to which was more to be prized than land titles. Sometimes he had to make shift with an inaccessible claim because the railway company refused to release for settlement its huge holdings adjacent to the tracks. The Homestead Act itself, hailed as a charter of Jeffersonian liberties, failed to protect the homesteader from his ignorance and poverty. The quarter section which, in the varied country of Ohio or Missouri, was enough to support a thriving mixed farm, proved totally inadequate for the single-crop tillage of the plains. To make his holding economic, the farmer had to acquire additional acres and the machinery to work them. But the cards were stacked against him. The price he obtained for his wheat, corn or cotton, sold on a world market, never seemed to bear an equitable relation to the cost of his manufactured supplies, protected by a high tariff. While on the one hand a series of 'trusts' jacked up the price of ploughs, harvesters and barbed wire, on the other a series of middlemen came between the farmer and the profits from the sale of his crop. Without storage space he was forced to sell his corn outright to elevator companies which were in a position to charge exorbitant rates and, like the proverbial miller, to downgrade his wheat or corn to their own advantage. The railway, which monopolized transport to distant markets, imposed heavy freight rates, the result, in part, of the high cost of shipping bulky, seasonal freight in a one-way traffic, but also, in part, of the advantage taken by the railway to charge what the traffic would bear. It took one bushel of corn to pay the freight on another on the journey from Nebraska to Chicago.[1] Freight rates west of the Missouri River were twice those east from Chicago: a fact with which railway and lake competition to the east had much to do. The railway's culpability was further confirmed when they slashed rates in wars with rival companies and when they granted specially favourable terms to large shippers who could guarantee a steady flow of freight over long distances. Where, as with the Santa Fé in Kansas and the Burlington and Union Pacific in Nebraska, the railway also controlled state politics, its hegemony was complete.

Few plains farmers had the capital to withstand the pressure of

---

[1] F. A. Shannon, *op. cit.* pp. 295–6.

these fixed charges. Most farmers carried on by buying machinery on instalment, by mortgaging their crops, land and buildings, and occasionally their wagons and teams, at oppressive interest rates. The money was borrowed from eastern speculators who, in the good times of the late '70s and mid-'80s, could not find enough farm mortgages to satisfy their desire to join the band wagon lumbering west. Finance companies from St Paul to Kansas City did such 'land-office' business that by 1890 there was one mortgage to every two persons in Kansas and South Dakota.[1]

But the boom had its inevitable nemesis. The Utopian hopes of the receding horizon were often dashed by the grim reality of the advance. Once again the West developed too fast. Attracted by the blandishments of railway and land companies, the settler had taken on land that never should have been farmed. His human instinct to recoup himself for bad years by sowing an ever larger acreage resulted in over-production which minimized his profits even in good years. A cycle of unusually wet years, which had encouraged the settlement of much semi-arid land, was followed by a return to more normal conditions of drought over the higher plains, which brought disaster to the Middle Border. Crop failures pricked the speculative bubble in 1887, ushering in nearly a decade of poverty and bitter adjustment. This slump, which merged with the industrial depression of 1893, put a stop to the westward surge and set up an undertow of bankrupt and demoralized settlers returning with their pitiful sticks of furniture to start again in some kinder, more easterly neighbourhood. As late as 1891, 18,000 prairie schooners, moving east, entered Iowa from Nebraska. In western Kansas twenty towns were totally abandoned, and whole counties virtually depopulated. Even in Wichita, according to one historian's memory, 'for years after 1900 houses . . . were seen rotting away miles from the city limits on what had once been sold as city lots'[2]. Over the entire Middle Border marginal land was abandoned, and holdings were consolidated. Land which had been under the plough reverted to scrub or the grazing of cattle and sheep. The land which fell to foreclosed mortgages passed from the settler through banks

[1] F. A. Shannon, *op. cit.* p. 306.
[2] *Ibid.*, p. 308.

and finance companies to more substantial men with capital. In the twenty years after 1880, the percentage of tenant farmers in Kansas increased from 16·3 to 35·2.[1] Although by no means all tenant farmers consisted of those who had failed to succeed on their own, the increasing proportion indicates that tenancy was a rung on the way down the ladder of agricultural success, and reflects the inadequacy of the Homestead Act to foster a sturdy yeoman class in the Far West. The individualism of the older West seemed to be outmoded on America's last frontier. In view of his bitter experiences, the farmer of the Middle Border cannot be blamed for laying his sufferings at the door of external forces over which he had no control—not the weather only, but railways, elevator companies, jobbers, commission agents, land and finance companies, banks and trusts: the baleful agents of an impersonal, monopolistic and eastern capitalism, intent on defrauding him of his livelihood.

Each advance to the West was followed by painful adjustments not merely on the frontier, but in older agricultural regions which felt the competition from the bumper harvests of virgin soils dumped on the market by the railway. As the wheat frontier moved northwest, farmers in Indiana and Illinois turned to raise maize to fatten pigs and cattle; Germans in Wisconsin began to specialize in dairy farming; and Californians, who in the 1870s had raised enormous crops of wheat, followed the example of western New York before it by turning in the 1880s to that production of fruit and vegetables which has become one of the chief industries of the Pacific coast.

With the frontier's disappearance, the relative scarcity of new land and the disastrous experience of over-extension at last gave pause to this prodigal and spendthrift people. About the turn of the century, State and Federal governments stepped in to protect the wasting resources of the continent by reserving mineral rights, preserving and replanting timber, controlling floods and, through the U.S. Department of Agriculture, teaching farmers to cherish the soil and by such means as crop rotation, contour ploughing, and the renewal of vegetation, to prevent it being blown and washed away. With the use of fertilizers, irrigation, heavy machinery and stock breeding, farming became a more intensive and specialized

[1] F. A. Shannon, *op. cit.* Appendix.

business. Whereas the average value of farm land and buildings per acre increased only from 16·3 dollars to nearly 20 dollars in the forty years before 1900, it reached almost 70 dollars in 1920.[1] Agriculture became a consolidated interest in the nation's economy.

This specialization revolutionized both the marketing of farm produce and the making and selling of all kinds of manufactured goods needed by the farmer. In the lands colonized by the railway, buying and selling was concentrated hundreds of miles away, at the termini of the sprawling railway systems at Kansas City, Omaha, the Twin Cities and, above all, Chicago—great cities on the doorstep of the plains, market towns for half a continent. Such was the overwhelming volume of produce rolling east, and such the prairies' need for furnishings, that the old familiar order of rural middlemen was replaced by a complex of large-scale and highly-specialized industries which transformed the household economy both on the farm and in the city.

With the rise of the cattle empire, the centre of meat packing shifted from Cincinnati to Chicago and beyond to a whole range of slaughtering centres from St Paul and Des Moines in the north to Omaha and Kansas City in the south. The millers followed the advancing wheat frontier from Rochester and Buffalo to Chicago in the 1860s, and thence north-west to Minneapolis in the 1870s. The freight trains from the prairies, which converged on the marshalling yards of Minneapolis or Chicago, carrying annually millions of bushels of grain and hundreds of thousands of head of cattle, threatened to overwhelm existing facilities, but they also presented a supreme opportunity to enterprising business men in the decade after the Civil War. What the rails brought, they could distribute to the four corners of the continent by large-scale methods of processing. In Chicago, Nelson, Armour and the Yankee Swift who moved out west from Boston, used their profits from Civil War contracts to revolutionize meat packing. Pioneering with overhead belt conveyors and rationalized lay-outs, these firms in Chicago and its satellite towns slaughtered beef and pork with a scientific precision which utilized every part of the animal for the table and for innumerable by-products from lard to tennis rackets. Pioneering

[1] *Hist. Stats.*, Series E, 4.

with refrigerated freight cars, they distributed chilled meat across the continent, putting local butchers out of business. In Minneapolis, Pillsbury and Washburne perfected new techniques which enabled the mills at the Falls of St Anthony to distribute cheap, standardized flours to local stores from Georgia to Oregon.

Under the stimulus of the bonanza from the prairies, these millers, packers and canners started a chain of innovations in food processing which led directly to the modern packaged, canned, baked and frozen foods sold to the housewife, not by anachronistic butchers, bakers and grocers, but in a multiple supermarket. Germans in St Louis and Milwaukee took advantage of the abundant grain to brew light, lager beers, which became a national drink, not only for their nostalgic fellow-immigrants, but for native Americans.

It was the same with industries supplying the farmer's own wants. Cyrus McCormick had moved his reaper factory to Chicago from western New York as early as 1847 and by the 1870s McCormick's and other firms in Illinois were supplying the most remote farmer by rail with brightly painted machinery of steel, mass-produced by means of standardized, interchangeable parts. Thus an entirely new agricultural machinery industry replaced the blacksmith on the frontier and transformed him in older communities into a mechanic and a selling agent for big firms operating on a national scale.

The supply of agricultural machinery was not alone in being revolutionized by railway colonization. The plains farmer ordered his household wants from distant suppliers at the other end of the railway line where his needs stimulated a characteristic response. In 1872, Montgomery Ward, a travelling salesman in Chicago, hit on the idea of selling dry goods to farmers by post. Beginning in the loft of a livery stable, he was so successful that he extended his business to a hundred and one cheap, mass-produced articles.[1] Blue jeans, saucepans, farm implements, ordered from a temptingly illustrated catalogue, were delivered by rail and, after 1896 when the U.S. Government introduced rural free delivery, by the mailman's buggy, to many a farm mailbox at the edge of an isolated country road. Sears Roebuck, Montgomery Ward, and other mail-order

[1] See *DAB*.

firms expanded their business so rapidly that by the twentieth century their names were household words in poorer homes, not merely on the plains but in the east where the general storekeeper found himself starved for business by this combination of railway and mammoth warehouse.

The railways not only colonized a new west, but, by fostering a continental market, began that process whereby American life ceased to be rural, local and diverse and became, in important respects, national and standardized. The butcher, the baker, the candlestick maker,[1] not to mention the miller, the blacksmith and those other 'Happy Family' characters, the grocer and the brewer, capitulated to great economic empires like General Mills, Armour's, International Harvester, Montgomery Ward, Budweiser, the Atlantic & Pacific Tea Company, and Standard Oil. And with this specialization went the rise in the Middle West of great cities devoted to the handling of a nation's merchandise. Of these Chicago, with its stockyards, grain elevators, wheat exchange, docks and railway grid, stands supreme. By 1900, Chicago, with a population of a million and a half, had grown within living memory from a lake-side settlement of log cabins to be the second city in the United States. It had also become the true metropolis of the continent's heartland, with a newly authentic American spirit, voiced by its own poet, Carl Sandburg, son of a Swedish immigrant, who apostrophized his city thus:

> Hog Butcher for the World,
> Tool maker, Stacker of Wheat,
> Player with Railroads and the Nation's freight Handler;
> Stormy, husky, brawling,
> City of the Big Shoulders.[2]

Chicago got her brash, cocky spirit from the conquerors of the prairies, exultant in their power to control the rich and diverse resources of a continent. But the speed of that conquest still depended on the pull of unseen forces far beyond that distant continental horizon. The plains farmer, in his bitter struggle to survive, might recognize no other forces than the elemental buffets of nature and

[1] For the candlestick maker see ch. ix following.
[2] Carl Sandburg, *Chicago Poems* (New York, 1916).

the chicanery of middlemen; but those hard, clever or merely lucky adventurers who played the wheat pit or the fat stock market in Chicago were conscious that their chances in business depended on the telegraphic advices they received from across the oceans, from Liverpool, Odessa or Buenos Aires. The American frontier was still the frontier of Europe, and the pace of western advance was determined by what the increasingly industrialized countries of western Europe, especially Great Britain, could absorb. Despite the increased consumption of the American population, which grew from 35 million in 1865 to 76 million in 1900, over a third of the American wheat crop was shipped abroad in the latter year, most of it to western Europe; and in 1906 the export of beef products reached a peak of 732 million pounds.[1] The railway which brought grain to Minneapolis carried flour thence to a British tramp loading at Baltimore. Refrigerated cars carried fresh beef from Chicago to eastern cities; refrigerated steamers carried it a further three thousand miles to Liverpool and London. During the '80s and '90s, cheap American grains and beef, blanketing the English market, contributed to the prolonged depression which radically altered the pattern of British farming. British landlords, impelled by this impact to invest in American cattle ranching, added their money to the British funds already crossing the Atlantic to promote prairie railways or mining companies. Farmers and labourers, no longer able to make a living in England, joined a new exodus across the Atlantic to the United States. Thus even this last frontier of the United States on the remote continental plains, over two thousand miles from the eastern seaboard, bore an intimate relation to a wider, Atlantic world.

But the very frontier conditions which enabled American wheat and beef for a time to hold their own in western Europe determined that this should be only a transient phase of American farming. After about 1890, the pace of competition in world markets came to be set by other countries where the conditions of a moving frontier still obtained—by western Canada, where the wheat frontier was but an extension of that of the United States, by

[1] *Statistical Abstract of the United States*; W. Trimble, 'Historical Aspects of the Surplus Food Problem of the United States 1867–1902', *American Historical Association, Annual Report, 1918*.

Argentina and Australia. In 1912 the United States was exporting only 12 per cent of her wheat crop; the export of cattle dropped from over half a million head in 1904–6 to 18,000 in 1914; and by the latter year the U.S. was beginning to be a net importer of beef. The American farmer had to undergo a painful adjustment, trimming his efforts to the needs of a largely domestic market. The disappearance of the frontier radically altered his relation, not merely to American society, but to the Atlantic community as a whole.

CHAPTER IX

FROM WILDCATTING TO MONOPOLY
1850-1914

'The old nations of the earth creep on at a snail's pace; the Republic thunders past with the rush of the express.'

ANDREW CARNEGIE, *Triumphant Democracy* (1886).

IN 1816 a Committee of the United States Senate reported that it was as cheap to bring goods three thousand miles from Britain as to carry them thirty miles overland: 'A coalmine may exist in the United States not more than ten miles from valuable ores of iron and other materials, and both of them be useless until a canal is established between them, as the price of land carriage is too great to be borne by either.'[1] When coal from Virginia had difficulty in competing with coal from South Wales, it was little wonder that Americans relied on the iron, machinery and hardware of Birmingham and Sheffield. Until bulky raw materials could be hauled cheaply overland, seaborne commerce helped to preserve the agrarian character of American life. Only when canals and railways had knit together a single market out of local communities scattered over half a continent did heavy industry migrate across the Atlantic. In particular, it was the railway—itself the product of iron, coal and steam—which provided the prime force behind America's unprecedented industrial growth.

Until mid-century Americans drew their raw materials principally from forest, soil and ocean. Their houses, ships, even roads, were made of pine, oak or chestnut; their rooms were warmed by wood-burning stoves and lit by candles or lamps, the tallow or oil for which came from whales; their wagons and machinery were

[1] G. R. Taylor, *op. cit.* p. 132.

greased by vegetable fats and harnessed with leather and hemp rope; the wheels of their grist mills were turned by water. The mining of coal, iron and lead was still a parochial business. Coal was carried by canal barge from the Alleghenies to heat the homes of Philadelphia and from Philadelphia, by schooner to New York; but the cost of its freight still prohibited the use of steam in most of New England's cotton mills. Small, up-country furnaces continued to smelt bog ore into wrought iron for rural blacksmiths by means of charcoal burnt in the bountiful forest.

The railway of the 1850s, however, demanded iron, copper and coal; and by bringing iron ore to coal and enabling manufactures to be concentrated in towns, increased America's industrial potential. Anthracite and then coke, carried by rail from the Allegheny fields, fired the furnaces of Pennsylvania. In 1849, an Indian named Majigigig led prospectors to the literally named 'Iron Mountain' in the wilderness of northern Michigan. Ten years later, railway tracks to the shores of Lakes Michigan and Superior made it possible to bring richer ores from the new mines of Marquette and Menominie nearly a thousand miles by steamer across the Great Lakes to the Erie ports and thence by rail to the western gateway of the Appalachian coalfields at Pittsburgh which became the centre of the iron trade. This iron ore 'frontier' took another leap westwards in the 1890s beyond the furthermost reach of Lake Superior to northern Minnesota. Here, on the fabulous Mesabi Range, ore was, and is, obtained not by arduous underground mining but by using steam shovels to scoop the rich iron-earth into freight cars bound for lake steamers at Duluth. Superior ores—80 per cent of America's total in 1913[1]—were responsible for a tenfold increase in production in the thirty years after 1875 and encouraged the U.S. Steel Corporation in 1907 to build a new steel manufacturing town at Gary, on Lake Michigan, five hundred miles west of its Pittsburgh headquarters. The copper-mining 'frontier' moved even farther west. New England shipwrights got their copper sheathing from small, local deposits until in the mid-'40s railways created a copper-mining boom in Michigan. By the time of the Civil War, copper from the Calumet mine, delivered by rail and ship to the smelters

[1] V. S. Clark, *History of Manufactures in the United States* (New York, 1929), vol. III, p. 18.

of Bridgeport, Connecticut, and later of Cleveland on Lake Erie, provided copper and brass for the castings, piping and wire of the young engineering industry. Twenty years later the building of the Northern, and Southern Pacific railways made possible large-scale copper mining in Montana and Arizona, and copper production jumped from 30,000 tons to 130,000 tons in ten years.[1]

When in the 1850s Americans began to feel the lack of cheaper illuminants and lubricants than the products of the whale, petroleum oil was a quack Indian remedy. But in the summer of 1859, a certain Colonel Drake drilled an adapted salt-boring rod through the oil-saturated earth at Titusville in the Pennsylvania mountains to a lake of subterranean petroleum. The resulting fountain of oil was the signal for a new and most gruelling race for the prizes of industrial wealth. Within three years a flock of 'wildcatters', fighting for claims and risking a hideous death from explosion, had made of Pithole Creek a grotesque forest of derricks and had started a wild oil boom on the Philadelphia exchange. But getting oil out of the ground was one thing; marketing it was another. To cart barrels over mountain roads or to float them down the Allegheny River was tedious and expensive. Not until branch railway lines had connected the oil region with trunk railways at Pittsburgh and Erie was the refining of oil possible on an extensive scale. The oil industry was the creature of the railway. The cost of pumping and refining was negligible beside that of transporting the bulky, heavy liquid, even by the newly invented tank car, over the long distances from well to refinery and from refinery to consumer. Favourable railway rates were vital to oil refiners; and the lower rates which Cleveland could command, owing to the competition of two railways and lake shipping, enabled that lake-side city to wrest the leadership in refining from Pittsburgh which was at the mercy of a single railway.

The oil frontier also began to push westwards. So quickly were the early oil reservoirs exhausted that Pithole City which, at the height of the boom, had a bigger postal business than any other Pennsylvania city except Philadelphia, reverted to an open wheat field. In 1891, over 31 million barrels of oil were pumped from the Pennsylvania mountains; but thereafter the pace was set by new

[1] *Hist. Stats.*, Series G, 112.

fields farther west: by Ohio in 1895, and then, about the turn of the century, by far-off California which increased its production to 73 million barrels in 1910. Still later, oil from newer fields in Texas, Oklahoma, Louisiana and Illinois entered the nation's pipeline in response to a revolutionary demand for petrol for motor-cars which came just when, through the growing use of electricity, urban oil lighting declined. This development strengthened in a new way the uniquely close connection between oil and transport in American life. But that belongs to a later chapter. Before 1910, apart from what went into machine oil and axle grease, most of the annual 200 million barrels or so of oil from American wells was consumed in homes where cheap oil fuel was a boon. In prairie farmhouses kerosene stoves warmed kitchens and cooked the food and kerosene lamps provided for the first time an adequate pool of light for evening reading round the family table.

At this time, it was said, many of the whalers of New Bedford, Massachusetts, with generations of seafaring blood in their veins, sold their ships and gear and invested the proceeds in the oil wells of Pennsylvania.[1] At the same call, two English immigrants, Maurice Clark and Samuel Andrews, with experience in refining vegetable oils, formed a partnership in 1863 with a twenty-six year old commission dealer in Cleveland called Rockefeller to enter the refining business. Within a decade, oil manufactured by the Rockefeller firm was lighting English homes and lubricating English locomotives. Once again, with important results for both sides of the Atlantic, the pull of the continent proved stronger than that of the ocean in the careers of Yankees and Englishmen.

The exploitation of the continent's mineral wealth made possible the migration of heavy industry across the Atlantic. As we saw in Chapter IV the first machine-driven, factory-housed industry to be established on the western shores of the Atlantic was cotton. By 1850 the American textile industries had passed far beyond the 'colonial' stage, although wool lagged behind cotton. From early days British machinery had been improved upon and superseded by important native inventions such as ring spinning, which was

---

[1] E. P. Oberholtzer, *United States since the Civil War* (New York, 1917–26), vol. I, p. 255.

already beginning to make Lancashire mill-owners take notice. The factory system of Waltham, Massachusetts, was more integrated than that of Oldham, Lancashire, and skilled artisans from the Pennines were now less conspicuous. The industry, which consumed something like a quarter of the cotton crop, supplied the home market with most of its coarser cloths.

American machine shops were beginning to turn out articles which impressed the world with their ingenuity. At the Great Exhibition of 1851 British manufacturers were impressed by the McCormick reaper and the Singer sewing machine. These two inventions were the first ambassadors of a characteristically American technique which was in time to transform the industrial productivity of the western world. 'Already', wrote Professor Clapham, 'the well-informed knew that an American was more likely than an Englishman to get tiresome and expensive handicraft operations done for him by machinery.'[1] In the 1850s the manufacture of standard articles by means of interchangeable parts, invented by Eli Whitney, perfected by Samuel Colt, and extended from small arms to clocks and watches at one end of the scale and farm machinery at the other, made possible also the sewing machine which, in turn, revolutionized the making of clothing and boots and shoes. And experience in making the accurate gauges, calipers and cutting tools involved created that vital prerequisite to modern engineering, a machine-tool industry.

But until the Civil War these advances were limited. It is true that the twin influence of the railway, marrying coal to iron ore and demanding iron for rails and rolling stock, greatly expanded the iron trade. More up-to-date methods crossed the Atlantic. The immigrant David Thomas had brought the technique of anthracite smelting from South Wales to Pennsylvania in 1839 and his example encouraged hundreds of his fellow-countrymen to bring their skills and talent for choral singing to Scranton and Wilkesbarre. As a result furnaces and rolling mills began to turn out the heavier iron needed for railways ten times as fast as the old charcoal furnaces and foundries had done; and in the '60s the production of pig-iron

[1] Sir John Clapham, *An Economic History of Modern Britain* (Cambridge, 1952), vol. II, p. 12.

more than doubled.[1] But domestic production was not cheap enough to choke off the flow of railway iron from Britain which, in spite of the high tariff of 1862, continued to play a prominent part in railway construction for another twenty years. In 1860 the iron trade ranked only sixth among American industries, being less important than timber and flour milling[2]; and industry as a whole occupied the energies of only a minority of Americans, of whom sixty per cent were still engaged in agriculture and a high proportion of the rest in commerce and transport.[3] The industrial advance of the '50s was a mere portent of what was to come.

The Civil War marks a new departure. It was not simply that war demands were a tonic for engineers, ironmasters, canners, boot, shoe and clothing men who found themselves, after Appomatox, with capital and plant ready to capture new markets in West and South. The triumph of the Republican Party gave the manufacturer his chance in American public life. Secession meant the final eclipse of those mercantile interests which had hitherto dominated commerce and politics. The cotton Whigs of New York, committed to an Atlantic trade based on the southern staple and the continental distribution of imported manufactures, found themselves crowded off the stage by a thrusting class of industrialists, determined to use their capital and 'know-how', not to trade, but to manufacture and sell. These gentry were obsessed, not with the Atlantic, but with the continent and its wealth of raw materials and 30 million consumers. Through spokesmen like Simon Cameron, the wealthy ironmaster-politician of Pennsylvania who became Lincoln's first Secretary of War, this class wrote a new and radical version of the American system into the programme of the Republican Party. The Pacific Railway Act of 1862, reaffirming in a new guise the old national policy of internal improvements, set the framework for completing the continent's transport system. The National Bank Act of the following year, by substituting Federally-chartered for State-chartered banks, provided a more stable network of credit. In 1864 a contract labour law, counteracting the safety-valve mechanism of

---

[1] *Hist. Stats.*, Series G, 96.
[2] Taylor, *op. cit.* p. 245.
[3] *Hist. Stats.*, Series D, 4–5.

the Homestead Act, encouraged industrialists to make use of cheap, immigrant labour, by permitting them to import European and Chinese workers under contract to work at what often amounted to sweated wages, a practice reminiscent of indentured service. Although the Morrill Tariff of 1861 was designed merely to provide the Government with war funds, the influence of manufacturers' lobbies so increased duties on imported manufactures that by 1865 the average rate had doubled and some commodities were taxed at as much as 100 per cent of their value. With the return of peace, such was the mood of impatient optimism, so great were the prizes of industrial enterprise and so tempting the bribes which seeped into Washington from business profits, that for a generation the politician became virtually the servant of the business man.

After Appomatox a new surge of westward expansion gave increased momentum to the economy. The central factor in that expansion was the railway. It was the demand of the railway for rails, bridging, locomotives and rolling stock which was to transform the modest iron trade of 1860 into the great steel industry of 1900; and it was steel which, in the ramifications of this chain reaction, was to industrialize American society.

When in 1864 young Andrew Carnegie, son of an immigrant Scots handloom weaver, returned from wartime railway duties in Washington he decided to leave the Pennsylvania Railroad, in which he had risen from telegraphist to divisional superintendent, in order to join one of the Pennsylvania's engineers in the building of iron bridges. With his railway connections Carnegie was soon manufacturing bridges and rails for the Pennsylvania and other lines. Carnegie was an upstart ironmaster in an established industry; but his rapid rise was symptomatic of the close relation of iron and railways. During the first post-bellum railway boom, which culminated in the collapse of 1873, the demand for railway iron seemed insatiable. In the four years ending in 1873, 25,000 miles of new track were laid, considerably more than half the entire mileage in 1868. As a result, pig-iron production more than trebled between 1860 and 1873 when it approached three million tons, of which more than half went into railways.

But iron was only a first step. In spite of the tariff and domestic production, the import of British rails increased over seven times in the five years after the War.[1] One reason was that most of these rails were made of steel. In 1873, Andrew Carnegie, when selling American railway bonds in England, was impressed by the record of a steel rail in use at Camden Town Station after wear which had broken down seventeen iron rails, and decided to take advantage of the Schenck Tariff of 1871 to turn over to steel. Carnegie was a laggard in this, believing that 'pioneering doesn't pay'. The principle of making steel cheap enough, not merely for needles and sword blades but rails, had been worked out by an American iron-master, William Kelly; but conditions were not ripe for its develop-ment. The wartime desire to convert the Union's ironclad monitors to steel armour led to the introduction from England of the superior Bessemer process which manufactured steel by subjecting molten pig-iron to a blast of hot air. The new accessibility of Lake Superior ores, which had the necessary low phosphorus content, enabled a number of firms to begin making steel and by 1873 American Bessemer 'converters' were turning out some 140,000 tons of steel a year, 85 per cent in the form of rails.[2] Even the long depression of the mid-'70s failed to stunt the industry's growth; and in the subsequent prosperity the half-million tons of 1877 were dwarfed by the two and a half million of 1886 when, only twenty years after the erection of the first pilot plant, the United States replaced Great Britain as the greatest steel producer in the world.[3] By the turn of the century the Carnegie Steel Company alone produced four-fifths as much steel as the entire British industry.

British business men had been sceptical about American indus-trialization. In 1866 Sir Morton Peto, the railway engineer, after visiting the United States to survey the prospects for British invest-ment in American railways, still maintained that 'it is on corn and cotton and not on manufacture that America has to place depend-ence'.[4] In 1874 a Middlesbrough ironmaster, Sir Lowthian Bell, stoutly asserted that iron would never be made more cheaply in the United States than in Britain because of the high cost of labour and

[1] V. S. Clark, *op. cit.* vol. II, pp. 74, 88–9.
[2] *Ibid.* vol. II, p. 75.
[3] *Ibid.* vol. II, p. 247.
[4] Sir Morton Peto, *The Resources and Prospects of America* (London, 1866), p. 400.

of transporting ore to coal.[1] But these pronouncements were not
without historic irony. Already freight cars running on Middlesbrough rails and financed by British capital were making it economic to yoke ore and coal beds a third of a continent apart. Before
long the steel men of Britain, feeling the competition in their
American markets, were singing a different song. In 1891 a Yorkshire ironmaster, Sir James Kitson, was forced to admit the reasons
for the sudden and unexpected transatlantic mastery. He concluded
that although Americans depended largely on British inventions
they had improved upon them and, 'studying their competitors
abroad in a way that British makers would not deign to study their
competitors in America, they profited by the errors of their rivals'.[2]
American business men had conquered a multitude of problems in
their own fashion. An expanding continental market encouraged
them to 'think big', and to invest their profits in building even
larger blast furnaces, more up-to-date rolling mills. Carnegie had a
new steel mill dismantled and rebuilt because his lieutenant, Charles
Schwab, had learnt from its construction a way of saving a dollar,
instead of the fifty cents, per ton on the output of the original
design.[3] There was a drive for maximum output which taxed the
resources of masters and furnacemen. Carnegie forced the pace by
causing a broom to be hoisted over the most productive furnace.
When one furnace broke all records his telegraphic comment was
simply 'what were the other ten furnaces doing?'[4] Better equipment and a ruthless drive increased the output per man of American
blast furnaces thirty times between 1850 and 1919, and the price of
steel rails fell from 160 dollars a ton in 1875 to 17 dollars in 1898.[5]
An American furnace produced twice as much as the equivalent
furnace on Tyneside. At a dinner of British manufacturers in the
'90s, Carnegie, in response to a complacent speech about the excel-
lence of British equipment, told British ironmasters what he
thought to be amiss with their steel trade: 'Most British equipment

[1] Clark, op. cit. vol. II, p. 286.
[2] Reported by Clark, op. cit. vol. II, p. 311.
[3] Charles M. Schwab, 'Andrew Carnegie, His Methods with His Men', quoted in
B. J. Hendrick, The Life of Andrew Carnegie (London, 1933), p. 408.
[4] Hendrick, op. cit. p. 182.
[5] C. W. Wright, op. cit. p. 583.

is in use twenty years after it should have been scrapped. It is because you keep this used-up machinery that the U.S. is making you a back number.'[1] The best American steelmen had, indeed, made their mills, in Kitson's words, 'models of arrangement and efficiency'. The old shortage of skilled craftsmen had become a blessing in disguise. It had forced American ingenuity to devise labour-saving machinery and rationalized lay-outs which permitted the employment, at low wages, of those unskilled immigrants from Eastern Europe whom America's industrial prosperity had attracted to the United States. Machine methods also, in time, created a new cadre of machine-minded operators even more valuable than the old-fashioned craftsman. As Kitson put it: 'The high standard . . . especially of technical education . . . undoubtedly is much to their advantage.'[2]

The most spectacular example of transatlantic migration was tin-plate. American manufacturers of tin cans for the petroleum and food-processing industries imported their tinplate from South Wales where the method of tinning steel plates had been perfected. Taking advantage of the McKinley Tariff of 1890, the can manufacturers determined to make their own tinplate, importing for the purpose Welsh technicians. The experiment prospered so well that within two years over three million pounds of tinplate was being manufactured by nineteen works.[3] The marriage of cheap domestic steel with an expanding market for canned goods was consummated. The McKinley Tariff and the low cost achieved by American producers through superior manufacturing techniques, in spite of a far heavier wages bill, had a devastating effect on the industry in South Wales where old-fashioned craft methods were employed to make tinplate largely for the American market. American imports rapidly died out and the Welsh industry was badly hit. Several Welsh tin-plate firms moved across the Atlantic taking with them hundreds of immigrant Welsh tin-platers. Thus basic, heavy industry was attracted to the United States and another stage in the expansion of Europe into North America was complete.

[1] Hendrick, *op. cit.* p. 407.
[2] Clark, *op. cit.* vol. II, p. 311.
[3] *Ibid.* vol. II, pp. 372–6.

Meanwhile, the furnaces and rolling mills which darkened the skies and grimed the hilly streets of Pittsburgh were turning out iron and steel so cheap as to invite a multitude of new uses. Orders for rails might be reduced to those needed for replacements; but the Baldwin and other companies did not lack orders for ever heavier locomotives and rolling stock which, along with such varied components as boilers, steel shafting and armour plating, immensely expanded the heavy engineering industry. When in 1888 the Carnegie Company acquired the giant steel works at Homestead the new plant was entirely converted from the production of rails to that of structural shapes for bridges and buildings. Iron and steel came to the aid of the now densely populated cities in the form of standardized iron girders for that wonder of the New World, the Brooklyn Bridge, and for the elevated railways and six-storey buildings of New York. But conventional buildings of six storeys were dwarfed in Chicago by the erection in 1891 of a towering structure of steel girders, the cantilevered framework of the new twenty-storey Masonic Temple. The skyscraper revolutionized urban building and made it possible to house, in busy 'downtown' areas of great cities, the inflated office staffs which transacted the expanding business of America by means of telephones and typewriters, inventions which themselves were the product of pressed steel, copper wire, electricity and the principle of interchangeable parts. When Taft became President in 1909 the railway had ceased to be the chief impulse in American economic life and the ramifications of iron and steel were lost in an acceleration of industrial change brought about by a multiplicity of interacting factors from electricity and machine production on the one hand to capital aggregations and the appetites of an increasingly urban people on the other.

Overnight, it seemed, this nation of farmers and horse traders had mastered the intricate mysteries of a technical civilization. During the twenty years after 1870 the United States experienced the most rapid rate of industrial growth the world had seen. By 1900 the greatest producer of raw materials and foodstuffs had also become the greatest manufacturer. In the 1870s farming contributed 20 per cent, mining and manufacturing only 14 per cent, to the national income; but thirty years later the farming contribution, reduced to 16 per cent, was equalled by that of finance and surpassed by the contribution of 21 per cent from mining and manufacturing. The American people multiplied from 40 million in 1870 to 92 million in 1910. Although of this teeming increase many an Ohio farmer or Swedish immigrant tried his hand at pioneering in the new West, many more farmers from Vermont or New Jersey or immigrants from Poland or Wales moved into the industrial centres of the East and the Middle West. In 1860 sixty per cent of the Americans who worked were on farms and only 26 per cent in industry and transport; whereas in 1900 only 37 per cent were on farms and some 46 per cent in industry and transport.[1] There also grew up a new order of industrial centres like the coalmining towns of West Virginia, the iron towns of Pennsylvania or the light engineering towns of New England. The population of the great cities was swollen by a new influx of workers employed, for instance, in the clothing trades and machine shops of New York, the copper works of Cleveland or the steel mills of Chicago. In the last forty years of the nineteenth century the towns and cities of the United States grew more than twice as fast as the nation as a whole; and in 1900 they housed about a third of the American people.[2] In the East especially, the number of towns 'gave to the entire region a strongly urban cast',[3] and already in 1890 four out of every five persons in Massachusetts were townsfolk. Of the great metropolitan cities, New York, Chicago and Philadelphia, each had over a million citizens. Brightly lit shops, restaurants and theatres dazzled the farmer in from the country. Electric trams, overhead railways and the underground—copied by Boston from London and Budapest—carried office workers down town to the ten- and twenty-storeyed buildings where, with ticker tape and telephone, they transacted the business of an entire continent. It was little wonder that Broadway and the Chicago Loop, with their quickened pulse, their variety and sophistication, should attract, as they still attract, a yearly influx of career seekers, like characters in a Dreiser novel, disillusioned with the prospects of Main Street or the farm. By the

[1] P. K. Whelpton, 'Occupational Groups in the United States. 1820–1920', *Journal of the American Statistical Association*, XXI, No. 155; quoted in Shannon, *op. cit.* p. 351.
[2] Shannon, *op. cit.* p. 357.
[3] A. M. Schlesinger, *The Rise of the City 1878–98* (New York, 1933), p. 68.

turn of the present century the farmer had become a somewhat forlorn figure in American life. The new romance of business had dispelled the old romantic ideal of the American countryman. Once
the unique object of Jeffersonian aspiration, the farmer had become
little more than a 'hick', 'hayseed', a figure of music-hall fun. His
place in American folklore had been usurped by a new stereotype:
the white-collared business man.

The cult of business owed its power to the example of the tycoon.
Before the Civil War there were few really rich men and the fortunes of these were, on the whole, modest. Of the hundred or so
millionaires, most of whom had made their money in foreign trade
or land speculation, only a handful could even approach the twenty
million dollars fortune, made in furs and multiplied in Manhattan
property, which John Jacob Astor bequeathed to his children in
1848.[1] Fifty years later a new social order of wealth had been created
out of the exploited resources of the continent. Fortunes made in
real estate, like Marshall Field's in Chicago; in timber, like the
Weyerhaeuysers'; in milling, like the Pillsburys'; in meat-packing
like the Armours'; in mining or simply in speculating in the wheat
pit, brought an aristocracy of *nouveaux riches* to the Gold Coast of
Chicago or San Francisco's Nob Hill. Still greater riches from
railways, steel, copper or oil proved an irresistible weapon in the
hands of the *arrivistes* who clamoured for admission to the glittering
society of New York's Four Hundred or the summer season at Newport. Here the princely families of industry vied with each other in
conspicuous display the like of which had never been seen before,
even at Versailles or St Petersburg. Men in silk hats and piped
waistcoats emerged from Fifth Avenue mansions reminiscent of the
châteaux of Touraine. In one of them Henry Frick, the steel
millionaire, was wont to sit, turning the leaves of the *Saturday
Evening Post*, on a canopied throne of the Renaissance, surrounded
by great masters exported to him by Duveen of London. George
Vanderbilt erected a palace at Asheville, N.C., with forty master
bedrooms, a banqueting hall and a court of palms, and spent more
money on his estate there than Congress appropriated to the U.S.
Department of Agriculture. It was the whim of Mrs Belmont to

[1] Taylor, *op. cit.* pp. 394–5.

construct a Chinese lacquer tea-house on the cliffs at Newport to which tea was brought by a concealed miniature railway from the pantry of her house.[1] Such were the visible tokens of the fabulous wealth disposed of by these masters of American capital. Carnegie's annual income at the time he retired was twenty-five million; and if Carnegie was the richest of them all there must have been a score or so with more than a hundred million capital. The wealth of these magnates was in effect untold, since it was impossible to capitalize accurately the true extent of their holdings; and the power they exerted over American life was revolutionary. Their position was the result of concentration of capital inherent in the process of industrial growth.

The story of that concentration begins in the little court off Lombard Street in the City of London where, in 1837, George Peabody had started that merchandising business which was to be the foundation of his career as a merchant banker, financing Anglo-American trade and selling American railway bonds. In 1864 the firm passed into the hands of another Yankee dry-goods trader, Junius S. Morgan, who brought it new power and authority in 1870 by successfully underwriting a formidable French government loan. A year later Morgan's clever, mathematically-minded son, John Pierpont, who had been sent to represent the firm in New York, organized there the banking house of Drexel, Morgan and Co. American business still depended on British capital for its expanding activities. British funds were forcing the pace of railway building with all that this meant for the migration of heavy industry across the Atlantic, and for settling the Greater West whence the movement of crops was, in turn, financed by British credits. By 1910 some 6,000 million dollars of foreign capital was invested in American enterprise, well over half of it British.[2] The migration of capital across the Atlantic was a basic, formative condition of the industrial transformation of the United States; and it is hardly surprising that we should turn to Lombard Street for the original impulse to that capital concentration which was ultimately to release

[1] These examples have been selected from F. L. Allen, *The Big Change. America Transforms Itself 1900–50* (London, 1952).
[2] Sir George Paish: 'The Trade Balance of the United States', *National Monetary Commission Document No. 579* (Washington, D.C., 1910), pp. 173–5.

Wall Street from the Old World's leading strings. Pierpont Morgan's powerful London connection gave the start to a career which was to end in domination of the American money market.

Within a few years the Morgan combination, by successfully refunding the U.S. Government's Civil War debt, reopened this American market to British investors. Morgan thereupon turned his forceful talents to American railways. In 1879 he rescued William Vanderbilt by secretly disposing of a quarter of a million of his New York Central shares to British clients of Junius Morgan; and he soon followed this first venture by more active intervention. As shown above, the generation of Gould, Huntington and Russell Sage, always speculators, not operators, had played ducks and drakes with the American railway system. Competing lines bled each other white in ruinous rate wars. Even where the volume of traffic justified the heavy investment, profiteering from stock manipulation ruined sound roads and sometimes almost brought traffic to a standstill. Most railway stock was heavily watered, and in the panic of 1893 more than half of the country's railway mileage went into receivership. The good name in London of the House of Morgan, resting as it did on the gleaming prospects of America, was in jeopardy. For, in John Moody's words, the Morgans had always been 'bulls on America'.[1] Therefore, to protect the investments of his British and other clients, 'Jupiter' Morgan took on his broad shoulders the affairs of railway after railway, reorganizing their finances and management, raising new capital, buying up competing lines and consolidating each group he handled into a single, economic unit exercising effective and often monopolistic control over a growing traffic region. What began as a means to an end became an end in itself. By acquiring blocks of voting shares Morgan emerged in the '90s as the august controller of a continent-wide network of railways which included such giants as the Northern Pacific, the Erie and the Southern. In addition he had a powerful voice in the affairs of the New York Central, the Baltimore and Ohio and other lines.

Morgan was not, however, the only banker to build an empire by reorganizing moribund railways. Another New Yorker, Edward H. Harriman, after pocketing the votes of an important group of

[1] See J. Moody, *Masters of Capital* (New Haven, 1919), p. 29.

Dutch stockholders, insinuated himself into the direction of the
Illinois Central and with a mortgage on this revived company
annexed the bankrupt Union Pacific to a network which began to
reach across the continent. At this point he met his match in another
railway chieftain, James J. Hill, who, to the north, was building up a
parallel satrapy from the Pacific to the Mississippi. Hill started, not
as a banker, but as a railroader. Canadian-born, he joined two British
adventurers, George Stephen and Donald Alexander Smith, in
building the Great Northern from Duluth to Seattle.[1] From the
profits of his well-run railway Hill acquired important interests in
New York's First National Bank and in Morgan's Northern Pacific
which flanked his route to the south. Whereupon in 1900 Harriman,
after a vain attempt to come to terms with Hill over a joint monopoly of railway traffic in the Greater West, set about defeating his
rival by quietly buying up Northern Pacific stock in the open market, an operation which meant finding between eighty and a hundred million dollars in cash. It was a battle of titans. James Hill,
who learnt from the ticker tape of the gyrations of his Northern
Pacific stock while railroading in the Pacific North-west, cleared
the line for his private train, which broke the record between
Seattle and the Mississippi on the way to New York.[2] Here his
fight with Harriman to buy up stock created a wild boom on the
exchange which brought its nemesis in a spectacular panic. Only a
last-minute truce between the two averted the ruin of the entire
banking and broking structure of Wall Street. This truce lasted
until the return from Europe of Morgan, with whom Hill was
already associated and whose commanding financial power alone
could resolve the deadlock. In 1901 Morgan arranged a compromise. Harriman and Hill were given joint control of the
Northern Pacific and the Great Northern by means of a gigantic
holding corporation with 400 million dollars capital called the
Northern Securities Company. This great merger, which put an
end to railway competition throughout the Greater West, was the
coping to Morgan's imposing edifice of railway consolidation. The

[1] Stephen and Smith, who were cousins, after making fortunes in Canada, ended
their careers in the House of Lords as Lords Mount Stephen and Strathcona.
[2] G. Kennan, *E. H. Harriman* (New York, 1922), vol. I, p. 303.

important railways of the entire continent were now grouped into five great systems under the control of one set of financial powers. Morgan's doctrine of a 'community of interest' to create order and a steady profit out of chaos and ruthless competition could go no further.

Harriman's fight with Hill had been financed by the City Bank of New York; and behind the City Bank lurked the great and swelling resources of the Standard Oil Company. For the drive to combination was by no means confined to the pull of banking towards industry. The reverse process also operated. The accumulation of capital from profits in the new industries impelled the emerging tycoons, not merely to strive towards monopoly within their own industry, but, by launching into banking, to extend their power into further reaches of the economy.

Fifteen years after starting his first refinery at Cleveland, John D. Rockefeller commanded a virtual monopoly of the sale of oil. Rockefeller's achievement is a tribute to his long, if narrow, vision, his book-keeping mind, his ruthless pursuit of money power, his horror of waste and respect for order. But it had to be someone's achievement. The wildcatting conditions of early days could not continue. Where a hundred and one producers with primitive equipment faced sudden death, physical and financial, to market oil at wildly fluctuating prices, only the toughest survived. Rockefeller, perceiving that the refinery, not the well, was the nodal point of the industry, and that the man with the extra reserve of capital would emerge stronger from each successive market slump, forced his wife to wear last year's bonnet so that he could put every cent of profit into more and better refineries. This put him in a position to exploit the one overriding condition which determined the sale of oil. The greatest element in its price was the cost of transport. Oil was also valuable freight to railways. Since Rockefeller could guarantee a larger and steadier flow of oil traffic, the railways operating out of Cleveland granted him secret rebates which enabled him to undersell his rivals. Such is the simple secret of Standard Oil's initial success. By exploiting its strong position to improve its product, by using lake steamers, by building pipe lines, Standard emerged in 1879 as the controller of over 90 per cent of refined oil, able to dictate its own terms to the railways. Thenceforward for a generation, in one legal form or another, Standard Oil exercised a virtual monopoly over the sale of oil both at home and abroad. The Company's earnings were so gigantic that, in spite of the voracious needs of the oil business, they spilled over into a multitude of enterprises—in railways, in copper, in iron ore, in public utilities. So dominant on Wall Street were the 'Standard Oil crowd', where their National City Bank alone came to dwarf all other banks in the country, that for a time they rivalled the power of the great Morgan himself.

In steel, too, the pace of concentration was equally forced. Exploiting his talent for cultivating influential connections and for picking partners, Andrew Carnegie forged ahead, sinking the profits from his simple partnership into more efficient plant than his competitors. Already the leading producer of basic iron and steel, he began in the 1880s to extend his control over all departments of this complex industry. His partnership with Frick brought him coalmines, coking plants and railway. He bought ore fields in Michigan and, finally, after a tussle with Rockefeller, leased the great Mesabi Range in Minnesota. He built a fleet of ore boats on the Great Lakes; a new port, Conneaut, on Lake Erie; and, finally, to be free from the Erie Railroad, a private line of his own from the lake to Pittsburgh. Carnegie was, however, faced with powerful combinations of manufacturers of steel wire, tubes, tinplate and similar products who were in a position to bargain about the price of his steel. In some of these combinations was to be discerned the hidden hand of Morgan; and in the end Carnegie came face to face with that massive banking power. For some time Carnegie had wished to retire and devote himself to philanthropy. After rejecting offers from various syndicates to buy out the Carnegie Company, including one from Rockefeller, Carnegie determined to force the financial world to buy him out on his own terms. Believing that combination was the only solution for the steel industry and that he was in a stronger position than his rivals, he proceeded in 1900 to announce a series of expansion programmes aimed directly at the independents. The threat of this war of attrition served its purpose. At this time Carnegie was making a quarter of the Bessemer steel and half the structural steel and armour plate in the country and, having built his empire entirely on his own resources, his financial position was impregnable. Wall Street and the steel trade were in a panic. Even his partner, Schwab, believed that Carnegie's day, which was that of a one-man business, was done and that he should go. In the upshot Schwab and Gates, one of the threatened independents, persuaded Morgan that he alone could command the resources to buy Carnegie out. In a memorable interview with Morgan, Carnegie named his price—450,000,000 dollars—which Morgan accepted without demur. To raise the money he gathered together all the important steel interests, including the Rockefeller group, to launch the greatest company the world had seen. The United States Steel Corporation of 1901, with a capitalization of over a thousand million dollars, controlled seventy per cent of the American iron and steel industry.

With U.S. steel, Morgan succeeded in concentrating into one group the chief banking and industrial resources of the United States at that time. In industry after industry the attraction of a 'community of interest' brought together the robust survivors of a chaotic competition in combinations the financial power of which interpenetrated the entire economy. In the later stages, financial came to dominate industrial leadership. The banker alone had the power to complete the overarching structure of industrial capitalism. In spite of the strength of Standard Oil, it was Morgan, whose career originated not in American industry but in the financial support of the City of London, who consolidated America's first industrial revolution.

In the first decade of the present century, Morgan applied his talents to the creation of 'trusts' in other fields such as that of agricultural machinery. Morgans and Standard Oil were by no means the only powerful groups on Wall Street engaged in such activities. But when in 1907 the less happy activities of smaller men led to another disastrous panic it was Morgan who, mobilizing his own resources with those of other giants such as Rockefeller, Harriman and Frick, preserved intact the immense structure they had created. Wall Street had become one of the great money markets of the world.

The Great Experiment

When, at the outbreak of war in 1914, the stock markets of half the world closed, the blood of Wall Street brokers ran cold at the thought that foreign investors would try to dispose overnight of their four thousand million dollars' worth of American securities in the United States. The Exchange closed its doors; and it seemed as though Wall Street were still financially dependent on Lombard Street. But when four months later the Exchange timidly reopened, the unexpected occurred. Stocks not only remained firm, but boomed. The American capital market proved resilient enough to take the strain of a world at war. In 1915 an Anglo-French purchasing commission arrived in New York seeking a loan to finance their American supplies. The sum proposed was unprecedented; but a loan of 500 million dollars was successfully underwritten by the House of Morgan who also undertook to handle Allied purchases of food and materials, while at the same time the American steel industry, under Charles Schwab, geared itself to turn out overwhelming quantities of armaments and ships.

Under the stress of war, the centuries-old flow of capital and manufactures from the Old World to the New was dramatically reversed: once, Junius Morgan in London had supplied credits and British rails for American railways, whereas now his son Pierpont, in New York, was raising vast sums to supply Britain and France with the armaments of war. It was the beginning of a new age.

222

CHAPTER X

THE DEMOCRATIC IDEA
AND THE IMMIGRANT
1880-1921

'They all had one thing in common. Their sense of identity
did not derive from their relation to their environment. The
meaning which their lives had for them was inner and individual. They did not need to be supported, framed, consoled,
by the known, the habitual, the loved—by the ancestral
village, town, river, field, horizon; by family, kin, neighbours,
church and state; by the air, sky and water that they knew.'

THORNTON WILDER.

WHEN President Franklin Roosevelt, that scion of colonial
Dutch patroons, addressed the Daughters of the American
Revolution as 'fellow immigrants' he made pointed reference to a common origin and an uncomfortable but fundamental
article of faith which those dignified matrons, beguiled into a super-
stition that they alone cherished the true, the antique, the somehow
indigenous American values, never forgave. The incident marks a
subtle change which has come about in the last fifty years in the status
of the immigrant in American society.

During most of their past Americans accepted the experience of
migration, across the ocean as well as across the continent, as a
central formative element in American life.

In the first place, the native American needed the immigrant
for the resources he brought. Between 1814 and 1914 some 35
million Europeans crossed the Atlantic in the greatest migration of
modern times to play a vital part in the American epic. He was a
rare immigrant who, like Robert Owen or Morris Birkbeck,
brought a fortune to squander in the wilderness. But from the day

in 1790 when Samuel Slater introduced his memorized textile plans to Rhode Island[1] to the day in 1890 when Welshmen taught tin-plating in St Louis, Americans enticed the skilled craftsmen of Europe to the western shores of the Atlantic. Such men were exceptional, lost in the broadening stream of immigrants who brought little but their hands. The immigrant's most heroic gift to his chosen land was unskilled labour. The fabulous prosperity of the American people was built upon foundations dug with picks and shovels by young men recruited from the villages of Europe. The forced labour of the felon, the indentured servant, the Negro slave and the oriental peon, was followed by the labour, technically free but often as breaking to body and spirit, of the Irish navvy, the Austrian miner, the Polish foundry hand or potato picker. In America the most recently arrived were always the most expendable; and without their blood and sweat, without the tears of their women, the United States would not yet be a Great Power.

Secondly, migration played an ever more important role in forming the American character. The American Revolution had its roots in that instinct to reject customary authority which was the primary motive of Atlantic migration. In this respect the immigrant was united in spirit with the Lexington 'minute man' triggered by the instincts of seventeenth-century Independency. Each had become American by virtue of an initial rejection of custom; and each came to share with his fellows a feeling of solidarity against the Old World. In an important sense each new immigrant arriving at Castle Garden was already more American than the native-born son of the Republic in that he himself had shown the will to make a clean break with the past. The immigrant was a sign that the great experiment was renewing itself. Although many, perhaps most, were too ignorant and bewildered to comprehend it, for a significant minority the journey was a pilgrimage of faith. The philosophic radicals who chose New York rather than London as a field for reform, the Utopian socialists who sought the asylum of the American wilderness for their experiments, the 'come-outers' in religion who crossed the Atlantic in search of a promised land, all contributed to the dynamic faith in progress and democracy

[1] See p. 80.

which characterized America's age of ferment. Although by no means every New York artisan facing immigrant competition, or every Yankee contemplating North Boston slums filled with superstitious Irish Catholics, responded to this conviction, or could have taken fire at de Crèvecoeur's rhapsody over the American—this new man in whose veins coursed the blood of half a dozen European 'races'—the United States Government neither encouraged nor discouraged immigration but assumed it to be integral to the process of creating an American nation. Where, on the eve of the Civil War, every seventh person had been born in some 'Old Country', it was invidious to distinguish too closely between native- and foreign-born.

In the third place, the problem of assimilation was not acute. The immigrants were drawn for the most part from stocks already represented in America at the Revolution. In 1850, of the two million foreign-born, two-thirds were English-speaking people from the British Isles and over a quarter were Germans.[1] During the following forty years, although there was a wider response to the pull of the New World, especially eastwards across the North Sea, English yeomen and labourers predominated in an exodus still largely from north-west Europe and Germany. As Professor Hansen pointed out, this uprooting had a common denominator in agricultural depression, in part induced by cheap food from the New World, coupled with a common land system: 'Its origin was Germanic, for the emigrants came from regions where the early Teutonic tribes had fixed the customs that governed agricultural practice and land succession. . . . This exodus was Teutonic in blood, in institutions, and in the basis of its language, forming the most homogeneous of all migrations to America.'[2] And the map of the journey was still determined by the old trade routes radiating from the British Isles. In 1890, of eight million foreign-born, three million had come from the British Isles, nearly three million from Germany and nearly a million from Scandinavia. The English quickly made themselves at home, and the educated and the forceful

[1] U.S. Census, *A Compendium of the Seventh Census* (Washington, D.C., 1854), p. 119.
[2] M. L. Hansen, *The Atlantic Migration, 1607–1860* (Cambridge, Mass., 1940), p. 10.

among them became social leaders in the American community. Such was their influence that in the last quarter of the century an 'English vogue' characterized all ranks of the people.[1] Although the Irish—a separate element, distinct from the Teutonic migration —congregated in the slums of the cities and adhered to the still alien Roman Catholic religion, they at least spoke English and took the business of politics seriously. Although the Germans spoke a guttural English, read newspapers in their own language and drank their own beer in the fellowship of *turnvereins*, German speech and ways had long been a familiar part of the American social landscape. Although the Norwegians of Minnesota clung together in narrow communities, preserving a Lutheranism which became archaic in Europe, they made good farmers and loyal citizens. There were few to doubt that, in time, the immigrant would be indistinguishable from the native-born.

But at precisely the time when, in 1886, the Statue of Liberty, the gift of France, was erected on Bedloe Island in New York harbour, the incoming ships were beginning to disembark from their steerage crowds a new kind of immigrant whose presence was to instil doubts about the efficacy of the melting pot. For the perfunctory immigration check at Castle Garden on the tip of Manhattan was substituted segregation and a more severe scrutiny at Ellis Island which, across the water, posed an ironic qualification to the Statue's welcome at the gateway to the New World. Before many years had passed, the sentimental verses on its plinth would seem to be little more than a quaint survival of an outmoded faith.

The new immigrants were not Teutonic or Celtic peoples from north-west Europe and Germany, but Slavs, Magyars, Jews, Latins from the remote interior of the European continent: from Bohemia, Hungary and the Balkans, from Poland, Russia and the Ukraine and from Mediterranean Italy and Greece. Some were driven out by political persecution in Poland or Bohemia; others, like the Jews from the ghettos of Poland or Russia, by religious persecution culminating in pogroms; still others by new demands for military service. But the majority were peasants stirred by a new breeze of opportunity from the West to make a better living in that fabulous,

[1] M. L. Hansen, *The Immigrant in American History* (Cambridge, Mass., 1940), p. 149.

if vaguely apprehended, 'Amerika' where land was freehold and streets paved with gold. The main impulse was economic, in the form of the 'pull' of the New, rather than the 'push' of the Old World, and the waves of emigration followed the trade cycle. For the power of the transatlantic economy had begun to quicken, not merely the Atlantic basin, but the great heartland of Europe. News of the New World was brought to villages on the Russian steppes or to mining towns in the Carpathians in advertisements placed against church or post office by the agents of steamship companies in search of passengers and by industrial concerns in search of immigrant labour cheaper than the Irish. Once the first adventurous youths had successfully negotiated the journey, letters and remittances from America stimulated what often became a folk migration in crowded, but by now highly organized, immigrant trains to Danzig, Bremen, Odessa or Naples and thence by steamer to New York. So smooth were the new means of communication that the emigrating stream became a torrential flood. Whereas in 1882, a record year, only 600,000 immigrants entered the United States from Europe, in 1907, the high-water mark of European migration, some 1,200,000 Europeans entered a country whose total population was only 87 million. A much greater proportion of these new immigrants, in 1908 some 400,000 in number,[1] were only sojourners who after a few years returned to their native Sicily or Slovenia, sometimes disillusioned, sometimes with the chink of dollars in the pockets of their store clothes. But the great majority stayed to swell the proportion of new immigrants among the foreign-born. In 1910, of eleven and a half million born in Europe over five million had come from some part of Europe east or south of Germany.[2]

Few of the new immigrants, landing at the piers of lower Manhattan, still held to the naïve plans they had started with. The buffetings of the journey had knocked away most of the certainties of these bewildered villagers, had revealed their helplessness before forces greater than they knew, had dispelled the mirage even of a homestead in the golden west. Unforeseen expenses had emptied the savings stocking and the only course was to take the first job that

[1] *Hist. Stats.*, Series B, 352.
[2] *Hist. Stats.*, Series B, 286–91.

offered in the hope of earning dollars to bring over families, to strike out for a life they knew. Many, taking the offer of a pick or shovel, went to work on the railway or in construction gangs in New York, Cleveland or Chicago, only to find themselves bound to unscrupulous contractors who saw to it that their earnings never repaid the cost of transport and subsistence in the unruly construction camp. Others earned a precarious pittance in stockyards, docks or haulage, only to be turned away in the first slack period. Those who had been specially recruited to work in textile mills, steel works or mines were less overwhelmed. Where the future was planned there was at least promise of security and relief from the nagging demand for continual personal decisions in an alien world. Some, like the Hungarian miners of Pennsylvania or Colorado, worked at trades which were in their blood. And if the improvised, ramshackle and dirty huddle of wooden shacks, muddy roads and broadwalks which was to be their home town contrasted bitterly with the ordered landscape of an ancestral village there was a countryside, sometimes of rugged, mountainous beauty, to breathe in. Even so, in his company town, where housing was never built fast enough for the new workers, where wages were sometimes paid in truck and must be spent at a company store, where prosperity depended on one industry, a single concern, and where hands were turned loose at the first weekly drop in orders, the ex-peasant found himself bound to a new kind of feudalism in which the lord had rights but no duties.

However, the centre of the immigrant problem lay in the great cities. Many immigrant families, lacking resources to get more than walking distance from the landing stage, fetched up like flotsam in run-down residential districts near the docks in Boston, in Philadelphia, above all in New York. With their bundles and family chests they moved first into boarding-houses and the converted stables of old brown-stone terraces. But as new shiploads thronged the port districts, rents rose and landlords made the most of each building lot by constructing six- and eight-storeyed tenements built in what became a standard 'dumb-bell' plan which permitted a maximum of box-like room-space for a minimum of air. Such tenements, often without indoor sanitation or garbage disposal, and with communal cold-water taps, became the New World homes of thousands of immigrant families. In no time they were slums. And as new arrivals poured into these overcrowded districts, colonies of Poles, Jews, Italians, Ukrainians, Slovaks and Greeks crept up the east and west sides of Manhattan to the Bronx, over the East River, following the streetcar and 'elevated' across Brooklyn to Flatbush. However far they went—along the shore to Bridgeport or New Haven, inland to Cleveland, Cincinnati or Chicago—each national group was huddled together in poverty-stricken communities, oddly uncouth in speech and dress and habit, nations within in a nation. It was the New Yorker's boast, misplaced in view of the conditions in which most of them existed, that there were in his city more Italians than in any city except Rome, more Germans than in any city except Berlin, more Irish than in any city except Dublin, and more Jews than in any other city in the world.

Few of the new immigrants really came to terms with American life. Conditions were weighted against them from the start. Crowded into tiny flats, six or eight to a bedroom, amid filth and vermin, the peasant wife lacked the barest amenity to quicken her housepride, and for her, as for her husband, there was no privacy; only the fire-escape to the roof to temper the oven-like heat of summer, or the dram of spirits in the local saloon to keep out the raw American winter. But poverty was only the beginning. Except for the Jews who had grown up in the ghettos of Riga, Lublin or Warsaw few had lived in towns, let alone the slums of a great city. They had known dirt; but it had been clean, country dirt. They had slept in crowded cottages; but they had worked in the fields, not in some sweat shop or abattoir, and they had taken their ease according to bucolic custom, not on some asphalt corner lot, streetcar ride or ferryboat trip. Hard manual work they also knew; but although the strong young men took pride in shouldering heavy loads, although the women submitted to eighteen-hour days of making paper flowers, laundering or sewing, the work, dissociated as it was from any pattern they knew, held no virtue. If the three or four dollars a week they earned was pitifully small it was enough had it been a token of better things to come; but the repeated cycle of casual unemployment brought them back to where they had started, without hope of betterment.

At the prompting of some obscure impulse the peasant had rejected his birthright without fully comprehending the extent of his sacrifice. The immemorial discipline of the seasons, the sequence of growth and decay in nature, the unquestioned degrees of position and property, no longer gave unity and meaning to the daily incidents of living. The changing sky, now a mere patch above a tangle of telegraph wires, no longer prompted him to new duties; it was merely an index of a heat or cold to be passively suffered. The alternation of work and idleness was determined, not in the natural rhythm of the seasons, but by the whim of the hiring foreman. Holidays were no longer saints' days rich in folklore, but arbitrary interruptions dedicated to a strange hagiography. The birth of an heir lost some of its solemnity where there was no holding to transmit; and the terror of death was increased when one's bones could not rest in the peace of an ancestral graveyard. No longer familiar and trustworthy, authority, in the shape of the Pinkerton agent, the grafting policeman on the beat, the occasional sudden raid of the paddy wagon, was to be feared and avoided. Jeered at by streetcar conductors for his halting English and strange manners, he felt menaced by the great city world he could not understand. Experience for the transplanted peasant had lost its purpose; it was irrational, fragmented. The mirror of self-respect was shattered. Little wonder that some lost their sense of manhood, became broken in spirit and assuaged their loneliness by drink, drugs or by indulging a nostalgia for the past.

Thus the 'first generation' immigrant remained suspended between the Old and the New Worlds. Unable and unwilling to return to the old, he made the most of a truncated existence on the threshold of the new; but in salvaging what he could of the life he had known he brought richness and variety to American society.[1]

Although he came to recognize that most of those he came up against, however alien their language and physique, however odd their customs, shared the same predicament as immigrants, his inner refuge was the community of his own people. Separate languages and folkways kept Poles, Greeks, Slovaks and Italians segregated in

---

[1] I am indebted for much of the material of this chapter to Oscar Handlin's *The Uprooted* (Boston, 1951) and to Alfred Kazin's *A Walker in the City* (London, 1952).

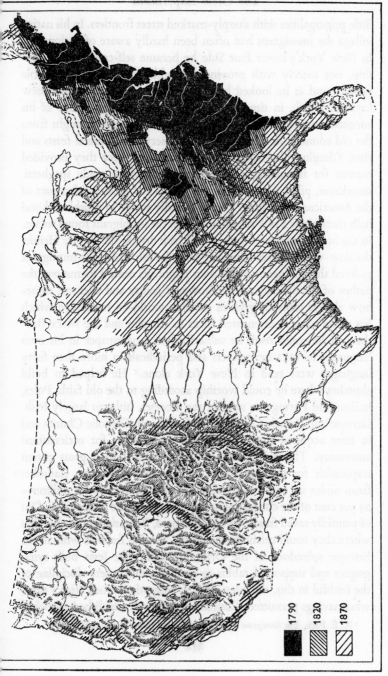

5. **The United States: Area of Settlement.** The shaded areas show a population of two or more persons per square mile, in 1790, 1820 and 1870

1790

1820

1870

little principalities with sharply-marked street frontiers. In his native village the immigrant had often been hardly aware of nationality. In New York's lower East Side he became self-conscious of kinship, not merely with provincial neighbours, but with a whole people; and as he looked back across the Atlantic he sensed new loyalties which, in time, were to affect the foreign policy of his adopted country. To propitiate the *lares* and *penates* brought from the old country, immigrant families observed traditional feasts and rites. Clinging obstinately to their native cookery they provided custom for innumerable little restaurants which made spaghetti, sauerkraut, pilau, goulash, borscht, salads and kosher dishes part of the American way of life. Out of friendly socials in neighbourhood halls there grew a folk theatre in which the immigrant found solace. In the broad caricature of the genial Irish drunk, the clumsy Heinie, the slow-witted Swede, the over-sharp Jewish trader, the immigrant re-lived the poignancy of his own plight. Its central theme was the pathos of the little man who, however jaunty and talented, somehow always came to grief in an alien world—a stereotype which has come to us in attenuated form in Chaplin and the Marx Brothers. If he could read, he subscribed to a newspaper in his own language. In 1922 newspapers and periodicals in more than forty languages were read in New York alone.[1] He helped to build churches where he could worship according to the old faith. Poles, Italians and Portuguese swelled the dioceses, hitherto largely Irish, German and French-Canadian, of the Roman Catholic Church and in time acquired their own priests and fought for ecclesiastical autonomy. The new influx of immigrants is to a great extent responsible for the increase in the number of Roman Catholics from under six and a half million in 1880 to twenty-six million—25 per cent of the churchgoing population—at the present day. Out of painfully saved funds, Greeks, Russians, Bulgarians built churches where they could celebrate the great Christian festivals with all the baroque splendour of the Orthodox faith. The Jews built synagogues and supported rabbis to maintain the austere discipline of the faithful in this, the latest of their migrations. And after a time, when savings permitted, Church after Church established parochial

[1] R. E. Park, *The Immigrant Press and its Control* (New York, 1922), p. 7.

schools where immigrant children could be preserved from the secular influences of American public education. Stubbornly determined to preserve the elemental human decencies, they passed round the hat to provide a fitting burial or to compensate one whose arm was crushed in a machine. And out of this clubbing together there grew friendly societies which were to become the basis of great insurance companies.

Some immigrants never became American citizens; but most, after the minimum five years or perhaps as many as fifteen, took the oath which made them naturalized Americans, and submitted to rudimentary instruction in the symbolism of the Flag, the principles of the Constitution, the sentiments of the Declaration of Independence, of the Gettysburg Address, spelling out the lucid, rounded periods, so different from the garbled English of their everyday speech. These were the talisman of their new existence.

For most, the vote was a novel privilege: a weapon to carve out the promised independence, to extend the precarious bridgehead they had established in the New World. Little wonder that they used it to support the men who promised a measure of security from the menacing out-world: the 'boss' labourer in the Navy Yard who was in a position to give jobs for votes; the second-generation politician who spoke the same language and yet moved easily in the greater world of city politics, protecting the rights of Italian street vendors, of German saloon keepers, saying the secret word at City Hall to release a fighting-drunk Polack from the 'cooler', putting through a measure to build a bath-house in his block; the genial, often physically big and confident, Irish ward healer who distributed turkeys and groceries to the needy at Thanksgiving and saw to it that the widow's boy got a start in the Sanitary Department. For the immigrant these were real benefits. That they often depended on collusion between voter, politician and underworld interests prepared to pay big money for their form of 'protection' was a fact beyond the immigrant's comprehension or care. For him machine politics were a natural and benevolent order to which he gave unquestioned loyalty, just as he gave a cold reception to the reforming canvassers who appeared briefly on his street corner at election time, prating of vice and corruption, and offering tax reductions and a non-partisan administration.

The immigrant was conservative. Although diffident and uncertain, he accepted America as it was, recognizing limited gains and clinging to his major premise that the New World offered the prospect of a better life, if not for him, at any rate for his children. Apathetic to the broader issues of politics and with a peasant's caution, he provided a powerful element of inertia to change. Reform left him cold. Just as the city immigrant suspected and did not understand the cause of municipal reform, so in the midwestern countryside of the '80s and '90s most immigrant farmers were unmoved by the agrarian crusade. And when it came to women's suffrage the immigrant was not merely unmoved but, retaining as he did his ancestral family assumption that the place of women was in the home, he was stubbornly hostile.

It is true that the old radical strain, so conspicuous among immigrant artisans and intellectuals of the Jackson period, persisted. One German, the Marxist Joseph Weydemeyer, provided leadership for the labour movement in the 1870s; another, Johann Most, introduced the anarchistic 'Black International' in the early 1880s. There was indeed a small, but much publicized, anarchist fringe. In 1886 a bomb was thrown into a meeting, in the Haymarket at Chicago, of strikers against the McCormick Harvester Company, and, although nothing was proved against them, eight anarchists, in the habit of practising Sunday bomb throwing in the sand dunes of Lake Michigan, were held guilty of inciting to murder and seven of them were sentenced to death. This famous incident, together with the subsequent action of the German-born Governor Altgeld of Illinois in pardoning three anarchists who had not been executed, fostered a suspicion in the public mind that there were subversive individuals among the immigrants. This suspicion revived with each of the bitter strikes which punctuated America's industrial history.

But the radical immigrant was an exception. Most of the first generation identified capitalism with the American way of life and believed in it as a ladder to success, however precariously their feet might be placed on its lowest rung. For in rejecting custom they had set their faces against ordered relationships in economic life. In spite of insecurity they continued to prize a system which guaranteed complete freedom in hiring and firing and to believe that, given time and good fortune, they or their children would be able to sell their labour to better advantage and to enjoy a high standard of living in some independent pursuit. Like earlier waves of immigrants and migrants before them, they also in their way showed a marked speculative strain. Only a lifetime of repeated disillusionment could instil a conviction that most of them were destined to remain members of a labouring class. For this reason, in addition to the more obvious difficulties in the way of organizing a polyglot labour force, unskilled labour remained largely unorganized until our own time. As for skilled labour, the man who directed the American Federation of Labor away from unprofitable political action into the conservative channel of industrial bargaining was Samuel Gompers, an immigrant of Dutch-Jewish extraction from the East End of London who made his way up out of the cigar trade of Manhattan's East Side tenements.

As the new immigrant made but a limited adjustment to America, so his sons and daughters had to withstand powerful tensions between the Old and the New Worlds in their determination to become Americanized. The 'second generation' immigrant child in the city grew up in a no-man's land of streets and vacant lots between the citadel of his tenement home and the *res publica* of school. He soon became aware that the precepts of the class room often conflicted with the values of the home. Submitting rather than responding to imperfectly understood lessons in Anglo-Saxon values, he became conscious at the same time of a certain *gaucherie* in his immigrant background which intensified the familiar conflicts of adolescence. The traditional authority of the European father, already shaken by insecurity, could not withstand the new authority of school and the codes of childhood cliques. The second generation were often passionate in their determination to obliterate all traces of their foreign origin, and to become '100 per cent Americans'. Their American education went far beyond the stilted instruction in respect for the Flag, in the Declaration of Independence, Washington's Farewell Address, Webster's Reply to Hayne, in the historical folklore of Betsy Ross and Johnny Appleseed, imbibed in public school and public library—although the existence of these institutions was itself a basic education. The world of the streets with its multitudinous nationalities, its babel of street-corner orators advocating a whole range of political and religious nostrums, provided an essentially American education in eclecticism, in curiosity, in the imperative need for tolerance and humour, in the rights of minorities and in the deeper, social, values of the American form of democracy. Second generation immigrants, believing implicitly in progress through experiment and the open mind, were to renounce their fathers' conservatism for the liberalism of La Follette and Franklin Roosevelt.

There was, however, an obverse to the coin. The second generation's desire to be American sometimes resulted in an urge to get rid of the conspicuous foreignness by superficial conformity to some idealized and unreal American pattern of manners. The tyranny of childhood cliques, of those street gangs, which when they occasionally went wrong became the cause of juvenile crime and adult gangsterism, sometimes encouraged in the growing youth an exaggerated yearning to conform, not only in speech, in dress, in the easy rhythms of deportment—so different from the tight, brisk carriage of the newly-arrived European—but also in deeper ways. Rejecting, as he so often did, the religious and social framework which had given definition to his father's half-way house he found himself without genuine institutional bearings. Instead, in his insecurity, he strove to act out an existence in conformity with what, in his ignorance, he thought to be 'American'. Taking on protective colouring he changed his name from Kabotznik to Cabot, from Silva to Wood; he acquired in exaggerated form the idioms of current usage—from the newest slang to baseball lore, from a false *bonhomie* to golf and the latest mechanical gimmick. His standardized responses made him fair game for the new art of advertising and helped to establish a uniquely fair field for the new technology of mass production. He became a 'regular guy'. In his inner loneliness he responded to the gregarious quality of American life. He became an enthusiastic 'joiner' of Lions, Elks, Freemasons, Odd Fellows, Woodmen—any society which would give him a sense of belonging to some in-group in a fluid and mobile community.

In time, the new immigrant family became fully assimilated into American society, contributing to it richness and variety. But the process was long and arduous and took two, sometimes three, generations. The native Americans who flourished between 1890 and the First World War may be forgiven for doubting the continued capacity of their society to absorb an unlimited influx of immigrants of the newer stocks. These doubts produced, in time, a revolution of opinion second only to that which brought about American independence.

From time to time throughout their history American voices had been heard in protest against the immigrant. As early as the 1830s the Whigs had branded the workingmen's parties as alien and seditious on account of their immigrant element. In the mid-1850s an 'American Party' of nativists had carried congressional seats in a wave of hysteria against the Catholic Irish. American workmen had objected to cheap immigrant competition, and the main achievement of the Knights of Labor had been to force the repeal of the contract labour law in 1885. At about the same time (1882), riots by unemployed against San Francisco's Chinatown had forced Congress to pass an Act excluding Chinese immigrants, a piece of racial discrimination carried a stage further in 1907 when, after the introduction of segregation for Japanese in Californian schools, Theodore Roosevelt negotiated the famous Gentlemen's Agreement whereby Japan undertook to prevent further emigration to the United States. Such hostile manifestations could hardly be said to challenge the traditional immigration policy. However, oriental exclusion was a portent. For although the United States had always limited the privilege of naturalization to people of Caucasian race,[1] the exclusion of Chinese and Japanese immigrants, as such, introduced the principle of 'racial' discrimination. It was tempting to extend this principle to 'ethnic' discrimination as the hordes of 'new' immigrants in turn presented special problems of assimilation.

An increasing number of interests and prejudices were aroused.

---

[1] Although in the hey-day of Reconstruction this was extended to persons of African descent.

The fear of industrialism in a society still rural in outlook was directed, in part, against the immigrants who made up the bulk of the unskilled labour force in industry. The hostility of native crafts-men to immigrant competition was sharpened as mill managers introduced machinery manned by unskilled immigrants; and their protests became ever more vocal with the growth of the American Federation of Labor. During the long depression of the 1890s there was much unemployment, especially among the unskilled; and the unwonted spectacle in mill towns of sorry lines of immi-grant workers standing in queues for bread and soup, caused many to wonder whether the importation of cheap labour had not been overdone. On the one hand, native union organizers resented the immigrant's docility, ignorance and the complex of linguistic and ethnic loyalties which prevented any organized stand against the demands of capital. On the other, the general public, taking fright at chronic industrial unrest—at the Haymarket Riot, the great strikes, such as those at Pullman, Homestead and Cripple Creek— became conscious of something new and explosive in American society for which the immigrant was inevitably blamed; and the occasional appearance of immigrant agitators, often anarchists and Marxist socialists, confirmed the timid in their suspicions that among the immigrants were undesirables, carriers of seditious, un-American doctrine.

Fear of the city, offspring of industrialism, was also, and more plausibly, directed against the immigrant. It was in the 1890s that Americans first became conscious of the urgent problems of great cities which had grown so fast that, overnight, it seemed, they had got beyond the power of civic government to control. The slums were a predominantly immigrant problem. Social workers like Jane Addams, of Hull House in Chicago, and 'muck-raking' journal-ists like Jacob Riis, by calling public attention to the evils of land-lordism, to the prevalence of disease, prostitution and crime, of ignorance and shiftlessness, made many echo Jefferson's old cry that the city—and by implication the immigrant—was a danger to the American way of life.

Fears that the new immigrant was too alien in social habit, too ignorant of Anglo-Saxon speech and education, ever to make a good citizen were exacerbated by his willingness to be led by machine politicians. Reformers fighting corruption in city government came up against not merely the inertia of the immigrants themselves, but the boss, often 'second generation' himself, who controlled the machine. The Irish control of Boston and, later, the Italian hegemony over Manhattan made Beacon Hill and Washington Square wonder whether the sacred traditions of the Republic were being perverted by ignorant foreigners.

When Church leaders of the old 'native' denominations reflected that an overwhelming proportion of the new immigrants were Roman Catholic, Greek Orthodox or Jewish in religion they shook their heads over the possibility that the old Protestant faith, so fundamental to the American ethic, would be swamped by alien dogma, idolatrous and superstitious. In particular, anti-Catholic sentiment, which had never entirely slumbered, became powerful on the eastern seaboard in the 1890s when the American Protective Association began to resist the influence of Catholics in politics, and the demand for Catholic parochial schools.

And when immigrant groups, self-conscious about their origins, banded together to proclaim their blood brotherhood with the Fatherland, like the Germans in their *Deutsche Bund,* or like the Czechs or the Sinn Feiners, to support with money and advice irredentist or revolutionary parties abroad, and to lobby the State Department at home, there were Americans of the older stocks who questioned the loyalty of 'hyphenated' Americans.

The movement for restriction, which grew out of these fears, acquired an articulate social theory. The climate of belief about the American experiment had changed radically since those far-off days of the Enlightenment when de Crèvecoeur was confident in the power of the uncorrupted wilderness to mould a new race of men out of the nations of Europe. For the first time large numbers of Americans were sceptical. However sharp the east-European peasant's break with his past, however eager he might be to make good in the freedom of the New World, the experience of migration in itself no longer seemed sufficient guarantee of his conversion to American values. To become American in the true sense would take time, might even be deferred to his children. It would take education. Meanwhile men began to distinguish degrees of 'Americanism', a distinction based on a kind of 'points' system involving considerations of ethnic stock, number of native generations, religion, education and economic status, and ranging all the way from the '100 per cent' of the older stocks down through the 'hyphenated American' of the first immigrant generation to the 'un-American' of the German-trained socialist or the Italian sojourner intent only on earning dollars to take back to Sicily.

For to be an American meant, not merely taking the oath, but living according to the cultural tradition of American life. And that tradition was predominantly Anglo-Saxon and Protestant: a fact which the new immigration brought home with full force to the men of English, Scots and Scotch-Irish blood who still dominated American public, professional and business life. In a post-Darwinian age, which was beginning to think of society in evolutionary and organic terms, these classes, taking their cue from historians such as John Fiske or Herbert Baxter Adams, saw American society as the triumphant end-product of a process of biological growth and mutation with origins in remote Anglo-Saxon ancestry. To protect that tradition they gave weight and authority to the movement to restrict immigration.

This restriction movement took some forty years to develop; for resistance to a programme offensive to important blocks of immigrant voters as well as to deeply held conviction was formidable. As early as 1882, Congress had introduced the principle of selection in the unexceptionable form of excluding idiots, convicts and persons likely to become public charges: a list to which were added over the years new categories such as polygamists, diseased persons, anarchists, alcoholics. But numerous bills to impose a literacy test failed of passage or, in four cases, were vetoed by successive Presidents who held firmly, in Cleveland's words, that such a test was 'a radical departure from our national policy'. It was, however, finally imposed over Wilson's veto in 1917. The Immigration Act of that year, which established in full the principle of qualitative selection, marks the transition from freedom of entry to the drastic restriction, based on ethnic discrimination, which was to come.

At the time of the First World War, American opinion was

especially sensitive about the immigrant problem. Some German communities preserved an attitude of passive resistance to a war against the Fatherland; Poles, Czechs, Irish and other groups, active in supporting governments in exile and revolutionary movements, brought their special interests to bear on American diplomacy. There was apprehension concerning the prospect of a renewed and heavy influx of immigrants from a post-war Europe in upheaval. Moreover, the short, sharp, post-war depression of 1920 brought inevitable labour troubles. There were violent clashes in textile towns and on the waterfronts between strikers organized by the International Workers of the World, suspected of being led by foreign agitators, and self-constituted vigilantes composed of 'nativist' trouble-shooters of the ex-service type. These incidents further dramatized the immigrant danger to the popular mind. It was also no accident that the old demand for cheap industrial labour was dying away at the time when Henry Ford was successfully demonstrating his methods of mass production by machinery.

In this climate of opinion Congress passed a new Immigration Act of 1921 which, augmented and modified by the subsequent Acts of 1924 and 1929, finally reversed the traditional policy of the United States towards immigrants. Under the new legislation the number of immigrants who might be admitted in any year was limited to 150,000, apportioned by quota among the various European countries according to the percentage of their national stocks in the American population in 1920.

Thus, the American people, by shutting the sluice-gates against the immigrant stream and by regulating the future trickle in favour of the English, Irish, Germans and Scandinavians and against the eastern and southern Europeans, abandoned their time-honoured faith in the importance of the immigrant to their society. As a result the whole concept of American nationality underwent a subtle change.

CHAPTER XI

THE DEMOCRATIC IDEA AND THE HEGEMONY OF BIG BUSINESS

1890-1917

'What America needs above all is a body of laws which will look after the men on the make rather than the men already made.'

WOODROW WILSON, *The New Freedom* (1913).

WHEN that scion of the patriciate, Henry Adams, returned from Civil War service in London as secretary to his father, the American Minister to the Court of St James, he was dismayed to find that the old social landmarks by which he had expected to follow the well-worn family path to political honour had been obliterated; and that a new, brash, money-getting America no longer had any use for the wonted services of an Adams. In that 'Gilded Age' there seemed only two choices open to the class to which he belonged, a class which had hitherto never been quite jockeyed out of its inner position on American politics. Henry Adams eventually became, not a statesman in the White House, but a man of letters in a comfortable family mansion on the other side of Lafayette Square. Here, through carefully chosen friends, he could feel the pulse of power in the new America. Here, and later abroad in restless travels, he turned to history to discover why the promise of that austere and classical republic which his family had helped shape had become dissipated, and in more speculative studies he pursued his quest for the meaning of a universe which could condemn an Adams to at any rate a pose of obscurity. His brother, Charles Francis II, chose the other course. He held his nose, and became a railway executive. For power was drawn increasingly into the hands of those business men who had emerged from the desperate game of wildcatting, rate wars, pools, gentlemen's agreements and trusts as the recognized controllers of America's mighty economy. Before the century had run out it began to look as though America were becoming the domain of a new plutocracy, richer and more powerful than any the world had seen.

For thirty years the business interests largely dominated American politics. As we have seen, the prizes for both business man and politician were so glittering that there was collusion between the two at all levels of the game for the speedier exploitation of the nation's wealth. Tariff walls were built for the asking, the national domain was parcelled out, the nation's soils, minerals, forests, were squandered to make private fortunes. Like the business man, the professional politician perfected techniques of large-scale organization as a means for delivering the vote. The rise of new cities like Chicago and the spread of old ones like Philadelphia, crowded with countrymen and immigrants, provided the opportunity for the building of great city machines, the instrument, not merely for exercising a rewarding dictatorship in municipal government, but for control of the national parties. Political bosses like Platt of New York, Quay of Pennsylvania or Hanna of Cleveland rose to the heights of Senator and president-maker; and their connection with powerful business interests, local and national, was invariably close. On this issue, whatever might be said in principle at election time, in practice there was little to choose between the different parties. Although the worst cases of corruption at the national level passed with the Grant Administration of 1868-72, the relation between government and business continued intimate during the long period of Republican ascendancy as well as in the two short Democratic interludes under Cleveland. The chief distinction in party warfare was between the 'Stalwarts'—bosses who were the creatures of private interests—and 'Half-Breeds'—independent bosses who used their control of votes to win favours from business. Stalwarts and Half-Breeds together crowded out the 'Mugwumps', well-meaning reformers who had nothing but a high-toned oratory to exercise against the power of organized politics. In these circumstances it is hardly surprising that the capitalist class had its way in determining the broad outlines of national policy, or that before the turn of the present century any attempts to limit the power of capital, such as measures to reduce tariffs, to regulate railways or to outlaw monopoly, were effectively sterilized.

The power of business did not, however, depend solely on the venality of politicians. The generation which survived the Civil War gave an overriding priority to the subjugation of the continent; and, far from being resentful, looked with admiration and envy on the triumphs of business moguls. In the popular image these men were pioneers. Just as the frontiersman had won his manhood by using brawn and wits to wrest a profitable livelihood out of the wilderness, so a new generation proved themselves by exploiting the riches which pioneering had laid bare. The fight to make money was a projection of the fight against a hostile nature. In that mobile society where there were few institutional means of conferring prestige, where power lay overwhelmingly in business rather than politics and where so much money was newly made, riches were considered a sign of intelligence, nerve and courage. Men made money to prove their manhood; and after making one fortune, went on to make another, to show that, although ageing, they were not past it. And the money, once made, was not, as in Europe, conserved as a tool for social advancement and transmitted to heirs, but spent, even squandered like the physical resources of the continent. This attitude to wealth was profoundly different from that of Europe, no more, no less materialistic. For if in European eyes the American vice has been conspicuous waste, the European vice in American eyes has been avarice.[1] The mid-Victorian beliefs in individualism, competition and *laissez-faire* as the conditions of progress found their ideal climate in North America which became a forcing house for capitalism.

That climate not only fostered a complacency towards the state of politics but had a benign influence on the law itself. Business men found not only pliant legislators but sympathetic judges. In the 1880s, the Supreme Court itself was a formidable bastion in the defence of business. Accepting the corporation-lawyer's interpretation of the word 'person' in the Fourteenth Amendment to cover

[1] See W. H. Auden, 'Huck and Oliver', *The Listener*, 1 October, 1953.

businesses as well as freed Negroes, the court declared unconstitutional important legislation regulating railway rates and hours and conditions of work on the ground that such measures deprived business corporations of property without due process of law. Judges also began to grant injunctions to employers in labour disputes on the ground that stoppages were detrimental to property rights. In these and other ways the courts went to great extremes to protect property and to write the principle of *laissez-faire* into the Constitution.

But by 1890 many Americans had come to recognize that *laissez-faire*, far from perpetuating competition, seemed to encourage a concentration of power stifling to the open conditions on which progress had been thought to depend. The future was in the hands, not of the independent business man, but of the great corporation. As we have seen, American life in this generation was characterized by a shift in scale and specialization. Americans were grappling with the problem of sheer size: the bigness of the continent itself, its railways, its crops, its teeming cities, its political interests and machines. Men and women brought up in a horse and buggy age found themselves projected, suddenly and breathlessly, into an age in which much of their inherited stock of ideas, their parish-pump politics, their village-store economics, seemed irrelevant. The old simple relation between landlord and tenant, buyer and seller, employer and workman, voter and politician, had ceased to exist. The inherited beliefs seemed only to have fostered a mass society in which the individual was anonymous, defenceless before the impersonal power of business corporation, slum landlord or city boss. The chief problem for Americans of this generation was to come to terms with these 'over-mighty subjects' which this period of forced growth had raised in their midst.

The new plutocrats did not understand that a problem existed. It was not only that the more ruthless and cynical of the buccaneers refused to recognize a social responsibility at all, like the younger Vanderbilt when he said 'the public be damned'. As the structure of business took shape its controllers began to assume that their power had been vouchsafed to them by Providence in the best interests of the American people. The more simple-minded among them were content to accept the view expressed by George F. Baer, President of the Philadelphia and Reading Railroad, when he referred to 'the Christian men to whom God in his infinite wisdom has given control of the property interests of the country'. But more sophisticated minds constructed a *rationale* which justified pluto-cracy to the satisfaction of the plutocrats and their admirers. It must be remembered that the self-confidence of these men derived, not merely from their success in defeating their rivals in the struggle for mastery of the new technology but from a consciousness that they were the chosen instruments of progress. The motives of the great tycoons were as various as their temperaments. But in their drive to bigness and to monopoly they were impelled, not only by an overriding ambition to make money, but by a profound belief in the virtues of efficiency and security. The generation which experienced the waste involved in wildcatting, the ruin of rate wars, the fevers of speculation, had an exaggerated respect for the stability of pools, gentlemen's agreements and trusts as well as for the economies of large-scale production. By establishing great industrial machines turning out cheap goods for ordered markets they believed they had carried civilization on to a higher plane. Far from being apologetic about monopoly they accepted it as part of a natural order. 'It is too late to argue about advantages of industrial combinations,' said John D. Rockefeller before the Industrial Commission in 1899, 'they are a necessity.'[1]

This acceptance of order and control, of a 'community of interest', presented something of a contradiction to a generation brought up to believe in the virtue of an open society governed by competition, *laissez-faire* and a free market. But the tycoons easily believed, and a large part of the American public with them, that their success was due to superior qualities. There could be no question but that they were smart men. As William Vanderbilt said of the Standard Oil crowd, he 'never came in contact with any class of men as smart and able as they are in their business and I think a great deal is to be attributed to that'.[2] John D. Rockefeller was brought up to be

[1] Testimony of John D. Rockefeller, 30 December 1899; *Report of the U.S. Industrial Commission*, I. 796–7.
[2] Testimony of William H. Vanderbilt, 29 August 1879; *Proceedings of the Special Committee on Railroads* (Hepburn Committee), II, 1668–9; quoted in T. G. Manning

smart: 'I cheat my boys every time I get a chance,' said his father. '... I trade with the boys and skin 'em and just beat 'em every time I can, I want to make 'em smart.'[1] A whole generation brought up on the stories of Horatio Alger—a transatlantic Samuel Smiles—believed that industry, thrift and probity would bring any office-boy to the top of the industrial tree; and there were enough examples to make the belief plausible. Of the gang with whom the boy Carnegie played in Rebecca Street, Allegheny, on the 'wrong side' of the river from Pittsburgh, Robert Pitcairn became Vice-President of the Pennsylvania Railroad, David McCargo was the driving force behind the Allegheny Valley Railroad and Henry Oliver made a vast fortune in oil and iron mining. Rockefeller was an Alger hero, with his fifteen-hour day at the refinery, his scrupulous book-keeping, his Sunday-school teaching, his ten per cent of income for charities, his single-minded preoccupation with 'oil, oil, oil'. If priggishness was also one of his qualities this, too, fitted the Alger pattern: 'Don't be a good fellow,' he warned his Bible class, '... every downfall is traceable, directly or indirectly, to the victim's good fellowship, his good cheer among his friends, who come as quickly as they go. We have to apologise every day for this class of men who fill our hospitals, our asylums, our poorhouses and the very gutters of our streets. Look on them and don't be a good fellow.'[2] Carnegie believed that the talent for organization was rare and that the energetic individual who possessed it would amass great wealth in which he should be protected. 'Upon the sacredness of property civilization itself depends', he wrote, '—the right of the laborer to his hundred dollars in the savings bank and equally the legal right of the millionaire to his millions.'[3] In his autobiography, in *Triumphant Democracy* and in popular, ghost-written articles this immigrant steel magnate took it upon himself to justify to the English-speaking community the accumulation of wealth as a social force: 'Individualism, Private Property, the Law of the Accumulation of wealth and the Law of Competition ...

and D. M. Potter, *Government & the American Economy 1870–Present* (New York, 1950), p. 81.
[1] Allan Nevins, *John D. Rockefeller* (New York, 1940), vol. I, p. 93.
[2] *Ibid.* p. 80.
[3] Andrew Carnegie, 'Wealth', *North American Review*, CXLVIII, (1889).

these are the highest results of human experience, the soil in which society so far has produced the best fruit.'[1] He believed that wealth and the power which went with it were best exercised in the hands of the superior individual who had the talents not only to confer great material benefits on society in the field of production but to dispose of that wealth in the interest of the highest culture. 'Without wealth there can be no Maecenas', he wrote. With this went the corollary that the superior individual had a duty to dispose of his wealth to the advantage of the community—or, as he would have said, the 'race'. 'No man,' he said, 'should die rich.' Carnegie practised what he preached. In his retirement, which he spent shuttling between New York and Scotland, he devoted the bulk of his steel fortune to philanthropy in the Atlantic world, especially in the realm of education which, as a self-made Scot, he felt to be the indispensable basis of the career open to talent. His example, copied by others of his peers, developed into the great tradition of private foundations for the support of education and the arts, for the amelioration of poverty and disease, which has become an integral part of American, and indeed of Atlantic, culture. The benefactions of Rockefeller and Harkness in oil; Frick in steel; Sage, Huntington, Stanford and Hill in railways; Whitney, Morgan and Mellon in banking; Ford in automobiles, are only a few of the more prominent memorials to magnates who believed in Carnegie's gospel of wealth.

Carnegie never faced the full implications of concentration. For him the life of a business was the superior individual who gave it force to survive. He did not sufficiently take into account the fact that great corporate aggregations might perish after the dynamic impulse had lost its thrust; and he was too sanguine about the opportunities for the enterprising but unestablished individual in a mature economy. For although Carnegie belonged to a generation remarkable for its self-made men, it now seems clear that inherited money and social connections have been more important in American business success than folklore of the Alger kind allows.[2] But even

[1] Andrew Carnegie, *loc. cit.*
[2] See Dwight C. Mills, 'The American Business Elite: A Collective Portrait', *Journal of Economic History*, vol. V, 1945, Supplement.

Carnegie recognized that competition tended to operate, not as a perpetual system of self-adjustment, but as a knock-out contest: 'While the law (of competition) may be sometimes hard for the individual, it is best for the race, because it insures the survival of the fittest,'[1] or, as Rockefeller put it: 'The American Beauty rose is only brought to flower by sacrificing the early buds.' These assertions are tell-tale evidence of a new mode of thinking which appeared from across the Atlantic just in time to reconcile the embarrassing discrepancy between the teaching of classic economic theory and the monolithic facts of the economic landscape, between individualism and the anonymity of a mass society. This was the doctrine of evolution.

In 1882 when the Englishman, Herbert Spencer, landed in New York on a lecture tour, he had to be spirited away by friends from the press of the curious and the admiring. He was the author of *Social Statics* which, by extension and analogy, applied the ideas of Charles Darwin to the study of society. Darwin and Spencer together revolutionized attitudes to institutions in the United States. Instead of a mechanical universe kept in equilibrium by self-regulating contrivances there was substituted the idea of an organic universe in constant growth and mutation from lower to higher forms of life. The idea that institutions were social organisms, subject to the dynamic processes of evolution, was arresting to a generation which had experienced such rapid changes. In particular, Darwin's law of the survival of the fittest appealed to men who had begun to feel that they had to deal, not with a market place, but a jungle. Herbert Spencer provided a convincing reconciliation between individualism and *laissez-faire* on the one hand and corporate monopoly on the other. American writers began to acclimatize these ideas to American conditions. William Graham Sumner popularized the Darwinian version of *laissez-faire* from his chair of political and social science at Yale in the 1880s and '90s: 'The "strong" and the "weak" are terms which admit of no definition unless they are made equivalent to the industrious and the idle, the frugal and the extravagant . . . If we do not like the survival of the fittest, we have only one possible alternative and that is the survival

[1] Carnegie, *loc. cit.*

of the unfittest. The former is the law of civilization; the latter is the law of anti-civilization.'[1] John Fiske, popular historian and lecturer, sounded the old messianic theme of American history in the new tonality of evolution. He saw American institutions as the triumphant result of a process of trial and error stretching back through English history to the German forests of Tacitus. Moreover, by his conviction that Providence had guided the evolution of America he reconciled to evolutionary ideas an important body of people, especially in the Churches, who had resisted Darwin because he associated man with the lower animals, and Spencer because he seemed by his materialistic determinism to rob man of his divine spark.

Such views encouraged a belief in divine right among the *nouveaux riches*, a faith that the concentration of business had created a ruling class with the power and the duty of controlling the destinies of the Republic. There were greater extremes between riches and poverty than America had ever known. As a result of these growing inequalities there was a hardening of class barriers separating a powerful metropolitan upper class from the mass of rural dwellers and industrial labourers, with a small 'white collar' class in between. As Carnegie himself put it: 'We assemble thousands of operatives in the factory, in the mine and in the counting-house, of whom the employer can know little or nothing and to whom the employer is little better than a myth. All intercourse between them is at an end. Rigid castes are formed and, as usual, mutual ignorance breeds mutual distrust. . . . Human society loses homogeneity.'[2] The rich frankly accepted these new conditions and justified their power in aristocratic terms. The men in frock-coats, who watched the ticker-tape and spent long hours studying complex case-histories of business, had an exceptionally self-conscious sense of *noblesse oblige*. When Morgan quietly organized the syndicate of bankers which saved Americans from the worst consequences of the 1907 panic he believed with simple sincerity that he was doing his duty not merely to family and class but to the nation and to an

[1] Quoted by M. Curti, 'The Literature of Ideas', R. E. Spiller and others, *Literary History of the United States* (New York, 1948), vol. II, p. 976.
[2] Carnegie, *loc. cit.*

Episcopalian Deity who had singled him out for special service. The philanthropy of a Carnegie or a Rockefeller was the result of public-spirited, even pious, conviction. As the pressure of Wall Street was replaced by the leisure of Long Island, new family dynasties, allied now to the older patrician stocks and to European noble houses, cultivated a refinement of manners and taste which brought fame and fortune to architects, prima donnas, art dealers and restaurateurs. An hierarchy of clubs, social lists, débutante seasons and schools reinforced the exclusiveness of the 'best families' from New York to San Francisco.

But this class did not constitute an aristocracy. The tycoons for the most part never transcended their business origins. Business remained their overriding passion. Unlike their English counterparts whose ambition was to rise in the social scale by acquiring landed estates, marrying their daughters into county families and sending their sons into Parliament, successful American business men stayed with their businesses and brought up their sons to believe that the manly life was to be found, not in the aristocratic code of hunting, war, government and the arts, but in pioneering new industrial frontiers. The continuing success of American enterprise owes much to this fact. This meant, however, that they had no resources left over to play a larger part in American society. Charles Francis Adams, that true patrician in business, delivered a devastating judgment on them from this point of view: 'I have known . . . a good many "successful" men—"big" financially—and a less interesting crowd I do not care to encounter. . . . Not one that I have ever known would I care to meet again, either in this world or the next.' Their training, education and tradition were not such as to make it easy for them to see beyond their own narrow interests to those of society as a whole. Indeed, like business men before and since, they identified the interests of the State with their own. They considered politics no career for a 'gentleman' and the armed services and departments of state as refuges for moral weaklings. Their attitude to the State is symbolized by the surprise of J. P. Morgan when President Theodore Roosevelt brought an action against him under the Sherman Act in the *Northern Securities* case. 'If we have done anything wrong,' he said to the President, 'send your man to see my man and they can fix it up.'[1] He could not believe that Roosevelt would be so ungentlemanly as to challenge the established code of business behaviour; nor that there was anything odd about No. 23 Wall Street's negotiating on equal terms with the White House. These plutocrats had, indeed, no roots in American society save those in the business which had originally nourished them. Their purchase of country estates on Long Island or on the Maryland shores carried with it little sense of identity with, and responsibility towards, a local community and larger interests. Many simply played the stage role of English squire with all its costumes and properties in an elaborately half-timbered mansion behind the high walls of a closely guarded estate. Nor was their pursuit of the arts anything more than superficial. Instead of acting as patrons to living American painters—let alone writers and musicians—they preferred to collect old masterpieces with a rarity value to satisfy a millionaire's desire to combine monopoly with conspicuous display. They left culture to their wives and daughters whose tastes were not aristocratic, but either vulgarly ostentatious or discreetly genteel, retarding rather than advancing the growth of a genuine vernacular.

There was no place for an aristocracy in America even had the plutocracy been of slower growth, more stable in its membership and broader in its interests. In spite of the tendency of industrialism to accentuate class differences, American society was still too fluid, too mobile, too diverse in its regional interests, too dynamic in its attitude to change, too set in its aspiration after individual values, too hostile to concentrated power, to allow of loyalties to an aristocracy. Consequently the plutocracy, however powerful, failed to acquire a recognized ascendancy. It remained one 'interest' among many in the body politic, only one of many 'in' groups claiming superiority over the menacing 'out' groups of an open society. Even the 'exclusive' societies of the plutocracy, which appear to be analogous to those of European aristocracies, bear more relation to much humbler American counterparts, like the Masons, the Elks and the Grand Army of the Republic. The elaborate formalities of the débutante, whether in New York or St Paul, bear little relation

[1] L. Corey, *The House of Morgan* (New York, 1930), p. 316.

to that of the Court of St James; the Racquet Club of New York and the Harvard Club of Boston are too self-conscious for the denizen of Pall Mall to be entirely at home in them and the traditions of the First Troop Philadelphia Cavalry are too mannered even for the members of the Honourable Artillery Company. Groton is too patently an imitation of an English public school ever to produce natural leaders for the American community: and its alumni have been doomed to preserve their exclusiveness without acquiring an easily recognized responsibility. America's plutocrats failed, inevitably, to acquire the natural ascendancy of aristocrats. And although in their hey-day they were not gainsaid, they could expect sooner or later, in the American system of balanced interests, to meet with a check.

The group of Americans whose interests were most directly affected were the workingmen who were forced to make inhuman adjustments to the machine order without benefiting, at least in the first generation, from the increase in productivity. When capital was tied up in elaborate plant and machinery, in raw material and distribution 'pipelines', the workingman suffered. 'Under the law of competition,' wrote Carnegie, 'the employer of thousands is forced into the strictest economies, among which the rates paid to labour figure prominently.'[1] Craftsmen were replaced by machines tended by semi-skilled workmen hired by the day and were turned loose to face starvation at the first sign of a fall in orders. When he was working, the average industrial hand earned in 1890 only twelve dollars for a sixty-hour week, and the unskilled labourer only eight dollars. In steel, men worked a twelve-hour day seven days a week as late as in the 1920s. In a sweated trade like clothing wages were as low as four and five dollars—not a wage to exist on by any contemporary standard—and women and children rarely earned more. Often workers had no choice but to live in tied cottages and to shop in company stores. The heavy risk of accident from unguarded machinery added to the worker's insecurity. No wonder that, in Carnegie's words, 'often there is friction between the employer and the employed'. But if the worker attempted to improve

[1] Carnegie, *loc. cit.*

his bargaining position by collective action, he was frustrated by company agents, and by mercenaries, hired from that enterprising English immigrant Allan Pinkerton, effectively armed and mobilized at trouble-points by means of railway and telegraph. The employer could often dispense altogether with an obstreperous labour force. Blacklegs were rushed from other parts of the continent, including Canada, to break strikes; natives were replaced by immigrants brought in under contract; and later, such was the mobility of American industry that whole factories moved to areas of cheaper labour-supply, as when cotton and steel companies moved south to Alabama and Carolina to take advantage of docile Negro workers.

Before the present century the workingman could look for no outside help in resisting the overwhelming pressure of capitalism. As we have seen, public opinion as a whole believed profoundly in *laissez-faire*. The dissident views of workingmen made little headway against those of the farmers, traders, business and professional men who in 1890 still constituted two-thirds of the gainfully employed. The occasional immigrant anarchist or socialist who raised his head in labour disturbances was enough to convince most Americans that labour troubles were the work of foreign ideas and agitators. The courts still relied on the old common-law of conspiracy to deny adequate rights of collective bargaining, and permitted extravagant use of the injunction to forestall direct action by labour in industrial disputes. As for the sympathies of politicians, in 1894 the liberal-minded Cleveland, on the advice of his Attorney-General, Richard Olney, himself a railway lawyer, sent Federal troops to put down the Pullman strike in spite of the bitter protests of Governor Altgeld of Illinois who denied that they were necessary.

Workingmen were handicapped by confusion about their long-term interests. The greatest impediment to collective action was not simply the craftsman's suspicion of the unskilled labourer, nor that of the native against the immigrant prepared to work for lower wages, nor the immigrant's ignorance and the difficulty of getting co-operation between Ukrainians and Austrians, Poles and Italians, but the lack of conviction among most workingmen that they constituted a separate class. Whether skilled craftsman, Nebraska farm boy, or European peasant, the industrial worker believed his job to be only a temporary makeshift, a stepping-stone to better things. The absence of a stratified social hierarchy which in Europe disciplined the workingman to membership of a working *class*, enabled his American counterpart to dissociate his job from his social status. This fact helps to explain the slow pace of unionization.

This psychological attitude, however, gave the American workingman strength to pit himself against the might of capitalism when conditions became intolerable. Like the settler before him who struck out for the west rather than submit to an order of squires and yeomen, the workingman refused to accept as natural a social hierarchy of bosses and labourers. He reacted to intimidation with independence and a sense of outrage. When bullets ricochetted off the walls of Colorado canyons; when the steelmen of Homestead repulsed an amphibious assault by an army of Frick's strike-breakers sent up the Allegheny River in barges; when the vagabond agents of the I.W.W.—called 'bindle-stiffs' because they carried their belongings in a bundle—went from job to job organizing migratory workers at harvest time in the Far West; when feuding hillbilly families of the Appalachians like the Hatfields and McCoys took sides in the bitter guerrilla warfare between Molly Maguires and vigilantes in the West Virginia coalfields, there is a sense in which the labour movement must be regarded as one of the last American frontiers.

The incipient labour movement after the Civil War, like that in Jackson's time, began by following the will-o'-the-wisp of political action. The National Labor Union and the Knights of Labor welcomed to their ranks all who accepted a platform which included not only an eight-hour day but woman suffrage and farmers' co-operatives. But, following the earlier pattern, their successes came in the organizing of strikes for higher wages and shorter hours during rising periods of employment after the War and in the late '70s and the early '80s. The National Labor Union forced the Federal Government to accept an eight-hour day for its employees and to repeal the contract labour law. The Knights made history by forcing Jay Gould to negotiate an agreement across the table with the railwaymen of his network; and as a result of this and other triumphs they boasted a membership of something like 700,000. But these gains were more apparent than real. The Knights had neither discipline nor organization to withstand hard times. Moreover, public opinion was whipped into new hostility by the embarrassing activity of the Black International. The Haymarket affair of 1886 excited such hysteria in the general public, which associated all labour activity with anarchism and worse, that employers like Gould took back their concessions, the Knights lost their initiative and within a few years had dwindled into insignificance. The grandiose attack on all fronts and on a national scale was a failure.

By contrast, the next group of labour crises were *ad hoc* attempts by workers to protect themselves from the hard times of 1892–3. The severity of this depression left a profound mark on both capital and labour, second only to that of 1929–33. The sudden contraction which followed the expanding years left even sound businesses over-extended and risking bankruptcy. Faced with a shrinking market, the Carnegie Company itself, under the generalship of Carnegie and his lieutenant, Frick, took characteristic action in 1892 by announcing ruthless wage cuts. The great Homestead strike which resulted in the summer of that year was a fully-mounted war; it was won by the iron-willed Frick only after an attempt on his life by a Polish anarchist had so turned opinion against the strikers that their nerve broke. So decisive was the victory that the steel industry was able to outlaw unions for another forty years. In 1894 Eugene Debs's railway union organized a strike of workers at the 'model' company town of the Pullman Palace Car Company near Chicago with the object of having wage cuts restored and conditions improved. This strike also was broken after the gratuitous intervention, mentioned above, on p. 254, of the Federal Government with the backing of public opinion. Such were the high-lights of a period of violent strike action which once again failed to make an impression against the entrenched power of capitalism.

Meanwhile, however, another attack achieved limited gains. Homestead and Pullman were strikes by a whole industry; and although they failed they provided certain lessons. The Homestead strike had been started by, and fought in the interests of, skilled steelmen supported by unskilled immigrants who had little to gain. In the end, although the unskilled lost their jobs the skilled were reinstated. The failure at Pullman broke up the railway union but led to the formation of a whole series of small, well-disciplined craft 'brotherhoods' of engineers, trainmen and conductors which, by keeping themselves exclusive and bargaining on specific issues, won an unchallenged authority by the time of the First World War. Skilled men were in a better bargaining position than unskilled.

The skilled steelworkers of Homestead were affiliated to a new organization which had already begun to carry a stage further the principle of organizing unions on the basis of craft skill as opposed to industry. The American Federation of Labor, founded under that name in 1886, consisted of a loose confederation of individual craft unions often crossing industry boundaries. This association of the aristocrats among workmen, which became the first successful national labour force in the United States, ultimately reconciled Americans to the principle, at any rate, of unions. It was the child of Samuel Gompers, who remained its president and mentor until his death in 1924. This conservative-minded immigrant accepted the new industrial order and concentrated the energies of the Federation on the practical task of improving the position of labour within it. He never tired of insisting that he had no ideological aims but was concerned simply with practical gains in terms of wages, hours and conditions of work. 'We have no ultimate ends. We are going on from day to day.' His concept of a partnership between labour and management has contributed not a little to the characteristic receptiveness of the American workingman towards new methods of increasing productivity. Under his brilliant leadership, the American Federation of Labor, steering clear of politics and violence, emerged alongside the independent railway brotherhoods as a recognized spokesman for the interests of skilled workmen. By 1920 these two groups had a combined membership of nearly five million.

But these five million were less than a third of the total labour force; and, for the rest, union recognition was a slow, uphill struggle concluded only in our own time. Even the skilled trades in steel and in the Ford plants were successfully forbidden to unionize until the

1930s. The story of the miners is one of violence, partial successes and heartbreaking setbacks. The United Mineworkers Union, organized by John Mitchell in 1898, has a history of engagements which 'sound like battle honours'—the Cripple Creek War of 1893–4, the Reading Anthracite Strike of 1902, the Trinidad Coal Strike of 1913–14. The French Canadian textile workers of New England, facing the competition of southern Negroes, lived through a fierce epidemic of strikes at the time of the First World War, organized by the International Workers of the World (Wobblies), a scattering of syndicalist agitators whose only programme, expressed in slogans and songs sung to popular hymn tunes, was violent protest. Even worse was the plight of the unskilled who could be aided only by industrial unions. Between the '90s and the early 1920s attempts were made, again by the I.W.W., to lead this defenceless and largely inert mass into battle. But the 'one big industrial union' of which the Wobblies sang was as Utopian as their methods were ineffective. Unskilled workers had to wait until our own time when, as a result of the 1929–33 depression, a new national organization, the Congress of Industrial Organizations, unionized their ranks.

The brutal history of these years softened public opinion towards the workingman's efforts to protect his interests. Already in 1902 President Theodore Roosevelt had reversed Cleveland's attitude towards strikes by forcing the Reading Railroad to accept his arbitration in the anthracite strike of that year. Under Wilson, a start was made in protective labour legislation and new authority was given to the Federal Department of Labor. Employers themselves discovered the need for a body representing labour with which they could bargain; and though, in the reactionary 1920s, many followed the example of Rockefeller who, after the Trinidad Coal Strike of 1913, invented a tame 'company' union to perform this function, the more thoughtful accepted the inevitable in the early 1930s. Slowly and reluctantly Americans came to recognize organized labour as an 'interest' proper to a capitalist democracy.

But the collectivist programmes, discernible in Europe before the First World War, could not thrive in the American political climate. The idea of 'welfare' as the responsibility of the State was still alien to a society which thought of moral worth in terms of individual effort. In that expanding economy it was assumed that the true hope of betterment for workingmen lay in the increased productivity of private industry, which alone could provide jobs and a higher standard of living; and that the weak should be cared for out of the profits of industry by private philanthropists best able to judge the merits of local claims. It is true that Eugene Debs, whom a prison sentence after the Pullman strike made into a socialist, attracted something like a million votes to his Socialist Party in the Presidential elections immediately before and after the First World War. But although many of these were the votes of workingmen, the labour movement as a whole was no longer beguiled by political action. Instead, it followed Gompers' lead in acting as a separate interest to obtain favours from the party which offered most, from the municipal to the Federal level. For labour, acting alone, could never hope to be a decisive influence in American politics which have been susceptible to control only by combinations of interests. Only by making common cause with the other great group victimized by capitalism—the farmers—were workingmen likely to exert effective political pressure to better their condition.

American farmers were the most unrepentant of individualists. Yet their plight was such, especially in West and South,[1] that even they were forced to combine to withstand it. To begin with, the loneliness of prairie or back-country farm was insupportable. When two clerks resigned from the Department of Agriculture to promote a secret society called the Patrons of Husbandry, designed to help farmers enrich their social resources, they found a ready response in the hard years of 1872–5. By the mid-'70s not less than 800,000 farmers and their wives—women were characteristically included on the same basis as men—were meeting together round stoves in oil-lit schoolhouses from Minnesota to Mississippi to talk farm 'shop', listen to lectures and concerts, organize libraries and plan beanfeasts. Farmers, meeting together in these Granges as they were called and in other associations, impatient with mere morale-building activities, began to think of ways to defeat the power of the

[1] See ch. viii.

railways, middlemen and bankers which threatened their well-being.

In order to eliminate middlemen the Granges negotiated with manufacturers to sell direct to their members. The great mail-order house of Montgomery Ward, which was founded in Chicago in 1872 with the purpose of dealing direct with the Grangers, managed so to cut prices that other manufacturers had to follow suit. As a result of manufacturers' concessions, Grangers in Illinois could buy reapers for 275 dollars less than the standard price. In Iowa, farmers even experimented in the co-operative manufacture of farm machinery. When at the behest of grain merchants railways refused any longer to allow farmers to shovel their grain into cars for direct sale, the farmers retaliated by building co-operative elevators to side-step the monopoly of private companies. By 1905 there were more than a hundred of these co-operative elevators in Illinois alone. Co-operative selling of dairy products spread from pioneers in western New York to the Middle West, especially to Wisconsin, where by 1900 nearly two-thirds of the creameries were co-operative; and a beginning was made in the co-operative marketing of livestock and fruit. Farmers also undertook their own insurance, telephone and electricity services, and organized their own retail stores on the Rochdale plan. In 1907 about half the farmers of America were involved in some form of co-operative enterprise; and a community of Swedes at Svea, Minnesota, went far to achieve a complete co-operative existence, with their own creamery, store, bank, insurance, telephones and grain elevator.[1] These achievements were characteristic of that spirit of rural self-help which, from the days of the early 'communitarian' experiments onwards, has enabled farmers to take a stand against what has appeared to them to be an out-of-State, urban, capitalistic tyranny. And though, like the old communities, many of the co-operatives were such in name only, or lapsed into private hands, the spirit of co-operation has been important in North American agrarian radicalism down to the present day.

But there was one monopoly which farmers could not tackle by market action. The railways' privileges were backed by law, and

[1] F. A. Shannon, *op. cit.* p. 346.

the only way to remedy abuses was through politics. The Grange frowned on politics; but its members stayed behind after meetings had been formally adjourned to discuss political action against the railways. In the 1870s the Grange and other independent farmers' organizations began to work for anti-monopoly parties in the Middle West which had railway regulation as their object. As a result of such lobbying, measures permitting the State regulation of railways were passed in the agrarian States of the North-west. A bitter struggle with the railways to make the enforcement of these Granger laws effective culminated in a series of Supreme Court decisions, beginning in 1876 with *Munn* v. *Illinois*, which established the right of States to regulate rates even in inter-State traffic. However, in the Wabash case of 1886, the Supreme Court reversed itself to the extent of denying the right of States to regulate the inter-State traffic of railways originating in the State. This placed the urgent issue of railway regulation at the door of the Federal Government. The result was the Inter-State Commerce Act of the following year, which outlawed rebates, unreasonable rates, long- and short-haul discrimination, pools and traffic agreements, and established an Inter-State Commerce Commission to administer the law. By this Act the Federal Government, under pressure from the mid-western farm States, set bounds to the illicit profits which the railways could make at the farmer's expense and established the principle that railways, because they were peculiarly monopolistic, should be subject to special government regulation. But in practice the law contained too many loopholes and its police powers were too weak to be effective; and although in the '90s the farmer gained some relief from falling rail charges, the practice of government regulation of railways remained to be worked out in the twentieth century.

The farmer's limited gains against middlemen and railways brought little relief from the hard times which set in about 1881 when farm prices took a new downward turn. After this year the price of cotton never again reached ten cents a pound during the rest of the century. As a result many a poor yeoman farmer in the South, already in the grip of his merchant creditor, sank to the level of tenant or share-cropper. Low prices for wheat, corn and beef cattle, which hit the prairies and High Plains, ended the land boom in 1887 and brought its crop of farm mortgages into the banker's hopper. The methods of the Grange were not militant enough to satisfy men faced with ruin. Instead, out of the farmers' clubs there arose a new set of associations with the object of attacking the agents of capitalism on a broad political front: the Grand State Alliance of Texas, the Agricultural Wheel which originated in Arkansas, the Farmers' Clubs of South Carolina—all of which emerged as the Southern Alliance—and the National Farmers' Alliance of the North-west. Both these main groups advocated the same comprehensive list of reforms, including the nationalization of the railways, laws to end speculation in farm produce, to prevent alien ownership of land and recovery of railway land grants, national aid to irrigation, a graduated income tax and the secret ballot. From 1890, the Alliances voiced the aggressive temper of farmers in local and State politics throughout the West and South. Stump orators like 'Sockless' Jerry Simpson ousted their established opponents from Congress, and Mary Elizabeth Lease, speaking from her hard-travelling buggy, exhorted Kansas farmers to 'raise less corn and more hell'. Out of a convention of the Alliances of St Louis in 1892 was born the Populist Party which, under James B. Weaver, attracted more than a million farm votes in the Presidential Election of that year. An effective protest-party had arisen. It remained to be seen whether it could build up power enough to capture the national administration.

Before all else, the Populists became obsessed with the need for monetary reform. The foreclosures and bankruptcies of those years seared into the farmer's consciousness the conviction that the cause of his troubles went beyond the oppression of railways and middle-men to the manipulation of the nation's money and credit system in the interests of the capitalist class. The old hostility of the agrarian debtor to his absentee, and apparently parasitic, creditor was intensified by the persistent deflationary trend of prices between 1865 and 1896. The appreciation of the dollar was attributed, in part correctly, to the failure of the currency supply to keep pace with the needs of an expanding society. The United States completed its return from the paper, 'greenback' currency of the war years to a gold standard by 1879 in spite of protests by farmers demanding a 'managed' currency. Falling prices, high interest rates and the increasing burden of farm debt were inevitably attributed to the inadequacies of a currency based on a limited supply of gold which seemed patently designed to benefit the money-lending and property-owning classes. Abandoning the paper money issue, the inflationary opposition shifted its attack to advocating a currency in which ample supplies of silver from the western mines would once again be allowed to circulate on the same basis as gold. Silver became the central issue of American politics; and to the opposing standards of silver and gold there rallied in the 1890s hostile armies which cut across party allegiances and represented a greater social cleavage than America had known since the time of Jackson.

Silver gave the Populists the chance to break through the conventional party structure and capture national power; for it attracted to their cause, not merely the rural States of West and South but the new silver-mining States of the Far West; and the inclusion of a labour programme was expected to attract the workingman. But in 1896 at its Chicago Convention the Democratic Party, which under Cleveland had been loyal to gold, was captured for the Populist interest by the young spell-binding orator from the Platte River, William Jennings Bryan, whose famous peroration, 'You shall not press down upon the brow of labor this crown of thorns, you shall not crucify mankind upon a cross of gold,' stirred wild emotions from the Dakotas to the Gulf; and the Populist Convention had no alternative but to endorse the Democratic ticket. As the election approached, conservative Republicans of wealth and social standing in eastern cities gave Mark Hanna a record war chest and prepared to do battle in defence of the citadel of property and sound—which meant gold—values. In the event, the efforts of these neo-Hamiltonians were sufficient to save the day. Bryan was narrowly defeated; and with McKinley in the White House they could dismiss the nightmare of insurgent government by 'hayseeds' from the 'sticks' who would nationalize railways and play fast and loose with the dollar.

The Populist attack of 1896 proved to be the last convulsion of the old, rural, individualistic America. For all the remarkable success of the silverites—Bryan secured some 45 per cent of the popular vote—their defeat was decisive. It revealed weaknesses too great to enable the Populists to continue as a third party in American politics. The emphasis on silver as a panacea drew attention away from more realistic reforms and entangled the movement in an alliance with western silver kings who had no true sympathy with agrarian radicalism. Southern separatism not only prevented a union of the Southern with the North-west Alliance on account of the problem of Negro membership, but encouraged that fusion with the Democrats which in 1896 robbed the People's Party of independent action and ensured that the spearhead of Populism as an insurgent movement should be blunted by the body armour of the conventional party machine. The Populists failed entirely in their bid to attract vital labour votes from eastern States. If the moribund Knights of Labor flirted with the Alliance, the American Federation of Labor would have nothing to do with a political movement which included employers. Although farmers and workingmen had a common interest in redressing the balance of power against capitalism, they were still too far apart in basic sympathy to combine effectively. Manifold as were the farmer's problems, there was little, as D. W. Brogan has pointed out, that dollar wheat could not cure; and indeed an upturn in prices in the summer of 1896 made its own contribution, through a slackening of interest in the autumn elections, to the defeat of Bryan at the polls. The enthusiasm of farmers for insurgent action in politics quickly evaporated in the warm sun of the prosperous first decade of the twentieth century, just as the enthusiasm of the Knights of Labor evaporated at the prospect of effective bargaining for a larger share in the profits of capitalism. Workingmen and farmers went their own ways. America had to wait another thirty years for her first effective farmer-labour party; and that, too, was only to be a temporary liaison, born of crisis.

In spite of the decline of Populism, much of its programme was adopted in States and nation within the next twenty years. The evils of the new industrial order became evident not merely to its most immediate victims but to a more general public increasingly impatient for reforms.

The Democratic Idea and the Hegemony of Big Business

The creation of an informed public was in part the work of that characteristic American hero—the crusading journalist. Ever since the days of Jackson, when first a 'public' opinion became effective in politics, there had been men to use the crude material of broadsheet and gazette in protest against oligarchy. The trumpet of Horace Greeley's *Tribune*, played in muted and genteel style after the war by E. L. Godkin's *Nation*, was followed about the turn of the century by a whole brass band of journalists giving contrapuntal expression to a single set of themes.

It all started with the publication in 1881 in the *Atlantic Monthly* of an article entitled 'The Story of a Great Monopoly'. This 'exposure' of Standard Oil, by a Chicago free lance named Henry Demarest Lloyd, followed in the '90s by his book, *Wealth Against Commonwealth*, and by Ida Tarbell's history of the oil trust, established the conventionally hostile judgment on the ethics of the Rockefeller associates which has persisted until the present. Lloyd's example led in the early years of the new century to the publication of a spate of money-making articles in magazines such as *Cosmopolitan*, *Everybody's* and *McClure's* dealing with the seamy side of 'modern' American life. Lincoln Steffens, who exposed the corruption of machine government in the cities, and Jacob Riis, who went into New York's immigrant slums to describe 'How the Other Half Lives', were only two of the more famous journalists 'covering' every newsworthy example of exploitation they could find, from trusts to prostitution. With these 'muck-rakers', as Theodore Roosevelt contemptuously and unfairly dubbed them, must be linked a new generation of didactic novelists such as Frank Norris, who exposed the Southern Pacific in *The Octopus* and the Chicago wheat exchange in *The Pit*, or Upton Sinclair, who attacked the Chicago stockyards in *The Jungle*. These writers did for the America of the bitter 1890s what Dickens did for the England of the Hungry Forties.

The reading matter of the thoughtful American went beyond journalism to popular tracts offering nostrums for the agues of capitalism. Edward Bellamy's socialist Utopia, *Looking Backward*, expressing that yearning for a 'change of heart' which is one response to the brutish facts of an acquisitive society, was devoured by a mass public on both sides of the Atlantic,[1] and Bellamy Clubs sprang up on every hand. Even more famous in English and American households was Henry George, whose *Progress and Poverty* (1879) made a characteristically western contribution to the Anglo-American armoury of socialist ideas. Writing in California at the outset of the agrarian crusade, obsessed by the railway monopoly of land, and heir to the land reformers, George advocated a single tax on unearned increment from land ownership. Although Bellamy and George comforted millions of earnest, if ill-educated, readers rocking on the porches of small-town America, thoughtful minds in well-to-do city homes patronized more sophisticated writers such as Herbert Croly, founder of the *New Republic*, whose *Promise of American Life* (1909) preached the need to translate the Declaration of Independence into economic terms.

Alongside this chorus of protest and advocacy there was to be detected a newly critical and rebellious temper in the rapidly growing universities and colleges where scholars were bringing a more 'scientific', detached and relativist approach to social problems. The young historian, Charles Beard, back from Oxford where he had helped to found Ruskin College for workingmen, began those elementary researches into the financial interests of the Founding Fathers which, when published in 1913, were to shake the official hagiography and visit academic ostracism upon their author. These years, during which a Princeton professor of politics was acquiring experience to be President, were the golden age of 'political science' when men believed that the evils of tyranny and war could be cured by the science of political engineering. The same scientific attitude, when applied by men like L. H. Morgan, who had learned anthropology from studying Indians, or Lester Ward who, like Spencer, started with Darwin, produced the first American sociology. Perhaps the most characteristic response to the problems of these years was that of a Norwegian immigrant's son from Minnesota called Thorstein Veblen who, in a lifetime spent suspended unhappily between his rejected family background and the world of mid-western Philistines, evolved in his *Theory of the Leisure Class* and *Theory of Business Enterprise* a social theory for American

[1] It prompted William Morris to reply in *News from Nowhere*.

capitalism. Combining the ideas of anthropology, psychology and evolution, Veblen saw economic growth as the result of conflict between the predatory and the industrious elements in society.

But though this new generation of intellectuals were rebels they were not revolutionaries. They rejected the outmoded absolutes of natural rights, the old dogmas of religion; but they by no means embraced the determinism offered them by evolution in biology and Marxism in politics. They kept faith with Emerson by retaining a stubborn sense of free will and belief in the autonomy of the individual in an open society. But instead of a lonely individual working out his salvation in a society preserved from anarchy only by a few fixed forms, they substituted an individual shaping his destiny by means of voluntary, co-operative interdependence with his fellows in a society which was dynamic, evolutionary and plural.

Their open-minded, relativist and above all pragmatic temperament was given philosophic form by a Harvard scholar who came to speculative thought by way of medicine and psychology. William James attempted to reconcile science with religion by inquiring into the psychological nature of religious experience. From his severely pragmatic approach he concluded that there were no absolutes in belief. Truthfulness in ideas depended on their effectiveness in action for one particular individual in one particular set of circumstances. Further, he considered that mind was not the antithesis of body but a function of the human organism, governed by instincts and habits. Rejecting determinism, however, he believed that the mind had a residual choice, a freedom of will, in the formation of habit, which enabled the human organism to adjust itself to social change. He thought of that adjustment in terms of self-help, initiative, competition, tolerance for dissidents, zest for living and the 'glories of choice and risk' in a never-finished, open universe.[1] In politics, James adhered to *laissez-faire* which was the best milieu for the struggle to live. But in his search for a moral equivalent to war which would satisfy the combative instinct he laid great stress on a co-operative attack on physical obstacles for the common social good, and in this he felt American society would become gradually more 'socialistic'. All in all, James's pragmatism, although owing

[1] M. Curti, *loc. cit.* to which I am indebted for this paragraph.

much to the English empirical tradition, was a characteristically American synthesis of old and new which gave his countrymen a satisfactory basis for action as they moved off into the twentieth century. It certainly provided a *rationale* for Progressivism in politics.

Progressivism was not an organized 'movement' so much as a yeast working in the parochial levels of politics. Populist sentiment lent emotional power, and the Progressives achieved their most outstanding success in Wisconsin, where, for over thirty years, led by the La Follettes, prosperous German farmers and small-town businessmen, conservative and stubbornly independent, hostile to big business operating from out-of-State Chicago, provided the Republican Party with its most liberal element. But as the character of its Wisconsin adherents indicates, Progressivism, although it took over the Populist programme, was more urban, middle-class and sophisticated, and its influence more pervasive and orthodox than its insurgent predecessor.

Independent citizens organized 'non-partisan' leagues to break the power of corrupt machines and restore the proper working of representative government. Cities such as Cincinnati and Toledo tackled the problem by appointing 'managers'—professional administrators with high salaries who stood a better chance than elected party men of resisting the seductions of spoilsmen. Some States, like Oregon under Governor U'Ren, tried by reforming their electoral machinery to restore and increase the power of the independent citizen over legislature and judiciary. In Madison, capital of Wisconsin, Robert M. La Follette built up a professional civil service and established close relations between the State Capitol and lively young social scientists such as Richard Ely and John R. Commons down the avenue at the State University. With their political machines thus revamped, Progressive parties followed the lead of Wisconsin in putting through advanced programmes of social and economic legislation—regulating railways, breaking up monopolies, fixing minimum wages and maximum hours, drawing up workmen's compensation schemes, factory and child labour acts and measures conserving the State's natural resources.

By 1900 the tide of reform was lapping at the Federal bastions.

But complacent after the Populist collapse, Washington slumbered on railway regulation, monopolies, land conservation, civil service reform and labour legislation. Reforms on a national scale were difficult to bring off. Even local reform parties, often improvised by well-meaning but inexperienced amateurs, tended to disintegrate after a seeming success, leaving old evils to return like weeds in an untended garden. Only where, as in Wisconsin, a Progressive party rested upon powerful interests could reform persist over the years. And at the Federal level it was even more imperative that some means should be found of working through the existing party structures. In the new age of bigness it was as foolish to baulk at machine politics as at the great corporation. Reforms, to be effective, had to be dramatized, made respectable and also made acceptable to the political bosses.

Fortunately, in 1901 at the moment when La Follette became Governor of Wisconsin and Tom Johnson was the reforming mayor of Cleveland, the assassination of President McKinley brought to the White House a statesman remarkably well qualified to bring the Progressive programme to the forefront of national politics. Theodore Roosevelt, descended from the Dutch patroons of New York, was of patrician birth; but, unlike his friend Henry Adams and his own Groton and Harvard contemporaries, he insisted on making a career in the distasteful business of politics, determined, as he told his family, to be a member of the ruling class. With his admired friend Henry Cabot Lodge, Senator from Massachusetts—who like himself was an accomplished historical writer—he represented something long absent from the American scene: the educated gentleman in public life. He had worked his way up in the Republican politics of New York as an advocate of honest government. His views on reform had led him to office as Civil Service Commissioner and New York's Police Commissioner. But unlike the 'do-gooders' and 'mugwumps' whom he so much despised, he was an effective, practical politician who understood and accepted the terms on which power was offered. Although as Governor of New York he quarrelled with Boss Platt, and although Boss Hanna tried to geld him by promoting him Vice-President, Roosevelt had as shrewd a sense of the value of party backing as the bosses had of his personality in winning elections. And his personality made him a great President.

Roosevelt had surmounted a sickly childhood with an assertive will and a passionate, boyish energy to meet physical and moral challenge. For 'T.R.' life was an unending struggle in which the fittest could only survive by imposing civilized values upon a world always threatened by reversion to decadence and chaos; a conviction which, as a Victorian, he expressed in terms of 'keeping in trim', 'decencies', 'gentlemanliness', and the antithesis between 'healthy' and 'morbid'. He was a conservative; and although in America, as he recognized, there was no place for the aristocrat, he was justifiably proud of being a 'gentleman democrat'. He thrust his ungainly, bespectacled figure into a wild variety of exploits, from hunting, bird-watching and sailing to writing, soldiering and politics, so absorbed that the encounters in which he appeared as the protagonist, part hero, part buffoon, seemed larger and more dramatic than life. In his energy and simplicity of moral vision he epitomized his generation. Determined to enforce the laws on the statute book, passionately interested in every nook and cranny of government, and standing foursquare on moral ground, Roosevelt kept a roused public opinion on tenterhooks with his aggressive campaign of reform.

Inveighing against 'malefactors of great wealth', he reinvigorated the Sherman Act of 1890 to force the dissolution of trust after trust, beginning with Morgan's Northern Securities Company in 1902, in order to prove that the United States Government was mightier than any business corporation. He put an end to the abuse of railway rebates. He arbitrated in the anthracite coal strike, recommended workmen's compensation laws and a pure food and drug act. But nearest the heart of this naturalist and ex-rancher was the conservation programme which Gifford Pinchot put through under his direction. By this some 235 million acres of mineral and forest land were placed in reserves, worn-out land was reclaimed and arid land irrigated, national parks, game preserves and bird refuges were marked off. In thus fending off western timber and mining interests he reversed the age-old drive for exploitation and set Americans on their new course of soil conservation and flood control which has led directly from his own Salt River project in Arizona to his cousin's Tennessee Valley Authority.

By his zest and imagination, his phrase-making and posturing, Roosevelt by 1909 had so successfully asserted the Presidential initiative and created so genial a climate for reform that his chosen successor, William Howard Taft, was able quietly to continue his efforts against the trusts. But 'T.R.'s' own wilfulness in 1912, when he led his progressive Republicans out of the party to fight his own, Bull Moose, campaign, made possible the most remarkable interlude of Democratic rule during all the long years of Republican ascendancy and ensured that the Progressive movement should burgeon into full flower at the hands of the party whose green fingers had tended its young shoots in the Populist decade.

The Republican split brought to the Presidency a man with some of Roosevelt's statesmanlike qualities. Like 'T.R.', Woodrow Wilson had an articulate, scholarly, gentlemanly mind, used to dealing in general principles, capable of an overall view and conscious of high moral purposes; and like 'T.R.' he was relatively uncommitted to 'interests' and determined to conduct good, honest government. Temperamentally, however, the two men differed greatly. Whereas Roosevelt had the choleric passion and the generosity in command which characterize the aristocrat, Wilson combined the phlegmatic intellectualism of the academic middle class with the stubborn rectitude of the Calvinist. For Wilson was born not in the expansive home of a Dutch patroon family, but in a Virginian manse to a Presbyterian minister of Scotch-Irish descent. After trying his hand at the law to no purpose, the young, studious and ambitious Wilson returned to his *alma mater* at Princeton as a teacher of history and politics and it was natural that, given his intellectual stature and concern for public life, he should have become President of the College. His logical and uncompromising mind, intent on reforming Princeton's fraternity system, brought him into head-on collision with his trustees at a moment when Boss Smith of New Jersey was looking round for a gubernatorial candidate who would placate the rising demand for reform in that machine-ridden State. It was characteristic of Wilson, not only that he should feel it his duty to accept the candidature, but that on becoming Governor in 1911 he should refuse to recognize any obligation to the men who had engineered his election and should instead embark on an effective reform programme which attracted to him the national spotlight. In view of his eminent 'availability' it was not surprising that he should become Democratic candidate for the Presidency in 1912.

Wilson's first administration was the high noon of the Progressive spirit in American life. Following the lesson he had learnt from studying the British Constitution, he appeared before Congress in person, the first President to do so since John Adams, and like a Prime Minister from the Treasury Bench proceeded to outline a comprehensive corpus of legislation designed to tilt the balance of power against big business. Where Roosevelt had been content to use the Sherman Act as his weapon against the trusts, Wilson not only engineered the Clayton Act of 1914, which extended the range of unfair practices and exempted labour unions from the charge of monopoly, but he set up the Federal Trade Commission with police powers which threw on business the onus of proving its innocence in the courts. As a Democrat and a southerner, as well as a believer that high tariffs breed monopoly, he sponsored the first radical reduction of the tariff since the Civil War, the Underwood Tariff of 1913. The Federal Reserve Act, by making the banking system more flexible and trustworthy, soothed radical suspicions about the existence of a 'money trust'. Mindful of its support from the American Federation of Labor, the administration passed La Follette's Seamen's Act, established a board of mediation for railway labour disputes and passed the Adamson Act which provided an eight-hour day for railway workers. Even more extensive was the help given to the farmers—Federal grants-in-aid to expand their technical advisory services and to help in the construction of rural roads; cheap Federal mortgages; and official warehouses where, after the manner of the Populist subtreasury plan, they could store their produce as security for bank loans. Lastly, Roosevelt's conservation programme was further developed by the appointment of a Federal Water Power Commission to supervise the private development of water power sites.

By 1916 the pace of reform had slackened as the conservatives in the Democratic Party re-asserted themselves, and as Wilson, like his reforming successor twenty years later, became pre-occupied with foreign affairs. The entrance of the United States into the war a year later put an end to reform for almost a generation. For with the post-war reaction, Americans had emerged into a new age of unrestrained business rule.

The Progressive spirit had achieved much. A vigilant public opinion had developed safeguards against the grosser forms of corruption in public life, and in certain States had succeeded in bringing business under some form of regulation to the advantage of workingman, farmer and consumer. At the national level, too, although the Federal authority never kept pace with the centralizing tendency of private business, nevertheless as a result of the efforts of two courageous, independent statesmen, Roosevelt and Wilson, the Presidency once again re-asserted its authority against the overmighty corporation. The farmer was given that relief for which the Populists had struggled. Although the workingman had long to wait for full rights of collective bargaining, the principle of Federal regulation of hours and conditions of work, and of arbitration between labour and capital, was established. Although, as always in American politics, organized interests like agriculture and labour benefited most, nevertheless the general public was newly protected against business irresponsibility in numerous fields from food and drugs to banking. And in the sphere of conservation the Federal Government assumed unprecedented responsibility not merely to protect the nation's resources from private greed but to develop them in the public interest.

But there were limits to direct government control of big business. It was recognized that railways were common carriers with a special measure of public interest, monopolistic in their nature, and that government was justified in regulating them. But on the question of big business in general the Progressives were confused. Many looked on industrial combinations as unnatural monsters whose tentacles should be severed by the public chopper before they strangled the life of a healthy, individualistic, competitive order. Others, more realistic, recognized that combinations were integral to modern life, and distinguished between size and monopoly.

They hoped to break up monopolies and force the pieces to compete against each other by legislative action. The effectiveness of 'trust busting' in these early days is in dispute. Certainly the American faith in the power of statute to alter human and business nature was unjustified. Even where suits were successfully prosecuted under the law, combinations persistently re-formed in new and more subtle forms. Yet there are grounds for believing that the actions of Roosevelt and Taft had a real deterrent effect, and sometimes the dissolution of a trust appears to have stimulated new forms of competition at least for a time.

Both Roosevelt and Wilson fully understood the effective limits of government control in American life. Roosevelt recognized that industrial combinations, like political machines, had come to stay. He distinguished between good and bad trusts in terms of their honesty, efficiency and public service, and had no quarrel with size as such. A nationalist with a due sense of the responsibilities of power, he had no intention of throwing sand into the works of American enterprise. Yet his impressive record of forty-four anti-trust actions set the pattern for the more thoroughgoing anti-trust enforcement of the present time. Wilson, too, was aware of the impersonal forces which threatened the vital individuality of American life; and in his speeches, published in 1913 as *The New Freedom*, he attempted to sketch the conditions of survival for that individuality. Starting from academic and Calvinistic convictions about the virtues of competition he came to recognize that size and monopoly were inevitable. He recognized the hopelessness of 'making big business little' and concentrated his efforts on the process whereby little business became big with the object of keeping that process lively and socially healthy. 'What America needs above all,' he wrote, 'is a body of laws which will look after the men on the make rather than the men already made', laws which would prevent business 'growing big by methods which unrighteously crushed those who were smaller'. He chose neither the futility of atomism nor the rigidity of regulation. Instead, he hoped that by an enforced competition among regulated giants in mature industries and by the natural competition of small pioneers in new fields, business could be civilized and yet continue to play its dynamic part in the open society of America. In this hope he was justified. For when, after the First World War, the American economy moved into a new phase of play in which the signals were called, not by railways and steel but by automobiles, electricity and chemicals, the old monopolies of 1900 ceased to look so threatening. It was not 'trust busting' so much as an expanding economy which preserved Americans from their nightmare of a business tyranny.

CHAPTER XII

THE GREAT DIVIDE
1890-1920

'Now the idea of a new Europe on the other side of the Atlantic affects every speculation, however much the new people keep themselves aloof from European politics. . . . European governments can no longer have the notion that they are playing the first part in the stage of the world's political history. And this sense of being dwarfed will probably increase in time.'

SIR ROBERT GIFFEN, 1904.

IN July 1893 Henry Adams received in Switzerland a telegram from his brother Brooks calling him home to face the financial panic. While these two Boston *rentiers* awaited the outcome for their investments in the ancestral home at Quincy that summer, they thrashed out perceptive ideas concerning the radical changes taking place in America's relation to the Atlantic world.[1] Brooks moved from his immediate pre-occupation with the stability of the gold dollar to a simple determinist thesis that 'the economic centre of the world determined the social equilibrium' and to a suspicion that the all-important 'international centre of exchanges', long established in London, might be shifting to New York and with it 'the economic capital of civilization' to the New World. Henry developed the idea of the concentration of capital as the release of physical power which determined the rise and fall of civilization. The dynamo which so much impressed him on a visit to the Chicago World's Fair the same September became the symbol of a new

---

[1] See especially Brooks Adams, *The Law of Civilization and Decay* (1895) and *America's Economic Supremacy* (1947 ed.); for Henry Adams see essays published posthumously in Henry Adams, *The Degradation of the Democratic Dogma*, with an introduction by Brooks Adams (1919).

phase in the history of human society. Using the theories of nineteenth-century scientists much as Milton used the Ptolemaic cosmogony, he arrived at a suggestive interpretation of history based on the harnessing of physical power. He saw human society passing through successive eras—religious, mechanical, electrical and finally 'ethereal'—each a stage in the progressive dissipation or 'degradation' of energy which would bring ruin to civilization unless man could establish some control 'of cosmic forces on a cosmic scale'. In this *dénouement* he saw the United States as the leader of western civilization in its mass, technocratic phase; and in his more speculative flights predicted not only world war and the eclipse of Britain and Germany but atomic fission and a new polarization of power in North America and asiatic Russia. However elementary their economic determinism, however fallacious their science, the Adams brothers were already in the 1890s noting humdrum signs like the relative production of pig-iron which heralded the rise of their country as a world power. In June, 1898, Henry, after examining the statistics of the British Board of Trade, wrote to his brother in a characteristic mood of wishful and pessimistic exaggeration: 'This year at last settles the fact that British industry is quite ruined and that its decline has at last become a debacle. . . . The world has entered on a new phase of most far-reaching revolution and our only danger is lest the ruins of the old empires should tumble too quickly on America.'[1] Six years later across the Atlantic the retired chief statistician of the Board of Trade, Sir Robert Giffen, was speculating on similar lines: 'The phenomenon' (of America's growing population) 'is also without a precedent in history . . . The increase is not only unprecedented in numbers but it is an increase of the most expensively living population that has ever been in the world . . . [It] is perhaps the greatest political and economic fact of the age. The fact has altered . . . the whole idea of the balance of power of the European nations.'[2] In 1914 the United States had become the greatest industrial power in the world and the gross

[1] Henry to Brooks Adams, dated London, 11 June 1898; *Henry Adams and His Friends: A Collection of His unpublished Letters*, compiled with a Biographical Introduction by H. D. Carter (Boston, 1947), p. 438.

[2] Robert Giffen, *Economic Inquiries and Studies*, vol. II, p. 22, London, 1904. The quotation which heads this chapter is taken from the same source.

value of her manufactures exceeded that of Britain and Germany put together.[1]

The generation between 1890 and the end of the First World War stands out in sharp relief as a period of profound crisis for the American people. In 1893 Frederick Jackson Turner closed his famous lecture on 'The Significance of the frontier in American History' with the words: 'And now, four centuries from the discovery of America, at the end of a hundred years of life under the constitution, the frontier has gone; and with its going has closed the first period of American history.'[2] From being primarily an area of geographic expansion the United States emerged as a powerful nation State in a position to exercise a decisive influence in Atlantic affairs. In one short chapter the age-old process of European expansion into North America was reversed, and as we move into what might be called Chapter Three, which began in the 1920s and is not yet concluded, the dominant theme is no longer the influence of western Europe on America but the return impact of America on western Europe.

The disappearance of the frontier of settlement, although it did not come about as suddenly as the census-takers of 1890 supposed, altered the whole balance of American life and its relation to the outside world.

The Americans had paid for their railways and industry largely by selling abroad the grains, beef and cotton of the Greater West; but by 1900 the scarcity of new land was beginning to modify the ancient practices of extensive agriculture. The mounting costs of farming, competition from new frontiers in Canada, South America and the Antipodes, the need to feed the growing population of America's own towns and cities and above all the transatlantic migration of industry, combined to transform the character of American trading relations abroad. Between 1880 and 1925, the proportion of agricultural products, including cotton, in American exports declined from seven-eighths to a half, with a proportionate increase in manufactures. On the import side, manufactures fell

[1] C. W. Wright, *op. cit.* p. 550.
[2] Frederick Jackson Turner, *The Frontier in American History* (New York, 1920), p. 38.

from nearly a half to a third, being replaced in importance by raw materials, such as tin and rubber, for America's own industries. With this shift in commodities went a shift in markets. Up to 1914, Great Britain remained the United States' closest associate, taking more than half as much again of her exports as Canada and Germany, her nearest rivals, and making the greatest contribution to American imports; but by the 1930s Canada had eclipsed Great Britain as the greatest importer of American goods, just as Asia had eclipsed Europe as the greatest contributor to American imports. The Atlantic was beginning to decline in importance for American foreign trade. Even more significant was the fact that already in the 1870s Americans were consistently selling abroad more of the abundant cheap produce of the West than they needed to pay for imported manufactures. For the first time since the Virginia settlers began shipping tobacco to England the Americans had become creditors in terms of their commodity trade.

It was many decades, however, before this shift from the status of debtor to creditor was reflected in the total balance sheet. Americans still needed large drafts of foreign capital. From 1878 to 1914, between 3,500 and 5,500 million dollars of foreign funds, largely British, flowed into the United States—into railways, and later into industries and public utilities. The interest and repayment on this vast commitment, together with the drain of foreign shipping charges owing to the decline of the American merchant marine, the increase in immigrant remittances to Europe and in American tourist expenditure abroad, kept the United States a 'mature debtor' until the time of the South African War. But so great were the funds accumulating from American business enterprise that the cost of capital rapidly decreased and at last, after three centuries, the difference between interest rates in America and in Europe disappeared. From 1900 onwards, not only was foreign capital of rapidly declining importance in American investment but American bankers were themselves investing abroad in Canada and South America to the tune of some 2,000 million dollars by 1914. The European War, which brought the French and British missions cap in hand to Morgan for loans to finance their purchases of American munitions, hastened dramatically the transformation of the United States from the world's greatest borrower into the world's greatest lender. As peace returned, the United States found that her favourable balance of trade, in those years of rehabilitation, had reached the unprecedented total of over 20,000 million dollars, that her old indebtedness to Europe had been partly written off, and that instead she was Europe's creditor to the extent of some 10,000 million dollars in foreign loans. Truly, as Brooks Adams had predicted, the 'international centre of exchanges' had shifted westwards across the Atlantic from Lombard Street to Wall Street.

It was unfortunate that popular ignorance, concern for the American standard of living and the pressure of industrial interests should have prevented the United States Government from adjusting her foreign policy to this economic revolution. The Hawley-Smoot Tariff of 1920, which raised to an absurd height a tariff structure originally erected to protect infant industries, obstructed the efforts of foreign customers to pay for the American cotton, wheat and machine-tools, the tobacco, films, typewriters and cars on which they had come to rely, as well as to pay off war debts owed to the U.S. Government. Unable to pay their way in goods, foreign countries were forced on the one hand to demand some relief from the payment of war debts and on the other to balance their American accounts by periodic shipments of gold which only increased the imbalance between the dollar and other currencies, notably sterling. The system was only kept functioning by virtue of the extensive American investment abroad, especially in central Europe during the 1920s. As the twentieth century wore on, the British were worried by a shortage of dollars; whereas at the time of the Revolution Americans had been worried by a shortage of sterling. There could be no more ironic demonstration of the reversal of Anglo-American economic relations.

The persistence of a debtor mentality in a creditor State, of small-town banking ethics in the most powerful nation in the world, was one inevitable result of the strains imposed on a people so suddenly arrived at world power. It bedevilled not only Anglo-American relations but hopes for world prosperity for another thirty years.

As with capital, so with the westward movement of labour across the Atlantic. Although the scarcity of new land for homesteads was of little concern to immigrants pouring into New York's East Side, the passing of the frontier and the restriction of immigration thirty years later were not unconnected. The herding together of immigrants in cities instead of their dispersal on the prairies forced the immigrant problem newly on the attention of the public. Difficult as assimilation proved to be, the American-born expressed little concern over Czechs in Nebraska, Ukrainians in Montana or Finnish miners in Minnesota. But when such unaccustomed groups invaded the cities and the New England countryside, the problem became national and serious. At the same time trade unions were beginning to make effective protests against immigrant competition, and industry, which had been the chief agent for immigration in its last great phase, no longer had so urgent a need for cheap, docile, unskilled labour. A population of 118 million without a western outlet provided industry with more native-born workers than ever before. Machinery was replacing the manual strength of the section- or factory-hand. Throughout the '20s and '30s it was still foreignborn huskies of Polish, Italian, Slovak and half a dozen other national groups who, along with Negroes, sweated it out building highways, loading ships and manhandling steel ingots; but Europe sent no substantial replacements. The general public, aroused by the threat to social stability of a new, post-war immigrant flood, took the revolutionary step of lowering the sluices. For the first time America was able to dispense with the labour of European immigrants.

The rejection of the immigrant's unqualified right to embrace United States citizenship subtly altered the whole concept of American nationality. The idea of the United States as an asylum and an experiment gave place to that of a folk society, a nation State. Although the United States might be a dedicated nation with a 'manifest destiny' on the American continent she was, for the purposes of defence and expansion, of the same character as the nations of the Old World. And for Europeans, Ellis Island came to represent something more than an immigration flood control point. It demonstrated that America was for the Americans; no longer an asylum from intolerable custom, but a Never Never Land to be experienced vicariously through its by-products. Instead of the emigrant letter there came the Hollywood film and *Life* magazine. The old inter-relation between America and Europe, based on the conviction that the United States was an extension of Europe on a different plane, was broken.

These developments were accompanied by an outward turning, a quickening of consciousness, on the part of Americans concerning the quality of their own way of life and its relation to Europe.

One of the first responses to affluence of the rising business family was the urge to take ship across the Atlantic. Between 1896 and 1914 cabin-class Americans, outward bound from New York or Boston, spent about as much money on foreign travel as the immigrants, close-packed in the steerage whom they passed in the bay, were to send back to their families in Europe. Many of these tourists, like their post-bellum predecessors described by Mark Twain, protected their New World innocence from the clever, ruthless and devious foreigners by means of a yankee-doodle brashness and humour. A more select number followed the habitual pilgrim's way for cultivated Americans, which ran from Liverpool to Brown's or Fleming's Hotels and the architectural, scholarly and, with suitable introductions, human monuments of London; and thence to Paris and the galleries of Florence and Rome or possibly to a winter spent exercising unwonted German in the lecture halls of Heidelberg or Berlin.

The few used their great riches to bring Europe and especially England closer to the Long Island shore. In Scotland Andrew Carnegie entertained public figures like John Morley at Skibo Castle, and other millionaires shot grouse or stalked deer on rented estates in preference to joining the plebeian crowd of duck hunters in the forests of Maine. Those with what Henry James called 'the sense of Newport' took country houses in Sussex, pestered Americans living in England to present their daughters at Court and fished for titled suitors who (like Mr Duveen's pictures) could be carried back as trophies. The English upper classes, always respectful of great wealth, relaxed their condescension to American democracy to the extent of admitting to fashionable society a chosen few whom ambition, riches and a talent for conformity had made acceptable.

Certain scions of great houses went further, and with the boldness and realism of aristocrats joined the European throng of titled and decorated fortune-hunters in the cotillions of New York. When in 1879 Lord Randolph Churchill paid suit to Jenny Jerome, daughter of a New York broker, he set a precedent for marrying into trade —if the trading were American—which was followed in 1895 by the spectacular wedding at St Thomas's Church, Fifth Avenue, New York, of his nephew, the heir to the impecunious dukedom of Marlborough, to Consuelo, daughter and heiress of William H. Vanderbilt. American beauties, with or without dowries, became fashionable brides for English public men such as Joseph Chamberlain; and in the portraits of their expatriate fellow-countryman, Sargent, they remain in the gallery of Edwardian grace. When American Rhodes Scholars appeared at Oxford, Harvard crews at Henley, Meadowbrook at Hurlingham, and British and American yachts raced the ocean off Long Island, an impeccable social atmosphere had been created for diplomatic *rapprochement*. The birth in 1903 of that celebrated banqueting society, 'The Pilgrims', with its two branches in New York and London representing all that is most staid in public life, symbolizes the transformation of Anglo-American social relations. No longer the neglected territory of poor emigrants, of drummers, of earnest evangelicals and radicals, and a few merchant bankers, the field had been annexed by that fashionable and official Britain which had hitherto despised the whole connection. It was indeed a new age.

The compulsion towards the European metropolis acted at deeper levels. The American intelligentsia had never lost touch with the European tradition of letters and art received largely by refraction through the English prism. But the New England Renaissance, which from Emerson's 'Atlantic seat' had preserved the balance between European authority and western exuberance, was overwhelmed by the Civil War and by the stampede for riches which followed it. For forty years a genteel veneer provided the only cultural coating for naked appetites. Although a Boston Brahmin like Henry Adams could, with the help of excursions as far afield as Samoa, maintain his quizzical, fastidious poise in Washington, there were men and women of sensibility who, withering in that Gilded

Age, so thirsted after the refreshing springs of Europe that they left the United States to live abroad. Whistler, son of a West Pointer turned railway engineer, settled down after study in Paris to paint the mysterious moods of the Thames and to transform Edwardian interior decoration. Edith Wharton, impatient with the limited values of the smart, brittle New York society of her novels, was irresistibly drawn to the greater subtlety, depth and range of the Faubourg Saint-Germain and Mayfair. And in 1915, the young T. S. Eliot, working in a London bank and experimenting with symbolist poems, represented a new generation of expatriates who were to hold their own in the metropolitan world of letters. For this Boston Eliot, born and brought up in St Louis, the pilgrimage from Mark Twain's Mississippi by way of the rocky shrines of his Puritan forefathers to the Anglo-Catholic discipline of Little Gidding was a progress from the eclecticism of the frontier to the spiritual authority of the European tradition. In T. S. Eliot the strain of Puritanism is discernible throughout. But George Santayana's flight from a Harvard chair to Europe in 1912 represented the rejection of his mother's Puritanism for the Latin Catholicism of his Spanish father. Yet in continuing to assert his Americanism this, America's most elegant philosophic writer, was only showing that expatriation cannot destroy the fundamentals of American character.

The expatriate who made articulate the international theme in American life was the novelist Henry James. James was no ingrained Yankee but the son of a well-to-do Irish-American with transcendentalist connections. Unlike his brother William, he never settled down on American soil after a peripatetic education in half the countries of Europe. As a young apprentice writer he abandoned the United States in 1875 for more rewarding subjects, Italian galleries, Paris salons and that cultivated society which moved so gracefully between Mayfair and the parklands of the English shires. Outsider though he was, James's fine-grained imagination, responding to immemorial traditions, social nuances, brilliantly-tuned intellects and exotic flowerings, gave all and more than its due to the European *haut monde*. Yet for all his reverence, indeed obsequiousness, towards the metropolitan world, James lost neither his sense of moral purpose nor his conscious American judgment. The theme of his greatest novels was the conflict of American with European standards and its resolution in a purification of values. In the relations of his innocent, clear-eyed American heroines with their elegant, sometimes good-hearted, sometimes devious and over-bred protagonists, James, by a tremendous effort of skill and imagination, brought together all that was best in America and Europe. It is true that he preferred Americans who had been impelled to seek Europe and that on his visit to the United States in 1904 he liked his own country little better than before. Yet in spite of living at Rye in Sussex, in spite of becoming a British subject, and of the Order of Merit so promptly conferred, James was never altogether committed to the Old World. He threw himself almost hysterically into the British cause on the outbreak of war in 1914; but there is reason to suspect that this totally unexpected Armageddon shook his faith in the whole society which could not escape responsibility for it. When he died in 1916 his will disclosed the wish to have his ashes buried in New England.

James's American contemporaries were blind to his great gifts to American culture. 'Thank Heaven Henry James is now an avowedly British novelist', wrote Theodore Roosevelt; and even so liberal a critic as Parrington, writing in the 1920s, could lament his failure to serve an American purpose. Yet the international theme he explored had its own importance for that quickening of the vernacular spirit in American letters which took place between the 1890s depression and the close of the First World War.

In 1911 Robert Frost was forced to leave New England for Old England in order to write and publish, in the congenial company of Georgian poets, the poems which, on his return to America in 1915, were to give him a sudden, belated recognition among his fellow-countrymen. At the same time other American poets, who had travelled to London from as far afield as Arkansas, were, under the leadership of Ezra Pound, helping to give poetry a new start not only in England but in Boston and Chicago. Harriet Monroe's revolutionary publication *Poetry: a Magazine of Verse*, which first appeared in Chicago in 1912, gave currency not only to Yeats, Pound, D. H. Lawrence, H. D. and Amy Lowell, but to a number of American poets who, owing nothing to *imagisme*, were beginning to fashion a new vernacular style out of the directly felt experiences of American living, which would show up the insipidities of the genteel tradition: Edward Arlington Robinson, who preserved his granite-like New England integrity and perfected his craftsmanship in Bowery doss-house and subway construction gang until he was recognized by Theodore Roosevelt; Vachel Lindsay, who, while peddling verses for meals throughout America, developed out of popular rhythms such as revivalist hymn-tunes the exciting new rhetoric of *General Booth Enters Heaven*; Edgar Lee Masters, who translated into poetry the characters and experiences of his native 'Spoon River' community in Illinois; Carl Sandburg, son of an immigrant Swede, whose feeling for the pioneer-bred American found expression not only in poetry and song but in his evocative biography of Lincoln.

This stirring at the grass roots also influenced prose. Hamlin Garland's stories of the life of the Middle Border were precursors of a regional quickening which owed little save craftsmanship to Europe. Willa Cather's novels of frontier Nebraska and of New Mexico, Ellen Glasgow's novels of old-stock families in the upland South, Sherwood Anderson's candid portraits of the citizens of Winesburg, Ohio, Sinclair Lewis's satire on life in the even more famous literary small town Gopher Prairie, were eloquent proof of a vernacular literature. The slightly later work of Hemingway, Faulkner, Scott Fitzgerald, Eugene O'Neill and others in the 1920s, far from submitting to European tutelage, gave important leads to European letters. With Mencken's exulting research into the American language, the criticism of Edmund Wilson and the uniquely American thrust which John Dewey gave to pragmatism as philosophy and as educational theory, and with the influence of Louis Sullivan and Frank Lloyd Wright in architecture, Americans at last acquired their own culture.

In 1915 the young critic Van Wyck Brooks wrote a pungent criticism of American values which ended on the wry hope that: 'When the women of America have gathered together all the culture of the world and the men have collected all the money— who knows?—perhaps the dry old Yankee stalk will begin to stir and send forth shoots and burst into a storm of blossom.'[1] He could not then know that this self-criticism was in itself a portent of 'America's Coming-of-Age'.

This national self-consciousness found expression in politics also. The existence throughout the nineteenth century of that Anglo-American partnership which enabled the American people to solve the problems of continental growth with the maximum of aid and the minimum of interference from across the Atlantic, should not obscure the fact that the Americans had throughout pursued an aggressively independent and expansionist foreign policy. Its theatre was not, however, the Atlantic where, with British co-operation, the Monroe Doctrine protected Americans from European inter-ference, but the American continent. The friction with Britain which makes up so large a part of American diplomatic history in the nineteenth century was mainly due not to oceanic but continen-tal issues—the Canadian boundary, Texas, Oregon, which were part of a larger parcel of issues involving not only British but Mexican and Russian claims in North America. The Monroe Doc-trine was only the negative arm of a foreign policy of which the positive arm was that programme of westward territorial aggrand-izement known at its most critical period as 'Manifest Destiny'. Americans, with their backs to Europe and their faces set towards the western horizon, combined in their instinctive make-up two ultimately incompatible strains: on the one hand a revulsion from European entanglements which underscored their belief in neutral-ism and isolation; on the other an aggressive expansionism westwards to the Pacific shore.

But by the turn of the present century there was no further room for continental expansion; and the United States had developed the sinews of a great metropolitan Power. The expansionist urge, hitherto fully extended in rounding out territorial limits, in over-coming civil conflict and in building an economic empire, found new expression not only in a westward projection across the Pacific towards Hawaii, the Philippines and the Far East, but in wider

[1] Van Wyck Brooks, 'America's Coming-of-Age', in Van Wyck Brooks, *Three Essays on America* (New York, 1934), p. 112.

responsibilities for the defence of the Western Hemisphere. These responsibilities, overcoming the isolationist instinct, were to bring back the United States across the Atlantic into a European War as a major world power.

The new nationalism exploded with dramatic suddenness in the summer of 1898. It needed little more than William Randolph Hearst's exploitation, as a newspaper stunt, of the sinking of the battleship *Maine* in Havana harbour to bring the United States to the aid of the Cubans fighting for independence from Spain. Most Americans, save those troops laid low by yellow fever in the Cuban swamps, enjoyed this exuberant little adventure in 'colonial warfare' which, at so small a cost, gave the nation a sense, thirty years after Appomatox, of fighting together in a patriotic, just and profitable cause. But for all its *opéra bouffe* character the war set the American people on new paths. By acquiring responsibility for the Spanish territories of Cuba and Puerto Rico in the Caribbean, Hawaii and the Philippines in the Pacific, the United States emerged overnight as a Great Power with strategic frontiers pushed far beyond her Atlantic and Pacific shores. The acquisition of a colonial empire of 'backward' peoples who did not qualify for statehood within the Union presented embarrassing problems to a nation whose whole existence was bound up with anti-colonial sentiment; and although their strategic interest in these territories was to remain permanent the Americans quickly repented of their imperialistic mood. Cuba became technically an independent republic as early as 1901, though subject to repeated interventions due to a mixture of strategic and economic motives; the Philippines received their long-promised independence in 1948 and Hawaii now looks forward to admission into the Union as a forty-ninth State. With her immense economic power the United States has exerted a great and often disturbing influence on adjacent territories, but 'dollar diplomacy' must be distinguished from colonialism.

If the desire to shoulder the white man's burden was only a passing whim, the determination to exert a strategic influence in world affairs commensurate with new-found power struggled increasingly to overcome the inhibitions of isolationism.

One important result of the Spanish-American War was the discovery of a new national hero. The part played by Colonel Roosevelt and his regiment of Rough Riders in capturing San Juin Hill may not have been as decisive for the Cuban campaign as the Colonel believed; but it brought him the New York governorship and ultimately the Presidency. It was 'T.R.' who, along with like-minded associates such as Lodge, expressed the jingo mood by giving a newly-assertive twist to American foreign relations. The quality of Roosevelt's patriotism bore more resemblance to that of Kipling than to that of John Quincy Adams.[1] His pride in his country's achievements was bound up with his sense of its mission as heir-general to Anglo-Saxon virtue. His boyish exuberance concealed a shrewd understanding of national power. He was convinced that life for nations as well as for individuals was an unending struggle for survival. He soldiered in Cuba to demonstrate his belief in martial virtues for a great nation; and when he became President he did all he could to put the United States in a combative posture towards the other Great Powers whose rivalries threatened to encroach on American interests. Since his early days as Assistant Secretary of the Navy and student of Admiral Mahan he had advocated a big navy. As President he modernized and doubled the fleet and improved its bases. Above all he transformed its striking power by cutting a canal through the Isthmus of Panama on territory dubiously acquired through manipulating a revolution in Panama. This policy of speaking softly while wielding a big stick created new respect for the United States among the Great Powers; and Roosevelt played an unwonted part for an American President by mediating between Japan and Russia at the Peace of Portsmouth (New Hampshire) and by sending a representative to the Algeciras Conference.

These adventures were accompanied by a marked growth in Anglo-American diplomatic understanding. From 1895 onwards Lord Salisbury and his successors at the Foreign Office, preoccupied by the rise of German power and convinced at length that Britain had nothing to fear from the United States, did all they could to entice that country into a tacit *entente* in which American naval

---

[1] Roosevelt was both attracted and repelled by Kipling, whom he considered 'an underbred little fellow' and 'at bottom a cad': *The Letters of Theodore Roosevelt*, ed. E. E. Morison and Others.

power would supplement the force behind the *pax britannica*. British friendliness over the Spanish-American War; Sir Julian Pauncefote's accommodating agreement to abrogate the Clayton-Bulwer Treaty which stood in the way of full American control of the Panama Canal; the reduction in 1903 of British naval forces on the West Indies Station with its tacit corollary of U.S. naval control in the western Atlantic; the unsuccessful attempt to interest the United States in joint action in China; all these were tokens of a new adjustment between these Atlantic nations, now both world powers. The United States was wooed by other Powers, notably Germany, that third offshoot of the Anglo-Saxon race for which many Americans, along with their President, had great respect. But in seven years of office Roosevelt moved from something like impartiality towards Britain and Germany to a conviction that the Kaiser threatened world peace and that hope lay in the co-operation of British and American naval power which, as he wrote to an English correspondent, 'is a menace to no Power, but on the contrary is a distinct help in keeping the peace of the world'.[1] Roosevelt was too shrewd a politician to contemplate any move against the traditional policy of eschewing entangling alliances. Indeed, in urging preparedness he was more in advance of public opinion than his cousin was to be thirty years later. By the close of his term Americans had lost their enthusiasm for diplomatic adventure, and the moment passed when the United States might have exercised a decisive influence for peace. Yet Roosevelt's rejection of isolation in favour of rights asserted by a proper use of force, of neutralism in favour of *ad hoc* co-operation with foreign powers in pursuit of strategic security, was an expression of a conservative nationalism which was to have an increasing voice in foreign affairs as the United States came to use its overwhelming power in the twentieth century.

When on 1 August 1914 Americans read the two-inch banner headlines announcing the incredible outbreak of war in Europe, the few who, like Roosevelt, understood the Atlantic Ocean to be a strategic highway were lost among the crowd who took comfort

---

[1] Theodore Roosevelt to Arthur Hamilton Lee, 17 October 1908: *Letters*, vol. VI, p. 1294. The letter was never sent.

in the idea of a watery barrier, three thousand miles broad, separating Sandy Hook from Ushant Rock. The prevailing breezes once again blew from the continental quarter, whispering their beguiling message of isolation and neutralism. Mid-western farmers who had never seen the sea; immigrants who had sacrificed so much to be free of Europe and military service; Boston Irish, drunk with the prospect of rebellion; Germans, Austrians, Magyars, conscious of their own unpopular sympathies; all these brought new force to the ancient conviction that war in Europe was no business of the United States. President Wilson was re-elected in 1916 because he had kept the United States neutral 'in thought and deed'. His policy consisted of attempts to secure a negotiated peace and to assert American neutral rights. Although commander-in-chief of a great navy he tried to persuade the belligerents to recognize that old maritime policy of the freedom of the seas for neutral trade which had been appropriate, if ineffective, in the days of weakness during the Napoleonic Wars; and in Note after Note he complained to Whitehall about the ruthless blockade and to the Wilhelmstrasse about the unscrupulous submarines.

Yet the American people could not remain neutral. Economically, they were providing the Allies with money and munitions; culturally, the dominant stocks felt a sentimental sympathy for France, a more intimate kinship with Britain; and immigrant Poles, Czechs and Serbs looked for emancipation of their people in the defeat of the Central Powers; morally, many were confirmed in their view of the violators of Belgium by indiscriminate U-boat campaigns; and strategically, as German pressure intensified by land and sea, Americans began to glimpse what German domination of Europe and, even more, the collapse of British naval power in the Atlantic would mean for American independence. By 1917 anger and concern had risen to such a pitch that it only needed the German announcement of a new, all-out submarine campaign in February to bring about a break in American diplomatic relations, followed, on 6 April, by the formal declaration of war against Germany. In May American destroyers reported for convoy duty with the Royal Navy at Queenstown, and on 7 June the first American troops ever to set foot in Europe on active service landed in

England before moving across the Channel to set up General Pershing's headquarters in France. It was truly a revolution in the Atlantic world.

The spirit in which the American people entered upon the European War was very different from that of Roosevelt's time. The simple nationalism which had taken Panama was reinforced in 1917 by a crusading idealism. Wilson's leadership was never shown to better advantage than in the way he patiently and scrupulously looked for the moment when the United States could intervene with a unified and overriding moral purpose, expressed so aptly in his famous war address before Congress: 'The world must be made safe for democracy. Its peace must be planted upon the tested foundations of political liberty . . . We desire no conquest, no dominion . . . We are but one of the champions of the rights of mankind.' In this spirit of high purpose Wilson sought, not to bring the New World to redress the balance of the Old by making alliance with other self-interested Powers such as Britain, but to establish a peace based upon those abstract principles of political morality which Americans regarded as their peculiar boon. Conscious as ever of a separate and dedicated status, the United States remained an 'associated Power' throughout hostilities, and at the Peace Conference Wilson endeavoured, as a detached arbiter, to draw up a settlement in accordance with the principles of American liberalism. The American boon of an open society in which individuals and minorities of all kinds would find freedom was translated into the principle of the self-determination of peoples in accordance with ethnic boundaries. The American boon of a rule of law enshrined in a written, Federal constitution was translated into the written Covenant of the League of Nations.

The failure of Wilson's larger aims was an American, as well as a personal, tragedy. The characteristically American ideal of a world order transcending the anarchy of power had no chance without the participation of the United States. But Wilson's stubborn righteousness of purpose prevented American support for his peace settlement at the moment when crusading idealism was evaporating in a feverish search for peacetime normality. The American people had been exposed too briefly and too superficially to the threat against their continental security to assume the continuing duties which their austere President had assigned to them. Instead they withdrew into isolation, jettisoning not merely the League but that tacit Anglo-American alliance which had been the basic instrument for winning the war and which had painfully to be built up from the beginning in face of the renewed threat to western society in 1939.

The man primarily responsible for scotching American member-ship of the League was Senator Henry Cabot Lodge. Lodge, who had been Roosevelt's friend, represented those conservative national-ists who believed American interests best served, not by a moral crusade for a universal 'collective security' but by the protection of American strategic interests, narrowly interpreted. In the mood of the 1920s conservative nationalism swung back from Roosevelt's interventionism to an isolationist phase from which it only re-emerged after the attack on Pearl Harbor.

But the new nationalism by no means stifled the older, liberal tradition. This continued to express itself in those Wilsonian terms which, after a renewed cataclysm, were to find a new embodiment in the United Nations and the Marshall Plan. Since 1920 the new nationalism and the old liberalism have warred to establish ascen-dancy over American foreign policy. The 'great debate' which, intermittently but with increasing intensity, has agitated American opinion since the First World War has been over the choice be-tween the pursuit of a solitary course in world affairs, of isolation behind the bastions of imperialism and, on the other hand, the assumption of leadership in a co-operative enterprise to achieve some system of world order. The isolationist-imperialist choice would represent victory for that concept of Americanism which has its sanction in the tribal compulsions of what is merely the latest, most powerful and, in some respects, the least stable of the nation States. The choice of international leadership would represent a victory for that older concept of Americanism bequeathed by the founders of the Republic. This, the dominant American tradition, is based upon the premise that the United States is more than a nation State; that it is a society of free men under oath to adhere to certain rational principles in the ordering of human relations; that all who adhere to those principles, of whatever race, religion or economic circumstance, are entitled to equal status within that community; that this society, therefore, cannot be and never has been isolated from the rest of the world; that by its very nature as an asylum for the outlaws of Europe it has a peculiarly intimate relation with the peoples of the older continent.

CHAPTER XIII

DEMOCRACY IN MODERN AMERICA

'France was a land, England was a people, but America,
having about it still that quality of an idea, was harder to
utter. . . . It was a willingness of the heart.'

F. SCOTT FITZGERALD.

IN 1916 an informed observer might have understandably taken
the view that the American people were settling down to a
humdrum maturity. It is true that the population, then 106
million, appeared to be doubling every thirty years as it had since
the Civil War; but war in Europe had already quartered the supply
of immigrants, and talk of severe restriction was already in the air.
The rate of natural increase was also declining. Since 1860 the birth-
rate had fallen from 41 to 25 per thousand whites, the death-rate (in
Massachusetts) from 20 to 15, and life-expectancy at birth had increased from forty to fifty years.[1] The American people were
becoming older.

They also appeared to be moving about less. Although the peak
of Homestead land-sales only came in 1913, a quarter-century after
the frontier had vanished, and the Oklahoma land-rush was still a
recent memory, the westward movement was losing momentum.
The proportion of easterners living west of the Mississippi was
falling: it decreased from 10 per cent in 1890 to 7·7 per cent in
1920.[2] Regional characteristics had never been more marked. For
proper Bostonians the West began at Albany, for Minnesotans the
East at Chicago; only in relation to the frontier between South and
North were all Americans agreed upon an exact line, drawn so long
before by Messrs Mason and Dixon. These psychological frontiers
marked great contrasts in ways of life. The Yankee families of New

[1] *Hist. Stats.*, Series C, 25 and 53; C. W. Wright, *op. cit.* p. 457.
[2] *Hist. Stats.*, Series B, 199.

England, in retreat before barbaric waves first of Irish and French-Canadians, then of Italians, Poles and Jews, became ever more aware of their colonial past; and their self-conscious antiquarianism received support from metropolitan New Yorkers who, turning to New England as a vacation land, began that process of restoring farmhouses, painting picket fences white and shutters green, which had made rural New England into an American Cotswolds. Southerners of William Faulkner's generation lived out their sequestered rural lives, handing on the manners and myths of ante-bellum chivalry and preserving the barriers of colour by means of poll taxes and share-cropping. Even the Midwest had acquired a past. In Michigan the decline of copper-mining left decaying towns served by a railway whose opulent parlour cars no longer carried their traffic of business magnates. Mid-western historians were reconstructing the forgotten trails of Indians and *voyageurs*, and the most brilliant of them, F. J. Turner, was finding recognition for a new, mid-western theory of history at Harvard. Mid-western poets and novelists were interpreting a long-established regional culture. Indeed it was a series of regional cultures, not a single national culture, which produced the most lively literature of the time. And in the regions were preserved pockets of more primitive communities, like the mountain folk of the Appalachians and Arkansas highlands, the crackers of Georgia, or the Mexican peons of the South-west, which appeared to have a continuing and unchanging place in the multiple society of America.

The economy also seemed to have settled down. Agriculture had become a stable and prosperous minority interest. The industrial landscape, with its coal mines and oil fields, steel works and cotton mills, stockyards, elevators and marshalling yards, presented features long familiar. After a rapid rise following on 1880 real wages had remained more or less stationary since 1900. In that trust-forming age economic power appeared to be concentrated once for all in the twenty-storey skyscrapers of Wall Street and it was hard to see how a new generation of Carnegies, Rockefellers and Harrimans could ever make their way thither.

Socially Americans had become more, not less, differentiated. The drift from country to town continued without marked change.

Nearly one in every three Americans was a city-dweller, taking the streetcar to office or shop, saving to install electric light, eating a lighter diet which included the new fruits and vegetables more suited to a sedentary life than the heavy farm diet of meats, potatoes and pies. In the urbanized East the disparity in income between the common labourer's twelve dollars a week and the ten thousand a year of even the moderately rich accentuated class distinctions. The well-to-do cultivated formal Edwardian manners, dressed for dinner and the opera, patronized good works or culture, pursued extravagant pleasures and suffered expensive worries. They lived a life altogether different in kind not only from their Italian parlourmaids and Swedish deliverymen, but from substantial tradesmen and clerks in their celluloid collars. These differences were not merely economic. The well-to-do still belonged for the most part to the early American stocks who assumed a superiority over the more recently arrived. If 'lace-curtain' Irish and German 'forty-eighters' were handicapped socially, what chance was there for the even exceptionally ambitious Swede, Italian or Polish Jew? And though education at a public high school was becoming more common the eastern college was still the preserve of rich and gentle folk. It looked, in short, as if the United States in her maturity was developing a vertebrate class structure like those of the Old World.

But in 1916 the American people were about to experience a new upsurge of growth which enabled them to develop further the social values they had acquired during the march across the continent. In the event the lack of a moving land frontier hardly lessened the dynamic pace of change. Mobile, adjustable, resilient and forward-looking, they used their unrivalled resources of capital, labour, raw materials and the greatest market in the world to exploit new 'frontiers' in technology. Mass production, by raising the standard of living, lessening the contrast between rich and poor, and increasing the choices open to ordinary people, fostered in new ways the practice of the American democratic idea.

Other innovations now replaced railways in giving direction to capital and enterprise, creating fresh markets, and starting all over again that driving process which led from pioneer competition to oligopolistic control. It was characteristic of continental growth that the new impulses should derive on the one hand from the harnessing of natural resources to provide a new form of power and on the other from a new form of transport. Steam was supplemented by the dynamo and the internal combustion engine.

America's first industrial phase, that of textiles, depended on water power; her second, iron and steel, upon coal; her third supplemented coal by cheap hydro-electric power generated in the great natural water basins of the continent. With electricity industry gained a new flexibility in production techniques and a new mobility which enabled it to move west and south, closer to materials or cheap labour, or to both when cotton manufacture migrated from New England to Carolina. New industries began manufacturing heavy electrical plant and the electric irons, refrigerators and vacuum cleaners which became standard household equipment in the 1920s. Telephones, all but universal in middle class homes by 1920, revolutionized business and social intercourse. The chain reaction detonated by electricity reached ever-widening fields, from motion pictures and radio to the electronics of the Second World War and the television of the post-war boom.

But the greatest impetus came, as always in the American continent, from a new form of transport. After the steamboat came the locomotive and now, in the direct genealogical line, the motor-car. The impact of the motor-car both on social habit and on technology was peculiarly American. The former is left for later discussion; the latter is touched upon here.

The scientific research which made possible the great innovations in electricity as well as in chemicals and synthetic fabrics was very largely the work of European, not American, genius and enterprise; and the contemporary history of electronics, penicillin and above all of atomic energy has continued to demonstrate that America is still in a measure dependent, as it was in the days of cotton and then of steel, on the westward migration across the Atlantic of ideas and of men. In its very early stages this was also true of motor-cars. But although Selden's American patent of 1879 had less influence on design than the experience of Daimler and French and British makers, drawn on behind the protection of the Dingley Tariff of

1896, the American automobile industry quickly made its own remarkable contribution to American technology.

Henry Ford did not stand out from the many farm mechanics, carriage and bicycle makers who, around the turn of the century, were competing to build workable motor-cars, until he abandoned the spectacular racing cars which brought him fame and capital in order to build a cheap car in large quantities. By the close of the First World War, he had completed a characteristically American revolution in manufacture. Starting from the novel principle of 'taking the work to the men instead of the men to the work', he evolved a power-driven assembly unit which in 1913 cut the time needed for assembling the Ford engine from nearly ten to nearly six hours.[1] The assembly line made it possible to employ a smaller and less skilled labour force and favoured a class of managers and engineers trained to look afresh at the problems of production from the point of common sense rather than traditional skill.[2] This was, however, only half Ford's innovation. By speeding assembly and the flow of raw materials and by emancipating himself from body and accessory makers, he was able not only to cut costs but to take the risk of narrowing the margin of profit on each car in the expectation of a rapidly expanding market. And all this was financed out of his accumulated profits. By more than doubling wages in 1914 he intended not merely to raise the shaky *morale* of his new, machine-geared labour force, but to put money into the pockets of ordinary people which would expand the demand for manufactures, including Ford cars. By building a network of sales agencies, by advertising and, ultimately, by financing hire purchase, he sustained a national market for his car.

Henry Ford demonstrated most dramatically the benefits of mass production; but he was only the most outstanding exponent of an American attitude towards manufacture previously expressed by the meat packers with their conveyor belt and the farm machinery makers with their interchangeable parts; an attitude carried further

[1] Henry Ford, *My Life Work* (New York, 1922), pp. 80–82.
[2] This attitude must be distinguished from that of the expert. Ford distrusted experts and wrote that 'we have most unfortunately found it necessary to get rid of a man as soon as he thinks himself an expert—because no one ever considers himself an expert if he really knows his job'. (Henry Ford, *ibid.*, p. 86.)

The Great Experiment

by others of his generation such as F. W. Taylor, who preached the importance not only of standardization but of saving time and motion. In the booming '20s business men making a host of products from refrigerators to tinned goods came to recognize the advantages of persuading the customer to accept a cheap standard article. Mass production methods quickly outpaced Ford's original plan. Other automobile makers, copying his methods, were soon able to offer more comfortable and stylish cars than the dependable but ungainly Model T which could be bought in any colour so long as it was black. And as techniques improved a shift in emphasis from a single standard article to the mass production of components permitted a new variety of end products so that, contrary to popular belief in Europe, standardization has promoted rather than limited the range of choices open to the consumer.

The motor industry, the output of which grew from just over 100,000 vehicles a year in 1909 to four and a half million in 1929, exerted perhaps the greatest force on economic growth in the 1920s. The influence of Detroit ramified far beyond the demand it created for new steel alloys, for glass, for complex machine-tools, for accessories, for garaging and servicing. The demand for petrol opened up an entirely new and much richer market for oil at a time when electricity was making the oil lamp obsolete even on the farm. It was the signal for a new series of oil rushes. Almost overnight new sky-scrapered cities reared up on the parched plains of Texas and Oklahoma, and a thousand Main Streets acquired their familiar clusters of filling stations. The new mobility sent city dwellers in search of suburban homes far beyond the streetcar terminus; and the result was a building boom which created great conurbations such as Los Angeles, a hundred miles across and dependent almost entirely for transport on private car and service vehicle, and new tourist resorts of which the Florida coast was the most spectacular example. The need for motor roads forced State and Federal governments to embark on a vast capital expenditure to superimpose a system of long-distance concrete highways on the old intricate network of local 'dirt' roads maintained by county and township; and along these highways fleets of heavy trucks drummed their way by night and day across the continent. The long-distance truck driver took his place, along with the high-tension linesman, in the modern folklore of Hollywood which succeeded the ballads of canal-boatmen, lumbermen and railroad engineers.

The industries which grew out of these innovations followed a familiar progress from a feverish wildcatting to a sedate condition of oligopoly. Electric power repeated in modern guise many of the features of continental pioneering. Small companies, manufacturing power from steam-driven generators for local municipalities, were drawn into a struggle for regional control; sending out platoons of linesmen to build power networks across country, they engaged in fierce rate wars, straining after the capital on which depended not merely success but survival itself. Holding companies like the rickety Insull empire in the Midwest reproduced the worst features of speculative finance, rocking the stock market with their operations. With the advent of hydro-electric power the few remaining giant companies exerted the old familiar influence on government for the rights to develop the great mountain and river basins from Appalachian to Sierra slopes. Telephone services, operated not by the post office but commercially, provided opportunity for further empire-building; the American Telephone and Telegraph, cutting into the market of the already established telegraph monopoly, had in 1930 become the biggest holding company in the world. Beginning with commercially operated pioneer stations, broadcasting developed inevitably, not as in Britain in the direction of a centralized State monopoly, but towards a federal system. Innumerable local stations scattered across the continent, locally owned and operated by private enterprise, broadcast local programmes intermixed with programmes 'piped in' from national networks, the whole financed, not out of taxation, but from advertising revenue. Within ten years broadcasting had become one of the major industries. Two companies so dominated radio purveyance that in 1941 one of them, N.B.C., was forced under the anti-trust laws to divest itself of one network, which was taken over by a separate company. With broadcasting was linked the manufacture of radio equipment; and this again expanded rapidly, bringing the Russian-Jewish immigrant David Sarnoff from a telegraphist's cabin on Nantucket Island to the presidential suite, high over Manhattan, of the mammoth Radio Corporation of America. The struggle was nowhere more bitter than in the automobile industry, where, of the twenty-two firms making cars in 1922, only three giants and a few smaller 'independents' survived in 1929 to share the market between them. Of the three giants Ford, like Carnegie before him, paid his way entirely from accumulated profits, Chrysler was financed by a Wall Street syndicate, while control of General Motors was bought by Dupont out of the overflowing financial power of their expanding chemical industries. Although Wall Street had less to do with the development of these industries than the new money which they themselves generated, the end-result, as with oil and steel, was a 'community of interest' based on financial power.

Like cotton, canals and railways before them the new innovations induced a spectacular prosperity. The boom of the '20s, which beguiled most Americans into the belief that blue skies had become a constant feature of the economic climate, was more complex than the cotton-canal boom of the 1830s or the railway boom of the 1850s and 1880s. Yet many of the old features of continental expansion were still discernible. Once more innovation in transport led to speculation in land. Although men did not make motor-cars, as they had built railways, to pocket capital gains from rising land values, motor-cars not merely affected industrial development but induced a speculative fever in urban building which was the true successor to the boom in farm lands of the early 1880s. Also that speculative temper which had tempted the pioneer settler to sink the proceeds of his 'improvements' in a new tract of unimproved land farther to the west, in turn prompted his city-bred grandchildren to prove their nerve and 'smartness' by investing profits and savings from higher wages and salaries in corner lots, oil wells and stocks and shares of new manufactures. The 'booster' mentality, the dazzling prospects of the new technology, the lack of adequate financial and governmental controls to act as a flywheel to the accelerating machine, all combined to reproduce, in even more exaggerated form, the violent pattern of upward swing followed by demoralizing collapse so characteristic of the successive phases of American economic growth.

So integrated had the economy become by the time of the 1929 crash that the exhausting effects of over-expansion were felt by all sections of the community. The semi-paralysis of 1933 affected profoundly the economic views not only of working men, of whom over twelve million were unemployed, or ruined stockbrokers, but of professional people worried about their grocery bills. So slow and halting was recovery that politicians, business men and economists, preoccupied with the problems of 'over-production' and contracting demand, came to fear that the long, dynamic expansion of the economy, the very foundation of the American way of life, might be at an end.

But from the vantage point of 1953 it seems clear that these fears were either unjustified or at least premature. With the initial stimulus of British and French war orders in 1939 and the American defence programme of 1940 the United States embarked on yet another phase of unprecedented economic expansion. In response to the demands of the Second World War, field, mine and shipyard, factory and laboratory surpassed all previous records of production. And this titanic war effort was superimposed on a peacetime economy which provided Americans with a standard of living higher than ever before. As the arsenal of democracy, the United States revealed to the world not merely the richness of her natural resources but the full brilliance of her production achievement. Although at the conclusion of hostilities many Americans feared the onset of depression, they enjoyed instead a new phase of prosperity which raised the national income to yet greater heights.

In the quarter-century after 1929, despite depression and war, the output of all goods and services increased from 172 to 345 billion dollars, industrial production doubled and agricultural output rose by 50 per cent. The number of workers in jobs increased from almost 48 million to 61 million and, although the working week dropped from about forty-eight to forty hours, each worker turned out on the average 80 per cent more goods and services. The resultant increase in well-being is illustrated by the facts that the number of homes with mechanical refrigerators increased from 10 per cent to 80 per cent, the number of electrified farms from 10 per cent to 96 per cent, and expenditure on education, health and medicine nearly doubled. Altogether the average annual income (after taxes) increased from a little more than 1,000 dollars to 1,500 dollars per capita.[1] Whatever may be the dangers of instability, it seems likely that the full measure of American economic growth has not yet been reached.

In spite of many turbulent eddies and stagnant backwaters the rising tide of material prosperity since the First World War has lifted Americans to new levels of opportunity. It has also accentuated many of their dominant traits. The full benefits of mass production have depended not only on a single great market, but on the existence of a mobile society comparatively free from rigidities of tradition and of class, whose members are prepared to adjust themselves to new and ever more standardized methods of getting and spending. In turn mass production has itself promoted that mobility—geographic, occupational and social—which conditioned American growth during the period of the great migration. The social compulsions of the caravan have continued in important ways to govern American habit.

American society has become revolutionized by the freedom afforded by the automobile. By 1929, with one car for every five Americans, it was a very poor or eccentric family which did not possess one and the whole rhythm of daily life has come to depend on them. Cars which remain an amenity in Europe have become in America a necessity not merely for the farmer and the well-circumstanced suburban dweller but for the clerk, the salesman, the student and the industrial worker, with whose transport needs bus and streetcar long ago failed to keep pace. The housewife's dependence on the car has changed the pattern of domestic economy. Mail-order houses have switched from the catalogue and postal service of the railway age to the emporium with its extensive parking lot on the outskirts of town. Down-town and corner stores have lost trade to the suburban supermarket whence a week's or a month's supplies can be laid in at once by means of car and domestic refrigerator. So with leisure. The golf and country club, the baseball

[1] The President's Annual Economic Report submitted to Congress, 15 January 1953. All figures are calculated in terms of 1952 prices.

304

park, even the football stadium—often several hundred miles distant —the week-end ski- or hunting-lodge, the summer lake-side cottage, have become easily accessible. The habit of long summer vacations has become normal, and to satisfy a new curiosity to explore the American continent, tourism has become a major industry, its whole apparatus of tourist cabins and wayside restaurants geared to the passing automobile. Those retired people who in their motor caravans seek the Florida sun in winter and the Rocky Mountain air in summer, are only the most extreme products of this automotive society. No wonder that the roomy American car, with its heater, radio and other gadgets, sometimes outrivals the apartment itself as the primary object of home-building. Faced with the necessity of travelling vast distances, always restless, always on the point of 'going places', Americans continue to devote a greater proportion of their income to travel by car, train and now by plane, than any other people.

This mobility extends beyond daily routine and travel. Although never perhaps shaking off nostalgia for the Kansas prairie, Mississippi bluff, Minnesota lake or Vermont hillside of childhood's memory, most Americans have been less bound by loyalty to ancestral places than the Welshman in his valley or the Mancunian in his back street. Inheriting something of the pioneer's yearning for 'God's Country' they have been more prepared than Europeans to migrate in search of opportunity. When a Detroit fitter thinks little of driving his family and few household chattels the three thousand miles to California to find better prospects, when Negroes drive north in their jalopies in search of industrial jobs and when even the ragged army of migrant fruit pickers and harvesters pursue their exiguous livelihood throughout the great West in motorized columns, it is clear that American industry enjoys the benefits of a highly mobile labour force.

Mass production, with its rationalized lay-outs, its scrupulous economies of time and motion, its semi-automatic machines, its assembly lines, its long runs in the manufacture of standard articles for a continental market, has increased the American's occupational mobility. It has created more jobs of elementary skill. The fall in the proportion of unskilled workers from 14·7 per cent in 1910 to

10·7 per cent in 1940 and the rise in the proportion of semi-skilled workers from 14·7 to 21 per cent is evidence of growing opportunity for the sons and grandsons of those immigrants who had been condemned to an unrewarding manual labour.[1] The fact that such jobs are easily learned has given a greater chance to the worker of moving from factory floor to factory floor, industry to industry. A mechanical turn of mind fostered by cheap technical education has enabled industrial workers to take readily to technological innovation and to take pride in resulting increases in productivity. The replacement of craft skills by machinery has been resisted, as in Europe, by conservative craftsmen, and 'featherbedding' is a feature of some craft unions; but this tendency has not been important for industry as a whole. The American worker has been much more ready than the European to move from a depressed to an expanding area, to tackle new jobs and to face novel conditions such as night shifts.

Mass production has not merely increased mobility on the factory floor; it has greatly increased the opportunities for white collar jobs. The old, dingy, one-room office, the book-keeper in his green eye-shade and alpaca jacket perched over a ledger, the 'lady' stenographer, the boss abroad half the day seeking orders in person, have been replaced by the great factory-office with its batteries of telephones and office machines, its battalions of clerks, secretaries and executives.[2] And it is not only the office staff which has been transformed. The commercial traveller, the advertising copywriter, the saleswoman in the department store, the attorney in the law-factory, the doctor and nurse in the hospital, the research worker in industry and university, have become members of a vastly expanded and specialized white collar force: a great pyramid in the occupational structure with an apex of powerful executives and professional experts and a mass-base of clerks, typists, salesmen, nurses and schoolteachers. This 'new middle class' of salaried workers has entirely eclipsed and largely absorbed the 'old middle class' of property-owning farmers, small business men and independent professionals who formed the basis of, and provided the ideal for,

[1] Wright, *op. cit.* table on p. 598.
[2] For this paragraph see C. Wright Mills's *White Collar: the American Middle Classes* (New York, 1951).

American society in the later nineteenth century. The white collar class increased from 6 per cent of the labour force in 1870 to 25 per cent in 1940 at the expense both of the 'old middle class' and of wage workers. If this social upheaval has caused distress to innumerable small farmers, businessmen and shopkeepers, for whom running their own business was the essence of self-respect, it has provided the opportunity of the increased status which comes from clean hands and street clothes, and in particular the opportunity of a career for unmarried women.[1] In the higher echelons of business, mass production has created more 'general knowledge' jobs of a relatively varied character. Success in business calls increasingly for general skill which can be applied almost anywhere; and as a result, able technicians and executives have wider opportunities for pursuing ambitious careers. Thus, in spite of specialization there still persists something of the open-mindedness, the jack-of-all-trades mentality of frontier days. The shift from a society of small property owners to one of salaried employees has only accentuated the traditional belief that wealth is to be earned and spent rather than owned and preserved. The old custom whereby youths of all backgrounds earn pocket money or pay for their education by temporary jobs—from delivering newspapers to clerking in summer hotels—has continued to drive home at an early age the ancient American distinction between tentative commitment to a job and total commitment to status which militates against class consciousness.

Mass production has worked against the tendency towards social stratification. There has been a marked redistribution of the national income. Since 1935-6 the real incomes of families and single persons in the lowest two-fifths of the income range have increased 90 per cent while the increase in the top fifth has been about 40 per cent.[2] As for the very poor, although some of the traditional black spots remain, notably in backward rural areas and in urban

---

[1] C. Wright Mills, however, takes a more pessimistic view, arguing that with the application of mass-production methods to the office there has been an increase in the number of dead-end jobs of diminishing skill and that the lower strata of white collar workers are coming to present a major problem of 'alienation' in American life.

[2] President's Annual Economic Report, 1953.

slums among under-privileged minorities such as Negroes and Puerto Ricans, the incidence of poverty is more generally the result of specific physical and social handicaps and is more widely spread at different social levels than in 1900, when the gulf between rich and poor more nearly corresponded to that between capital and labour. Certainly it seems that since the outbreak of the Second World War 'millions of families' have climbed out of the 'under 1,000 dollars a year' bracket into the two, three and even five thousand bracket; and although many of these have been farmers and white collar workers, probably the most important group have been industrial workers whose average weekly earnings rose from 11 dollars in 1914 to 44 dollars in 1945.[1] And because social barriers are so much less formidable than in Europe the industrial worker with a 'middle class' income has quickly and confidently adopted 'middle class' modes of living. Though the statistical chances of an office boy's becoming general manager are remote, there are still enough heroic examples to preserve something of that speculative habit of frontier days, that stubborn faith in the 'break' which, exploited with skill and courage, will turn machinist or commercial traveller into millionaire manufacturer.

Mass production has worked in more subtle and pervasive ways against the hardening of class distinctions. In response to the blandishments of advertising, Americans have increasingly come to reject expensive 'custom-made' articles and services, catering to individual tastes and pockets, in favour of the standard and the mass-produced. As a result, more and more Americans, whatever their income group, have learned to follow similar patterns of living. There has been both a levelling down and a levelling up. The homes, furnishings, cars, sports, holidays, even clothes of quite humble people have come increasingly to be the same as, or merely cheaper versions of, those of the well-to-do; and the rich conform to a more casual style of life. This unifying process has gone beyond material well-being. Mass production methods have invaded the realm of ideas. Best-sellers and book-of-the-month clubs, magazines like the *Readers' Digest* or *Life*, with circulations of roughly five millions,

---

[1] F. L. Allen, *op. cit.* p. 213; *Hist. Stats.*, Series D, 119.

the columns of commentators syndicated in thousands of small-town newspapers, films, radio and television programmes, have provided Americans not only with a universal folklore but with popular enlightenment. Americans are coming increasingly under the cover of a single, undifferentiated culture which, for want of a better term, one must describe as 'middle class' or the all-American norm.

This easily acquired apparatus of living has hitherto proved beneficial, by providing a greater freedom of choice to the mass of Americans, rather than stultifying by standardizing responses. The sons and daughters of the new immigrants have been enabled to conform to accepted standards of American social behaviour and, as their income increases, to move with comparative ease up the social scale; the gap between Negro and white in the North has lessened, and the dirt farmer and even the hillbilly of the back country have been given wider horizons.

More especially has it completed the emancipation of women. The granting of the vote to women by constitutional amendment in 1920 was merely the final stage in that feminist struggle, referred to in Chapter V, to assert the right of women to educational, professional and political equality with men. It remained for twentieth-century technology to emancipate the housewife and mother from the drudgery of the home. Ever since the early days of urban over-crowding in the 1830s and '40s, when families were content to live in boarding-houses, Americans have been more used than the English to apartment life; and since the First World War, as urban values have risen and as the supply of immigrant servant girls has run out, families have tended to move from roomy frame houses into small streamlined apartments as well as to suburban villas. In their new labour-saving homes, with a variety of mechanical devices, from vacuum cleaners, refrigerators and electric mixers to automatic furnaces, and with a wide variety of processed foods, American housewives have discovered the boon of leisure. The self-reliant, vigorous woman of pioneer days has now both time and energy for pursuits outside the home. If bridge, golf and women's clubs have sufficed for some, more have discovered outlets in multifarious forms of social work, from parent-teacher associations to marriage-guidance clinics. And a younger generation, co-educated with their husbands, are seeking a more satisfying life in a combination of home duties and part-time jobs. The American woman, always dominant in the home, has become a powerful social force in the local community and in the nation at large.

These changes, together with the general practice of birth control, have influenced family life in general. Children enjoy a greater independence; grandparents are less often supported in the family home, and resorts in the mild climates of Florida and California cater for old people living independently on modest means. This increased flexibility of family life has tended towards a more contractual attitude to marriage reflected in a rise in the marriage rate, a lowering of the marriage age and an increase in divorce.

The most important contribution to social mobility and one, moreover, without which mass production itself would hardly have been feasible, has been made by mass education. The germ of the idea of free schooling for all, embedded in the North-west Ordinance, has grown into a luxuriantly spreading vine. The little red school house has become the grade and high school with—in rich States—unsurpassed plant and equipment. In 1870 a little over half, in 1950 over four-fifths, of American children were attending public elementary and secondary schools. In 1950, 71 per cent of those in their seventeenth year were attending high school.[1] In higher education, the agricultural colleges and schools of mines made possible by the Morrill Act of 1862—many of which have developed into great State universities—and the innumerable institutions founded by religious bodies and wealthy benefactors, have joined the nucleus of private colleges of ancient charter to form a complex system which provides a further education for one boy or girl in every ten. This system contains within it an abundant variety of types and levels of education. Historically the basis of American education was the familiar English selective progress from the three Rs, by way of the grammar school to the college grounded in the humanities; and modern America still has a galaxy of institutions

[1] U.S. Bureau of the Census: *Current Population Reports*, Series P, 20; quoted in Gordon C. Lee: *An Introduction to Education in Modern America*, p. 26.

adhering to this traditional discipline, from schools like the Boston Latin School, country day schools, boarding 'preparatory' schools, to liberal arts colleges like Amherst or Smith and universities such as Harvard and Chicago with a distinguished tradition of learning. But taken as a whole, the American system had begun, by the close of the nineteenth century, to depart radically from this familiar norm. American scholarship, more influenced than British by German scientific method, began earlier to specialize in the techniques of the natural and the social sciences; and upon the liberal arts college and the vocational school was built an immense super-structure of research.

These developments have been accompanied by a marked social-izing of the purposes of education. The practical bent of a largely self-taught people, asserted democratically through school boards, parent-teacher associations and State legislatures, has led to an em-phasis on the acquisition of 'useful' knowledge, and to a demand for more and more technical training not only at school but at universities, where the original degrees in agriculture and mining have been supplemented by degrees in a wide variety of subjects from business administration to embalming. In law and medicine the universities long ago stepped in to fill the gap caused by the early decay of the apprentice system which survives in Britain. On the other hand in engineering, great technical colleges, notably the California and the Massachusetts Institutes of Technology, have developed into important institutions of higher learning, the aim of which is to provide in modern form something of the 'universal' education of the ancient craft. In science the greatest achievements of American research have been, not so much in 'pure' fields where Europeans continue to give the lead, but in 'applied' fields of more immediate social relevance—in applied physics and chemistry, in biology, medicine and engineering. Above all, the social sciences of applied economics, sociology and psychology have in America their most favourable habitat.

This social emphasis has been equally important in primary and secondary education. In an open community with few institutional signposts to guide conduct, the role of school and college in setting patterns of social behaviour has been powerful. The frontier tradition of co-operation among those for the time being thrown together, reinforced by the imperative to make the immigrant child into a good American citizen, has become formalized in the schools into a training in group endeavour; and this has become the overriding educational aim. The idea of a free schooling for all has turned the aim of education away from the progressive selection of a talented *élite* and towards an education suited to the capacities of the average youth. The emphasis is not so much on intellectual distinction as on the pursuit of a wide variety of common 'projects', not so much on individual leadership as on being an acceptable and forceful member of a community of representative individuals. This tendency away from formal disciplines to the encouragement of spontaneous interests and to the development of a personality 'well-adjusted' to the demands of the professional and social group has become embodied in a theory of educational psychology which, associated with the name of John Dewey, has in varying degrees permeated most levels of education.

Born in New England and matured in the Middle West, Dewey gave a distinctly earthy and native twist to the pragmatism which in William James preserved something of a European temper. Beginning with evolutionary assumptions, Dewey treated thought as an 'instrument' of adjustment and survival, a plan of action which was true if it worked, false if it failed to work; not as an independent search for 'truth' but 'a process of making over one's environment into something more satisfactory to one's needs and desires'.[1] His teaching was followed by a revolution in educational theory and practice: traditional, cultural discipline was replaced by experiment, by a readiness to attack specific problems as they arose, to face new choices with an open mind. This carried to a logical conclusion the habitual assumptions of a flexible, forward-looking society.

The belief that education ought to develop a personality readily able to adjust to a rapidly evolving society is only one element in a comprehensive faith in the ability of man to dominate his environment. The Utopian spirit which characterized the Puritan strain and the messianic cult, the Jeffersonian 'enthusiasm' and the com-

[1] Brand Blanshard, 'Speculative Thinkers', in Spiller, *op. cit.* vol. II, pp. 1278–80.

munitarian experiment, has persisted into the twentieth century as a passionate humanism which sees no limits to material and moral progress. Just as technology has created undreamt-of material wealth, so the newly won knowledge in the social sciences, in medicine, psychology, education and sociology, should minimize human waste in all its forms and create a society to which each individual freely contributes his best. This idealism regards evil as negation rather than positive force, discounts the experience of the past as a precedent for the present and looks to a future when by human effort human nature can be changed for the better. Thus, in the expansiveness of the early twentieth century Americans have carried forward on to a new plane their faith in their great experiment.

The foregoing represents the dominant trend of American society between the two world wars. But the American people have remained too heterogeneous and too eclectic for any simple interpretation to have more than tentative validity. Account must be taken of the co-existence at all levels of powerful dissents which qualify and complicate the full picture. Americans who in one context respond to the standardizing, unifying force of modern technocracy, in another respond to minority convictions which are deeply felt and stubbornly persistent.

Regional influences continue to accentuate contrasts between dirt farmers in Nebraska, fruit growers in the San Fernando Valley, market gardeners in New Jersey; between the fishermen of Maine and of the Mississippi; between electricians in Hollywood and in Schenectady; miners in Appalachia and in Colorado, department store managers in Dallas and in Boston, attorneys in Duluth and in Manhattan. In these widely separated regions are still to be found cultural pockets which represent vestigial remnants of each of the overlaying stages of American settlement: the seventeenth-century hillbillies of the Great Smokies, the eighteenth-century Dunkers of Pennsylvania, nineteenth-century Norwegian Lutherans of Minnesota, and the newest of 'new' immigrants like the Mexicans of Arizona and the Puerto Ricans of New York's upper West Side. Provincial capitals like Memphis or Minneapolis still radiate local impulses which resist the power of transmission from the New York–Hollywood network. Ethnic contrasts, even where the assimilation process has been effective, remain important. Distinctions between Swedes and Poles, Finns and Austrians, Irish and Jews and between all the more recently arrived and the 'natives' of English and Scotch-Irish stock emphasize the security of belonging to an 'in-group', the need for minority solidarity. And as the Negro has moved north the caste distinction of colour has become an American rather than an entirely southern problem. Culturally, the all-American norm has by no means routed older strains. In education the reaction against Dewey, led by President Hutchins of the University of Chicago, has been intense; and in most universities the humanities keep up a spirited resistance to the aggressions of science. The conservative-minded, especially of the older stocks, continue to cherish European connections; and in every large city across the continent are to be found thriving Bohemias, in revolt against a surrounding Philistia, cultivating an eclectic *avant-gardisme* in fine arts and letters. In the sphere of religion a multitude of Churches, from conservative Presbyterians to the most exotic of cults, continue to dissent from the prevailing humanism. The revivalism and fundamentalism of frontier days are still potent forces in small-town and rural America. The famous anti-Darwinian trial at Dayton, Tennessee, in 1925 proved the continued resistance of fundamentalist opinion to the whole concept of evolution: and the temperance movement, which in 1920 forced the experiment in Prohibition on the nation, and which still preserves 'dry' States and counties, had its origin in that frontier revivalism which also contributed so largely to the woman suffrage amendment of the previous year. If it is argued that such sects and movements merely reflect the more eccentric spiritual aspects of American Utopianism there can be no denying that the modern expansion of Greek Orthodox and Roman Catholic Churches, largely the result of the 'new' immigration, has provided a powerful body of dissent from the dominant, and Protestant, ideal. In particular, the Roman Catholics, with their uncompromising Christian dogma, a congregation amounting to a quarter of the total church-going population, an hierarchical structure at once authoritarian and ultra-marine and an elaborate educational system, constitute a kind of official opposition to the governing ideal of humanism. And even within the Protestant fold, tones of doubt and pessimism are heard, as when the theologian Reinhold Niebuhr expounds the history of the American experiment in 'ironic' rather than epic or triumphant or even tragic terms.[1]

In politics the continuing practices of the open society have enabled both orthodoxies and dissents to find expression in the changing equilibria of power. Within the framework of the Constitution and its associated party system the practice of individualistic democracy continues to thrive. Unlike the British, whose politics are underpinned by a complicated and centralized structure of institutions, the politics of the American mobile society remain comparatively free from institutional hardening. Americans remain as distrustful of continuing loyalties to traditional institutions as they were when they 'disestablished' those they inherited from Britain at the time of the Revolution. Apart from the polling station and the court room they continue to govern their affairs largely on the voluntary principle.

The social compulsions of the caravan persist in the habit of *ad hoc* co-operation by those individuals for the time being thrown together for immediate, specific ends. The neighbourliness of the frontier expressed characteristically in the roof-raising, the harvest-help and the marriage-shower persists in the energetic, go-getting team spirit which drives not only Churches but an elaborate network of voluntary social services still bearing a large share of the welfare burden. The gregariousness of the frontier persists in the impulse to join one or more of a galaxy of associations and fraternities as different as Elks, Lions and Knights of Columbus, chambers of commerce and professional bodies, exclusive country clubs and the Daughters of the American Revolution. These characteristic American associations which cater to the 'un-American' desire to belong to some in-group affording protection from the menacing out-groups of a chaotic society take the place of the integrated class and institutional structure by which English society is articulated. The impulse of the 'joiner' has given rise to an elaboration of

[1] Reinhold Niebuhr, *The Irony of American History* (London, 1952).

highly geared associations representing all kinds of interests from religious bodies, ethnic groups and ex-servicemen to the lobbies of industry, trade and the professions which are in a position to exert pressure on politics in municipality, State and nation. These voluntary associations provide the machinery for the day-to-day formation of opinions which govern public policy.

In public affairs conflicting interests are still adjusted mainly by private, voluntary initiative outside the formal structure of politics. Of the three interests with the greatest influence on American life, business, organized labour and farming, only the third, conscious of its shrinking role, now regards legislation as a first resort. True to the tradition of Gompers, the American labour movement pursues its interests by means of industrial action, only intervening directly in politics when its rights of collective bargaining are threatened. Big business has been disciplined into some sense of social responsibility not only by government action to enforce competition but by the 'countervailing power' of other business interests, organized labour, and new forms of competition.[1] With the growing divorce between ownership and management and with the growing association of business with government the whole nature of business as an interest has become much more complex and diffuse than in the days of the tycoons.

In this process of mutual adjustment among dominant interests the State remains very much a power of last, and limited, resort. In spite of its changing custom the Federal Constitution perpetuates the tradition of limited government. Within its framework political decisions still resolve themselves in terms not so much of ideology as of bargaining and compromise, the result of that incessant and intricate diplomacy among effective interests which alone makes possible a single continental sovereignty. The chief function of the two parties, which have become ancillary to the Constitution, is still to resolve conflicts of interest before they reach the formal stage of politics; and although 'conservative' or 'liberal' ideas may from time to time dominate one or other of them they remain essentially parties of interest rather than of ideology, each containing

[1] For the term 'countervailing power' see J. K. Galbraith, *American Capitalism: the Concept of Countervailing Power* (London, 1952).

within it the whole gamut of effective ideas. It is true that since the 1920s the functions of government have enormously increased. Two world wars and economic crisis have enormously extended the power of the Federal Government at the expense both of the States and of private enterprise. As a result of the necessity to control the continent's resources, to put the unemployed to work and to provide for national defence the Federal Government has become the greatest single employer in the nation; and with new powers is in a position not merely to determine the relative roles of different interests, but to control the oscillations and direction of the economy as a whole. Yet it is important to remember that the powers of government are still limited by the Constitution and by public opinion. True to their revolutionary inheritance Americans remain suspicious of or irreverent to the authority of the State. In spite of the massive impersonality of modern life they maintain the important constitutional fiction that their democracy is a matter of immediate self-government. Like their Jacksonian forbears, who thought 'spoils' a healthy insurance against the pretensions of an office-holding class, they make no distinction between the 'we' of the governed and the 'they' of government; between private and official life. This temperamental attitude to power not only releases the Congressman from any inhibitions about intervening in the twilight zone which separates the legislative from the executive, and permits well-organized interests to make the most of whatever pressure they can command, but makes it proper for the private citizen to exercise a perpetual referendum on the day-to-day conduct of affairs. The American recognizes no *mystique* of government and prefers open muddle to hidden *expertise*. Secrets are considered discreditable and the Press has assumed the authority of a constitutional 'fourth estate'. Government is thought of not so much as an ultimate authority as a separate interest, a 'public' interest to be sure, but one which hardly differs in kind from other powerful interests in a multiple society. The American worker pays his taxes as he pays his union dues in recognition of two separate and limited obligations. Business men offer their services to government in time of crisis not in a spirit of allegiance to the public service but of tentative co-operation for an immediate end; and behind their condescension lies the long tradition by which talent, breeding and means have been recruited for the command of private corporations instead of for the higher ranks of the civil service which, lacking the prestige of its British counterpart, has had to be content until recently with pedestrian recruits.

Government, therefore, has not been, as in Europe, the natural instrument of public welfare. Americans do not regard their government as embodying the collective will of a unified people and they reject the whole concept of 'statism' as fervently now as they did in the eighteenth century. The idea of long-term planning in accordance with a fully conceived, doctrinaire programme is alien to them. Policy remains pragmatic, experimental, related to problems forced upon legislators and administrators by the pressure of interests and vocal opinions; and statesmen are judged by their skill in the political manipulation necessary for that minimum unity without which the government of a continent cannot be carried on: the kind of leadership which jeopardizes immediate gains for ultimate ends is not expected of them. The acts of government in the economic crisis of the 1930s were true to this tradition. In spite of the pseudo-Marxist thinking of some of its intellectual adherents, the New Deal resembled the Progressive movement to which it was the heir. Its policies were experimental, sometimes mutually conflicting, born of immediate crisis, of political expediency; but its underlying objective was to restore the operations of free enterprise. The object of public works was not to socialize industry but to give employment and to stimulate demand by creating purchasing power during the emergency—to 'prime the pump'. That most ambitious experiment in government planning and operation, the Tennessee Valley Authority, has won acceptance, not as the thin end of a socialistic wedge, but as a single venture, a 'yard-stick', which has set a standard for private enterprise, particularly in the field of electric power. It is true that the ill-fated experiment of the National Recovery Administration embodied important dissents from the prevailing doctrine of free enterprise and had some affinity with the 'corporate state' in Italy. But the Supreme Court declared NRA unconstitutional: and the interests which, in practice, NRA most benefited—big business and organized labour—continued to receive benefits in more traditional forms, by means of government capital provided through the Reconstruction Finance Corporation and a full code of collective bargaining embodied in the Wagner Act. The principle of collective welfare was established by the Social Security Act which provided a bare minimum of social insurance; but the New Deal administration got rid of its responsibility for relief at the earliest possible moment, eschewing unemployment benefit in favour of putting the unemployed to work, and more recently by concentrating on indirect manipulation to preserve full employment. State insurance for workmen's compensation and old-age pensions remains very much less important than private schemes; and the doctors continue to draw upon powerful public support in their resistance to a national health service. The chief beneficiaries of the New Deal were not private citizens, but organized interests such as agriculture, labour and business, able to make their wants known through political pressure.

In the mid-twentieth century the American people still pursue their Revolutionary ideal: a Republic established in the belief that men of good will could voluntarily come together in the sanctuary of an American wilderness to order their common affairs according to rational principles; a dedicated association in which men participate not by virtue of being born into it as heirs of immemorial custom, but by virtue of free choice, of the will to affirm certain sacred principles; a gathered community of Protestants, 'separatists', nonconformists, for whom the individual conscience alone is sovereign; a community of the uprooted, of migrants who have turned their backs on the past in which they were born, who have thrown off the disciplines of traditional authority, for whom continuing institutions command only tentative allegiance and have only an attenuated personality; a caravan on the move; squatters sojourning in a mansion where all the cluttering furniture of the past has been banished to the attic; a commonwealth where authority, reduced to a minimum, is hedged about with safeguards and government serves the limited purpose of a framework within which individuals find their levels in voluntary and ever-shifting groups and minorities preserve their identity in a plural order; a society fluid and experimental, uncommitted to rigid values, cherishing freedom of will and choice and bestowing all the promise of the future on those with the manhood to reject the past.

This is the most ambitious ideal ever to command the allegiance of a great nation; it is hardly surprising that it has never achieved full acceptance in practice. In the words of Thornton Wilder: 'It is difficult to be an American because there is as yet no code, grammar, decalogue by which to orient oneself. Americans are still engaged in inventing what it is to be an American. That is at once an exhilarating and a painful occupation. All about us we see the lives that have been shattered by it—not least those lives that have tried to resolve the problem by the European patterns.'[1] Even during the classic, formative period of territorial expansion its success was partial and marked by tragic failure: and with the continent conquered and isolation incompatible with the responsibilities of a Great Power, the American people face a crisis in their way of life even more acute than that of the Civil War. Is their ideal entirely dependent on an expanding economy with an ever-rising standard of living and with new opportunities to offset the inexorable tendency to private monopoly? Does the uniformity induced by mass production threaten that individuality which is the very basis of liberty? Does the ideal impose too great a responsibility on ignorant and appetite-ridden humanity, prone to seek security from an unbearable isolation by joining intolerant and irresponsible 'in-groups' and easily led by demagogues into tyrannous courses? Can the revolutionary concept of American nationality survive the end of immigration and the return to an older, more chauvinistic, xenophobic form of nationalism? Are the American people, temperamentally given to dynamic experiments, to impatient and Utopian solutions, capable of the nerve, discipline and experience demanded of a Great Power? Does the ideal, rejecting as it does 'feudal' authority, provide a solution to the problem of resolving order and liberty which is relevant to the international world? And above all are Americans determined merely to cherish their ideal at home at the risk of losing it altogether or are they prepared

[1] Thornton Wilder, 'Towards an American Language', extracts from the Charles Eliot Norton Lectures, *Atlantic Monthly*, July 1952.

to project it abroad in the hope of establishing some form of framework in which a free world may survive?

These are questions to which the historian has no answer; but reflecting on the grand, epic story of the American experiment he is left still believing with Walt Whitman that 'The United States are destined either to surmount the gorgeous history of feudalism or else prove the most tremendous failure of time'.

INDEX

Abolition, *see* Anti-slavery
Acts of Trade, British, 4
Adams, Brooks, 276, 277
Adams, Charles Francis, 242, 243;
quoted, 251
Adams, Henry, 242, 276, 283;
quoted, 277
Adams, Herbert Baxter, 240
Adams, John, 24, 31, 43, 55, 59;
quoted, 38
Adams, John Quincy, 71, 91, 140,
164n
Adams, Samuel, 18, 24, 30, 31
Adamson Act, 272
Addams, Jane, 238
Admission of States to Union, 129,
163, 164, 165
Agrarianism, 259–64; Southern, 158
Agricultural Wheel, 262
Agriculture, 104–5, 110, 192, 198,
202, 208, 303; and the farmer, 42,
108, 109, 215, 259–64, 272; and
the land, 104, 127, 193, 196; and
mechanization, 105, 160, 199; in
the South, 142, 147, 149, 178
Albany, N.Y., 2, 84, 97
Albany and Susquehanna Railroad,
187
Albion newspaper, 74
Alcott, Bronson, 83
Alger, Horatio, 247
Alien and Sedition Acts, 68
Allegheny River, 96
Almy and Brown, merchants, 80, 85
Altgeld, Governor John P., 234, 254
American Anti-Slavery Society, 133,
163
American Colonization Society, 146
American Federation of Labor, 235,
238, 257, 264, 272
American Fur Company, 103

American Party, 132, 166, 237
American Peace Society, 133
American Protective Association, 239
'American System,' 89, 102
American Telephone and Telegraph
Company, 301
American Temperance Society, 133
Anderson, Sherwood, 286
Andrews, Samuel, 206
Anthony, Susan B., 118
Anti-Masonic Party, 166
Antioch College, 119
Anti-Sabbatarianism, 132
Anti-slavery, movement, 122, 133,
134; opinion in the North, 122,
132, 163–4
Anti-trust policy, 270, 272, 273–5
Appomatox, surrender at, 174
Arizona, copper mining in, 205
Army, British in colonies, 21; re-
cruitment of officers in American,
41; Continental, 35, 36; Con-
federate, 171; Union, 170, 174
Articles of Confederation, 43, 44, 50
Assemblies, colonial, 11, 12, 24, 39
Astor, John Jacob, 103, 215
Atlantic Monthly, 265
Atlantic system, 4, 5, 9, 75, 89
Atlantic voyage, 1, 76
Automobile, industry, 298–302;
social effects of, 304–5

Back country, 14, 15, 29, 34, 35, 42;
and western lands, 44–5, 92, 97;
industry in, 85–6; religion in, 40;
significance to society, 26; stronghold of Revolution, 33
Bacon's Rebellion, 18
Baltimore and Ohio Railroad, 84,
88, 217
Bancroft, George, 126

Index

Chardon Street Convention, 134

Charleston, S.C., 2, 155

Chicago, Ill., 97, 99, 101, 198; growth of, 200, 214

Chrysler Corporation, 302

Church, 17, 26, 40, 106; disestablishment of, 40; in West, 106; Baptist, 48, 81, 156; Episcopal, 40; German pietist, 13, 26, 40; of Latter Day Saints, 121, 182; Lutheran, 40, 226; Methodist, 87, 156; Moravian, 17; Presbyterian, 17, 40; Roman Catholic, 166, 232, 239, 314; Unitarian, 27, 81, 136

Churchill, Lord Randolph, 283

Cincinnati, Ohio, 104, 120, 198, 268

Cincinnati, Society of the, 41

Citizenship, Jeffersonian concept of, 62, 68

City Bank of New York, 219

City manager, 268

Civil War, 170–5

Clark, Maurice, 206

Class structure, 17, 297; in South, 151, 152; 'white collar', 306, 307; plutocratic, 251–3

Clay, Henry, 69, 89, 140, 153, 164

Clayton Act, 272

Clayton-Bulwer Treaty, 290

Clemens, Samuel, 120, 282

Cleveland, Grover, 254

Cleveland, Ohio, 101, 205, 214

Climate, 3, 93, 194

Clinton, de Witt, 98

Clinton, Sir Henry, 35

Cobden, Richard, 72, 78, 173

Colden, Cadwallader, 29

Colleges in Revolution, 40

Colonial Currency Act, 24

Colonial System, British, 4, 9, 19

Colt, Samuel, 207

Columbia College, 49

Combe, George, 133

'Come-outers', 132

Committees of Correspondence, 30

Commons, John R., 268

Communities, experimental, 111, 112, 113, 135

Comstock lode, 182

Concord, Battle of, 31

Confederacy, 172, 173

Confederation, Articles of, 43, 44, 50; Congress of, 44

Congress, Continental, 31, 32, 35–6, 39, 43; of Confederation, 44; of the United States, 52, 53, 54

Congress of Industrial Organizations, 258

Connecticut, 25; founding of, 44

Conservation, 270, 272, 273

Constitution Construed and Constitutions Vindicated, 156

Constitution of the United States, 50–5, 316; drafting of, 48–51; structure of, 53, 54, 316; amendments to, 55, 175

Constitutions, State, 38, 39

Contract labour law, 208, 237, 255

Contract, theory of, 41

Cooper, Thomas, 68, 83

Co-operatives, farmers', 260

Copper, 204–5

Corn laws, British, 78

Corning, Erastus, 102

Cornwallis, Lord, 35, 37

Cotton, 92, 97, 104, 147, 173; area of production, 193; export of, 73, 278; price of, 141, 147; withholding of crop, 172; manufactures, 85, 298

Cotton gin, 146

Council Bluffs, Iowa, 89

Country store, 96

Crédit Mobilier Construction Company, 188

Crèvecoeur, Michel de (J. Hector St. John), 63, 225, 239

Crockett Almanac of 1838, 115

Crockett, David, 110

Croly, Herbert, 266

Cuba, 288

Cunard, Samuel, 76

Index

Mexican War, 166, 180–1

Michigan, 92, 204

Michigan Central Railroad, 84, 187

Middle Border, 192, 196

Migration, westward, 21, 25, 26, 91–105, 108; influence of, on American society, 26, 106–10, 115, 116; of planting families, 97–8; *see also* Frontier

Military strategy, in Revolution, 35–7; in Civil War, 172, 173–5

Military techniques in Civil War, 171

Miller, William, 121, 132

Milling, flour, 104, 198, 208, 215

Milwaukee, population of, 101

Mining, 99, 183, 197, 203–5, 228; silver, 182–3, 263; gold, 182

Minnesota, 92, 204

Mississippi Valley, 92, 98, 102, 131, 159, 180

Missouri, admitted to Union, 163

Missouri Compromise, 163, 164

Mitchell, John, 258

Molasses, 9, 10, 22, 23

'Molly Maguires, The,' 255

Monroe Doctrine, 71, 287

Monroe, Harriet, 285

Montecello, 60

Montgomery Ward, 199, 260; *see also* Mail order houses

Moravian Church, 17

Morgan, John Pierpont, career of, 216–22, 250; quoted, 250, 252

Morgan, Junius, 216

Morgan, William, 131

Mormons, 182; *see also* Latter Day Saints

Morrill Act, 193, 310

Morrill Tariff, 209

Morris, Gouverneur, 49

Morris, Robert, 31, 36, 39, 48, 49

Most, Johann, 234

Mount Vernon, 47

'Muckrakers, The,' 265

'Mugwumps, The,' 243

Munn v. *Illinois*, 261

Mutiny Act, 21

Nashoba experiment, 112

Nation, The, 265

National Bank Act, 208

National City Bank, 220

National Farmers' Alliance, 262

National income, 213, 214

National Recovery Administration, 318

Nativist Movement, 88, 132

Natural rights, doctrine of, 27, 28, 29, 38

Navigation Acts, British, 66, 73

Navy, British, 9, 45, 64, 66, 71; U.S., 41, 68, 70, 289

Nebraska territory, settlement of, 165

Negro, 145, 147, 152; problems of, after emancipation, 175–9; in North, 305, 309; *see also* Slavery

New Bradford, Mass., 2, 80, 82

New Deal, 318

New England, 13, 23, 25, 82; and Federalist Party, 59; influence of migration from, 100–1, 160, 161

New England Renaissance, 135–8

New Freedom, The, 274

New Harmony, Indiana, 112

New Jersey Plan, 52

New Orleans, 74, 75, 94–6, 102

Newport, R.I., 18, 215, 216

New Republic, The, 266

Newspapers, foreign language, 232; commentators, 309; *see also* Journalism

New York Central Railroad, 84, 102, 217

New York City, 18, 73, 87, 88, 102; population of, in 1860, 83; in 1890, 214

New York State, 44, 55, 98–9; influence of 'burnt-over' area, 122, 160

Neutrality, U.S., in Napoleonic Wars, 68; legislation, 69

Index

Index

Wall Street, 221, 296, 302
Waltham, Mass., 85
Ward, Lester, 266
'War Hawks', 69
War of 1812, 59, 69, 74
Washington, George, as landowner, 13, 24, 31, 33, 46, 47, 57; in public life, 35, 36, 37, 49, 55; quoted, 35
Wealth, accumulation of, 215
Wealth against Commonwealth, 265
Weaver, James B., 262
Webster, Daniel, 89, 164
Webster-Ashburton Treaty, 70
Weld, Theodore, 122
Welsh, as immigrants, 79, 207
Wesley, John, 17
West Indies, 2, 3, 4; British, 73; Dutch, 9; French, 9
Westover, Virginia, 6
Westward movement, *see* Migration
Weydemeyer, Joseph, 234
Weyerhaeuser, Frederick, 184, 215
Wharton, Edith, 284
Wheat, 72, 73, 97, 104, 105, 192-3, 197, 264
Whig Party, 89, 102, 125, 141, 143, 166-7
Whigs, Revolutionary, 31-4, 36, 45, 49
'Whiskey Rebellion', 59
Whistler, James McNeil, 284

Whitefield, George, 17
Whitman, Walt, 138, 139, 321; quoted, 64, 139
Whitney, Eli, 146, 207
Wigwam Convention, 167
Wilder, Thornton, 223, 320
William and Mary College, 40, 49, 155
Wilmot Proviso, 166
Wilson, Edmund, 286
Wilson, James, 48
Wilson, Woodrow, 275; career of, domestic, 271-2; in foreign affairs, 291-3
Wine Islands, 4
Wisconsin, 92, 99, 180, 268
Women, emancipation of, 309; rights for, 122, 133, 234; status of, in western communities, 117
Workingmen's parties, 86, 88, 166
World War I, 290-1
Wright, Frances, 81, 112
Wright, Frank Lloyd, 284
Wyoming Stock Growers' Association, 185
Wythe, George, 49, 155

Yancey, William L., 164
Yorktown, surrender at, 37
Young, Brigham, 182